ORACLE®

Oracle Press

OCP Oracle9*i* Database: New Features for Administrators Exam Guide

Oracle Press™

OCP Oracle9*i* Database: New Features for Administrators Exam Guide

Daniel Benjamin

McGraw-Hill/Osborne

New York Chicago San Francisco
Lisbon London Madrid Mexico City Milan
New Delhi San Juan Seoul Singapore Sydney Toronto

McGraw-Hill/Osborne
2600 Tenth Street
Berkeley, California 94710
U.S.A.

To arrange bulk purchase discounts for sales promotions, premiums, or fund-raisers, please contact **McGraw-Hill**/Osborne at the above address. For information on translations or book distributors outside the U.S.A., please see the International Contact Information page immediately following the index of this book.

OCP Oracle9*i* Database: New Features for Administrators Exam Guide

234567890 DOC DOC 0198765432
Book p/n 0-07-219531-2 and CD p/n 0-07-219532-0
parts of
ISBN 0-07-219530-4

Publisher
Brandon A. Nordin

Vice President & Associate Publisher
Scott Rogers

Acquisitions Editor
Jeremy Judson

Acquisitions Coordinator
Athena Honore

Technical Editor
Jay Norton

Project Manager
Jenn Tust

Composition & Indexing
MacAllister Publishing Services, LLC

Cover Design
Damore Johann

This book was composed with QuarkXPress™.

To God for infinite blessings.

To Carol for her great sacrifice.

About the Author

Daniel Benjamin has a master's degree and over fifteen years of experience providing training and consulting solutions in Management and Information Technology for various clients including the White House, the U.S. Senate, the Department of Navy, the Department of Army, the Federal Aviation Administration (FAA), the National Air and Space Administration (NASA), the Department of Treasury, Anteon Corporation, and the Washington Convention Center.

Dan developed the implementation strategy for President Bush's CFO Act of 1990. He also implemented a web-based learning facility in support of President Clinton's Distance Learning Initiative. He was also commended for implementing quality solutions at the White House.

Dan is an excellent instructor; he uses humor successfully to communicate enterprise level Internet solutions using Java, Oracle, and Microsoft technologies using UNIX and Microsoft platforms. As a senior staff member of the Rockwell University faculty, he helped create a Masters Degree program in E-Commerce and Internet Security. He is also a featured workshop presenter at the USDA Graduate School, government agencies, and private corporations.

Dan has also authored books on Java Programming (J2SE) and Java Enterprise Connectivity (J2EE). He is a certified Workshop Facilitator for Joint Application Development and a certified Project Management Professional (PMP). Dan is also an avid guitarist and songwriter.

You can find additional information at www.dantastic.com. You can send feedback to dantastic@erols.com.

About the Oracle Certification Exams

The expertise of Oracle database administrators (DBAs) is integral to the success of today's increasingly complex system environments. The best DBAs operate primarily behind the scenes, looking for ways to fine-tune day-to-day performance to prevent unscheduled crises and hours of expensive downtime. They know they stand between optimal performance and a crisis that could bring a company to a standstill. The Oracle Certified Database Administrator Track provides DBAs with tangible evidence of their skills with the Oracle database.

The Oracle Certified Professional (OCP) Program was developed by Oracle to recognize technical professionals who can demonstrate the depth of knowledge and hands-on skills required to maximize Oracle's core products according to a rigorous standard established by Oracle. By earning professional certification, you can translate the impressive knowledge and skill you have worked so hard to accumulate into a tangible credential that can lead to greater job security or more challenging, better-paying opportunities.

Oracle Certified Professionals are eligible to receive use of the Oracle Certified Professional logo and a certificate for framing.

Requirements for Certification

To upgrade from an Oracle8*i* DBA OCP to an Oracle9*i* DBA OCP, you must pass one test. This exam covers knowledge of the essential aspects of the SQL language, Oracle administration, backup and recovery, and performance tuning of systems. The certification process requires that you pass the following exam:

Oracle9*i* Database: New Features for Administrators (1Z0-030)

When you take the exam, you will have to answer correctly at least 38 questions out of a total of 56 in order to successfully complete the exam. The required number of correct questions can vary based on the difficulty of the questions administered in the particular exam you take. If you fail a test, you must wait at least 30 days before you retake that exam. You may attempt a particular test up to 3 times in a 12-month period.

Recertification

Oracle announces the requirements for upgrading your certification based on the release of new products and upgrades. Oracle will give six months' notice announcing when an exam version is expiring.

Exam Format

The computer-based exam is a multiple-choice test, consisting of 56 questions that must be completed in 90 to 120 minutes.

Contents at a Glance

Contents

Acknowledgments

It takes a team to accomplish an objective of this nature. There are many people who have contributed to the successful completion of this book.

First and foremost, I thank God who is the source of all wisdom.

Second, I am grateful to Carol, my wife, whose sacrifice made this book possible. Holidays and weekends were excluded from our vocabulary during the writing of this book. She also gave up the warmth of our basement, which became my hideout for writing this book.

Jay Norton, a renowned instructor and consultant at Oracle Corporation, spent many hours reviewing the draft documents for technical accuracy. His contribution is invaluable.

I am thankful to the staff of Rockwell University. There is the ever so optimistic Tarun Gera who believes I can do anything; and Subash Boda, a renowned author of Oracle books, who related to my addictive, nocturnal writing patterns. "Larry" Srinivasan a reputed Oracle DBA and trainer helped with Chapter 3 and "blessed" the initial drafts before they went to the publisher; and Krishna Mohan, a recognized Oracle/Java consultant and trainer, helped with Chapter 4.

There are many players at McGraw-Hill/Osborne that were part of the team. There is the dynamic Jeremy Judson who gave me the big picture. Then there is the enthusiastic Athena Honore who effectively kept me focused on the next task at hand, and managed to sneak in an encouraging word when some chapters never seemed to end. And optimistic Lisa McClain was instrumental in the planning of this book.

The staff at MacAllister Publishing Services also played a critical part. Michael Brumitt was a thorough Copyeditor; besides improving the readability of the materials, he also had the pleasant task of eliminating F.I.B.s (fatigue induced burps). Molly Applegate, the Project Manager, was always energetic anytime I needed copyediting related discussions. Karen Fields was the Layout Technician, Kelly Applegate was the Proofreader, and Jeff Yesh was the Graphic Artist for the production of this book.

I also appreciate many other friends who wished me well, wondered if I was insane, encouraged, and prayed for an uneventful return to normalcy.

It truly took an outstanding team to produce this book.

Introduction

This book is a valuable resource for IT Management and Technical Staff; it gives them a good insight into the many enhancements in Oracle9*i* to address the challenges introduced by the Internet. The database has to service millions of users from around the world without compromising security even though many of the users are anonymous, without degrading performance levels, and while letting each user have a personal experience in the time and language of their locale. You have to improve availability, because downtime can have significant economic and legal impacts. Since user loads are prone to increase (a good problem for a retailer) scalability is of paramount importance. The database also needs various facilities including replicated cluster configuration to ensure that the database is available and recoverable in a contingency. Part 1 of this book discusses a vast number of Oracle9*i* enhancements in the areas of: security, availability, manageability, performance, scalability, language, and globalization.

This book also meets the objectives set forth for the Oracle9*i* New Features for Administrators 1Z0-030 exam, to upgrade your OCP certification from Oracle8*i* to Oracle9i. As such, this book is an excellent tool to prepare for the exam. Besides the technical discussions, Part 1 has many aids to help you prepare for the exam. At the end of topics you will find a For Review section and a number of questions to confirm and retain your learning. At the end of chapters, you will find a good summary that will help you review the chapter, and a number of questions. Part 2 consists of 3 practice exams with a total of 180 questions. You can purchase additional practice tests from Oracle Corporation (see following instructions). When you take the exam, you will have to answer correctly at least 38 questions out of a total of 56 in order to successfully complete the exam. The required number of correct questions can vary based on the difficulty of the questions administered in the particular exam you take.

You can get the candidate guide, the test content checklist (objectives), and the exam details for the Oracle9*i* DBA certification paths from Oracle's OCP web site (see following instructions). The candidate guide presents the benefits of certification; describes the overall tracks and exams for each track; tells you how you can prepare, register, and take the exam; makes suggestions about steps to take after the certification, and discusses special testing opportunities where you can take the test at discounted prices.

Various job and salary statistics consistently show that OCP certification gives you an edge over the competition both in getting the job and in compensation levels. Oracle9*i* was just released in mid-2001; the database market is just beginning to understand the power of Oracle9*i* and is on the lookout for Oracle9*i* OCPs. This certification will give both the confidence and the recognition that tilts the job interview in your favor. The certification tells the potential employer that you have attained a competency and skills level that would be needed to accomplish the day-to-day task requirements. Certification also helps companies gain a competitive edge in the marketplace when they have a team of competent, certified professionals.

This book is a great resource for preparing for the upgrade exam and it is an excellent reference for the new features of Oracle9*i*.

Purchase Practice Tests

To purchase practice tests from Oracle Corporation:

1. **Go to www.oracle.com.**
2. **Click on** *Education* under *Customer Services.*
3. **Click on** *Oracle Certified Professional (OCP).*
4. **Click on** *Practice Tests* under *Candidate Guides Exam Objectives* in the box to the left of the page.
5. **Click on the word** *here* in the following sentence **Click** *here* to purchase the Self Test Software Practice Tests. It should take you to the www.selftestsoftware.com page for purchasing practice tests.
6. **Click on** *9i DBA* under *Products* and *Oracle* in the menu to the left of the page.

7. **Click on** *1Z0-030 Oracle9i: New Features for Administrators* link under the sentence *To upgrade your Oracle8i OCP certification to Oracle9i, you must pass this exam.*

Get the Candidate Guide

To get the candidate guide:

1. **Go to www.oracle.com.**
2. **Click on** *Education* under *Customer Services.*
3. **Click on** *Oracle Certified Professional (OCP).*
4. **Click on** *Candidate Guides Exam Objectives* under *Certification* in the box to the left of the page.
5. **Click on** *Oracle9i DBA* under the *Candidate Guide* column.

PART I

Oracle9*i* New Features Exam Guide

CHAPTER 1

Security Enhancements

The Internet introduces a number of challenges for assuring security of information. Some of these challenges follow:

- You now have to administer distributed data as opposed to managing a single database.
- You now have to provide data protection for web-hosted environments, where many companies can host their applications on one web-based database server as opposed to protecting data within just one company's servers.
- You have to manage millions of users as opposed to just a few hundred users.
- You have to grant access to a wide set of *anonymous* users where every user was specifically granted access.
- You have virtual connections with packets traversing different paths as opposed to a simple hardwired or wireless connection.

Oracle9*i* features several security-related enhancements to mitigate the security risks inherent on the Internet. Today, Oracle9*i* is the most secure database for managing and accessing information on the Internet. Oracle9*i* assures security by establishing multiple layers of security tools. This approach to mitigating security is called *deep data protection.* It ensures that security is not compromised even if one security tool is not effective. This chapter introduces you to several Oracle9*i* security enhancements, such as

- Privileged connections
- Virtual Private Database (VPD)
- Fine-grained access control
- Fine-grained auditing (FGA)
- Enhancements to encryption
- Optional security products such as Oracle Label Security, Oracle Single Sign-On (SSO), and Oracle Enterprise Login Assistant

Privileged Connections

The way you establish privileged connections has changed in Oracle9*i*. These changes include

- Deprecation of CONNECT INTERNAL
- Deprecation of Server Manager
- Stringent Default Security with the Database Creation Assistant (DBCA)

Deprecation of CONNECT INTERNAL

Previous versions of Oracle allowed the use of CONNECT INTERNAL and CONNECT INTERNAL/PASSWORD to authenticate database administrator connections to the database. CONNECT INTERNAL and CONNECT INTERNAL/PASSWORD are not supported in Oracle9*i*. If you attempt to use the CONNECT INTERNAL in Oracle9*i*, you get the ORA-09275 Oracle error "CONNECT INTERNAL is not a valid DBA connection."

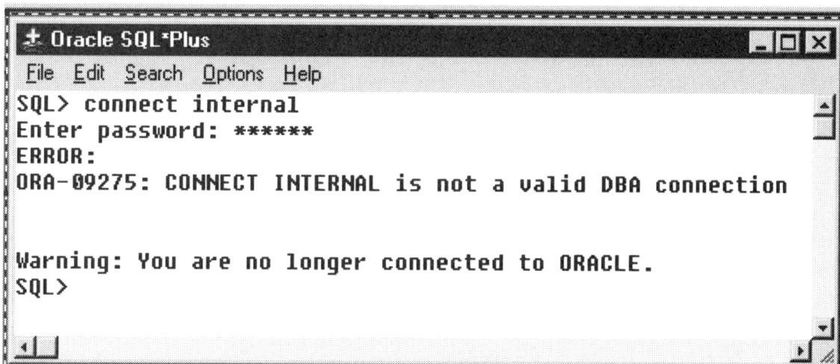

Instead of the CONNECT INTERNAL, you can use the SYSDBA or the SYSOPER privilege. The SYSOPER privilege is a subset of the SYSDBA privilege. To perform administrator tasks such as starting and stopping databases, you can use either the SYSDBA or SYSOPER privileges. To create a database, you need the SYSDBA privilege.

You have the choice of using Oracle's password file to authenticate users, or you can enable operating system (OS) authentication and use the OSDBA or OSOPER roles. Just as with the CONNECT INTERNAL connections in earlier versions, SYSDBA and SYSOPER connections are automatically audited.

To connect with DBA privileges over a nonsecure connection you must use Oracle's password file authentication. Here is the syntax:

```
CONNECT username/password AS SYSDBA
```

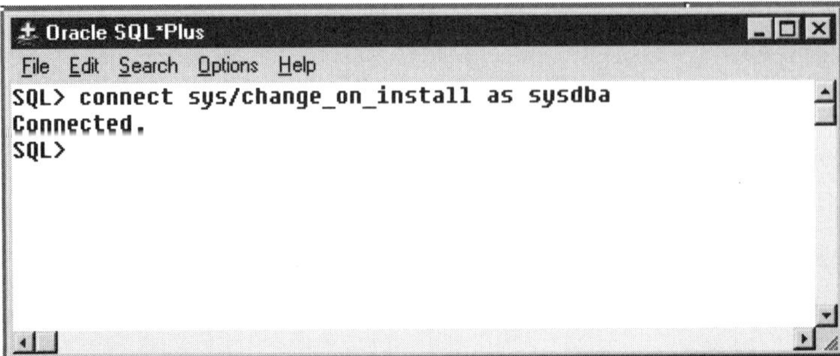

To connect with DBA privileges for a local database or over a secure connection for a remote database, you have the option of using the OS authentication. Here is the syntax:

```
CONNECT / AS SYSDBA
```

The / specifies that Oracle is to use OS authentication. The OS user should belong to the ora_dba group on the Windows NT/2000 OS or the *dba* group on the UNIX OS.

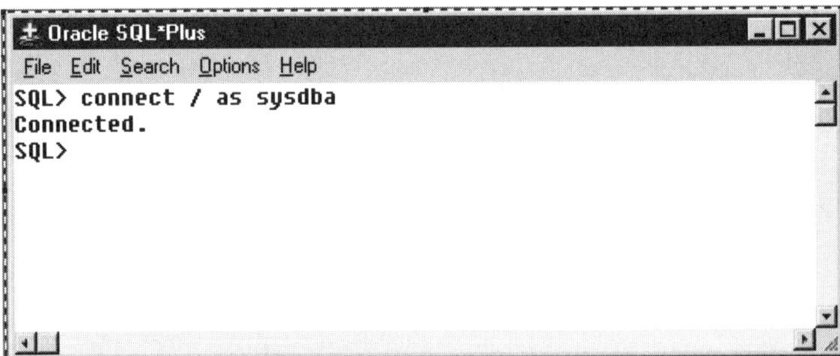

Deprecation of Server Manager

The Server Manager utility is deprecated in Oracle9*i*. You can use SQL*Plus to issue STARTUP and SHUTDOWN commands and to perform most Server Manager line-mode scripts. However, you should expect to modify your Server Manager scripts to adapt them to SQL*Plus.

For example, the Server Manager commands SET CHARWIDTH, SET DATEWIDTH, and SET LONGWIDTH that are used to change the width of all character, date, and long columns are not supported by SQL*Plus. To accomplish this in SQL*Plus, you must use the `COLUMN colname FORMAT` command. However, you cannot use the `COLUMN colname FORMAT` command to set the widths for all columns. You can only change the width one column at a time. For example, the SQL*Plus command to change the column width of a character column is COLUMN city FORMAT A15. You can use the SQL*Plus command SET LONG to specify how many characters of the LONG column you want to retrieve.

The Server Manager command SET STOPONERROR is not available in SQL*Plus. Instead, you can use WHENEVER SQLERROR or WHENEVER OSERROR in SQL*Plus to specify whether to CONTINUE or EXIT when an error occurs.

THE Server Manager commands SET MAXDATA and SET RETRIES are not available in SQL*Plus, and there are no SQL*Plus equivalents. These commands must be removed.

You can place comments at the end of a line after the semicolon, as follows:

```
SELECT * FROM book
 WHERE subject = 'Oracle';    /* Only retrieve Oracle products  */
```

This will trigger an error in SQL*Plus. You have two options to remedy this situation. The first option is to remove the semicolon and to put a / in the following line, as depicted here:

```
SELECT * FROM book
 WHERE subject = 'Oracle'     /* Only retrieve Oracle products  */
/
```

The second option is to move the comment to the following line, as follows:

```
SELECT * FROM book
 WHERE subject = 'Oracle';
 /* Only retrieve Oracle products  */
```

You must make many other changes to the Server Manager line-mode script file to make it compatible with SQL*Plus. Refer to the Oracle9*i* Migration manual for additional details.

Stringent Default Security with the Database Creation Assistant (DBCA)

Any developer or administrator with even a basic knowledge of Oracle knows about the SYSTEM/MANAGER account. Oracle placed the burden on the administrator to change the password upon installation. Unfortunately, many administrators did not make these changes, and the database was vulnerable to security breaches.

In Oracle9*i*, several enhancements were made to tighten the default security for the default user accounts to minimize the potential for security breaches.

Locked and Expired Default Accounts

When the Oracle DBCA installs or creates a new database, it locks and expires most default user accounts. Some accounts that are exceptions to this lock and expire rule are SYS, SYSTEM, and SCOTT.

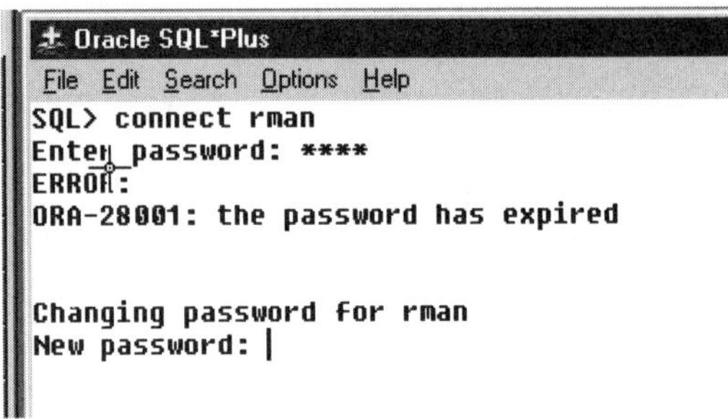

Before you can use these locked and expired accounts, you must first unlock the account manually and generate a new password.

Use the following syntax to unlock the account:

```
ALTER USER ctxsys ACCOUNT UNLOCK;
```

Use the following syntax to change the password:

```
ALTER USER ctxsys IDENTIFIED BY newpassword;
```

Elimination of Default Passwords

Prior to Oracle9*i*, DBCA assigned the SYS and SYSTEM user accounts the default passwords of CHANGE_ON_INSTALL and MANAGER respectively. You were responsible for changing the password when you completed the installation. In Oracle9*i*, the DBCA prompts you for the passwords for the SYS and SYSTEM accounts when installing a new database.

According to stated plans, Oracle9*i* is the last version of Oracle where the SYSTEM user account will be created automatically when installing or creating new databases.

Data Dictionary Accessibility

Oracle set the parameter 07_DICTIONARY_ACCESSIBILITY to TRUE in previous versions of Oracle. This enabled anyone who had the ANY privilege to use this privilege on the Data Dictionary. In order to limit access to just the SYSDBA privileged connections, you had to set this parameter to false using the following statement:

```
07_DICTIONARY_ACCESSIBILITY = FALSE
```

Oracle9*i* sets this parameter to false by default in order to enhance security.

Limit Privileges for PUBLIC

PUBLIC is the default role granted to every user. This means that if you grant a privilege to PUBLIC, every user who is connected to your database has this privilege. Execution privileges on many PL/SQL packages are granted to PUBLIC. Even though a given user may be restricted from many resources, the user may execute packages that provide access to resources that the user may not be able to access directly.

You should revoke EXECUTION privileges that were granted on powerful packages that have the potential for misuse.

For Review

1. Be aware of the deprecation of the CONNECT INTERNAL and about using CONNECT / AS SYSDBA. Also, state the difference between using the OS Authentication and using the Oracle password file.

2. Know how to make modifications to Server Manager line-mode scripts to make it compatible to work within SQL*Plus.

Exercises

1. **To connect to the database with administrative privileges, the syntax is**

   A. CONNECT / AS ADMIN

   B. CONNECT AS SYSDBA

   C. CONNECT / AS SYSDBA

   D. CONNECT / AS DBA

2. **To modify the SET CHARWIDTH command in the Server Manager script to adapt it for SQL*Plus, you would use the following:**

   A. SET WIDTH

   B. COLUMN first_name FORMAT A25

   C. SET CHARWIDTH

   D. SET COLUMN WIDTH

Answer Key
1. C. **2.** B.

Virtual Private Database (VPD)

Oracle8*i* introduced the Virtual Private Database (VPD) as a database server-based enforcement of fine-grained row-level access control. VPD in Oracle9*i* enables a number of clients to access data stored on a common, shared hosted database server, while limiting each client to their own data. Even though data of all the clients is stored in one single database, each client will interact with the database as if it were just their own database. In other words, the VPD provides the necessary data separation between clients in a shared, hosted database environment without the need for physically separating their databases on different servers.

To establish a VPD, you must specify a security policy and then associate the policy with Oracle tables or views. The ability to associate a policy with a table or view (as opposed to with an application) makes security a data issue as opposed to an application issue. If the policy were associated with an application, another application that did not enforce policies would have total access to information. By associating the policy with the table, the database will enforce the policy on any and every application or user who attempts to use the data. You can associate one policy for the SELECT statement, another for the INSERT statement, another for the UPDATE statement, and yet another for the DELETE statement.

Whenever any kind of attempt is made to access a table that has a security policy associated with it, the server invokes the function that implements the policy. This policy function returns an access condition or criteria that the server will add to the query. In other words, the original query is dynamically rewritten, and the access condition is appended to the WHERE clause of the query. This concept is depicted in the illustration that follows.

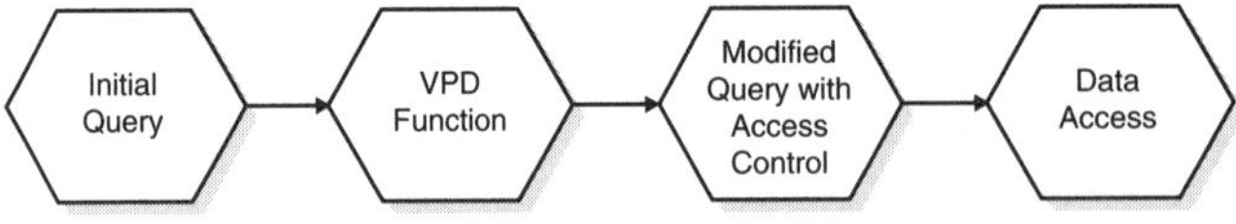

For example, let's assume that you are the Division Manager of the Accounting Group whose Division Code is 'AC', and the company policy limits your access to projects that are within your division. Let's also assume that you implemented a VPD by specifying a security policy that only enables you to access rows from the project table. Let's say you wrote the following query to access this table:

```
SELECT *
  FROM project;
```

Behind the scenes, VPD will dynamically write this query to now read

```
SELECT *
  FROM project
 WHERE division_code = 'AC';
```

The database processes this modified query and therefore limits your access to just the rows of the project table that are associated with the Accounting Division.

The VPD concept has been greatly enhanced in Oracle9*i* with the addition of the following features:

- A policy management tool
- Secure application role
- The global application context
- Multiple policies
- Partitioned fine-grained access control

Policy Management Tool

The Oracle Policy Manager is a GUI tool to create and manage security policies; it is part of the Oracle Enterprise Manager (OEM). The Oracle Policy Manager enables the administrator to create and manage security policies, associate them with tables and views, create and manage application contexts, and manage Oracle Label Security.

Secure Application Role

Oracle8*i* introduced the Secure Application Context to enable an application to tailor access control based on using the attributes of the user's session. This results in a VPD that is customized to the specific security needs of the application. For example, if an HR Manager changes from one division to another, the application must set the attributes for the application context to reflect the new division. The validation procedure determines that the HR Manager has the necessary privileges to access the new division. Oracle prevents users from bypassing this validation procedure by restricting application attribute changes to the procedure that implements the context.

Oracle provides the SYS_CONTEXT function to obtain information about the session. The syntax for this function call is

```
SYS_CONTEXT('namespace', 'attribute')
```

One example of the application context namespace (the first argument) is userenv. The second argument attribute specifies the particular attribute of the session about which you wish to obtain information. Some values for the attribute are CURRENT_USER, CURRENT_USERID, DB_NAME, HOST, IP_ADDRESS, LANGUAGE, and SESSIONID.

You can use application context to return an application-specific predicate that really is an application-specific security policy. You can use application context to obtain application attributes dynamically when you dynamically rewrite queries, instead of hard coding the values. If you were hard coding values, you would dynamically rewrite the following query:

```
SELECT *
  FROM project;
```

You would include the following hard-coded predicate:

```
SELECT *
  FROM project
 WHERE division_code = 'AC';
```

With application context, you would dynamically rewrite the query as follows:

```
SELECT *
  FROM project
 WHERE division_code = SYS_CONTEXT('personnel', 'division_code');
```

When the division code is not hard coded, your application has to set the context with the applicable division code, and the security policy procedure will obtain this division code from the application context and provide the predicate for the query.

Oracle9*i* takes the concept of the application context one step further; it provides a means of associating the application context with the security role. When you assign privileges directly to the user, you have to assign the same set of privileges individually to all users who perform a given function, such as the Customer Service Representative. If you encounter a need to change these privileges, you will have to make the same change to every user account. This is both a productivity and a quality issue; for example, you may accidentally miss updating one or two user accounts. Oracle has addressed this problem through the use of roles. You assign a specific set of roles for each application, and then you assign users to these roles. If the set of privileges needs to be changed, you only have to change the privileges that were assigned to the specific set of roles. Oracle9*i* gives you a way to integrate the Application Context with roles.

When your application starts up, you should enable the roles for application by using the SET ROLE statement. Prior to Oracle9*i*, your application would have to provide the password when using the SET ROLE statement. Your application would try to hide this password by encrypting it. The application itself became the weakest link in the chain. If someone discovered the password, any application could enable the role and gain access to the information. Any user that has access to the application code could in fact discover the embedded password. In Oracle9*i*, the SET ROLE does not use a password to enable a role; instead, it invokes the associated procedure that authenticates the role. This procedure can also use SYS_CONTEXT to access session information and set up fine-grained access control.

The first step to creating a Secure Application Role is to create a Secure Access Role as follows:

```
CREATE ROLE hr_manager IDENTIFIED USING hr.verify_hr_manager;
```

In this example, verify_hr_manager is not a password. It is the procedure that authenticates the role before setting it using DBMS_SESSION.SET_ROLE.

The second step is to create the verify_hr_manager procedure. The following code is a procedure that verifies that the session was initiated from an IP Address that begins with the string '172.141.' before authenticating the role:

```
CREATE OR REPLACE PROCEDURE verify_hr_manager
  AUTHID CURRENT_USER IS
       ipstring VARCHAR2(20);
BEGIN
  SELECT SYS_CONTEXT('USERENV', 'IP_ADDRESS')
    INTO ipstring
    FROM DUAL;
  IF SUBSTR(ipstring, 1, 8) = '172.141.' THEN
    DBMS_SESSION.SET_ROLE('hr_manager');
  ELSE
    RETURN;
  END IF;
END;
```

If the IP address begins with the string '172.141.', the SET ROLE statement sets the role to the specified hr_manager role and disables previous roles. If the IP address does not begin with the string '172.141.', the procedure exits silently without setting the role.

In real-life applications, it is important that you do not limit your authentication to just the IP address, since IP addresses can be spoofed. For the same reason, you should not use IP address validation as the primary method of authentication. Once you authenticate the role based on other attributes of the user session, you can use the IP address to further refine access control parameters.

For example, you can combine proxy authentication and the secure application role to enable role authentication only when a user accesses the database through a middle-tier application. The middle-tier logs into the database on behalf of the user, which is where the term proxy authentication originates.

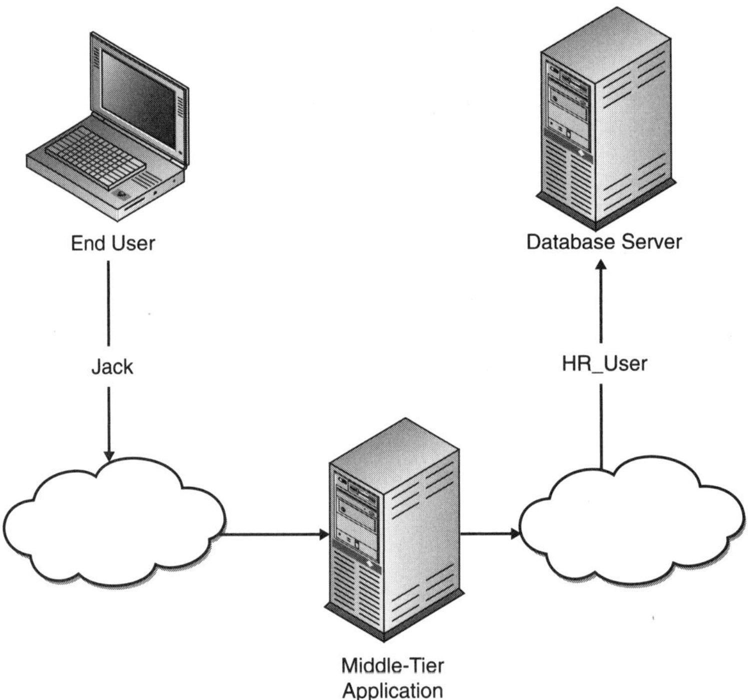

The secure application role can verify that this is a proxy user by invoking SYS_CONTEXT('userenv', 'proxy_userid') or SYS_CONTEXT('userenv', 'proxy_user'). The secure application role can also verify that the user has a connection to the database via a middle-tier application and that it is not connected directly. You can limit the user connection to certain IP addresses with the secure application role procedure defined earlier.

Global Application Context

We have seen that Oracle can establish fine-grained access control that is specific to each user whether the user is a database user or a proxy user. Setting up an individual session for each user constitutes a significant overhead. If this application were extended to the Web where hundreds of thousands of users can request access to the data, this overhead can become next to impossible; besides, the application will not scale well. Establishing a separate connection for each user, on the Web, can require significant overhead since the Web is stateless.

You can also implement user-based fine-grained access control in middle-tier applications where a single application user connects to the database and interacts with the database on behalf of the end users. The single user identity (HR_Manager) connection to the database is created for each individual user (Jack and Jill).

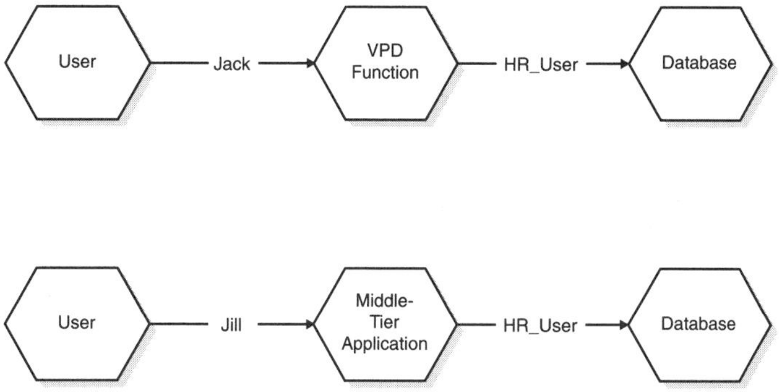

User — Jack → VPD Function — HR_User → Database

User — Jill → Middle-Tier Application — HR_User → Database

Security can be set differently for each user by invoking SYS_CONTEXT('userenv', 'attribute') to get information about the user's session. Since the user who is connected to the database is always HR_Manager, regardless of who connected to the middle-tier application, Oracle's capability to audit based on the individual user is eliminated. When the number of users is small, there is no need to reuse an existing connection to the database.

On the Web, when hundreds of users connect to the middle-tier, there will be a need to reuse an existing connection to the database. Oracle9*i* provides a facility for connection pooling, where many connections to the middle-tier can share application contexts. This concept of enabling many connections to share and reuse application contexts is called Global Application Context. In other words, the application establishes a specific number of Global Application Contexts that are connected to the database. The application reuses these Global Application Contexts instead of creating individual user sessions. This concept of pooling connections results in highly scalable applications.

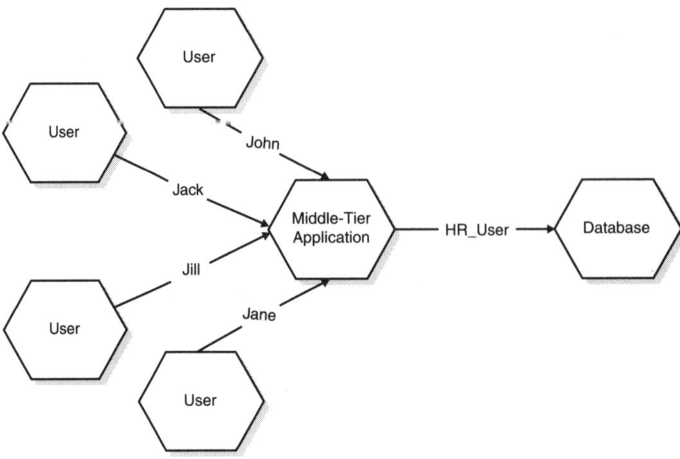

Oracle provides a number of interfaces in the DBMS_SESSION package that enable the application to set and manage global application context. These interfaces were enhanced to include a client identifier for each global application context. These interfaces include the following:

- SET_CONTEXT
- SET_IDENTIFIER
- CLEAR_CONTEXT
- CLEAR IDENTIFIER

The middle-tier application uses SET_CONTEXT to set the global application context for a specific client. Then it uses SET_IDENTIFIER to associate a pre-established global application context (an existing database connection) with the client session. The client identifier becomes an attribute (CLIENT_IDENTIFIER) of the user session information. Invocations of SYS_CONTEXT after the SET_IDENTIFIER will retrieve information about the context that was associated with the SET_IDENTIFIER. The client identifier becomes the basis for establishing global application context. Before exiting the interaction with the database, the application has to invoke CLEAR_IDENTIFIER to release the client's access to the global application context.

The steps to effect a global application context solution follow:

1. The first step is to establish a global application context as follows:

   ```
   CREATE CONTEXT hr USING hr.init ACCESSED GLOBALLY;
   ```

   This ACCESSED GLOBALLY qualifier specifies that the context that is created is available for reuse as a global application context.

2. The middle-tier application is the HR application. Upon startup, the HR application establishes connections to the database. Let's assume the user identity for these connections is HR_Manager.

3. A nondatabase user named jack logs on to the HR application and is authenticated by the middle-tier application, which provides a connection for jack.

4. The middle-tier HR application assigns a temporary identifier for the jack connection; let's assume this ID is 1357. The middle-tier application either returns the ID as a cookie entry on the browser machine or maintains the ID in the middle-tier application.

5. When the application invokes the hr.init package as part of the initialization of the application context, the package issues the following command:

   ```
   DBMS_SESSION.SET_CONTEXT('hr', 'id', 'jack', 'HR_Manager', 1357);
   ```

   The identifier for this application context is jack.

   It also issues a second SET_CONTEXT statement:

   ```
   DBMS_SESSION.SET_CONTEXT('hr', 'division_code', 'AC', 'HR_Manager', 1357);
   ```

   This second SET_CONTEXT call sets the application context to the Accounting Division (AC).

6. The application then picks an existing database connection for this user session (jack) with the following call:

   ```
   DBMS_SESSION.SET_IDENTIFIER (1357);
   ```

   The application uses an existing database connection that has the username identity HR_Manager.

7. At this stage, the application has established a context for jack. Any calls to SYS_CONTEXT will retrieve information about jack's context. For example, the following call

```
SYS_CONTEXT('hr', 'ID')
```

in a query will return jack, and the following call

```
SYS_CONTEXT('hr', 'division_code')
```

will return AC.

8. Let's say a second nondatabase user named jill logs on to the middle-tier HR application. The application authenticates jill, and provides a connection for jill with the identifier 3972.

9. The application issues a second set of SET_CONTEXT calls as follows:

```
DBMS_SESSION.SET_CONTEXT('hr', 'id', 'jill', 'HR_Manager', 3972);
DBMS_SESSION.SET_CONTEXT('hr', 'division_code', 'OP', 'HR_Manager', 3972);
```

The first SET_CONTEXT sets the application context to use jill as the identifier.

This second SET_CONTEXT call sets the application context to the Operations Division (OP).

10. The application then sets up a database connection for this user session (jill) with the following call:

```
DBMS_SESSION.SET_IDENTIFIER (3972);
```

11. At this stage, the application has established a context for jill. Any calls to SYS_CONTEXT will retrieve information about jill's context.

12. Any user with a client session ID set to 1357 who issues a SYS_CONTEXT call will retrieve information about jack's context, while users with a client ID of 3972 will retrieve information about jill's context. To determine the client ID, the user can use

```
SYS_CONTEXT('USERENV', 'CLIENT_IDENTIFIER')
```

in a query.

13. While the application has established contexts, it does not mean that you have controlled data access. The application has to specifically establish the VPD as discussed earlier in this chapter.

Multiple Policies

Prior to Oracle9*i*, you had to put all your policies into one comprehensive policy. Oracle9*i* allows you to associate several policies with a table or view. For example, you may associate one policy based on the Job Titles (functional responsibility) and another based on Division Code (area of jurisdiction). When an application or user attempts to access the data, the database must enforce both controls in tandem. In other words, every policy must grant you access before you can access the data. If you fail to make it through one policy, the database will not grant you access to the data. This is an all or nothing deal with an implicit AND between the policies.

This capability of setting up many policies against a table gives a great degree of autonomy to developers. Each group of developers can establish its own policy independent of other groups of developers.

Partitioned Fine-Grained Access Control

You have seen that you can set up many policies against a table, and that these policies are ANDed (that is, you must satisfy all these policies to gain access to the table). While Oracle does this to ensure maximum security, this could pose a problem for your application. The accessible rows for your application may be restricted because of the security policies of other applications.

You have also seen that multiple applications, each with multiple policies, can access the same table or view. When a certain application tries to access a table, it is important to identify which policies must be applied in order to gain access to the table or view. Oracle gives you the ability to combine a number of Security Policies into a Security Policy Group, which you can associate with an application context (also called the driving application context). When you access a table or view, Oracle refers to the driving application context to identify the associated security policy group; Oracle then enforces all the policies in the associated security policy group. Security policy groups enable you to partition fine-grained access control based on the needs of the driving application context.

When you establish a security policy, it is organized under a security policy group called SYS_DEFAULT, which is organized under the Policy Groups folder, which is part of the Fine-Grained Access Control folder in the Oracle Policy Manager. When you create a security policy group, it is added to the Policy Groups folder. When Oracle enforces all the policies in the associated security policy group of the driving application context, it also enforces all the policies in the SYS_DEFAULT policy group.

Let's assume you are hosting the Employee table for two customers on your Oracle server. The first customer requires you to restrict access to data that belongs to the same division as the user and then to data for employees who work on projects where the user is the project manager. Let's say you set up a driving application context C1_context and a policy group called C1_policy_group for the first customer. The second customer requires you to restrict access to data for employees who are supervised by the user and to employees whose status is part time. Let's say you set up a driving application context C2_context and a policy group called C2_policy_group for the second customer. As depicted in Figure 1-1, when a user with the application context C1_context accesses the Employee table, Oracle enforces all the policies in C1_policy_group and then enforces all the policies in SYS_DEFAULT. When a user with the application context C2_context accesses the Employee table, Oracle enforces all the policies in C2_policy_group and then enforces all the policies in SYS_DEFAULT.

If you do not set up the driving application context or if the driving context is NULL, Oracle executes all the policies that are applicable to the table or view that is being accessed. Oracle does this to ensure that an application cannot circumvent the policies and that the policies are applied, no matter what, when a table or view is accessed.

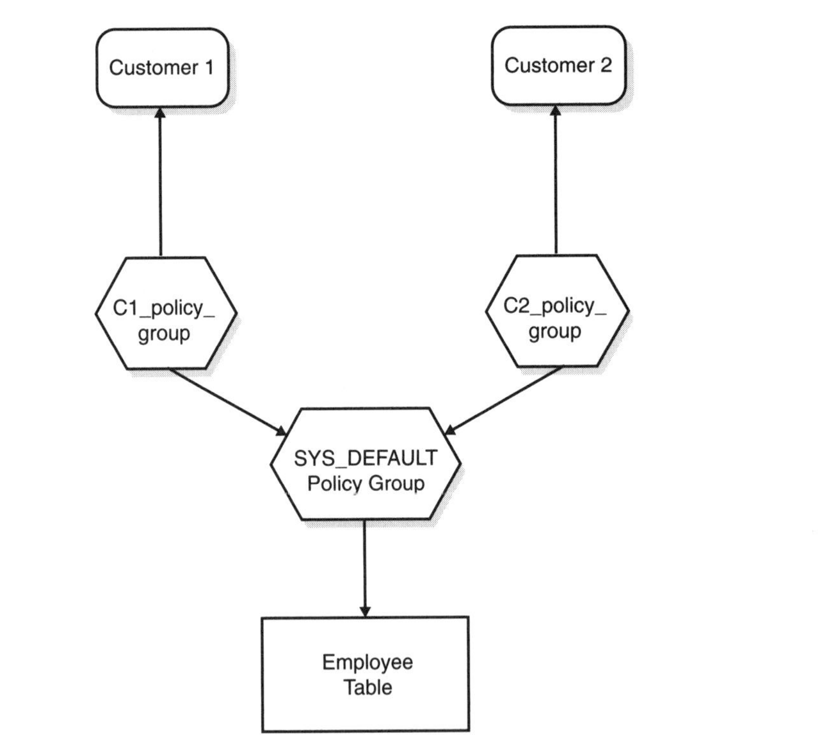

FIGURE 1-1. *Security Policy Groups and the Default Policy Group*

The DBMS_RLS package contains a number of interfaces to work with policy groups. You create a policy group with the CREATE_POLICY_GROUP interface. You add a security policy to an existing security policy group by using the ADD_GROUPED_POLICY interface. You add a driving application context to an existing policy group with the ADD_POLICY_CONTEXT interface.

Fine-Grained Auditing (FGA)

Prior to Oracle9*i*, value-based auditing was possible with before and after triggers for the INSERT, UPDATE, and DELETE operations. Oracle9*i* extended the concept of the fine-grained access control to the auditing function to enable you to audit SELECT operations. When a user attempts to access data that the user does not have authorization to access, the SELECT operation is unsuccessful. Oracle9*i* can specifically audit just the successful operations or the unsuccessful operations. In other words, FGA can audit attempts to access information even if the information itself was not accessed.

You are not restricted to auditing every SELECT operation; Oracle only audits those SELECT operations that satisfy an audit condition. Similar to the fine-grained access control, Oracle9*i* uses the concept of appending predicates to the WHERE clause of the query. This predicate is the basis for FGA, the query is audited whenever the audit policy condition is satisfied. The rows that satisfy the audit condition are referred to as interested rows.

Let's assume that you plan to audit all access to employee data for employees who have a security_clearance of TOPSECRET, and that the employee with an ssn of 123-45-6789 has a security_clearance of TOPSECRET.

Let's say you issue the following query:

```
SELECT last_name, first_name, phone
  FROM employee
 WHERE ssn = '123-45-6789';
```

Since the security_clearance for this employee is TOPSECRET, the audit policy condition *is* met. This query will be audited.

Let's say you issue the following query:

```
SELECT last_name, first_name, phone
  FROM employee
 WHERE security_clearance = 'SECRET';
```

This query only retrieves employees with SECRET clearance; it does not meet the audit policy condition that requires an audit of TOPSECRET. This query is *not* audited.

Let's say you issue the following query:

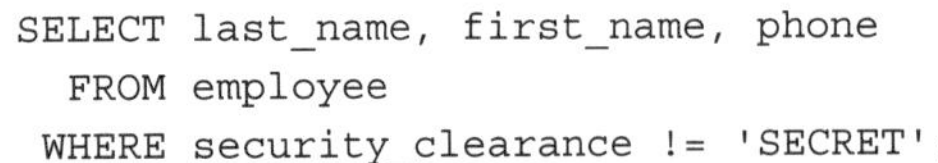

```
SELECT last_name, first_name, phone
  FROM employee
 WHERE security_clearance != 'SECRET';
```

This query retrieves any employees that do not have a SECRET clearance. Some of the non-SECRET employees are TOPSECRET, therefore it meets the audit policy condition that requires an audit of TOPSECRET. This query *is* audited.

You can specify auditing requirements with the interfaces specified within the DBMS_FGA package. These interfaces are

- ADD_POLICY
- DROP_POLICY
- DISABLE_POLICY
- ENABLE_POLICY

When you create an audit policy, you must specify the schema, object, name of the policy, and audit condition. Optionally, you can also specify the audit column, the event handler schema, the event handler name, and whether the policy is enabled. The policies are stored in DBA_AUDIT_POLICIES.

When you drop, enable, or disable an audit policy, you must specify the schema, object, and name of the policy.

For example, to audit queries that attempt to retrieve employee data for employees who have a security_clearance of TOPSECRET, you use the following statement:

```
DBMS_FGA.ADD_POLICY
 (
  object_schema   => 'hr',
  object_name     => 'employees',
  policy_name     => 'audit_dept100_employees',
  audit_condition => 'department_id =''100'''
 );
```

When the audit is triggered, the audit event data is inserted into DBA_FGA_AUDIT_TRAIL. Some audit information that is stored is the session id, username, timestamp, name of the policy, and the SQL query text.

Audit Column

You can also specify an audit column to restrict audits. Without the audit column, the query is audited if the audit condition is satisfied. If you specify the audit column, the audit is not triggered even if the audit condition is met, unless the audit column is referenced in the query. If you do not specify an audit column, Oracle9*i* will treat all columns as audit columns.

You specify the audit column with the audit_column attribute, as follows:

```
DBMS_FGA.ADD_POLICY
 (
  object_schema   => 'hr',
  object_name     => 'employee',
  policy_name     => 'audit_topsecret_employees',
  audit_condition => 'security_clearance = ''TOPSECRET'' ',
  audit_column    => 'ssn'
 );
```

In this example, you are not concerned about every query that references employees with TOPSECRET clearance. You are only concerned if they also reference the ssn column, since the ssn enables them to obtain detailed information about the employee.

Let's say you issue the following query:

```
SELECT last_name, first_name, phone
  FROM employee
 WHERE ssn = '123-45-6789';
```

Since the security_clearance for this person is TOPSECRET, the audit policy condition is met. Also, you are referencing the ssn column in the query. This query will be audited.

Let's say you issue the following query:

```
SELECT last_name, first_name, phone
  FROM employee
 WHERE security_clearance = 'SECRET';
```

This query only retrieves employees with SECRET clearance; it does not meet the audit policy condition that requires an audit of TOPSECRET. This query is not audited.

Let's say you issue the following query:

```
SELECT last_name, first_name, phone
  FROM employee
 WHERE security_clearance != 'SECRET';
```

This query retrieves any employees who do not have a SECRET clearance. Some of the non-SECRET employees are TOPSECRET; therefore, it meets the audit policy condition that requires an audit of TOPSECRET. In any case, this query is not audited since you are not referencing the ssn column.

Audit Event Handler

You can also specify an audit event handler as part of the audit policy. When the audit is triggered, Oracle9*i* invokes this event handler. You can define an event handler as follows:

```
CREATE OR REPLACE PROCEDURE hr.ts_access_alert
  (schema varchar2, table_name varchar2, policy_name varchar2) AS
 BEGIN
   /* You can enter your custom audit code here.
      For example, you may decide to send an email or alert a pager
      or update a special table for tracking special information
      Let's assume you want to send a pager alert.
                                                          */
   UTIL_ALERT_PAGER('TS Access Alert '||SYSDATE||' '||table_name);
 END;
```

You specify the event_handler in the audit_policy as follows:

```
DBMS_FGA.ADD_POLICY
 (
  object_schema   => 'hr',
  object_name     => 'employee',
  policy_name     => 'audit_topsecret_employees',
  audit_condition => 'security_clearance = ''TOPSECRET'' ',
  audit_column    => 'ssn',
  handler_schema  => 'hr',
  handler_module  => 'ts_access_alert'
 );
```

Enhancements to Encryption

The purpose of encryption is to make data secure; however, the resulting security is only as good as the strength of the encryption key that is used, the security of the connection when the key is transmitted, and the security of the location where the key is stored. Cryptanalysts (those who try to crack encryption codes) look for weaknesses in the encryption key that is used or for access to the keys that are not securely stored, before they cycle exhaustively through all the key combinations. The stronger your key, the more secure your key is.

It is important that you choose a strong key and that you store your key securely. The key must be easily accessed so your performance does not degrade significantly. On the other hand, the key must be stored securely, since a user who can retrieve your key has access to your data.

If you choose a key that is easy to predict, the key is considered to be weak. For example, random number generators that are based on the time of day and date are highly predictable. Oracle's DBMS_RANDOM.RANDOM function generates a random number, but it is weak since a given seed value produces the same random number. Oracle 9*i* adds the Federal Information Processing Standard (FIPS) 140 certified random number generator called GETKEY, which is a strong key. GETKEY is a part of the DBMS_OBFUSCATION_TOOLKIT package.

The DBMS_OBFUSCATION_TOOLKIT performs encryption and decryption on the server as opposed to client machine. You must secure the connection when you send your key to the server; otherwise, it is vulnerable to being picked off. The procedure that performs the encryption must itself be obfuscated to minimize the risk of discovery by unauthorized users.

Optional Security Products

Oracle Advanced Security is a comprehensive security architecture. Some of the components of this architecture are packaged as optional products. Oracle Advanced Security is extremely important to assure security in enterprise level database applications on the Internet. Oracle Advanced Security Release 8.1.6 has been certified at security Level 2 of the FIPS 140-1 standards specification.

Some of these optional products are

- Oracle Label Security
- Oracle Single Sign-On (SSO)
- Oracle Enterprise Login Assistant

Oracle Label Security

Oracle Label Security is an optional add-on product that is part of Oracle9*i*'s Advanced Security Architecture. The Oracle Label Security product replaces a previously available add-on product called Trusted Oracle that is used primarily by government agencies.

Oracle Label Security is built upon the VPD capability of Oracle 9*i*. You do not have to do any programming to implement security based on labels; you use Oracle Policy Manager (a GUI tool) for managing label security policies. Oracle Label Security provides a toolkit that is comprised of PL/SQL packages to build labels and associate the corresponding label security policy with a table or view.

When a user attempts to access data, Oracle Label Security verifies that the label for a row is validated against the label security privilege associated with the session. If the validation is satisfied, the session has authorization to that row, and the access to the row is granted.

The VPD provides data separation for shared tables in a shared hosting environment. The VPD requires programming and is dependent on using the programming. The Oracle Label Security provides another layer of data separation and access control on top of the controls implemented in the VPD. The Oracle Label Security does not require programming; it is based on data in the row labels. Since Oracle Label Security places the security within the data, it offers the benefit of ease and speed for implementing data separation across many applications. One common use for Oracle Label Security is to restrict data access to user sessions based on security clearance levels such as SECRET and TOPSECRET.

Oracle Single Sign-On (SSO)

The Oracle Application Server (OAS) is middleware software that services database requests. One important feature of OAS is the Single Sign-On (SSO) that enables you to sign-on once and has access to a number of web-based applications. This eliminates the need to have a password for every application. Multiple passwords are a stress on users since they have to remember a number of passwords; multiple passwords are also insecure, since users are likely to write passwords down. The SSO is useful in the Oracle Portal application where the user can have access to many applications when logging in to the portal.

Oracle SSO is made possible in a stateless Web environment through the use of cookies that can be created by the partner applications or by the Oracle Login Server. The Oracle Login Server is the fundamental component that enables you to implement SSO capability. It authenticates the user, then connects to the partner applications on the user's behalf, and passes the identity of the user to the partner application very securely. Since the Oracle Login Server uses cookies to implement SSO capability, the login server will not be able to implement SSO capability if the browser disallows cookies.

Oracle Enterprise Login Assistant

Oracle Enterprise Login Assistant (ELA) is a tool that is enables Oracle to authenticate a user for enterprise-wide application logins. When you start Oracle ELA, it looks for a wallet in the default folder. If it finds one, it prompts you for a password. If you enter the correct password, it logs you in, sets the state to logged in, and creates an obfuscated copy of the wallet on the local machine.

If the Oracle ELA finds an obfuscated copy of a wallet on the local machine when you start it up, it assumes that you are already logged in and sets the state to logged in.

If the Oracle ELA does not find a wallet in the default folder machine when you start it up, it prompts you for a directory service username and password.

Oracle ELA can authenticate you to an LDAP directory service, download the wallet, decrypt it, and establish an SSL connection to public-key infrastructure (PKI)-enabled applications without having to prompt you for a password over again.

Oracle ELA enables you to update the wallet password, the directory password, and the database password in the Oracle Internet Directory (OID) passwords. ELA can also upload a wallet to the OID.

For Review

1. You should be familiar with the concept of the application context and the Virtual Private Database (VPD). The VPD ensures data separation for data from many sources that reside on a single database. You establish a VPD by associating a security policy with a table or view.
2. You should know how to create a Global Application Context and the steps to develop an application that uses the Global Application Context to perform connection pooling.
3. You should be able to identify the process and the interfaces of the DBMS_RLS package that enable you to establish partitioned fine-grained access control.
4. You should understand the concept of fine-grained auditing (FGA), the purpose of the audit column, and the event handler.

Exercises

1. **The Virtual Private Database (VPD):**

   A. Is a way to put each company's data in their own database

   B. Is a way to provide data separation when data from many sources that reside in one database

   C. Associates a security policy with Oracle tables or views

   D. Is a policy function that returns an access condition or criteria that the server will add to the query itself

2. **To create a new application context, you use the following keyword or procedure:**

   A. DBMS_SESSION.SET_CONTEXT

   B. SET CONTEXT

   C. CREATE CONTEXT

   D. DBMS_SESSION.SET_IDENTIFIER

3. **To create a global application context, you use the following qualifier:**

   A. GLOBAL ACCESS

   B. ACCESSED GLOBALLY

   C. GO GLOBAL

   D. GLOBAL CONTEXT

4. **To create a security policy group, you use the following interface of the DBMS_RLS package:**

   A. CREATE_GROUPED_POLICY

   B. MAKE_POLICY_GROUP

   C. NEW_POLICY_GROUP

   D. CREATE_POLICY_GROUP.

5. **Oracle Label Security:**
   A. Enables you to label or name a security policy
   B. Enables you to validate row labels against session label security privileges before granting access
   C. Enables you to audit rows that contain row labels
   D. Enables you to use row labels to specify where you wish to save the results of the audit

Answer Key
1. B, C, D. **2.** C. **3.** B. **4.** D. **5.** B.

Chapter Summary

This chapter explored Oracle9*i*'s response to the security-related challenges of the Internet. We toured the spectrum from obvious, but simple, changes to sophisticated security technology. We began with an exploration of privileged connections and the deprecation of CONNECT INTERNAL and CONNECT INTERNAL/password. You use CONNECT / AS SYSDBA and CONNECT username/password AS SYSDBA in Oracle9*i* to establish a privileged connection.

We looked at the impact of the deprecation of the Server Manager, noting that you have to modify the Server Manager line-mode scripts so they can run in SQL*Plus. We also reviewed some changes that you must make to the Server Manager scripts to adapt them to SQL*Plus. For example, you saw that the Server Manager commands SET CHARWIDTH, SET DATEWIDTH, and SET LONGWIDTH are not supported by SQL*Plus. You use the COLUMN FORMAT command in SQL*Plus even though it behaves in a slightly different manner from the Server Manager commands. You also saw some of the changes required to make comments usable in SQL*Plus scripts.

Then we reviewed the risks inherent in the default administrator accounts such as the SYSTEM/MANAGER account. Upon installation, many administrators did not change the passwords, and the database was vulnerable to security breaches. We looked at the enhancements that were made in Oracle9*i* to tighten the default security for the default administrators accounts.

We focused on the implementation of the Virtual Private Database (VPD) to enforce fine-grained access control. You specify a security policy and associate it with a table or a view. When anyone attempts to access data in that table, Oracle enforces the policy. The policy function adds a predicate to the WHERE clause before Oracle executes the query. We saw that VPDs enabled us to provide data separation even when multiple companies share the same tables on a single hosted database. While VPD was available in Oracle8, Oracle9*i* added enhancements such as a GUI policy management tool, a secure application role, the ability to use multiple policies for a table, partitioning fine-grained access control, and the Global Application Context.

The essence of the policy management tool is to create and manage policies and associate them with tables.

Application Context enables an application to tailor the VPD based on attributes of the user's session. In effect, you can tailor the VPD to satisfy the security needs of the application. You can use the SYS_CONTEXT function to retrieve session attributes such as the user ID, the IP address, and the host name. You refine the security policy by tailoring the predicate based on the attributes of the session. This enables you to implement policies that are not hard coded and can change depending on the application context.

Oracle9*i* enables you to associate this application context with a role as opposed to a table; this results in Secure Application Roles. This enables you to set the application context based on the function performed by the user. In other words, the Secure Application Role integrates the application context with roles.

When an application is deployed on the Web, it would not be practical to set up an individual user session for each of the thousands of users. The users log in to a middleware application. The middleware application establishes a specific number of connections to the database server that are then assigned to a connection pool. The end user sessions are assigned to the first available database connections.

Oracle9*i* allows you to specify a number of security policies and assign them to a table or view. Prior to Oracle9*i*, you could only associate one policy with a table or view. When you assign multiple policies to a table or view, these policies are ANDed.

You can organize policies into groups and then associate a policy group to an application context. When you specify a policy, it is organized in the SYS_DEFAULT policy group.

Oracle9*i* extends the concept of fine-grained access control to the world of auditing. Fine-grained auditing (FGA) enables you to audit the SELECT statement if the query rows satisfy the audit condition. You can also specify an audit column; the audit does not take place unless this column is referenced. You can also specify an audit event handler, which is invoked when an audit is triggered.

Oracle9*i* provides the GETKEY random number generator, which is certified at Level 2 of FIPS-140 standards specification. This provides random numbers that are not easy to predict.

Oracle9*i* also has optional add-on products that are a part of Oracle's advanced security architecture. One of these products is Oracle Label Security, which grants access to data only after verifying that the row level label is validated against label security privilege associated with the session. Oracle Single Sign-On (SSO) enables you to sign in once and to have access to a number of associated web-based applications without additional logins. The Oracle Enterprise Login Assistant takes care of authenticating the user for enterprise-wide logins.

Two-Minute Drill

1. **Privileged Connections**

- CONNECT INTERNAL and CONNECT INTERNAL/password have been deprecated.
  - You can use CONNECT username/password AS SYSDBA.
  - You can use CONNECT / AS SYSDBA to use OS authentication.
- The Server Manager has been deprecated.
  - You must use SQL*Plus to issue STARTUP and SHUTDOWN commands.
  - You must modify the Server Manager scripts to adapt them to SQL*Plus.
  - The SET CHARWIDTH, SET DATEWIDTH, and SET LONGWIDTH Server Manager script commands are not available in SQL*Plus.
  - In SQL*Plus, you use the COLUMN FORMAT or SET LONG command.
  - Comments after commas were okay in the Server Manager. They may need to be reworked to be compatible with SQL*Plus.
- Locked and Expired Default Accounts
  - When DBCA creates a new database, it locks and expires most default user accounts.
  - You must unlock the account first, and then change the password before you can use the account.
- Elimination of Default Passwords
  - Prior to Oracle9*i*, the default passwords for SYS and SYSTEM were CHANGE_ON_INSTALL and MANAGER respectively.
  - In Oracle9*i*, THE DBCA prompts you for the passwords for SYS and for SYSTEM.

- Data Dictionary Accessibility
  - Prior to Oracle9*i*, 07_DICTIONARY_ACCESSIBILITY was set to TRUE by default.
  - In Oracle9*i*, this parameter is set to FALSE by default.
- Limit Privileges for PUBLIC
  - PUBLIC users can invoke PL/SQL packages whose execution privileges are set to PUBLIC.
  - This PUBLIC privilege may be able to execute packages that provide access to data to which the user does not have direct access.
  - Revoke EXECUTION privileges on powerful package.

2. Virtual Private Database (VPD)

- Fine-Grained Access Control
  - You specify a security policy and associate it with a table or view.
  - Enables clients to have data separation when they share tables on hosted database servers.
  - You can associate one policy for the SELECT statement, another for the INSERT statement, another for the UPDATE statement, and yet another for the DELETE statement.
  - The policy function returns an access condition or predicate that is appended to the WHERE clause of the query.
- Policy Management Tool
  - A GUI tool creates and manages security policies.
  - A GUI tool creates and manages application contexts.
  - A GUI tool associates security policies with a table or view.
  - A GUI tool manages Oracle Label Security.
- Secure Application Role
  - Secure Application Context tailors the VPD to meet the access requirements of the application.
  - The Secure Application Role integrates the Secure Application Context with roles.

- Global Application Context
  - Users log into a middleware application and the application creates a session for the user.
  - The middleware application establishes a connection to the database server.
  - The middleware application assigns an unused database connection to the user session.
  - Database connections can be reused.
- Multiple Policies
  - You can assign multiple security polices to a table or view.
  - When enforced, these policies are ANDed.
  - You must satisfy all policies to gain access to the table or view.
- Partitioned Fine-Grained Access Control
  - You can organize security policies into groups.
  - You can assign a security policy group to a driving application context.
  - You partition the fine-grained access control to be enforced for a given driving application context.

3. **Fine-Grained Auditing (FGA)**
   - Prior to Oracle9*i*, you could audit the INSERT, UPDATE, and DELETE operations with before and after triggers.
   - In Oracle9*i*, you can audit the SELECT statement, thanks to fine-grained auditing.
   - The query is audited if the rows satisfy the audit condition.
   - You can specify an audit column. The query is not audited if the audit column is not referenced by the query.
   - You can specify an audit event handler. This is a procedure that is invoked when the audit is triggered.
   - You typically use the event handler to send an e-mail or alert to a pager.

4. **Enhancements to Encryption**
    - Encryption is only as good as the strength of the encryption key, the security of the connection, and the security of the storage of the key.
    - The stronger the key, the more secure is the encryption, since it is less predictable.
    - Oracle9*i* adds the FIPS-141 certified random number generator GETKEY.
5. **Optional Security Products**
    - Oracle Label Security
        - The row label is validated against the Oracle Label Security privileges assigned to the session before data access is granted.
        - No programming is required.
    - Oracle Single Sign-On (SSO)
        - Sign on just once and have access to a number of associated web-based applications.
        - The core of the SSO is the Oracle Login Server.
        - The Oracle Login Server authenticates the user, connects to the partner applications on the user's behalf, and passes the identity of the user to the application in a secure manner.
    - Oracle Enterprise Login Assistant
        - A user is authenticated for enterprise-wide application login.
        - A wallet can be located and, if your password matches, can log you in.
        - A wallet password can be updated.

Fill-in-the-Blanks

1. To start and stop a database you can use either the SYSDBA or __________ privileges.
2. To establish a ____________________, you specify a security policy and associate it with Oracle tables or views.
3. Oracle provides the ____________ for you to obtain information about the session.

4. When you establish a security policy, it is organized under a security policy group called ________________.

5. Oracle9*i* allows you to associate multiple ______________ to a table or view.

6. You can specify auditing requirements with the interfaces specified within the _____________ package.

Chapter Questions

1. With respect to associating security policies with a table or view, which of the following is true?

A. You are restricted to associate only one policy with a table or view.

B. You can associate multiple policies with a table or view.

C. You cannot associate policies with a table or view.

D. Oracle does not establish a security policy; you need to grant permissions in the user and password table.

2. To establish partitioned find-grained access control with a driving application context, you:

A. Add a policy to an application context.

B. Add an application context to a policy group.

C. Add an application context to a policy.

D. Add a policy group to an application context.

3. To create an audit policy, you use the following interface of the DBMS_FGA package:

A. ADD_POLICY

B. CREATE _POLICY

C. MAKE_POLICY

D. NEW_POLICY

4. The Secure Application Context:

A. Uses SYS_CONTEXT to obtain information about the session.

B. Was introduced in Oracle9*i*.

C. Tailors access control based on the what the user requests.

D. Secures the location where the application is housed.

5. **Which of the following roles allows a user to create the database?**

A. DBA

B. SYSOPER

C. SYSDBA

D. CATALOG OWNER

6. **After creating the Oracle9*i* database, which of the following user accounts are not locked by default?**

A. HR

B. SCOTT

C. CTXSYS

D. OE

7. **Which of the following parameters needs to be set to TRUE in order to allow a user with SELECT ANY TABLE privilege to access the data dictionary views?**

A. QUERY_REWRITE_ENABLED

B. O7_DICTIONARY_ACCESSIBILTY

C. ORACLE_TRACE_ENABLE

D. SQL_TRACE

8. **To implement a Virtual Private Database, the security policy needs to be associated with which of the following?**

A. Roles

B. Users

C. Tables and Views

D. Indexes

9. **Which package contains the interfaces that you need to specify a Global Application Context?**

   A. DBMS_STANDARD

   B. DBMS_POOL

   C. SET_ROLE

   D. DBMS_SESSION

10. **Which of the following statements is true with the Secure Application Role?**

   A. SET ROLE invokes the associated procedure that authenticates the role.

   B. SET ROLE needs a password.

   C. A user with access to the application code can see the password.

   D. The Secure Application Role cannot ensure that the role was enabled by a proxy user.

Fill-in-the-Blank Answers

1. SYSOPER
2. Virtual Private Database
3. SYS_CONTEXT
4. SYS_DEFAULT
5. Security policies
6. DBMS_FGA

Answers to Chapter Questions

1. B. You can associate multiple policies with a table or view.

Explanation Prior to Oracle9*i*, you could only associate only one policy with a table or a view. Oracle9*i* allows you to associate multiple policies with a table or a view.

2. B. Add an application context to a policy group.

Explanation You first create a security policy using the DBMS_RLS.CREATE_POLICY_GROUP interface, then you add the policy to the group with the DBMS_RLS.ADD_GROUPED_POLICY, and you add the driving application context to the security policy group with the DBMS_RLS.ADD_POLICY_CONTEXT interface.

3. A. ADD_POLICY

Explanation You use the add policy interface to create a new policy. You must specify the schema, object, name of the policy, and audit condition. Optionally, you can also specify the audit column, event handler schema, event handler name, and whether the policy is enabled.

4. A. Uses SYS_CONTEXT to obtain information about the session

Explanation The SYS_CONTEXT function enables you to retrieve a variety of information from the session attributes.

5. C. SYSDBA

Explanation The SYSOPER does not have adequate privileges to create a database. You need the SYSDBA privilege to create the database.

6. B. SCOTT

Explanation DBCA database creation does not expire and lock the SCOTT, SYS, and SYSTEM user accounts.

7. B. O7_DICTIONARY_ACCESSIBILTY

Explanation You must assign a TRUE to O7_DICTIONARY_ACCESSIBILTY to allow a user with SELECT ANY TABLE privilege to access the data dictionary views.

8. C. Tables and Views

Explanation To implement a Virtual Private Database (VPD), you must first specify a security policy, and then assign the policy to a table or view. Anytime a user attempts to access data from that table, it will trigger that security policy.

9. D. DBMS_SESSION

Explanation The DBMS_SESSION package contains the SET_CONTEXT, SET_IDENTIFIER, CLEAR_CONTEXT, and CLEAR_IDENTIFIER interfaces that you need to specify a Global Application Context.

10. A. SET ROLE invokes the associated procedure that authenticates the role.

Explanation You specify a Secure Application Role with the following statement:

```
CREATE ROLE hr_manager IDENTIFIED USING hr.verify_hr_manager;
```

This statement creates a role called hr_manager. When an application sets to this role, the procedure verify_hr_manager will be invoked.

The SET ROLE needed a password prior to Oracle9*i*. In Oracle9*i*, it does not require a password.

CHAPTER 2

Availability Enhancements

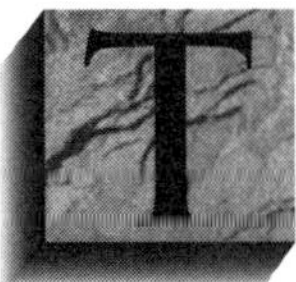

The downtime of production databases can have a significant impact on the organization: You can lose revenue, you can lose credibility, you can lose customers, you can lose orders, you may not deliver on obligations, you may violate contract requirements for uptime, and you may encounter legal proceedings. This chapter discusses the following:

- General high-availability technology
- Data guard
- Online operations
- Replication enhancements
- LogMiner

General High-Availability Technology

Oracle 9*i* introduced a number of enhancements to its comprehensive data availability solution. For example, Oracle9*i* realizes that downtime is an eventuality, and that one aspect of database availability is to minimize the amount of downtime by focusing on recovering from an outage very quickly.

Some of the high-availability enhancements are

- Minimal input/output (I/O) recovery
- Fast-start time-based recovery limit
- Oracle Flashback
- Resumable space allocation
- Export/import features

Minimal I/O Recovery

Oracle9*i* recognized that failure is a reality and focused specifically on recovering rapidly from the outage by optimizing the speed with which it can apply redo logs. One obvious solution is to use disks and drivers that can quickly access the logs and can transfer the data into memory rapidly. A second solution is to ensure that the redo logs reside in a contiguous area on disk. A third solution is to minimize the number of redo entries that must be read and applied; this concept is called *minimal I/O recovery.*

Oracle documents every change that is made to the database in the redo log. Changes are recorded in the redo log as redo entries, which are comprised of a set of change vectors. A change vector tracks a specific change that is made to a single data block. The redo logs also track the rollback segments in the database.

Oracle uses the redo log to recover from a database crash. Oracle scans the redo logs, reads the change vectors, and applies them to the corresponding data block in the database.

To recover from a crash, you must recover the data blocks in the cache that were dirty at the time of the failure. The entries that pertain to the dirty blocks in the data cache are documented in the redo log. However, the redo log is very likely to contain entries for dirty data blocks that were written back to disk before the crash, and therefore were not dirty at the time of the failure. Oracle9*i* optimized the recovery process to exclude the redo log entries that do not apply to blocks that were dirty at the time of the failure (see Figure 2-1).

Oracle first does a quick pass through the redo logs to identify the change vectors that pertain to the dirty blocks and then stores this information in the PGA. In a second pass, Oracle uses the information in the PGA to apply just the identified changes. Since Oracle only sequentially reads the online log and does not actually access the data blocks themselves, the overall time to recover is minimized by the two-pass approach.

Fast-Start Time-Based Recovery Limit

Oracle9*i* periodically stores the checkpoint redo byte address (RBA) in the redo log. A checkpoint is designated by a system change number (SCN) in the control file. The checkpoint assures you that all data blocks with an SCN that is less than or equal to

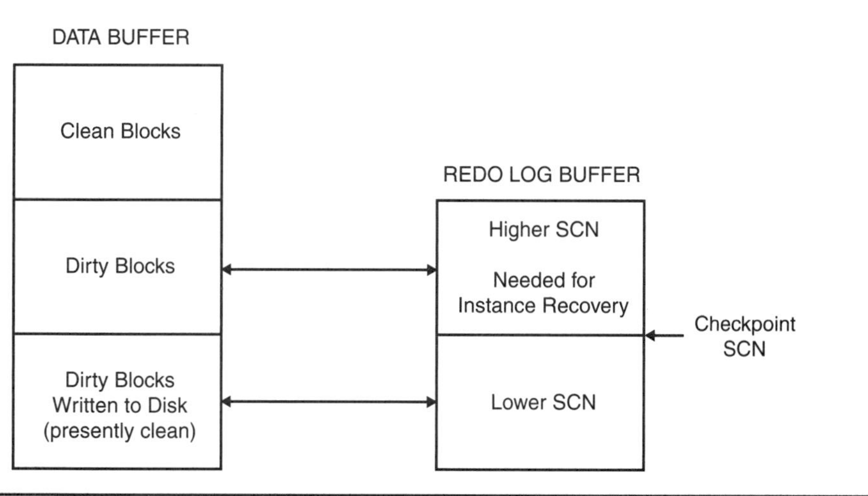

FIGURE 2-1. *Redo logs and instance recovery*

the checkpoint SCN have been written to disk. In the event of a failure, only redo entries with an SCN higher than the checkpoint SCN need to be read and applied. More specifically, the checkpoint RBA identifies the starting point in the redo log from which redo entries must be applied.

The time to recover is dependent on how recently the last checkpoint was done, since it determines the number of data blocks with a higher SCN than the checkpoint SCN. The time to recover is also dependent upon the number of redo log blocks that must be read to identify changes. Therefore, frequent checkpointing actions result in a lower time for instance recovery; the price for this benefit is the adverse impact on performance. This performance degradation occurs because checkpointing uses the database writer (DBWn) processes. You must make a trade-off between instance recovery time and operational database performance.

Oracle9*i* introduces the fast-start checkpointing architecture to implement fast-start instance recovery functionality. The fast-start checkpointing architecture performs incremental checkpointing, and it writes the oldest dirty blocks first to ensure that the most recent dirty blocks are associated with a higher SCN. You can now specify the target mean time to recover (MTTR) for the instance recovery by assigning the initialization parameter FAST_START_MTTR_TARGET a value between 0 and 3,600 seconds. When you set this parameter to 0, Oracle9*i* will not use this parameter to manage instance recovery time. The optimal value for FAST_START_MTTR_TARGET depends upon the database utilization, the system global area (SGA) size, and the Service Level Agreement (SLA) for that site. Your challenge is to optimize the FAST_START_MTTR_TARGET parameter such that it is in accordance with the SLA without an undue degradation in operational performance. You can verify checkpoint statistics with the Statspack and by querying the V$INSTANCE_RECOVERY view.

Oracle9*i* added the following three columns to V$INSTANCE_RECOVERY:

- **TARGET_MTTR** The user's setting for the FAST_START_MTTR_TARGET parameter
- **ESTIMATED_MTTR** The MTTR that is estimated based on the number of dirty blocks and the number of redo log blocks
- **CKPT_BLOCK_WRITES** The number of data blocks that were written by the checkpoint write operation

You can set the FAST_START_MTTR_TARGET parameter dynamically with the following statement:

```
ALTER SYSTEM SET FAST_START_MTTR_TARGET = 240;
```

Oracle internally uses the FAST_START_MTTR_TARGET parameter value to calculate and set the FAST_START_IO_TARGET and LOG_CHECKPOINT_INTERVAL parameters. If you specify the FAST_START_IO_TARGET and LOG_CHECKPOINT_INTERVAL parameter values, they will override the values Oracle calculates from the FAST_START_MTTR_TARGET parameter.

Some parameters that you use to manage instance recovery are as follows:

- The LOG_CHECKPOINT_INTERVAL parameter value specifies the maximum number of redo blocks that you can have after the checkpoint. You can eliminate checkpoint intervals by setting LOG_CHECKPOINT_INTERVAL to 0 (zero).
- The LOG_CHECKPOINT_TIMEOUT parameter specifies the maximum number of seconds of redo logging action after the checkpoint.
- The FAST_START_IO_TARGET parameter specifies the number of data blocks that must be recovered with the two-pass minimal I/O recovery.
- The DB_BLOCK_MAX_DIRTY_TARGET parameter specifies the maximum number of dirty data blocks that you can have in the buffer cache. This parameter has been retired in Oracle9*i*.

Oracle Flashback

Oracle Flashback enables you to query the database as of a certain time or a specific SCN in the past. All DML operations that were committed prior to that specific time or SCN are included, while data that was committed after the specific time or SCN is not.

Some applications where Oracle Flashback is useful are

- Decision support systems (OLAP)
- Document management systems and e-mail systems
- Database repair

When working with decision support systems, Flashback enables you to analyze data as of a past time period. When using databases, document management systems, and email systems, Flashback enables you to recover database rows, documents, or emails that were accidentally deleted by stepping back to a time or SCN before the deletion and save the document or email in the current period (see Figure 2-2).

Here is an example:

1. All the rows of the database are intact at 10:25; the database is at SCN#1.
2. The user accidentally deletes critical rows of information at 10:28; the database is at SCN#2.

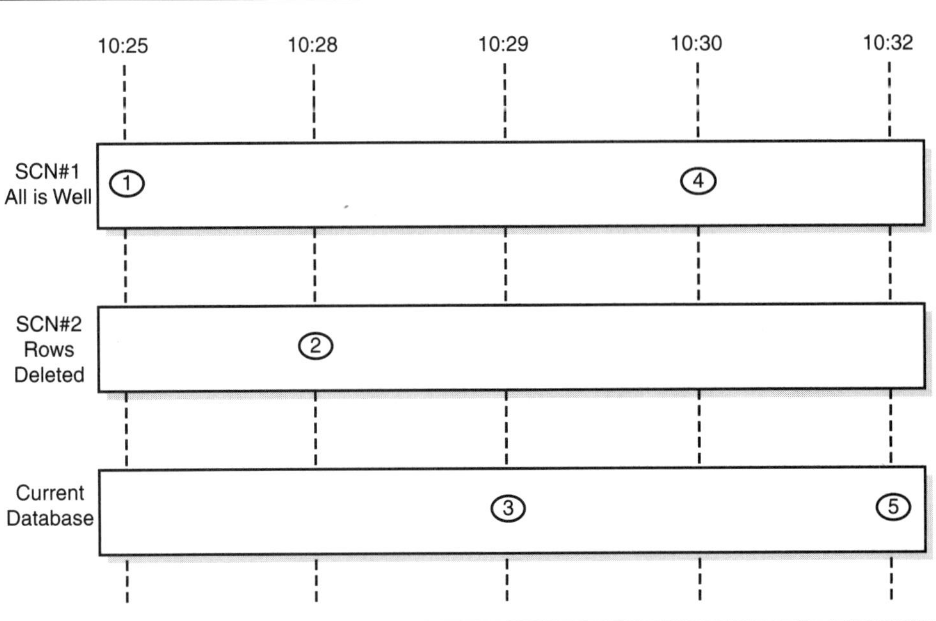

FIGURE 2-2. *Database recovery with Oracle Flashback*

3. The user recognizes this loss of information at 10:29.
4. At 10:30, the user flashes back to the database at SCN#1 before the information was deleted and retrieves the "missing" rows into a PL/SQL cursor.
5. At 10:32, the user returns to the current database by disabling the flashback and inserts the missing data from the PL/SQL cursor.

Requirements for Flashback

Here are some requirements in order to use Flashback:

1. You must use automatic undo management as opposed to the older technique of rollback segments:

   ```
   UNDO_MANAGEMENT = AUTO
   ```

2. You must set the initialization parameter UNDO_RETENTION to specify how far back in seconds Oracle should retain undo information and

therefore how far back you can perform a Flashback query. You can also update this parameter dynamically with the following statement:

```
ALTER SYSTEM SET UNDO_RETENTION=1800
```

3. You must have EXECUTE privilege on the DBMS_FLASHBACK package.

Using Oracle Flashback

Here are the steps for using Flashback to perform Flashback queries:

1. Invoke DBMS_FLASHBACK.ENABLE_AT_TIME to enable Flashback for the session and to access the database at the SCN that is closest to the specified time. You also have the option of invoking DBMS_FLASHBACK.ENABLE_AT_SYSTEM_CHANGE_NUMBER to enable Flashback for the session and to access the database at the specified SCN:

   ```
   EXECUTE DBMS_FLASHBACK.ENABLE_AT_TIME ('22-JAN-01 10:25:00');
   ```

2. Perform the query and access missing information in a PL/SQL cursor. You cannot perform any DML or DDL statements while in Flashback mode.
3. Invoke DBMS_FLASHBACK.DISABLE to disable Flashback and return to the current database:

   ```
   EXECUTE DBMS_FLASHBACK.DISABLE
   ```

Resumable Space Allocation

Resumable Space Allocation suspends a large operation in the event of a space allocation failure so you can take corrective action; execution resumes automatically once the action is corrected. An operational statementthat is resumable space allocation enabled, is called a resumable statement. In the absence of resumable space allocation, the space allocation failure would have resulted in the operation being rolled back.

Correctable Conditions

The following conditions can be corrected:

- **Out of space** You have an out of space error when you cannot get any more extents for various database objects in a tablespace.
- **Maximum extents reached** You have a maximum extents reached error when the number of extents in various database objects exceeds the maximum extents that you have specified for the object.

- **Space quota exceeded** You have a space quota exceeded error when you exceed the space quota that was assigned to you in the tablespace.

Resumable Operations

The following operations are resumable:

- Queries that run out of temporary space for sorting
- **DML** Insert, update, and delete statements
- **DDL** Create table as select, alter table, create index, alter index, create materialized view, and create materialized view log
- **Export/import** SQL*Loader operations

When an operation is suspended, the error is tracked in the alert log. You can invoke the DBMS_RESUMABLE.SPACE_ERROR_INFO function or you can query the USER_RESUMABLE or DBA_RESUMABLE views to obtain information about the suspended operation.

Oracle provides you with the AFTER SUSPEND system event to enable you to perform custom operations whenever an operation is suspended. You can specify a trigger that contains your custom code at either the database or schema level to respond to the AFTER SUSPEND system event. The SQL code within the AFTER SUSPEND trigger is autonomous and it is not resumable. Here is the code to specify an AFTER SUSPEND trigger:

```
CREATE OR REPLACE TRIGGER rsa_custom
  AFTER SUSPEND ON DATABASE
 DECLARE
    /* You would perform your transaction declaration here.
       This declaration will be an autonomous transaction
       since it is within a trigger.
*/

 BEGIN
    /* Your custom code goes here.
       Whenever the operation is suspended, this code
       will be invoked.
    */

 END;
```

Using Resumable Space Allocation

You set the session in the resumable mode with the following statement:

```
ALTER SESSION ENABLE RESUMABLE;
```

You will need the RESUMABLE system privilege to perform this operation. You can set this privilege as follows:

```
GRANT RESUMABLE TO hr;
```

You can use the following statement to specify a timeout in seconds after which the suspended operation will be rolled back and return an error:

```
ALTER SESSION ENABLE RESUMABLE TIMEOUT 1800;
```

You can also specify the timeout as the standard for the suspend operation as follows:

```
CREATE OR REPLACE TRIGGER std_rsa_timeout
    AFTER SUSPEND
    ON DATABASE
  BEGIN
    DBMS_RESUMABLE.SET_TIMEOUT(1800);
  END;
```

You can specify the timeout interval for resumable statements in a session with a DBMS_RESUMABLE.SET_SESSION_TIMEOUT procedure call. When you are done, you can also name the operation as follows:

```
ALTER SESSION ENABLE RESUMABLE TIMEOUT 1800 NAME 'load_purchase_orders';
```

You can abort the resumable statement with the `DBMS_RESUMABLE.ABORT` procedure. You can also get information about the error by invoking the SPACE_ERROR INFO function in the DBMS_RESUMABLE package or by querying the USER_RESUMABLE or DBA_RESUMABLE views.

Export/Import Features

Export places the ANALYZE statement in the dump file if statistics were requested to enable you to recalculate the database optimizer statistics for the table. Import uses the precalculated statistics that are in the dump file, as opposed to using the ANALYZE statement written by Export, to generate statistics. This is because the ANALYZE statement takes time to perform its job.

If you do not want to import precalculated statistics or the questionable statistics, you influence the import in Oracle8*i* with the ANALYZE statement and the RECALCULATE_STATISTICS parameter. Oracle9*i* introduces the new import parameter STATISTICS and the options for this parameter are as follows:

- **ALWAYS** The database optimizer statistics are always imported. This is the default.

- **NONE** The database optimizer statistics are not imported or recalculated.
- **SAFE** The database optimizer statistics are imported only if they are non-questionable.
- **RECALCULATE** The statistics are recalculated, not imported.

Oracle9*i* also introduces the following new parameters for performing exports and imports:

- **RESUMABLE** This parameter is used to enable or disable resumable space allocation. You enable it by setting `RESUMABLE = y`.
- **RESUMABLE_NAME** This is used to identify the resumable operation when you query the USER_RESUMABLE or DBA_RESUMABLE views. This applies only if you have set `RESUMABLE = y`.
- **RESUMABLE_TIMEOUT** This is used to specify the time period within which the situation that suspended the operation must be resolved. If it is not fixed within this time period, the operation is aborted. The default is 7,200 seconds. This applies only if you have set `RESUMABLE = y`.
- **FLASHBACK_SCN** This is used to specify that the export or import enables Flashback and applies to data that corresponds to that particular SCN.
- **FLASHBACK_TIME** This is used to specify that the export or import enables Flashback and applies to data that corresponds to the SCN that is closest to the time specified.

Oracle9*i* also introduces the TABLESPACES export parameter, which only exports tables within the specified tablespace. The corresponding indexes are also exported regardless of which tablespace they are located in. You must have the EXP_FULL_DATABASE role in order to use TABLESPACES.

For Review

1. You must know how Oracle9*i* improves recovery time by performing minimal I/O recovery.
2. Oracle9*i* only applies the redo log entries that pertain to datablocks that were dirty at the time of the failure.
3. You must be aware of the fast-start time-based recovery limit and how it helps the web-hosting site meet the demands of the SLA.
4. You must understand the trade-off between instance recovery time and operational database performance, and about how you can use the

FAST_START_MTTR_TARGET parameter to manage the instance recovery time.

5. You must know how Flashback works and how you can use it to perform database repairs when rows are deleted.
6. You must be familiar with the concept of resumable space allocation and how you can suspend operations, fix space-related errors, and resume operations.
7. You must be able to discuss the enhancements to the export/import utility.

Exercises

1. **The redo log:**
   - **A.** Records every change to the database.
   - **B.** Records changes to the SYS schema only.
   - **C.** Also tracks the rollback segments in the database.
   - **D.** Only tracks the rollback segments in the database
2. **Resumable space allocation:**
   - **A.** Suspends operations whenever any error occurs.
   - **B.** Suspends operations whenever a space allocation error occurs.
   - **C.** Allocates space automatically whenever any error occurs.
   - **D.** Allocates space automatically whenever a space allocation error occurs.

Answer Key

1. A, C. **2.** B.

Data Guard

Oracle8*i*'s standby database technology has been greatly enhanced and renamed to Data Guard in Oracle 9*i*. Data Guard technology is a critical component of the Oracle database availability solution; it enables you to establish and manage a standby database solution. In Oracle9*i*, Data Guard automates all the tasks in setting up this standby database solution, including setting up standby databases, managing standby databases, transferring the redo logs, and applying the logs to the standby database. Before Data Guard, you had to perform all these tasks manually; you had to manually clone the database, copy the archived redo log, and apply this copy of the archived log to the cloned database.

Data Guard provides you with a graphic user interface (GUI) to integrate a primary site with a number of remote sites in order to establish one cohesive standby database solution. You can create, manage, and monitor these sites with the Data Guard GUI tool. If the primary database should fail, Data Guard will failover or transfer control to the secondary database.

Data Guard manages three objects, as shown in Figure 2-3:

- The *database resource* object represents a primary or standby database instance; it is at the lowest level in the object hierarchy.
- The *site* object represents a collection of database resource objects that are resident on a single host system.
- The *configuration* object represents a collection of site objects.

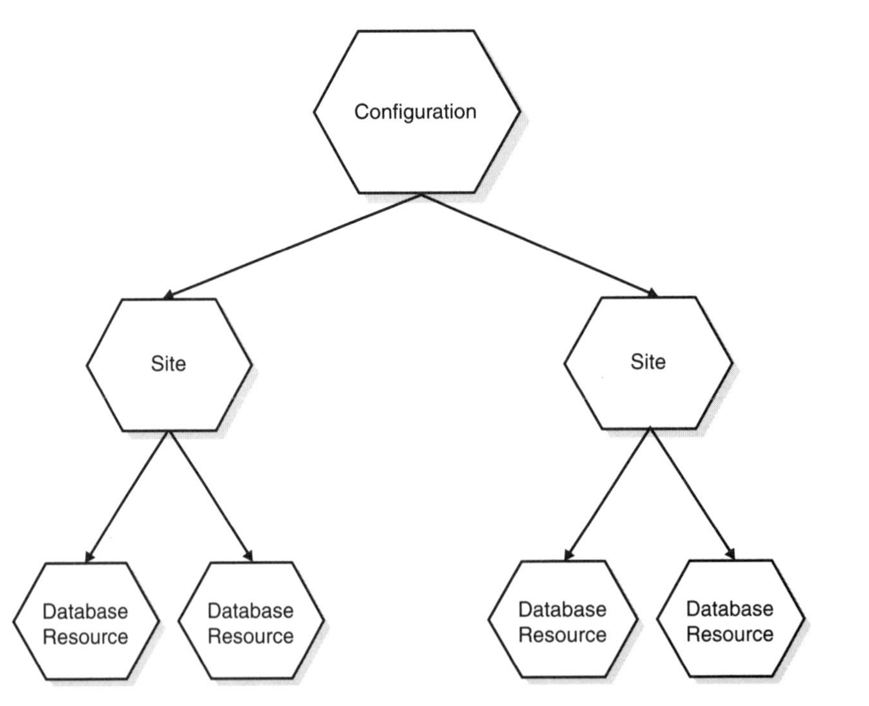

FIGURE 2-3. *Data Guard objects*

Oracle9*i* introduces a number of enhancements for Oracle9*i*'s Data Guard, which includes a comprehensive architectural framework to manage these objects. Some of these new features are as follows:

- A comprehensive architectural framework
- Data availability modes
- Database role transitions
- Archive log gaps
- Managed recovery process (MRP)
- Delayed redo logs

A Comprehensive Architectural Framework

Oracle9*i*'s Data Guard has a distributed and comprehensive architectural framework called the Data Guard Broker, which enables you to establish, configure, monitor, and manage standby database solutions.

Data Guard Components

The Data Guard Broker is comprised of three components (see Figure 2-4):

- The *Data Guard Manager* is a GUI interface component of the Data Guard framework, which is included in the Oracle Enterprise Manager (OEM). It enables you to establish and manage the Data Guard configuration by

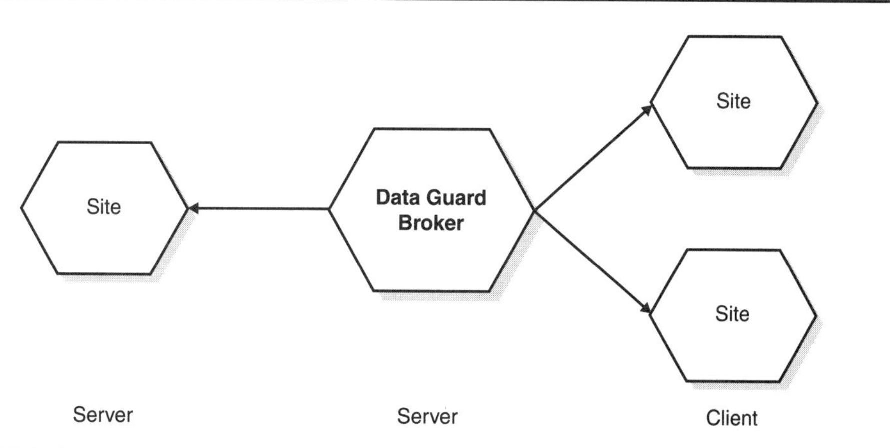

FIGURE 2-4. *The Data Guard Broker components*

pointing and clicking. It enables you to create a standby database, include an existing database into the configuration, monitor the configuration, and report events.

- The *Data Guard Command Line Interface* (CLI) enables you to use text commands to establish, manage, and monitor the Data Guard configuration. You need the SYSDBA privilege to start and shut down the Data Guard CLI.

  Some commands that you can use are CREATE & REMOVE (to create and remove Data Guard objects), ENABLE & DISABLE (to enable or disable Data Guard objects from being monitored), ALTER (to alter the state, online or offline, of Data Guard objects), and SHOW (to get information about objects or the configuration).

- The *Data Guard Monitor* is the component of the Data Guard Broker that is responsible for actually managing and monitoring the configuration. In order to perform this function, a Data Guard Monitor process (DMON) is initiated on each site that is in the Data Guard configuration (see Figure 2-5). When your local Data Guard Manager or CLI needs to interact with an Oracle instance or obtain information about the instance, it

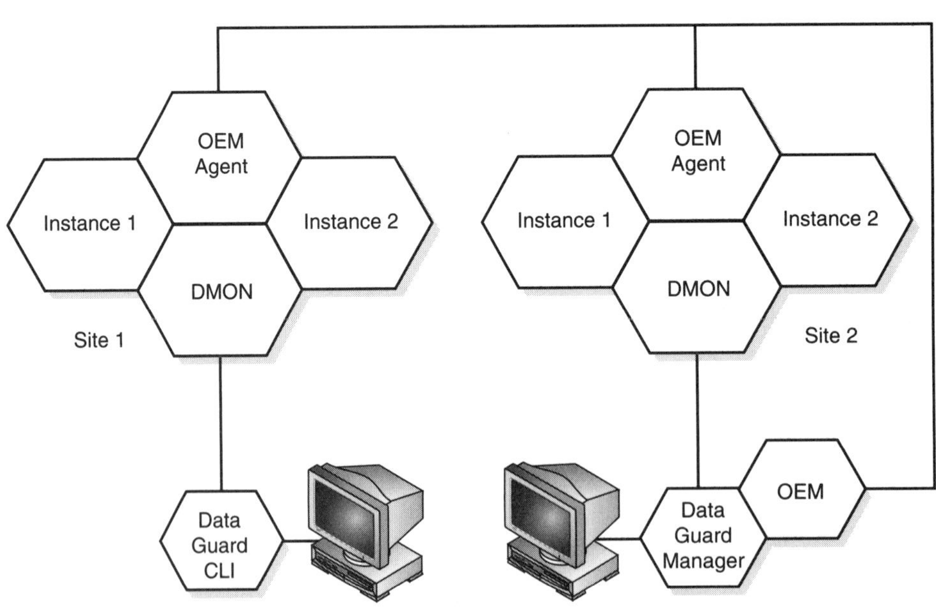

FIGURE 2-5. *DMON process interaction*

interacts with the DMON process on the server where the instance is running. The DMON processes maintain information about the configuration in a binary file on the site it monitors.

Data Guard Log Services Architecture

Once you create a standby database, the transactions are entered into the redo log files, and they should be reflected on the standby database. You also need to determine which database is the master and which one is the standby. Data Guard has three services for this purpose (see Figure 2-6):

- The *log transport service* is comprised of several processes. On the primary database site, the log writer updates the online redo logs with the transactions. It can also update the local archived redo logs and send online redo log transactions to the standby databases. The Archiver saves the online redo log transactions on either local or standby archive logs. The Fetch Archive Log (FAL) client gets redo log transactions from the primary database. When it detects an archive log gap on the standby database, it initiates a request to the FAL server to automatically send and archive the primary database's redo log transactions. The FAL server exists on the primary database server, and it services requests from FAL clients. These processes are depicted in Figure 2-7.
- The *log application service* applies the archived redo logs to the standby database; this action synchronizes the standby with the primary database. The log application service uses the Archiver on the standby database site to archive standby redo logs, as depicted in the previous figure. The Remote File Server (RFS) actually receives the archived redo logs from the primary database site. The Managed Recovery Process (MRP) process applies the archived redo log information to the standby database.
- The *role management services* enables you to change the database role from primary to standby and from standby to primary. You have four possible transitions: switchover, switchback, graceful failover, and forced failover. These transitions are discussed under the subheading "Database Role Transitions."

Data Availability Modes

Data Guard synchronizes the primary and standby databases by cloning the redo logs from the primary database to the standby database and then by applying the standby redo logs on the standby database. When the standby database is unavailable or the connectivity to the standby database is unavailable, redo log transactions can be applied against the primary database, but they cannot be

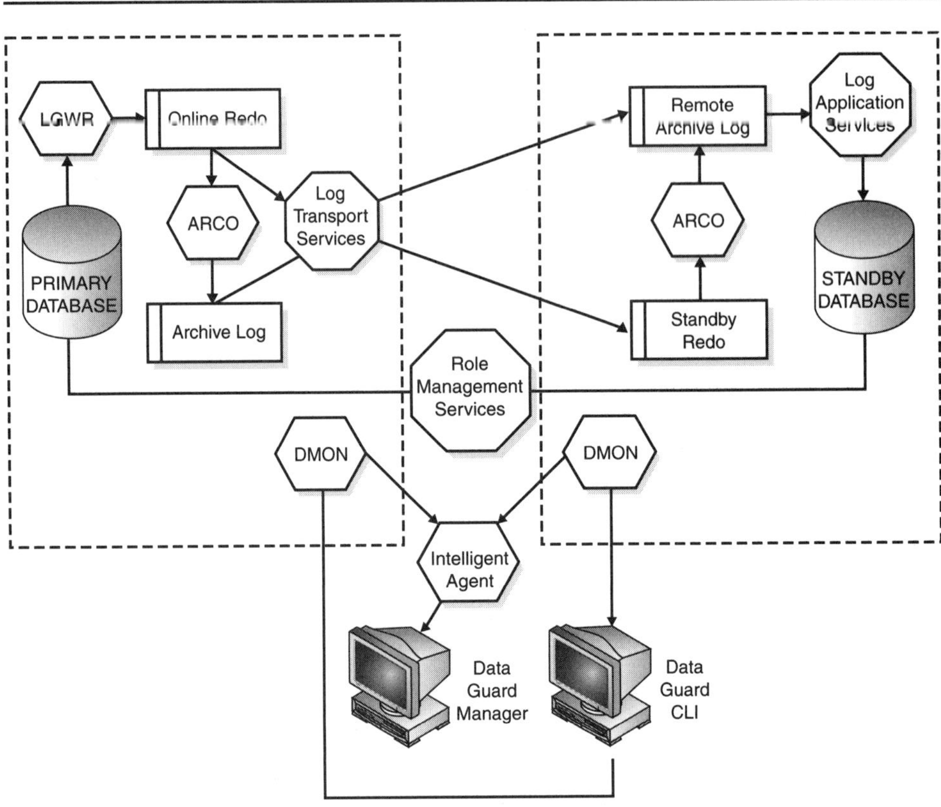

FIGURE 2-6. *Data Guard services architecture*

applied on the standby database. The primary database and the standby database are not totally synchronized at this point, resulting in *data divergence.*

When you failover from a primary database to a standby database that is in a data divergent state, you will encounter *data loss.*

A *zero data loss* requirement specifies that all transactions on the primary database must also be available on at least one standby database, even if it has not been applied to the standby database yet.

A *zero data divergence* requirement specifies that the primary and secondary databases must be synchronized at all times.

Exploring the Modes

Data Guard gives you control over the degree of data loss and data divergence through four data availability modes (also referred to as the database protection modes).

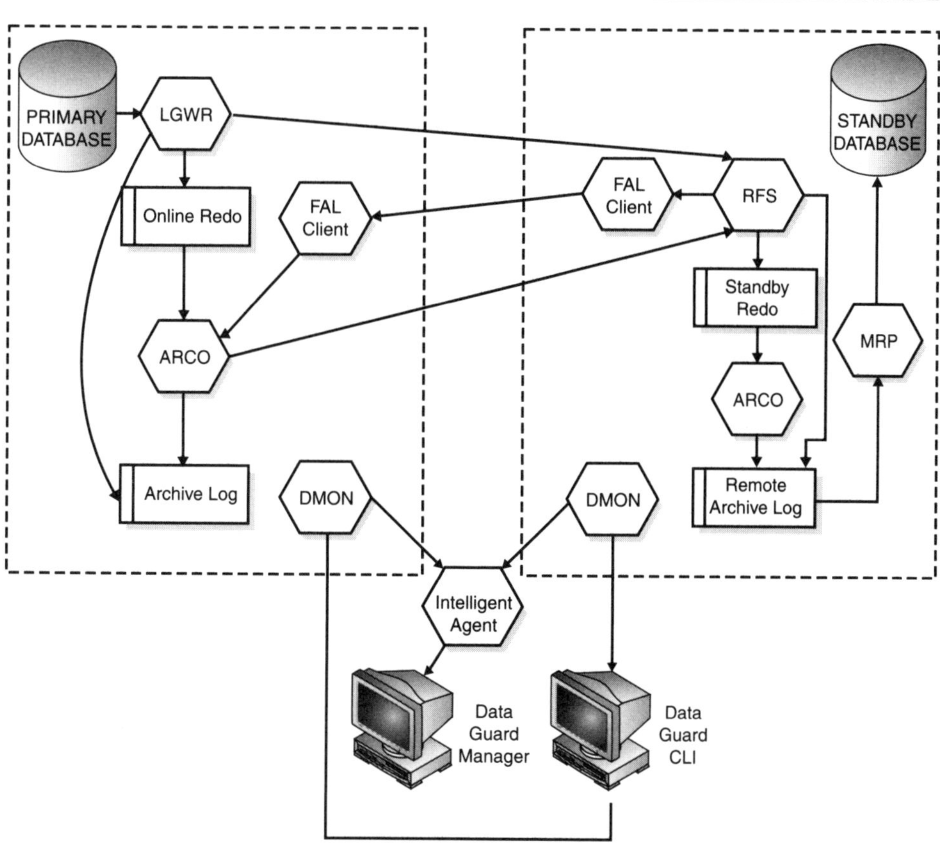

FIGURE 2-7. *Data Guard process architecture*

The *guaranteed protection mode* is the most conservativeof the four modes. It assures that the primary and standby databases are totally synchronized at all times. The transaction on the primary database is not committed until there is a confirmation that the log writer (LGWR) on the primary database site has transmitted the transaction, and that it has been applied on at least one standby database in the Data Guard configuration. In other words, this is a *zero divergence mode;* you are assured that every transaction, up to the last transaction that has been committed on the primary database, has already been applied to the standby database. If the standby database is unavailable, or if the connectivity to the standby database is unavailable, it prohibits all changes to the primary database. This mode has the most adverse impact on the performance of the primary database. Since there is zero data divergence, there is zero data loss.

Like the guaranteed protection mode, the *instant protection mode* assures you that all modifications to the primary database up to the last committed transaction, are also available on at least one standby database site by the log writer, even if the transactions have not yet been applied to the standby database. Unlike the guaranteed protection mode, the instant protection mode enables temporary data divergence. In a failover situation, the configuration retains full capability to synchronize the standby database.

Operations do not have to cease on the primary database when the standby database or connectivity to the standby database is unavailable. If the standby database or connectivity to the standby database is unavailable, the instant mode functions as the delayed protection mode. When they become available, it returns to the instant mode of operation. This mode has less of an impact on the performance of the primary database as compared to the guaranteed protection mode.

The *rapid protection* mode improves the performance of the primary database as compared to the instant mode; the log writer sends modifications on the primary database to the standby database site as soon as it gets a chance to do so. Data divergence is allowed here. Modifications to the primary database are finalized whether or not the standby database is available or the connection to the standby database is available.

Unlike the other modes, in the *delayed protection* mode, it is the archiver process (ARCH) that transmits the redo logs to the standby database site. You can specify a time lag from the point when you archive the redo log on the primary database, within which you cannot apply the redo logs on the standby database. This time lag can help with not propagating errors that may get fixed within the time lag specified. This mode has the lowest adverse impact on the performance of the primary database.

Comparing the Modes

Table 2-1 summarizes the features of the four Data Availability modes.

Guaranteed protection is the only mode that assures data protection. The price for the protection is the impact on the performance of the primary database. The delayed protection mode offers the least impact on the performance of the primary database.

Configuring the Modes

You configure the primary database to perform archiving on remote standby databases by setting LOG_ARCHIVE_DEST_n and LOG_ARCHIVE_DEST_STATE_n initialization parameters. Table 2-2 summarizes some attributes of LOG_ARCHIVE_DEST_n.

Mode	Redo logs to standby	Standby DB State	Primary DB State	Impact on Failover	Impact on Switchover
Guaranteed	LGWR	Available	Zero divergence	Zero loss	Zero loss
		Unavailable	Instance shutdown	Zero loss	N/A
Instant	LGWR	Available	Zero divergence	Zero loss	Zero loss
		Unavailable	Delayed mode	Some loss	N/A
Rapid	LGWR	Available	Some divergence	Some loss	Zero loss
		Unavailable	Delayed mode	Some loss	N/A
Delayed	ARCH	Available	Some divergence	Some loss	Zero loss
		Unavailable	Some divergence	Some loss	N/A

TABLE 2-1. *A Comparison of the Data Availability Modes*

Function	Attribute	Description
Standby failure	[NO] ALTERNATE	Specifies an alternate destination if destination is not accessible.
Archiving method	[NO] AFFIRM	Confirms that archiving has succeeded.
	MANDATORY	Archiving must succeed to continue log transport.
	OPTIONAL	Archiving does not have to succeed to continue.
Archiving process	ARCH	Archiving will be done by the archiver process.
	LGWR	Archiving will be done by the log writer process.
Transmission mode	SYNC	Log transport must be synchronous. Control is not returned until the log transport operation is complete.
	ASYNC = blocks	Log transport is asynchronous. Control is returned immediately. You specify the SGA network buffer size in blocks.
Reception	[NO] Delay [= minutes]	The time lag between archiving and applying redo logs on the standby database.

TABLE 2-2. *Attributes of LOG_ARCHIVE_DEST_n*

Table 2-3 summarizes the attributes you must set to configure the Data Guard solution for the various Data Availability modes.

You must make a number of decisions about the configuration and specify a number of parameters to establish the desired data availability mode for the Data Guard configuration. In the examples, we will assume that you wish to configure the Data Guard solution to function in the guaranteed protection mode, and that the name of the standby database is "friday." The main steps to specify a data availability mode are as follows:

1. Configure the primary database archivelog mode.
2. Specify the standby database.
3. Enable the Archive Destination state.
4. Specify the process to be used for archiving.
5. Specify the transmission mode.
6. Specify the archiving method.
7. Specify the reception log.
8. Specify the failure resolution policy.

Step 1: Configure the Primary Database Archivelog Mode The first step is to configure the primary database to run in the archivelog mode. You can do this with the following SQL statement:

```
ALTER DATABASE ARCHIVELOG;
```

You would also need to configure the redo logs themselves; you need to specify their size, how often they switch, and the minimum period before they can be reused.

Step 2: Specify the Standby Database The second step is to specify the process standby database, which is the archive destination for the primary database, using the following statement:

```
LOG_ARCHIVE_DEST_2 = 'SERVICE=friday'
```

Mode	First Implemented	Archiving Process	Transmission Mode	Archiving Method	Reception Log
Guaranteed	9*i*	LGWR	SYNC	AFFIRM	Standby
Instant	9*i*	LGWR	SYNC	AFFIRM	Standby
Rapid	9*i*	LGWR	ASYNC	NOAFFIRM	Standby
Delayed	8*i*	ARCH	ASYNC	NOAFFIRM	Archived

TABLE 2-3. *Attributes of the Data Availability Modes*

You enter this statement in prmyinit.ora, the initialization file for the primary database. If the database is already running, and you do not wish to restart the instance so it will invoke prmyinit.ora, you can use the following statement:

```
ALTER SYSTEM SET LOG_ARCHIVE_DEST_n = 'SERVICE=friday'
```

You use the SERVICE parameter to specify the database based on the Oracle Net service name. This service name must have an associated database SID. You can obtain the archive destinations and their characteristics from the view V$ARCHIVE_DEST.

Step 3: Enable the Archive Destination State You must enable the archive destination with the following statement:

```
LOG_ARCHIVE_DEST_STATE_2 = ENABLE
```

Step 4: Specify the Process to Be Used for Archiving In this step, you specify the process that the primary database site must use to archive the redo log; the options are the log writer (LGWR) or the archiver (ARCH). You set the initialization parameter with the following statement:

```
LOG_ARCHIVE_DEST_n = 'SERVICE=friday LGWR'
```

If you specify LGWR, it means that the log writer will create the archived redo logs and transmit them to the remote archive destinations (if the database is in the ARCHIVELOG mode) concurrently with adding entries to the online redo log.

If you specify ARCH, the log writer will add entries to the online redo log. The archiver will update the local archived redo log and transmit the redo log to the remote archive destinations. You can obtain configuration and runtime information about the archive log destinations from the V$ARCHIVE_DEST_STATUS view.

Step 5: Specify the Transmission Mode You can specify that the archive transmissions be performed synchronously (SYNC) or asynchronously (ASYNC) for that archive destination with respect to the primary database.

If you specify SYNC, the log writer will transmit redo information from the primary database to the remote archive destinations as it adds entries to the online redo log on the primary database. Control is returned to the transaction on the primary database only after it has been confirmed that the redo logs have reached the archive destination; hence, the performance of the primary database can be adversely impacted.

If you specify ASYNC, control is returned immediately. You can specify the synchronous (SYNC) mode by adding the following entry to the init file:

```
LOG_ARCHIVE_DEST_n = 'SERVICE=friday LGWR SYNC'
```

Step 6: Specify the Archiving Method In this step, you specify the method to be used when archiving the remote logs to disk. The AFFIRM attribute ensures that the remote archive log is successfully written to disk; in the event of a failover, this data is immediately available for recovery operations. You specify the AFFIRM attribute with the following statement:

```
LOG_ARCHIVE_DEST_n = 'SERVICE=friday LGWR SYNC AFFIRM'
```

Step 7: Specify the Reception Log When the Remote File Server receives the redo log information, it can either store this redo information as a standby redo log or an archived redo log. Storing to the standby redo log is a new feature that was added in Oracle9*i*. Writing to the archived redo log file was available in Oracle8*i*. If there is a failover, the data in the standby redo log is fully recoverable.

One disadvantage of the standby redo log is that it must be archived before the redo transactions can be applied to the standby database. This introduces an additional lag time for the standby database.

You must have at least the same number of standby redo log groups with the same sizes as you have on the primary database. It is a good idea to create additional standby redo log groups, since the primary database instance will be shut down if the RFS cannot allocate a standby redo log when the primary database is running in the protected mode.

You can evaluate the adequacy of the number of standby redo log groups by reviewing the contents of the RFS process trace file and the database alert log. If there were a number of waits for a group due to an incomplete archival, you should consider adding groups. When the primary database is created, the MAXLOGFILES parameter establishes the maximum number of standby redo log groups for each standby database. The LOG_FILES parameter can reduce the maximum number of standby redo log groups temporarily for the duration of the instance. The MAXLOGMEMBERS parameter establishes the maximum number of member files in each group on the standby database when the primary database is created.

You can create standby redo log files with the `ALTER DATABASE ADD STANDBY LOGFILE` statement. Here's an example:

```
ALTER DATABASE ADD STANDBY LOGFILE
  ('/oracle/dbs/log3a.rdo', '/oracle/dbs/log3b.rdo') SIZE 25M;
```

You can add standby log group members at a later point in time with the following statement:

```
ALTER DATABASE ADD STANDBY LOGFILE MEMBER
  '/oracle/dbs/log3c.rdo' TO GROUP 3;
```

You can review the standby redo logs by using the V$STAND_BY and V$LOGFILE views.

Step 8: Specify the Failure Resolution Policy The failure resolution policy specifies what should happen on the primary database if all the standby databases in the configuration are unable to archive the redo logs. To specify guaranteed protection, you must establish the PROTECTED mode for the primary database. The PROTECTED mode will establish a zero divergence and zero data loss configuration. You can place the primary database in the PROTECTED mode with the following statement:

```
ALTER DATABASE SET STANDBY DATABASE PROTECTED;
```

If you need to allow a degree of data divergence, you can set the primary database back to an UNPROTECTED mode with the following statement:

```
ALTER DATABASE SET STANDBY DATABASE UNPROTECTED;
```

The current mode of the database is contained in the STANDBY_MODE column of the V$DATABASE view.

Database Role Transitions

In a Data Guard configuration, a database can take one of two roles: primary or standby. The *role management service* (RMS) enables you to change the role of a database from primary to standby or vice versa. This change in roles is called a *role transition.* The role management service interacts with the log *transport service* and the *log application service* to ensure that the requirements of the data availability modes are accomplished during role transitions.

Role transitions can either be planned or they can occur as a result of the primary database becoming unavailable. A planned role transition is called a *switchover* and a role transition that occurs due to failure of the primary database is called a *failover.* You can perform a switchover without having to reinstantiate either database. A failover does require database instantiation. Based on the switchover and the failover, you have four options for role transitions:

- Switchover
- Switchback
- Graceful failover
- Forced failover

Switchover

You perform the switchover operation deliberately; you take the primary database offline so you can perform maintenance functions, and you transition a standby database to function as the primary database so users can access their databases while you perform the maintenance functions (see Figure 2-8).

In this transition scenario, there is no loss of data and you do not have to instantiate either database. Switchovers are important; they enable you to perform preventive maintenance functions on the primary database without encountering data loss or compromising availability. Regularly scheduled preventive maintenance actions minimize the chance of failovers, which are prone to data loss.

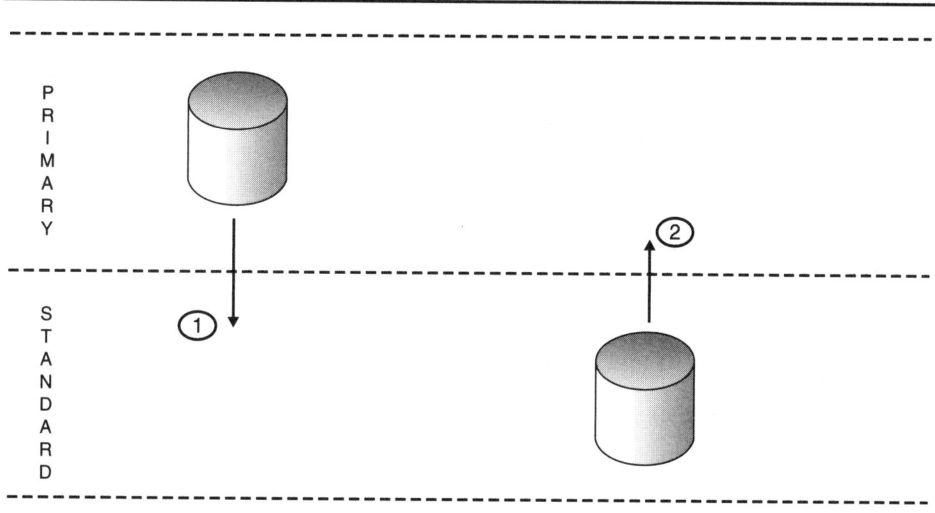

FIGURE 2-8. *The switchover role transition*

Suggested Actions Before You Begin the Switchover Operation Before starting the switchover operation, you must

- Plan the details.
- Perform a full backup on the primary database.
- Ensure that the primary and secondary databases have a minimal lag.

Required Actions Before You Begin the Switchover Operation Before you perform the switchover operation, you must meet the following requirements:

- When you get ready to restart the instance, you must perform an orderly shutdown of the primary database, that is, with a SHUTDOWN NORMAL, SHUTDOWN TRANSACTIONAL, or SHUTDOWN IMMEDIATE command.
- The online redo logs and control files of the primary database must be available.
- The initialization parameter file must be resident on the primary and standby database sites.
- The archive logs must be available since they are required for recovering the standby to the same state as that of the primary database in a zero data divergence configuration.
- You must have an active Oracle Net connection between the primary and standby databases. The FAL client on the standby database site needs this connection to request missing data or files from the FAL server on the primary database site, as it brings the standby database to the same state as the primary database.
- On every database site in the configuration, you must have entries for all databases in both tnsnames.ora and listener.ora.
- You can have only one active SQL session on the instance in which you are performing the switchover. You must terminate all other sessions.
- The standby database must be in both ARCHIVELOG mode and in managed recovery mode.

Performing the Switchover To perform a switchover operation, you have to perform the following tasks:

- Switch the primary database to standby role.
- Switch the original standby database to function as the primary.
- Complete setting up the new standby database.

Switch the Primary Database to Standby Role Use the following steps to place the primary database in the standby role:

1. Verify the possibility for a switchover.
2. Issue the switchover command.
3. Shut down the database instance.
4. Verify initialization parameters.
5. Start the database.
6. Mount the database as a standby database.

Step 1: You can *verify the possibility for a switchover* by looking at the SWITCHOVER_STATUS in the V$DATABASE view. Here is the query to review this column:

```
SELECT SWITCHOVER_STATUS
  FROM V$DATABASE;
```

If the column contains the string 'TO STANDBY', it is possible that you can switch the primary database to a standby database.

Step 2: You can *issue the switchover command* with the following statement:

```
ALTER DATABASE COMMIT TO SWITCHOVER TO PHYSICAL STANDBY;
```

This command closes the primary database, completes the archive task, inserts an `end-of-redo` marker, and backs up the current control file to the SQL session trace files for conversion to a standby control file.

Step 3: *Shut down the instance* using the following statement:

```
SHUTDOWN NORMAL;
```

Step 4: You must *verify that the initialization parameters* are appropriate for the new database role.

Step 5: *Start up the database without mounting it* using the following statement:

```
STARTUP NOMOUNT;
```

Step 6: *Mount the database as a standby database* using the following statement:

```
ALTER DATABASE MOUNT STANDBY DATABASE;
```

Switch the Original Standby Database to Function as the Primary You are now ready for the second part of the Switchover operation. You must place the original standby database in the primary role using the following steps:

1. Verify that you are ready for the switchover.
2. Place the database in managed recovery mode.
3. Issue the switchover command.
4. Shut down the database instance.
5. Verify initialization parameters.
6. Start the database.

Step 1: You must *verify that you are ready for the switchover.* Verify that the original primary database has been successfully switched to the standby role.

Also, verify that this database (the original standby database) has applied the switchover notification from the original primary database. Perform the following command:

```
SELECT SWITCHOVER_STATUS
  FROM V$DATABASE;
```

If the value in the SWITCHOVER_STATUS is SWITCHOVER PENDING, it means that the switchover notification was received from the primary database and that it has not been completely processed by this standby.

Then you must verify that it is possible to switchover this database. If the value in the SWITCHOVER_STATUS is TO PRIMARY, then it is possible to switchover the database.

Step 2: You can *place the database in the managed recovery mode* using the following command:

```
ALTER DATABASE RECOVER MANAGED STANDBY DATABASE
```

Step 3: You can *issue the switchover command* with the following statement:

```
ALTER DATABASE COMMIT TO SWITCHOVER TO PHYSICAL PRIMARY;
```

This statement ensures that all redo log files have been received and that they have been applied up to the `end-of-redo` marker. It also converts the standby control file to the current control file.

This statement also automatically creates online redo logs if they do not exist. This has an impact on performance. To minimize this time, one suggestion is to manually add online redo logs to the standby database prior to starting the switchover.

Step 4: You can *shut down the database instance* with the following statement:

```
SHUTDOWN NORMAL;
```

or just

```
SHUTDOWN;
```

Step 5: You must *verify that initialization parameters* are set up for this new database role of being the PRIMARY database.

Step 6: You can start the database with the following command:

```
STARTUP;
```

Complete Setting up the New Standby Database You can complete the switchover by setting up the new standby database with the following steps:

1. Place the new standby database in managed recovery mode.
2. Start the archive logs.

Step 1: You can place the new database in the managed recovery mode with the following statement:

```
ALTER DATABASE RECOVER MANAGED STANDBY DATABASE
```

Step 2: You can *start the archive logs* via the initialization parameters. If this was not done, use the following commands:

```
ALTER SYSTEM ARCHIVE LOG START;
ALTER SYSTEM SWITCH LOGFILE;
```

Switchback

Once you complete your maintenance functions, you have to switchover the original primary database (now a standby) back to the primary database role. This operation is called the switchback operation and is the reverse of the switchover operation. You perform the same instructions as the switchover, just in reverse.

Graceful Failover

The failover operation is initiated when the primary database is not available or not accessible. You failover the primary database to a standby database. This failover can be either a zero data loss or a minimal data loss failover, depending on the data availability mode the configuration was operating in prior to the failover. If the standby redo logs are available, then you must use the graceful failover option.

Whether standby redo logs are available or not, you do have unfinished standby redo logs because of the failure of the primary. You can recover these unfinished standby redo logs with the following statement:

```
ALTER DATABASE RECOVER MANAGED STANDBY DATABASE FINISH;
```

After a graceful failover, further redos from the original primary database are archived on the standby site, but cannot be applied to the standby database. You have to copy these logs onto other standby databases, register them, and apply them. You can register them with the `ALTER DATABASE REGISTER LOGFILE` statement.

Your next step is to designate the standby database as the new primary database in the configuration with the following statement:

```
ALTER DATABASE COMMIT TO SWITCHOVER TO PHYSICAL PRIMARY;
```

You must then focus on reconstructing the original primary database, which may have encountered data loss, from the new primary database, which was the original standby database.

Forced Failover

You use forced failover to change a standby database to a primary. If the standby redo logs are not available, you must use the forced failover transition option. If the primary database is accessible, you should archive the online redo logs, copy them, register them, and apply them on the standby database, which is to become the new primary database. You can issue the archive log with the following statement:

```
ALTER SYSTEM ARCHIVE LOG CURRENT;
```

Then you must set the standby database to UNPROTECTED if it was in the PROTECTED mode. You do this with the following command:

```
ALTER DATABASE SET STANDBY DATABASE UNPROTECTED;
```

When standby redo logs are not available, your only option is to activate the standby database using the following command statement:

```
ALTER DATABASE ACTIVATE STANDBY DATABASE;
```

A word of caution, you are likely to lose redo information since this statement resets the online redo logs.

Archive Log Gaps

Consider the scenario where the regular standby database is inaccessible and the archive logs are rerouted to an alternate database. At a later point in time, the regular standby database becomes accessible, and the archival logs are now sent to the regular standby database. Some archive logs are missing on the regular standby database. These missing archive logs constitute a gap in the archive log. In other words, you have an archive log gap whenever the primary database archives the online redo log, but it is also not archived to the standby database.

Manual Recovery of Archive Gaps

In Oracle8*i*, you had to manually apply the logs in the archive gap to the standby database before you could use managed recovery to apply subsequent logs. You had to manually detect this situation by querying the V$ARCHIVE_GAP view. Consider the following query:

```
SELECT thread#, low_sequence#, high_sequence#
  FROM v$archive_gap;
```

Here is a sample output:

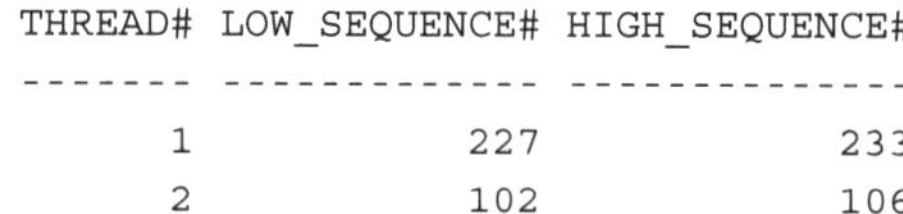

```
THREAD# LOW_SEQUENCE# HIGH_SEQUENCE#
------- ------------- --------------
      1           227            233
      2           102            106
```

You have two archive gaps: log numbers 227, 228, 229, 230, 231, 232, and 233 for thread #1, and log numbers 102, 103, 104, 105, and 106 for thread #2.

If the query returned no rows or if it returned a thread with the same value for the low- and high-sequence numbers, it means that there are no archive gaps for that thread.

Automatic Recovery of Archive Gaps

Oracle9*i* enables you to configure the log application service to automatically detect and recover archive gaps. You must establish a connection between the FAL server and the standby database. You must also set up initialization parameters for both the FAL server and the FAL client; you must assign the service name for the standby database to the parameter FAL_CLIENT, and you must assign the service name for the FAL server to the parameter FAL_SERVER. Assuming that the service name of the primary database is 'crusoe' and that the name of the standby database is 'friday', the entries that you must add to the initialization parameter files are as follows:

```
FAL_CLIENT = 'friday'
FAL_SERVER = 'crusoe'
```

When you enable Managed Recovery, the FAL client on the standby database detects an archive gap and automatically initiates a request for the FAL server to transmit the redo logs. The FAL server on the primary database responds to the request from the FAL client.

Managed Recovery Process (MRP)

You can place the standby database in managed recovery mode with the following command:

```
ALTER DATABASE RECOVER MANAGED STANDBY DATABASE;
```

This command creates a foreground session called a managed recovery process (MRP), which applies archived redo logs on the standby database site to the standby database.

To start a background process and return control to the foreground SQL session where you initiated the command, use the DISCONNECT option as follows:

```
ALTER DATABASE RECOVER MANAGED STANDBY DATABASE DISCONNECT;
```

This frees up the SQL session for other commands and tasks. As an option, you can add the qualifier FROM SESSION as follows:

```
ALTER DATABASE RECOVER MANAGED STANDBY DATABASE DISCONNECT FROM SESSION;
```

The FROM SESSION qualifier does not make any difference to creating the MRP process; it only adds clarity to the statement.

You can stop the MRP with the CANCEL option, as follows:

```
ALTER DATABASE RECOVER MANAGED STANDBY DATABASE CANCEL;
```

You can use the FINISH option to synchronize the state of the standby database with the state of the primary database; that is, you recover the standby up to the last committed transaction on the primary database.

```
ALTER DATABASE RECOVER MANAGED STANDBY DATABASE FINISH;
```

Without the FINISH option, MRP only applies the archived redo logs. With the FINISH option, MRP recovers all available standby redo logs.

Delayed Redo Logs

The MRP process applies the redo logs as soon as they are available on the standby database site. You can specify a delay or time lag between the time they are archived on the primary database site and the time they are applied at the standby database site.

This delay can prevent the propagation of unintended errors. For example, if you accidentally deleted a large number of rows on the primary database, this delay will prevent its propagation to the standby database. You can retrieve good information from the standby database within the time lag period and fix the primary database.

You can specify the time lag by using the DELAY attribute of the LOG_ARCHIVE_DEST_n initialization parameter:

```
LOG_ARCHIVE_DEST_2 = 'SERVICE=Friday DELAY=180';
```

Here the time lag is 180 minutes or 3 hours.

The time delay set by this parameter is overridden by the NODELAY or FINISH option of managed recovery. For example:

```
ALTER DATABASE RECOVER MANAGED STANDBY DATABASE FINISH;
```

or

```
ALTER DATABASE RECOVER MANAGED STANDBY DATABASE NODELAY;
```

will override the time delay specified with the LOG_ARCHIVE_DEST_n parameter.

For Review

1. You should be able to define data divergence and data loss.
2. You should be familiar with the Data Guard architecture.
3. Be able to define the four data availability modes.
4. Know the steps for establishing a desired data availability mode for the Data Guard configuration.
5. You should know the difference between a switchover and a failover role transition.

6. You should know how to configure a time delay for propagating changes from the primary database to the standby database.
7. You should be able to create a managed recovery process (MRP).
8. You should know what an archive log gap is and how to configure the system so that archive gaps are detected and resolved automatically.

Exercises

1. To place the primary database in PROTECTED mode, the syntax is:

A. ALTER DATABASE SET PRIMARY DATABASE PROTECTED

B. ALTER SYSTEM SET PRIMARY DATABASE PROTECTED

C. ALTER DATABASE SET STANDBY DATABASE PROTECTED

D. ALTER SYSTEM SET STANDBY DATABASE PROTECTED

2. To specify the archive destination for the primary database as 'friday,' you make the following entry in prmyinit.ora:

A. SET_ARCHIVE_DEST_2 = 'SERVICE=friday'

B. LOG_ARCHIVE_DEST_2 = 'SERVICE=friday'

C. LOG_ARCHIVE_DATABASE_2 = 'SERVICE=friday'

D. SET_ARCHIVE_LOG_DEST_2 = 'SERVICE=friday'

Answer Key

1. C. **2.** B.

Online Operations

Oracle9*i* improves availability by enabling you to perform a number of DBA operations while the database is up and running, as opposed to shutting down access to users while these operations are completed. Operations that fall under this category are called online operations. Some online operations that this book discusses are as follows:

- Rebuilding indexes online
- Using index-organized tables (IOTs) online

- Redefining tables online
- Validating the structure with the Online Analyze command
- Using the Server Parameter File (SPFILE)

Rebuilding Indexes Online

When you need to move an existing index to another tablespace or improve index performance by reducing intrablock fragmentation, you have two options. The first option is to drop the index and then create it over again. A second option is to rebuild the existing index, and this option has better performance characteristics.

You can rebuild the index while the users continue to have access to the data in the tables. In the past, the entire table had to be locked when performing such actions. The online rebuilding of indexes was introduced in Oracle8*i* to reduce the locking, but it had a lot of limitations. Oracle9*i* has extended this online index rebuilding capability to reverse key indexes, function-based indexes, key-compressed indexes on tables, and key-compressed indexes on IOTs. Oracle9*i* does not currently support online index rebuilding for bitmap or partitioned local and global indexes.

The user can perform all DML operations while the online index rebuilding is in progress, but users will not be able to perform DDL operations at this time. When you rebuild an index, you are in effect using the existing index as the source for building a new index. DML operations on the base table can continue to reference the existing index (see Figure 2-9).

The DML transaction holds a lock on the row(s) in the base data table, and the index rebuilding has to wait until the lock is released with a commit or rollback of

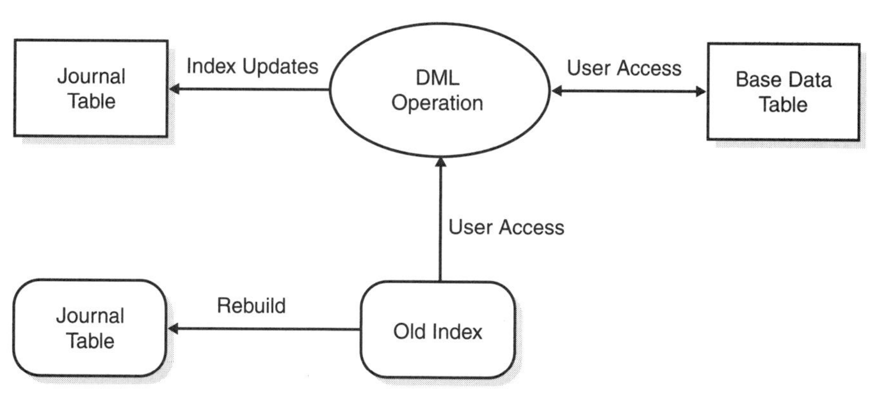

FIGURE 2-9. *Online index rebuilding*

the DML transaction. As such, DML operations that affect a large number of rows can adversely affect the performance of the online index rebuilding operation.

The index rebuilding operation builds a new index based on the information in the existing or old index. The user can still perform DML operations on the data table; the old index is still helping to enhance the performance of the DML operations. If changes are made to the table that affect the old index table, the updates that should be made to the old index are not actually made to the old index; instead, they are documented in an IOT.

Once the new index generation is completed, the rebuild operation will merge the journal table entries into the new index, associate the new index with the table, and get rid of the old index. The statement to rebuild an existing index "product_description_ix" is

```
ALTER INDEX product_description_ix REBUILD ONLINE;
```

Using Index-Organized Tables (IOTs) Online

Here are some of the Oracle9*i* enhancements to online operations on IOTs:

- Coalesce primary key indexes.
- Create and rebuild secondary indexes.
- Update logical ROWIDs for secondary indexes.
- Specify an OVERFLOW segment in a move operation on IOTs.

Coalesce Primary Key Indexes

A row within a regular table is fairly static and stable. Once created, it retains its position via the original physical ROWID. The index in a regular table stores both the column(s) data values and the physical ROWID.

On the contrary, a row within an IOT does not have a stable physical location; it maintains the sort order as leaves in a B-tree. The rows can be moved around to maintain this sort order. Because of the nature of IOTs, Oracle does not permit you to alter the primary key index of IOTs. This is a severe restriction; with time, the primary key index can experience poor performance because of intrablock fragmentation. Oracle9*i* introduces the capability to coalesce the primary key indexes. The rebuild operation creates a new tree to defragment the index, as opposed to the coalesce operation that coalesces the leaf blocks within the same branch of the tree.

You can coalesce the primary key index of an IOT with the following statement:

```
ALTER TABLE iot_product COALESCE;
```

Create and Rebuild Secondary Indexes

Secondary indexes in IOTs improve performance when accessing columns that are not the primary key. Because of the inherent nature of rows in an IOT to move around, a secondary index cannot use the physical ROWID. Oracle builds secondary indexes on IOTs using logical row identifiers that are based on the primary key. Oracle9*i* enables you to create and rebuild secondary B-tree indexes on IOTs online. To create the secondary index, use the following statement:

```
CREATE INDEX iot_product_secondary_ix
    ON iot_product (product_description) ONLINE;
```

where iot_product is the IOT.

To rebuild the secondary index, use the following statement:

```
ALTER INDEX iot_product_sec_ix REBUILD ONLINE;
```

Although the creation of secondary indexes was made available as of version 8.1.6, REBUILD ONLINE was introduced in Oracle9*i*.

Update Logical ROWIDs for Secondary Indexes

The logical ROWIDs used for secondary indexes in an IOT are based on the primary key and a best guess at the physical address via the database block address at which the row is most likely to be found. With time, the row can move to another datablock to maintain the sort order of the primary key index, and the best guess is no longer good. The index has become *stale*. Oracle9*i* enables you to update the logical ROWIDs to reflect the current state of the IOT.

You can update logical ROWIDs for secondary indexes with the following statement:

```
ALTER INDEX iot_product_sec_ix UPDATE BLOCK REFERENCES;
```

Specify an OVERFLOW Segment in a Move Operation on IOTs

When you store a non-key column in the primary key B-tree index of an IOT, it tends to diffuse the dense clustering of index rows in the leaf blocks, and index rows may have to move to another leaf block. If this diffusion is strong, it may not enable the leaf block to store the minimum requirement of two index rows.

To avoid this problem, Oracle9*i* enables you to specify an OVERFLOW segment as part of the move operation while the database is online. The index row holds the first few nonkey columns and a ROWID that references the overflow location with the remaining nonkey columns.

The statement to specify the OVERFLOW segment is

```
ALTER TABLE iot_product MOVE ONLINE
  TABLESPACE data1
  OVERFLOW TABLESPACE data2;
```

Redefining Tables Online

You will encounter the need to redefine a table that is in production. Traditionally, you had to lock the table in shared mode to perform this action, which shuts out all DML access. If the table is accessed often, this will have a severe impact on users who need access. However, Oracle9*i* enables you to redefine tables while the database is online. The table is accessible to DML operations for most of the redefinition process.

Online Redefinition Operations

Some online redefinition operations that you can perform are as follows:

- Add or rename columns.
- Drop nonprimary key columns.
- Convert a regular table into a partitioned table and vice versa.
- Convert a regular table into an IOT and vice versa.
- Recreate the table to reduce block-level fragmentation.
- Add parallel query capabilities.
- Change storage parameters and tablespaces.

Restrictions for Redefining Tables Online

Here are some restrictions for online table redefinition:

- The table must have a primary key.
- The source table to be redefined and the target table must have the same primary key column.
- The table cannot have a BFILE column or a LONG column. LOB columns are allowed.
- The table cannot have user-defined types.
- The table cannot be part of a cluster.
- The table cannot be an overflow table for an IOT.

- The table cannot belong to the SYS or SYSTEM schema.
- The table cannot have materialized views or have materialized view logs defined on the table.
- The new column that is being added cannot be declared as NOT NULL.
- The redefinition must belong to the same schema.

The Process of Redefining Tables Online

Here are the steps that you must follow to redefine a table:

1. Verify that the table can be redefined online by invoking the `can_redef_table` procedure in the `dbms_redefinition` package. One requirement for online redefinition is that the table must have a primary key. If this requirement is violated, you will get the following error:

   ```
   ORA-12089: cannot online redefine table "OE"."PRODUCT2" with no
   primary key
   ```

2. Create an interim table with the same schema definition and characteristics as the source table that you wish to redefine. Let's say the name of this table is `int_product`.
3. Start the redefinition process by invoking the `start_redef_table` procedure in the `dbms_redefinition` package. An example of this statement is

   ```
   dbms_redefinition.start_redef_table
    (
      'oe',
      'product',
      'int_product'
   );
   ```

   You can also enter the column mapping as an optional fourth argument. If you do not provide column mapping (as in the example), Oracle assumes that all columns are in both tables and with the same names.
4. Create indexes, constraints, triggers, and grants with different names on the interim table. All referential integrity constraints on the interim table must be created with the DISABLE option. Upon completion, Oracle will automatically ENABLE these constraints.
5. Optionally, you can periodically synchronize the interim database with the original table if a large number of DML operations were done on the original table. You can effect this synchronization with the `sync_interim_table` procedure in the `dbms_redefinition` package.

6. To terminate the redefinition process when you encounter errors or for any other reason, you must invoke the `abort_redef_table` procedure in the `dbms_redefinition` package.
7. Complete the redefinition by invoking the `finish_redef_table` procedure in the `dbms_redefinition` package. This is the only step where the table is locked in the exclusive mode for a brief period and is therefore unavailable to DML access.

   During this step, the original table is redefined with all the characteristics, indexes, constraints, triggers, and grants that you defined on the interim table. Also, the referential constraints are enabled.
8. As an option, you can rename the indexes.

Validating the Structure with the Online Analyze Command

You can use the ANALYZE command with the VALIDATE STRUCTURE option to verify the structural integrity of a table, index, materialized view, or cluster.

Oracle9*i* enables you to perform this VALIDATE command online. In other words, you can perform DML operations against the object while the ANALYZE command is validating the command.

The statement to do this is

```
ANALYZE TABLE product VALIDATE STRUCTURE ONLINE;
```

Using the Server Parameter File (SPFILE)

A server parameter file is a binary file that serves as a storage facility for initialization parameters. The Oracle database server maintains the SPFILE on the machine where the server is running. The SPFILE makes the initialization parameters persistent when shutting down and starting the database server. You should not manually edit the SPFILE with a text editor; if you do so, you will corrupt the file. This corruption will keep the new instance from starting and will cause the existing instance to crash.

Creating a SPFILE

You can create a SPFILE with the `CREATE SPFILE` statement as follows:

```
CREATE SPFILE FROM PFILE;
```

This statement creates the SPFILE from the parameters in the PFILE. You can provide specific names for both the SPFILE and the PFILE. Here is an example:

```
CREATE SPFILE = '$HOME:\ADMIN\PFILE\my_spfile.ora'
  FROM PFILE = '$HOME:\ADMIN\PFILE\init.ora';
```

At startup, the database server will look for the file specified by the new init.ora parameter SPFILE. Also, if just the STARTUP command is used without the PFILE clause to start the instance, the SPFILE is used if is found in the default location. To display the name of the file specified by the SPFILE parameter, you could use the following statement:

```
SHOW PARAMETER spfile;
```

Viewing the Parameters in the SPFILE

Since Oracle does not want you to edit the SPFILE with a text editor, they provide the V$SPPARAMETER view to display the contents of the server parameter file. Here are some columns of this view:

- **SID** Represents the SID for the parameter
- **NAME** Represents the parameter name
- **VALUE** Represents the value of the parameter
- **UPDATE_COMMENT** Represents the comments when last updated
- **ORDINAL** Represents the ordinal number of the VALUE if the parameter has a list of values (that is, CONTROL_FILES)

Here is an example query to display the parameter settings in effect:

```
SELECT name, value, ordinal, update_comment
  FROM v$spparameter;
```

Changing Parameter Values

You change server parameters with the `ALTER SYSTEM` statement. Optionally, you can specify the scope of the change as follows:

- **MEMORY** Only makes changes in memory for the current instance and not the SPFILE; it does not persist.
- **SPFILE** Makes changes only in the SPFILE and not in the instance.
- **BOTH** Makes changes to both the instance and the SPFILE.

If the initialization parameter file was used to start the database, the default is MEMORY. If the server parameter file was used to start the database, the default is BOTH. You can use the DEFERRED option to specify that the parameter is only applicable to future sessions. You can also specify a COMMENT, which is stored with the parameter specified.

Here is an example statement:

```
ALTER SYSTEM SET job_queue_processes = 70
 SCOPE=SPFILE COMMENT='Peak Load';
```

You can verify the parameter update with the following statement:

```
SELECT name, value, update_comment
  FROM v$spparameter
 WHERE name = 'job_queue_processes';

NAME                 VALUE                UPDATE_COMMENT
-------------------- -------------------- --------------
job_queue_processe 70                     Peak Load
```

Exporting a SPFILE

You can export a SPFILE to a PFILE with the following statement:

```
CREATE PFILE='editsp.ora' FROM SPFILE;
```

You can edit the PFILE with a text editor and then recreate the SPFILE from the PFILE.

For Review

1. You must be able to identify the different operations that can be performed online.
2. You must know about the online operations on IOTs.
3. You must also know about the need for secondary indexes on IOTs and about the need for updating logical ROWIDs.
4. You must be able to identify the restrictions on the table if it can be redefined online.
5. You must be able to specify a validation of the structure of a table, index, materialized view, or a cluster.

Exercises Template

1. **Which one of the following statements will rebuild online a secondary index named iot_employee_sec_ix on an IOT named iot_employee:**

   A. REBUILD INDEX employee_sec_ix ONLINE

   B. ALTER SECONDARY INDEX employee_sec_ix ON iot_employee

   C. REBUILD ONLINE INDEX employee_sec_ix

   D. ALTER INDEX employee_sec_ix REBUILD ONLINE

2. **Which of the following statements is not a requirement for redefining a table online?**

   A. The table must have a primary key.

   B. The table must have a foreign key.

   C. The table cannot have a LONG column.

   D. The table cannot have a LOB column.

Answer Key
1. D. **2.** B, D.

Replication Enhancements

A *distributed database* enables you to implement source tables and database objects on various nodes of a network, and to make this complex network of tables and objects appear as one database. For example, the HR division is located in Los Angeles, and you decide to locate the `employee` table on a server named `West` located in Los Angeles. The Training division is located in Washington, D.C., and you decide to locate the `training` table on a server named `East` located in Washington, D.C. The user does not need to be concerned with the location of the individual tables. To the user, this is a single database that has two tables: `employee` and `training`.

Distributed databases enable you to share data across the network as if you were working with just one database. Generally speaking, one table does not reside on more than one node; and if it does, one set of rows in that table does not reside on more than one node. Distributed database technology provides you with location transparency, individual site autonomy, and full transactional integrity.

A *replicated database* is built upon distributed database technology; it synchronizes objects and data across databases. In the example we just saw, when the Training division schedules an employee for training, the transaction would have to verify that the employee exists in the `EMPLOYEE` table on the server located in Los Angeles. This generates a lot of traffic across the net every time you add a row of data in the training table on the server located in Washington, D.C. Besides extra traffic, this introduces a time delay for the insert operation.

Since we know that distributed database technology enables site autonomy, let's assume that the staff at Los Angeles took the `West` server down for maintenance. In this case, your insert operation into the `training` table will take even longer. You can address this problem by maintaining a duplicate of the `employee` from the `West` server on the `East` server. This process of synchronizing the employee tables on both servers is called *replication*. Replication is also needed to propagate data changes across different levels of materialized views.

One direct benefit of replication is availability. If the `West` server is unavailable, the user could use the `employee` table from the `East` server. Replication offers a degree of protection in a failover situation.

Some database objects that can be replicated are

- Tables and views
- Indexes
- Procedures and functions
- Packages
- Triggers
- User-defined types

A *replication object* is a database object that you have configured to be replicated. A *replication group* is a collection of related replication objects. A replication object can only belong to one replication group. One replication group can reside on many *replication sites* (a server that contains replicated objects and groups). A replication site can be designated as the *master site* for one replicated group and as a *materialized view site* (dependent) for another group. A *master group* is the group that designates the replication site as a master site; it is the source for the replication mechanism.

Oracle replication enables you to perform replication in a configuration with many master sites, many materialized view sites, or a combination of the two.

Oracle9*i* introduces a number of enhancements to Oracle replication technology, including the following:

- Adding new masters without quiescing
- Row-level system change numbers
- Materialized view's fast refresh capability
- Object replication
- Job queue initialization parameters

Adding New Masters Without Quiescing

When you add a new master group object, you must quiesce (stop replication) for that master group. Oracle9*i* has reduced the number of operations that required you to quiesce the master group. For example, you can add a new master site to a master group without quiescing the master group.

You can query the tables and views in a quiesced master group, but cannot perform DML operations on objects in that master group. If you attempt to perform DML operations, you will receive the `deferred_rpc_quiesce` exception. Besides this adverse impact on availability when you quiesce a master group, you will also affect performance since the Oracle Server has to complete the propagation of all deferred transactions before it can quiesce the master group.

Required Conditions for Adding New Masters Without Quiescing

The following conditions must be true before you can add new masters without quiescing:

- All master sites in the replication configuration must be at Oracle 9.0.0 or higher.
- The master group to which you are adding the new master must be replicating in asynchronous mode.
- All the database links of the master group must have the same connection qualifier. The only other option is that none of them should have a connection qualifier.
- All links must be configured for parallel propagation (parallelism is 1 or higher). Serial propagation (parallelism is 0) is not supported for this action.
- You must have enough space for rollback segments or undo tablespace to support the export.
- Each master site must have adequate space for the largest deferred transactions queue that has not been propagated.

Restrictions on Adding New Masters Without Quiescing

The following restrictions are in effect when you add new masters without quiescing:

- You cannot add a new master to the group until the previous add new master operation is completed. To verify if the previous add new master is completed, look for the master group in the view `DBA_NEW_REPSITES`. If you do not find it, it means that the add master operation was completed. If you found the entry, it means that the operation is still underway, and you need to wait.
- You can only add one new master site at a time. You can add another master site separately and after the previous add new master is complete.
- Before you add a new master site, you must configure it for multimaster replication.

Choice of Full Database or Object-Level Export/Import

Before you begin adding a new master without quiescing, you must choose between performing a full database or an object-level export/import. You must use full database if each and every one of the following statements is true:

- The new master sites do not have any existing replication groups.
- The master definition site does not have any materialized view groups.
- All master groups have the same master definition site.
- You are adding all the master groups, and not just some of them, to the master site at the master definition site.

If any one of the previous statements is false, you must use an object-level export/import.

In this section, we will assume all four of these statements are true. Therefore, we will be using the full database export/import option. You have to satisfy one additional statement if you want to use the change-based recovery option: The existing master site and the new master site must be on the same operating system.

The Process to Add a New Master Site Without Quiescing

You will be using a number of procedures from the `DBMS_REPCAT` package to add a new master site without quiescing. The step-by-step process to perform this operation is presented in Figure 2-10.

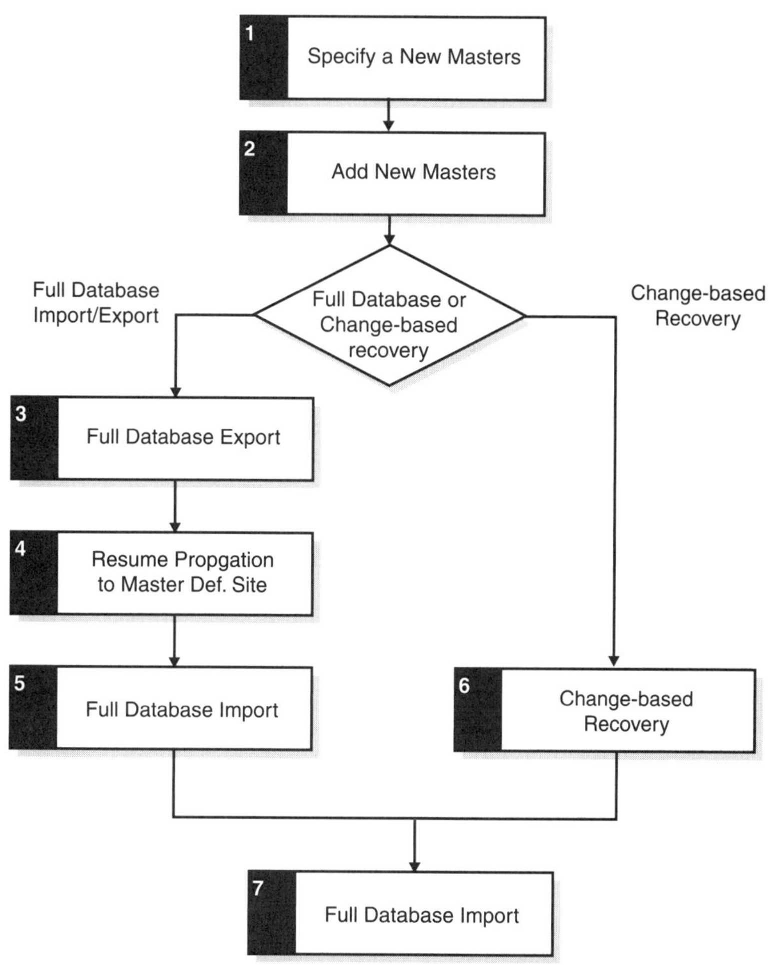

FIGURE 2-10. *Adding a new master without quiescing*

Step 1: Specify a New Master Site You specify a new master site by invoking the SPECIFY_NEW_MASTERS procedure within the DBMS_REPCAT package. Use the following statement:

```
DBMS_REPCAT.SPECIFY_NEW_MASTERS
(
  gname => 'grp1',
  master_list => 'mstr1, mstr2'
);
```

Oracle creates an extension_id to reference and track these potential new master sites in two data dictionary views: DBA_REPSITES_NEW and DBA_REPEXTENSION. You can query these views to monitor progress.

If you invoked SPECIFY_NEW_MASTERS and did not specify any masters in the master_list, it will remove all masters for the specified replication group from DBA_REPSITES_NEW.

Step 2: Adding New Masters You add new masters by invoking the `ADD_NEW_MASTERS` procedure within the `DBMS_REPCAT` package. Here is a sample call:

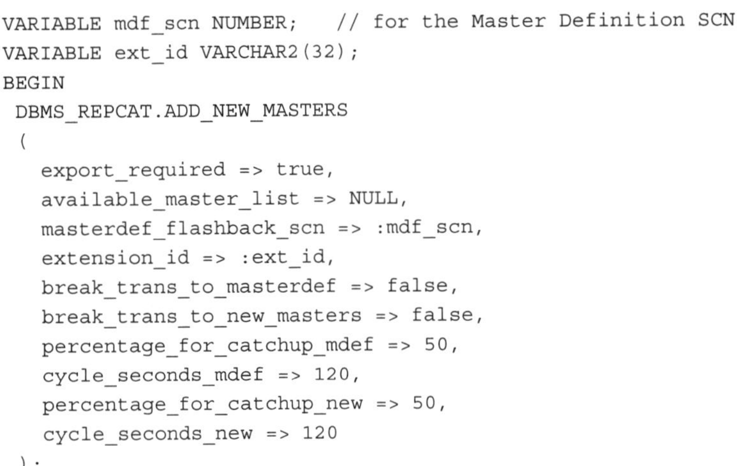

```
VARIABLE mdf_scn NUMBER;    // for the Master Definition SCN
VARIABLE ext_id VARCHAR2(32);
BEGIN
 DBMS_REPCAT.ADD_NEW_MASTERS
 (
   export_required => true,
   available_master_list => NULL,
   masterdef_flashback_scn => :mdf_scn,
   extension_id => :ext_id,
   break_trans_to_masterdef => false,
   break_trans_to_new_masters => false,
   percentage_for_catchup_mdef => 50,
   cycle_seconds_mdef => 120,
   percentage_for_catchup_new => 50,
   cycle_seconds_new => 120
 );
END;
```

Table 2-4 explains the parameters of the `ADD_NEW_MASTERS` procedure.

Parameters	Description
`export_required`	A full database or object-level export/import will be used for at least one of the new masters if this is true. If it is false, use change-based recovery for all new masters.
`available_master_list`	Specifies the sites that to instantiate with object-level export/import. You must set this parameter to NULL to instantiate all masters with full database export/import or change-based recovery.

TABLE 2-4. *Parameters for the* `ADD_NEW_MASTERS` *Procedure*

Parameters	Description
masterdef_ flashback_scn	Returns the Flashback SCN to be used later for a full database export or for change-based recovery.
extension_id	Returns the ID for the current ADD_NEW_MASTERS procedure without a quiescing request.
break_trans_ to_masterdef	If TRUE, existing masters can keep propagating deferred transactions to the master definition site for all replication groups to which you are not adding new masters. This parameter is applicable only if the export_required parameter is set to TRUE.
break_trans_to_ new_masters	If TRUE, existing masters can keep propagating deferred transactions to the master sites for all replication groups to which you are not adding new masters.
percentage_for_ catchup_mdef	This the percent of resources to be used for catching up propagation to the master definition site. This parameter is only applicable if both export_required and break_trans_to_masterdef are set to TRUE.
cycle_seconds_ mdef	This the number of seconds for propagation to master definition site to cycle between replication groups that are being extended and replication groups that are not being extended. This parameter is applicable only if the percentage_for_catchup_mdef parameter value is between 10 and 90.
percentage_for_ catchup_new	This is the percentage of resources to be used for catching up propagation to the new master site. This parameter only applies if both export_required and break_trans_to_new_masters are set to TRUE.
cycle_seconds_ new	This is the number of seconds for propagation to new master sites to cycle between replication groups that are being extended and replication groups that are not being extended. This parameter only applies if the percentage_for_catchup_new parameter value is between 10 and 90.

TABLE 2-4. *Parameters for the* ADD_NEW_MASTERS *Procedure*

The ADD_NEW_MASTERS procedure returns the SCN in the parameter MASTERDEF_FLASHBACK_SCN; you will need this SCN later on for instantiation. You can obtain the value for EXTENSION_ID by querying DBA_REPSITES_NEW and DBA_REPEXTENSIONS. You can get the SCN from the variable MDF_SCN as follows:

```
PRINT mdf_scn

MDF_SCN
----------
12743
```

You can also get the SCN from the DBA_REPEXTENSIONS view, as follows:

```
SELECT flashback_scn
  FROM DBA_REPEXTENSIONS;

FLASHBACK_SCN
----------------------------
12743
```

This call to the ADD_NEW_MASTERS procedure will add the new masters that are specified in DBA_REPSITES_NEW. This procedure also adds these new masters to the replication catalogs at all master sites. This procedure tracks the status in the data dictionary view DBA_REPCATLOG. If there is no information about this master in DBA_REPCATLOG, it means that this procedure has completed.

Once you invoke this procedure, you should not disable or enable the propagation of the deferred transactions queue until the add masters has been completed.

Step 3: Perform a Full Database Export Steps 3, 4, and 5 only apply if you are performing a full database export/import. If you are performing change-based recovery, go directly to step 6.

You will need to specify the SCN returned in step 2 when you perform a full database export. The ADD_NEW_MASTERS procedure returned the SCN in the parameter MASTERDEF_FLASHBACK_SCN. If you did not save this SCN away, you can also obtain it from the FLASHBACK_SCN column in the DBA_REPEXTENSIONS view.

We will assume that the scripts CATEXP.SQL and CATALOG.SQL have been run at least once since the database was created. These scripts create the export views, set up privileges for the EXP_FULL_DATABASE role, and then assign that role to the DBA role.

You must ensure that you have adequate disk space for the export. You can determine this by querying the USER_SEGMENTS view as follows:

```
SELECT SUM(BYTES)
  FROM USER_SEGMENTS
 WHERE SEGMENT_TYPE = 'TABLE';
```

We are only assuming that the data only resides in tables within this database. This query does not include space for data in other objects such as LOBs, partitioned tables, and VARRAY columns.

To perform this export, you will need the CREATE SESSION privilege, and the EXP_FULL_DATABASE role must be enabled.

Here is a sample specification for the export operation:

```
EXP SYSTEM/MANAGER FLASHBACK_SCN=257142 FILE=ADDMASTER.DMP FULL=Y
    GRANTS=Y ROWS=Y COMPRESS=Y STATISTICS=COMPUTE LOG=EXPADDMASTER.LOG
```

You cannot use the CONSISTENT parameter when performing this export.

Step 4: Resume Propagation to the Master Definition Site You need to enable ropagation for the master groups at the master sites with the following statement:

```
DBMS_REPCAT.RESUME_PROPAGATION_TO_MDEF
(
  extension_id => ####
);
```

where #### represents the extension_id from step 1. You can also obtain the extension ID for this master from the DBA_REPSITES_NEW data dictionary view.

Step 5: Perform a Full Database Import Since you have to instantiate the database at each new master site, you need to copy the export file ADDMASTER.DMP to every master site. You will need the DBA role or the IMP_FULL_DATABASE role to perform this import.

Here is a sample import statement:

```
IMP SYSTEM/MANAGER FILE=ADDMASTER.DMP FULL=Y DESTROY=Y
    GRANTS=Y ROWS=Y COMMIT=Y IGNORE=Y LOG=IMPADDMASTER.LOG
```

Now skip the following step and go directly to step 7.

Step 6: Perform a Change-based Recovery You will come here directly after step 2 if you decided to perform change-based recovery instead of a full database export/import. You must skip this step if you performed steps 3, 4, and 5 for a full database export/import.

You must perform the change-based recovery with the SCN returned by the ADD_NEW_MASTERS procedure in step 2. The SCN is returned in the parameter MASTERDEF_FLASHBACK_SCN. You can also obtain the SCN from the FLASHBACK_SCN column of the DBA_REPEXTENSIONS view. In step 2, we assumed that the returned SCN was 12743.

You can perform change-based recovery by either using the SQL*Plus RECOVER command or the Recovery Manager (RMAN) DUPLICATE command. To perform change-based recovery through the SCN 12743 with the RECOVER command, use the following statement:

```
RECOVER DATABASE UNTIL CHANGE 12743;
```

Here is an example with RMAN:

```
RMAN> RUN
2>    {
3>      SET UNTIL SCN = 12743;
4>      DUPLICATE TARGET DATABASE to MSTR1 NOFILENAMECHECK;
5>    }
```

Configure the New Masters to Receive Deferred Transactions You must configure the new masters for multimaster replication. You would need to set the proper global names for the new master sites, and you must ensure that you have the proper database links between the new master sites, existing master sites, and the master definition site.

To enable propagation of deferred transactions between other master sites and this new master site, you must invoke the PREPARE_INSTANTIATED_MASTER procedure, as follows:

```
DBMS_REPCAT.PREPARE_INSTANTIATED_MASTER
(
  extension_id => ####
);
```

where #### represents the extension_id from step 1.

Whether you used the full database export/import or change-based recovery, all the deferred transactions in the queue on the master definition site are already in the new master site. Accordingly, this procedure deletes the deferred transactions in the queue at the master definition site before enabling propagation of deferred transactions.

You must not invoke this procedure until the full database export/import or change-based recovery has completed. You should not use DML statements on objects in the master group or use DBMS_DEFER to defer transactions until the

PREPARE_INSTANTIATED_MASTER procedure has completed since the resulting transactions may not be replicated.

Row-Level System Change Numbers

Some transactions are independent, while others are dependent on each other. Let's consider two transactions within a company, A and B. Transaction A represents person A canceling an order, and transaction B represents person B canceling another order. These two cancel order actions are independent actions by two independent persons; transactions A and B are independent of each other. Let's introduce a third transaction, C, where the company returns person A's funds in response to the cancellation of transaction A. Transaction C is dependent upon transaction A.

When you are performing serial propagation, this is fairly straightforward. Transaction A is sent first; it is received and applied at the target database first. Transaction C is sent later; therefore, it arrives later and is applied later at the target database.

This situation quickly becomes complex when you perform parallel operations. If transactions A and C are sent concurrently on separate streams, you have no assurance that transaction A will arrive at the target database before transaction C.

Oracle introduces a dependency SCN to assure that transaction A will arrive before transaction C. Oracle tracks the SCN for dependent transactions; this dependency SCN is an indicator of which transaction was committed first. Oracle uses dependency SCNs to ensure that transaction A is propagated prior to transaction C. Oracle uses parallel propagation for independent transactions.

Prior to Oracle9*i*, this SCN was maintained at the block level. In other words, the block SCN tracks the most recently changed row in that block. Two transactions within one block have the same SCN regardless of which transaction came first; thus, you will encounter false dependencies. Oracle9*i* resolves this problem by providing a greater degree of granularity for dependency SCNs. It tracks dependency at the row level.

When you create a table, you can opt for block-level or row-level dependency SCNs. You do this with a ROWDEPENENCIES or NOROWDEPENDENCIES clause in the CREATE TABLE statement. Here's an example:

```
CREATE TABLE employee
(
  emp_id     CHAR(4),
  first_name VARCHAR2(15),
  last_name  VARCHAR2(15),
  phone      VARCHAR2(10)
) ROWDEPENDENCIES;
```

Row-level SCNs require an additional six bytes per row; row-level SCNs represents the last time a change to that row was committed. The use of row-level SCNs results in efficient propagation and therefore results in systems that are more scalable.

Materialized View's Fast Refresh Capability

A materialized view is a replica of a master table at a master site or a master materialized view at a materialized view site at a specific point in time. Although the tables in a multimaster replication configuration are updated automatically on an ongoing basis to reflect the changes to the master, you need to refresh a materialized view periodically to reflect the changes to the master tables or master materialized views.

You have three methods to refresh materialized views:

- Complete refresh
- Fast refresh
- Forced refresh

Complete refresh will execute the defining query for the materialized view, and the resulting data set replaces the data of the existing materialized view. There are no restrictions, so you can completely refresh all the materialized views.

Fast refresh only applies changes to the material view for the master rows that changed since the last refresh of the materialized view. The materialized view must have a materialized view log for you to perform fast refreshes. A *materialized view log* tracks all changes made to the master table or master materialized view.

Forced refresh does a fast refresh whenever it is possible. If it cannot perform a fast refresh, it performs a complete refresh. In any case, the materialized view is refreshed. The defining query is subject to some restrictions if the materialized view is to be fast refreshed.

Prior to Oracle9*i*, you could not fast refresh materialized views if they contained a join subquery where the inner table did not have a unique key constraint. This precluded materialized views that had many-to-many joins or one-to-many (outer-to-inner) joins from fast refreshing. Also, you could not fast refresh unique key-based materialized views that included set operators such as the UNION operator.

Materialized Views with Many-to-Many and One-to-Many (Outer-to-Inner) Joins

Replication has been enhanced in Oracle9*i*, and you can now fast refresh materialized views, that have subqueries with *many-to-many* and *one-to-many (outer-to-inner) joins*. To do this, you need to store the nonprimary key column of the subquery's join condition in the materialized view log.

Consider the following materialized view:

```
CREATE MATERIALIZED VIEW customers_with_orders REFRESH FAST AS
  SELECT *
    FROM customers C
   WHERE EXISTS
      (SELECT customer_id
         FROM orders O
        WHERE C.customer_id = O.customer_id);
```

This materialized view contains customers who have placed orders. The first column in the subquery's join condition is the `customer_id` column from the `customer` table. This column is a primary key and is handled easily by the fast refresh operation. However, the second column in the subquery's join condition is the `customer_id` column from the orders table. This is a foreign key and does not have uniqueness restrictions; you have to specifically identify this column to the materialized view log:

```
CREATE MATERIALIZED VIEW LOG
    ON orders (customer_id);
```

If you already have a materialized view log created for this table, you need to use the `ALTER` statement as follows:

```
ALTER MATERIALIZED VIEW LOG
   ON orders
  ADD (customer_id);
```

Materialized Views with Set Operators Such as the UNION Operator

In Oracle9*i*, you can also fast refresh unique key-based materialized views that include set operators such as the UNION operator. Consider the following materialized view:

```
CREATE MATERIALIZED VIEW customers_with_orders_and_credit REFRESH FAST AS
  SELECT *
    FROM customers C
   WHERE EXISTS
      (SELECT customer_id
         FROM orders O
        WHERE C.customer_id = O.customer_id)
     UNION
  SELECT *
    FROM customers
   WHERE credit_limit > 80;
```

This materialized view can be fast refreshed since the same columns are selected in both subsets of the UNION. However, since the customer_id column of the orders table is not unique, you must specify that column to the materialized view log, as you saw in the previous example.

EXPLAINing Fast Refresh Capabilities

You will encounter error messages from Oracle when you attempt to create a fast refreshable materialized view that is in reality not fast refreshable because it does not comply with the restrictions. Oracle provides you with an `EXPLAIN_MVIEW` procedure in the `DBMS_MVIEW` package to analyze why an existing or a potential materialized view is not fast refreshable. For example, use the following command to analyze the `customers_with_orders` materialized view:

```
EXECUTE DBMS_MVIEW.EXPLAIN_MVIEW('customers_with_orders');
```

If you just want to analyze a potential defining query for a materialized view that you have not yet created, specify the query as the parameter as follows:

```
EXECUTE DBMS_MVIEW.EXPLAIN_MVIEW
(
  'SELECT *
    FROM customers C
   WHERE EXISTS
     (SELECT customer_id
        FROM orders O
       WHERE C.customer_id = O.customer_id)'
);
```

After EXPLAIN_MVIEW completes the analysis, it posts the results in MV_CAPABILITIES_TABLE. If this table does not exist before you invoke EXPLAIN_MVIEW, you can create the table by running `utlxmv.sql`. You must query MV_CAPABILITIES_TABLE to see the results:

```
SELECT capability_name, possible, related_text
  FROM mv_capabilities_table;
```

The capability_name column has the following values:

- PCT
- REFRESH
- REFRESH_FROM_LOG_AFTER_ANY

- REFRESH_FROM_LOG_AFTER_INSERT
- REWRITE
- REWRITE_GENERAL
- REWRITE_PARTIAL_TEXT_MATCH

The value displayed in the column named POSSIBLE informs you whether or not it is possible for you to perform the capability displayed in the column named CAPABILITY_NAME.

Object Replication

You can create object types (or user-defined types) to address relationships in data. The customer, vendor, employee, consultant, intern, instructor, and student entities have something in common; they are people. As such, each entity tracks the first name, last name, address, city, state, zip, and phone. You can define an object type called person, which becomes a new user type that you can reference in each entity. Here is the statement:

```
CREATE TYPE person_type AS OBJECT
(
  ssn         CHAR(9),
  first_name  VARCHAR2(15),
  last_name   VARCHAR2(15),
  address     VARCHAR2(25),
  city        VARCHAR2(18),
  state       VARCHAR2(2),
  zip         VARCHAR2(9),
  phone       VARCHAR2(10)
);
```

This user-defined type is an object type; you can use it to define a column in a table as follows:

```
CREATE TABLE customer
(
  customer_id     CHAR(6),
  customer_info   person_type,
  credit_limit    NUMBER(6)
);
```

In this case, you created a table with an object column; `customer_info` is a column object.

You can also build a table with a single column with the user-defined type; the entire row is an object. Assuming that you will access people with just their social security number (SSN), you can define the following table:

```
CREATE TABLE people
(
  people_info person_type
);
```

Oracle9*i* enables you to replicate user-defined types, user-defined operators, and the following database objects:

- Tables that have column objects
- Tables with nested tables
- Tables with VARRAYs
- Tables with REF columns
- Object tables
- Object views including INSTEAD OF triggers
- Index types

You cannot explicitly configure the replication of the storage tables for nested tables. However, when you replicate a table that contains nested tables, the storage tables for these nested tables are also automatically replicated.

When configuring a master group, you first create the schema at the master site, and then you create the master group with the following statement:

```
DBMS_REPCAT.CREATE_MASTER_REPGROUP
(
  gname => 'cust_mstr_grp'
);
```

The next step is to add objects to this group. Use the following code to add the person_type (user-defined type) that we just created:

```
DBMS_REPCAT.CREATE_MASTER_REPOBJECT
(
  gname => 'cust_mstr_grp',
  type  => 'TYPE',
  sname => 'oe',
  oname => 'person_type'
);
```

Use the following code to add the customer table:

```
DBMS_REPCAT.CREATE_MASTER_REPOBJECT
(
  gname => 'cust_mstr_grp',
  type  => 'TABLE',
  sname => 'oe',
  oname => 'customer'
);
```

Job Queue Initialization Parameters

The job queue run this jobs at regular intervals. You can submit jobs to the job queue with the DBMS_JOBS package.

The SNP background process that you had in prior versions has been retired; it is obsolete with Oracle9*i*. The SNP process has been replaced with a family of processes. At the top of the family is a background process called the job queue coordinator (CJQ0). The coordinator selects the jobs from the DBA_JOBS view, sequences them based on start time, and dynamically spawns job queue processes (such as J002) to execute these jobs.

If JOB_QUEUE_PROCESSES (an initialization parameter) is set to 0 (zero), Oracle does not start a job queue coordinator process when the database is started. Since there is no job queue coordinator, none of the jobs in the job queue will be executed. If JOB_QUEUE_PROCESSES is greater than 0, it establishes the maximum number of job queue processes that can be spawned in that instance. The maximum value for JOB_QUEUE_PROCESSES is 1000. Since the coordinator scans the job queues continuously, there is no further need for the JOB_QUEUE_INTERVAL parameter; it has been eliminated in Oracle9*i*.

To set JOB_QUEUE_PROCESSES in the initialization parameter file, use the following:

```
JOB_QUEUE_PROCESSES = 30;
```

You can dynamically change this parameter with the following statement:

```
ALTER SYSTEM
  SET JOB_QUEUE_PROCESSES = 50
  COMMENT 'Temporary - to handle year end load'
  SCOPE = MEMORY;
```

This statement also specifies that the change is only made in memory. When you restart the database, JOB_QUEUE_PROCESSES will be set back to 30 by the initialization parameter file.

For Review

1. You must know the difference between a distributed database and a replicated database.
2. You must be able to identify the required conditions for adding new masters without quiescing.
3. You must know the process you must follow to add a new master without quiescing.
4. You must be able to state the purpose for row-level system change numbers.
5. You must know about the fast refresh capability of materialized views.

Exercises

1. **To specify a new master for replication, you invoke the following procedure:**

   A. `DBMS_REPCAT.SPECIFY_NEW_MASTERS`

   B. `DBMS_REPCAT.MAKE_NEW_MASTERS`

   C. `DBMS_REPLICATE. NEW_MASTERS`

   D. `DBMS_REPLICATE.SPECIFY_NEW_MASTERS`

2. **To analyze why a materialized view was not fast refreshable, you**

   A. Query the V$MVIEW_FAILURE view

   B. Invoke the `EXPLAIN_MVIEW` procedure

   C. Query the EXPLAIN_MVIEW view

   D. Invoke the `WHY_VIEW_FAILED` procedure

Answer Key

1. A. **2.** B.

LogMiner

The purpose of the redo log is to record every change that is made to the data and to the data dictionary. Oracle stores these changes as redo entries in the redo log, which is comprised of two or more redo log files. The database redo log is very critical in contingencies such as an unanticipated power outage, where the database could not write the dirty blocks back into the data files. After the power is restored and the Oracle database is started, Oracle recovers the database to the state of the database right when the power outage occurred.

LogMiner enables you to view the contents of the redo log files via the V$LOGMNR_CONTENTS view. You just query V$LOGMNR_CONTENTS to review and analyze the redo entries in the redo log files. To determine which redo logs are being analyzed, you can query the V$LOGMNR_LOGS view.

Some of the new features that were built into LogMiner under Oracle9*i* include the following:

- DDL statement support
- Capability to use an online dictionary
- DDL tracking in the dictionary
- Dictionary staleness detection
- Capability to skip log corruptions
- LogMiner viewer

DDL Statement Support

Prior to Oracle9*i*, DDL statements were recorded as a set of DML statements on internal tables. It was no simple task to review these DML statements and realize that a DDL operation had been performed. You could almost forget this when trying to determine the actual DDL statement that sourced these DML statements.

Oracle 9*i* records the original DDL statement in the redo logs, and LogMiner lists this DDL statement followed by the set of generated DML statements.

When you query V$LOGMNR_CONTENTS, you can see DDL under the OPERATION column, and the DDL statement itself under the SQL_REDO column. Here's an example:

```
SQL> SELECT operation, sql_redo
  2    FROM v$logmnr_contents
  3   WHERE username = 'OE' AND
  4         operation = 'DDL';

USERNAME OPERATION SQL_REDO
-------- --------- ----------------------------
OE       DDL       alter table customer add
                   birthday date
```

The capability to track DDL enables you to chart the evolution of the schema with DDL actions, such as adding or dropping columns. You can chart the evolution, but you cannot undo the DDL commands. As such, the SQL_UNDO column of the V$LOGMNR_CONTENTS view is NULL for DDL rows. It is important that you keep in mind that this capability to track DDL does not enable you to recover from a table drop or truncate, since the DDL statement does not specifically delete the individual rows.

Capability to Use an Online Dictionary

LogMiner requires access to a database dictionary in order to translate the information in the redo logs. If LogMiner can access a dictionary, it translates the object identifiers and datatypes to give you the name of the object and the external data formats; your data is then understandable. Without a dictionary, LogMiner returns the object identifier and hex data representations. You can extract the data dictionary to a flat file or to the redo log files by using the `BUILD` procedure in the `DBMS_LOGMNR_D` package.

The advantage of using a dictionary that is in a flat file is that it is more efficient than using a dictionary that is in the redo log. The disadvantage is that it may not correspond to the "version" of the information in the redo logs.

The following statement extracts the dictionary into a flat file:

```
EXECUTE dbms_logmnr_d.build( -
  DICTIONARY_FILENAME => 'dictionary.ora', -
  DICTIONARY_LOCATION => '$ORACLE_HOME\DATABASE', -
  OPTIONS  => DBMS_LOGMNR_D.STORE_IN_FLAT_FILE);
```

The options parameter to extract the dictionary to a redo log is DBMS_LOGMNR_D.STORE_IN_REDO_LOGS.

You also have a third option; you can use the online dictionary. This option ensures that you are using the current dictionary. However, you have a chance that the redo logs may not correspond to the current database dictionary if the database changed significantly since the logs were generated. You must use the DICT_FROM_ONLINE_CATALOG when you start LogMiner. The statement is as follows:

```
EXECUTE dbms_logmnr.start_logmnr( -
  OPTIONS => DBMS_LOGMNR.DICT_FROM_ONLINE_CATALOG);
```

DDL Tracking in the Dictionary

Prior to Oracle9*i*, the initial dictionary snapshot in LogMiner was static for the duration of that analysis. In other words, LogMiner could not translate objects that were created or affected by the alter command after the initial dictionary snapshot was taken.

With Oracle9*i*, the internal dictionary can be dynamically changed to reflect the DDL statements in the redo logs. LogMiner applies the DDL statements that it encounters in the redo logs to its internal dictionary.

If you are using the flat file dictionary or the redo log dictionary, you can perform DDL tracking in the internal dictionary by specifying the DDL_DICT_TRACKING option when you start LogMiner. Here is the statement:

```
EXECUTE dbms_logmnr.start_logmnr( -
  OPTIONS => DBMS_LOGMNR.DICT_FROM_REDO_LOGS -
          + DDL_DICT_TRACKING);
```

Dictionary Staleness Detection

Prior to Oracle9*i*, LogMiner had no way of verifying that the dictionary snapshot corresponded to the log files it had to analyze. Oracle9*i* addressed this problem by using an internal object version number, which is updated each time the object is changed in any way. In Oracle9*i*, LogMiner uses this object version number to verify if the dictionary definition for the object corresponds to the version of the object that you encounter in the redo logs. If they do not correspond, the dictionary is stale.

Capability to Skip Log Corruptions

LogMiner will stop when it encounters a corruption in the redo log being analyzed. You can instruct it to proceed past the corruption during the analysis by using the options parameter value SKIP_CORRUPTION as follows:

```
EXECUTE dbms_logmnr.start_logmnr( -
  OPTIONS => DBMS_LOGMNR.DICT_FROM_REDO_LOGS -
          + SKIP_CORRUPTIONS);
```

The rows that come after the corruption will be flagged with a `Log File Corruption Encountered` text string in the INFO column of the V$LOGMNR_CONTENTS view. LogMiner also displays the number of blocks that it skipped corresponding to each corrupt redo entry. By default, LogMiner does not skip corruptions.

LogMiner Viewer

LogMiner now has a GUI interface available via the Enterprise Manager. This GUI interface has two panes: a navigator pane on the left and a detailed pane on the right (see Figure 2-11).

You start by creating a query, and you get a dialog box with three tabs. The first tab is Query Criteria; it enables you to specify the query graphically (see Figure 2-12). For example, you can specify the name of the table, the owner of the table, the time period of interest, and the SQL operation of interest.

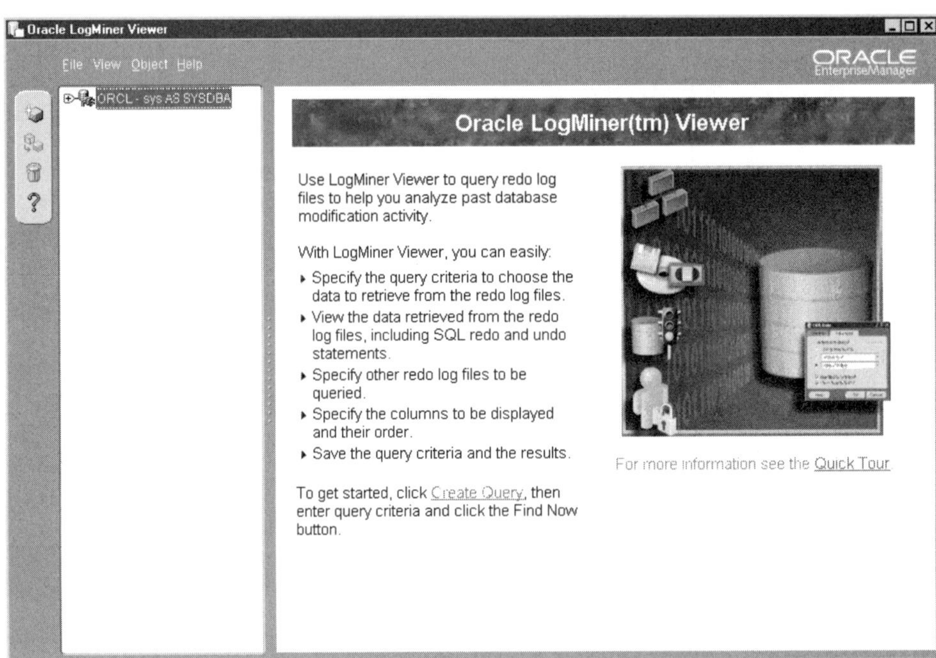

FIGURE 2-11. *The LogMiner viewer*

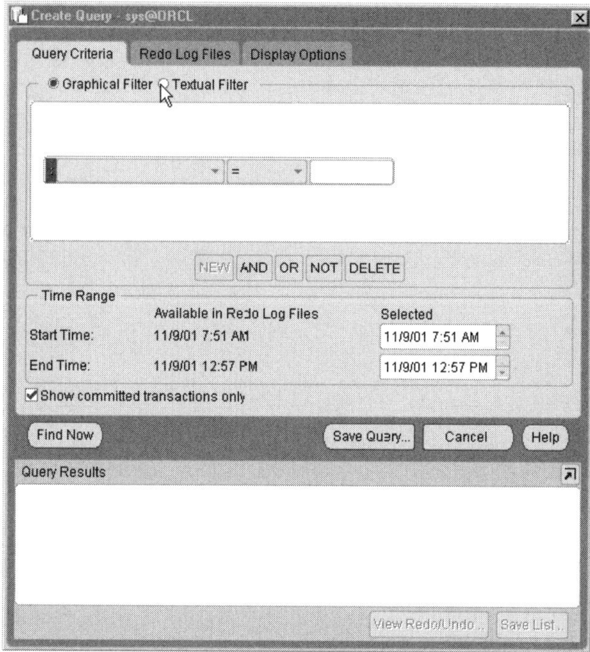

FIGURE 2-12. *LogMiner Query Criteria tab*

The Redo Log Files tab displays the online redo log files for the currently selected database (see Figure 2-13). You can remove these log files or specify additional redo logs.

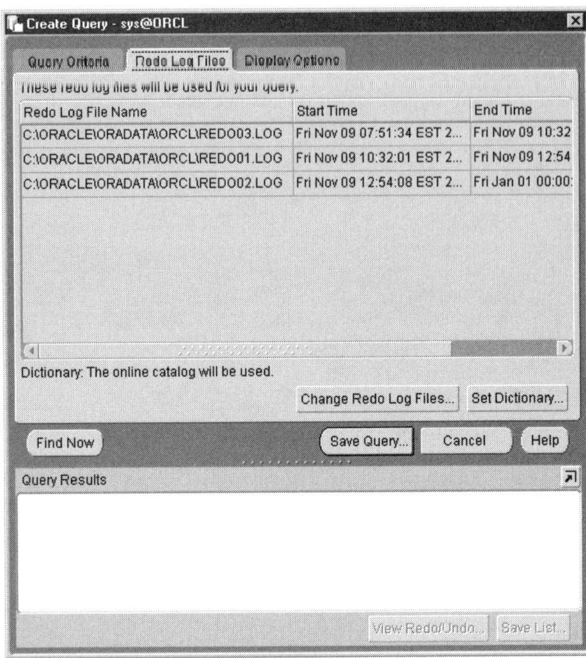

FIGURE 2-13. *LogMiner Redo Log Files tab*

The Display Options tab enables you to specify which columns of the redo log file data in the V$LOGMNR_CONTENTS view you want displayed in the results of the query (see Figure 2-14).

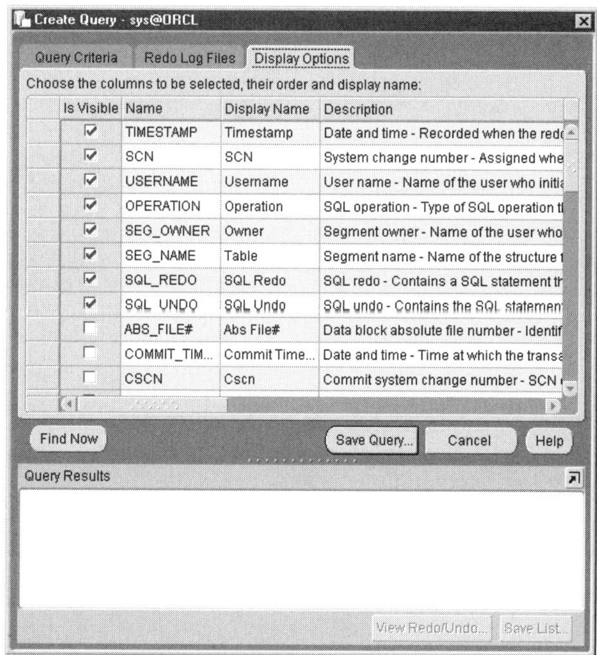

FIGURE 2-14. *LogMiner Display Options tab*

If you go back to the Query Criteria tab and click on the Find Now button, the query results will be displayed (see Figure 2-15). You can click on the View Redo/Undo button to view the redo entries (see Figure 2-16). You can click on the SQL Undo tab to view the undo statement (see Figure 2-17).

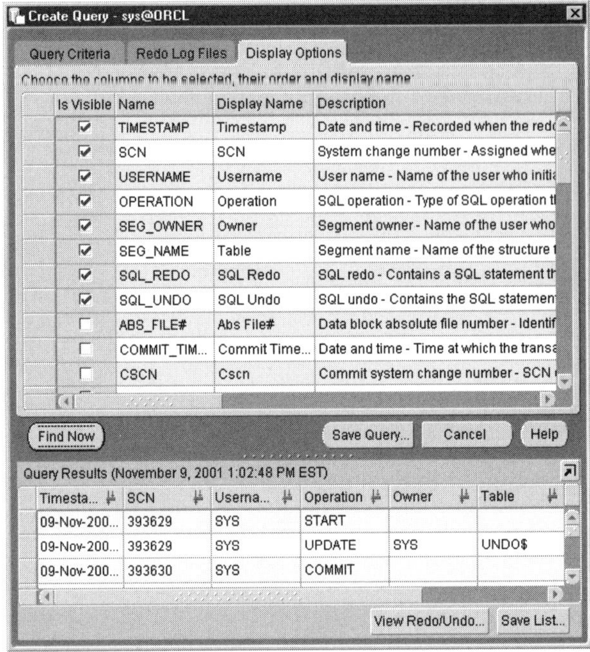

FIGURE 2-15. *LogMiner query results*

For Review

1. You must know how LogMiner can help you analyze redo logs.
2. You must know how Oracle9*i* addresses tracking DDL statements in the redo logs.
3. You must know why LogMiner needs access to a database dictionary.
4. You must know about how LogMiner applies DDL statements it encounters to its internal dictionary.

Exercises

1. LogMiner needs access to a database dictionary to:

A. Know which object it must delete.

B. Use hex values to identify the object.

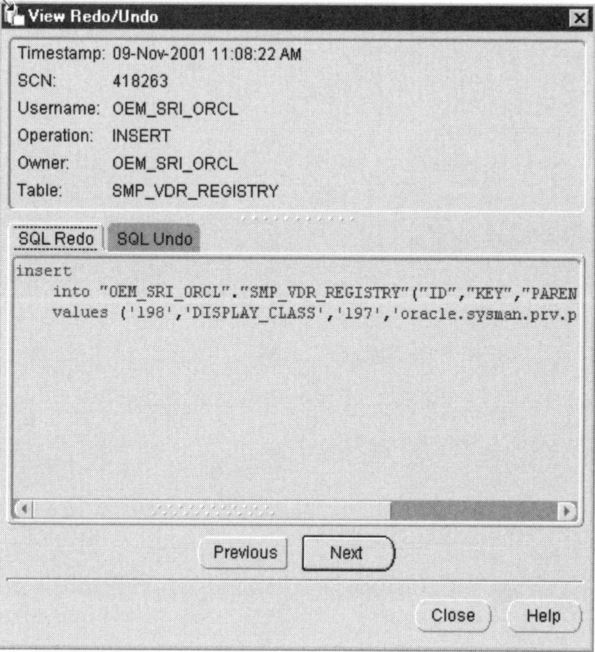

FIGURE 2-16. *LogMiner redo entries*

- **C.** Translate object identifiers to give you the name of the object.
- **D.** Drop columns from tables.

2. Dictionary staleness indicates:

- **A.** When the dictionary was last modified.
- **B.** When the redo log was last modified.
- **C.** When the database was last modified.
- **D.** The object version in the redo log is not the same as the object version in the dictionary.

Answer Key

1. C. **2.** D.

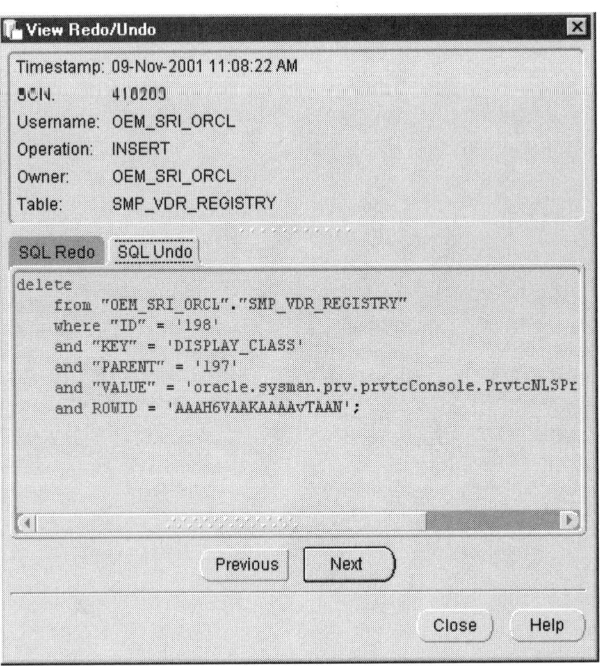

FIGURE 2-17. *LogMiner undo entries*

Chapter Summary

This chapter focused on the comprehensive approach that Oracle9*i* takes toward data availability. Oracle9*i* addresses the reality of instance and cache failures and provides enhancements that improve the recovery time. Oracle9*i* introduces minimal I/O recovery, which makes two passes through the redo log in order to apply just those redo entries that pertain to datablocks that were dirty at the time of the failure.

Oracle9*i* also provides the fast-start time-based recovery limit to help you optimize recovery time with the least possible operational performance degradation. Oracle Flashback enables you to return to the state of the database at a point in time or an SCN in the past, so you can retrieve data that was accidentally deleted. Oracle's Resumable Space Allocation (RSA) suspends a large operation in the event of a space allocation failure to give you an opportunity to fix the problem. Once fixed, operations resume automatically. Oracle9*i* also introduces the STATISTICS import parameter, which gives you control over recalculating database optimizer statistics.

Oracle gives you added control over recovery with LogMiner, which enables you to analyze the redo logs. Oracle9*i* records the original DDL statements in the redo log, and LogMiner lists these statements followed by the set of generated DML statements. Prior to Oracle9*i*, the redo logs did not record the DML statements; they only recorded a number of DML statements. LogMiner can now use the online dictionary to translate internal object identifiers into external names. The LogMiner's internal dictionary can now be dynamically changed to reflect the DDL statements in the redo logs. LogMiner can now verify if the version of the object in the redo log corresponds to the version of the object in the dictionary; this is called dictionary staleness detection. LogMiner can also skip log corruptions as opposed to coming to a halt in previous versions.

Data Guard enables you to establish and manage standby database solutions. This section provides an architectural overview, compares the data availability modes, and explores the process to specify a data availability mode. This section also describes the process of switching the standby database to function as the primary database in the event of a planned or unanticipated failure of the primary. Oracle9*i* can automatically detect and recover gaps in the archive log that happen when the primary database archives the online redo log, but does not also archive to the standby database.

Many database operations in previous versions required you to either take the object or the database offline. Oracle9*i* enables you to perform a number of these operations online while the user still has full DML access to the object. For example, you can rebuild indexes, perform IOT operations, redefine tables, and validate structures online. This chapter also described the Server Parameter File (SPFILE).

Replication enables you to enhance availability by establishing and synchronizing copies of the master database. The Oracle9*i* enhancements to replication enable you to add new masters without quiescing the database, use row-level SCNs for reliable parallel replication, fast refresh materialized views, replicate objects (including user-defined types, nested tables, and object tables), and better management tools for replication.

Two-Minute Drill

1. General high-availability technology

- Minimal I/O recovery
  - Only applies to redo entries that pertain to datablocks that were dirty at the time of the failure.
  - Performs two passes through the log, identifies pertinent redo entries in the first pass, and applies them in the second pass.

- Fast-start time-based recovery limit
    - The fast-start checkpointing architecture enables you to implement fast-start instance recovery functionality.
    - You can specify the mean time to recover for instance recovery with the FAST_START_MTTR_TARGET parameter.
- Oracle Flashback
    - You can query the database as of a certain point in time or as of a certain SCN in the past.
    - If critical data were deleted, you can go back in time and retrieve the information before it was deleted.
- Resumable space allocation
    - Large operations can be suspended automatically when it encounters a space allocation problem, so you can fix the error.
    - Once you fix the error, the operation resumes automatically.
- Export/import features
    - Oracle9*i* introduced a number of parameters: STATISTICS, RESUMABLE, RESUMABLE_NAME, RESUMABLE_TIMEOUT, FLASHBACK_SCN, and FLASHBACK_TIME.
    - The STATISTICS parameter enables you to control the recalculation of database optimizer statistics when performing an import.

2. LogMiner enables you to view and analyze redo logs via the V$LOGMNR_CONTENTS view.

- DDL statement support
    - Prior to Oracle9*i*, DML statements were recorded as a set of DML statements. It was next to impossible to determine the DDL statement that sourced these DML statements.
    - In Oracle9*i*, the redo log records the original DDL statement.
- LogMiner can use an online dictionary, which ensures that you are using the latest dictionary.
- LogMiner can dynamically apply the DDL statements it encounters in the redo logs to the internal dictionary.
- LogMiner can detect dictionary staleness. A dictionary is stale if the version of the object in the redo log does not match the version of the object defined in the dictionary.

- LogMiner can skip log corruptions. Prior to Oracle9*i*, LogMiner came to a halt when it encountered a corruption.

3. Data Guard technology enables you to implement and manage a standby database solution.

- The Data Guard broker is comprised of the Data Guard manager (GUI), the Data Guard command-line interface, and the Data Guard monitor.
- Data Guard uses the log transport services, the log application services, and the role management services to reflect redo logs on the standby database.
- Zero data loss implies that all transactions that are on the primary database must also be available on at least one standby database. Zero data divergence implies that the primary and standby databases are synchronized at all times.
- You can specify four data availability modes: guaranteed protection, instant protection, rapid protection, and delayed protection. Guaranteed protection is the most conservative; it operates in the zero data divergence mode.
- You have four options for database role transitioning: switchover, switchback, graceful failover, and forced failover.
- You have an archive log gap when the primary database archives the online redo log, but it is not archived on the standby database.

4. Online operations

- You can rebuild indexes online. Full DML access is available to the object while the rebuild is in progress.
- You can coalesce primary key indexes online for IOTs.
- You can create and rebuild secondary indexes and update logical ROWIDs for the secondary indexes online with IOTs.
- You can redefine tables online by using procedures provided in the `DBMS_REDEFINITION` package. Online operations include adding columns, dropping non-primary key columns, and converting a regular table into a partitioned table.

5. Replication

- You can add new masters without quiescing (stopping replication) for that master group.
    - This is not possible for all configurations; for example, all master sites in the configuration must be at Oracle 9.0.0 or higher for this capability.

    - You can either perform a full database export/import or an object-level export/import.
    - The procedures for adding new masters without quiescing are provided in the `DBMS_REPCAT` package.
- Data Guard can use row-level SCNs to assure the timing integrity of transactions in a parallel propagation.
- Prior to Oracle9*i*, you could not fast refresh materialized views that contained a join subquery where the inner table did not have a unique key constraint.
    - This limitation was removed in Oracle9*i*, so you can now fast refresh materialized views that have a subquery with a many-to-many or a one-to-many (outer-to-inner) join.
    - This is also possible where the materialize view includes a set operator such as the UNION.
- Oracle provides you with the `EXPLAIN_MVIEW` procedure to analyze why an existing or a potential materialized view is not fast refreshable.
- You can now replicate objects such as user-defined types, nested tables, tables with VARRAYS, object tables, and object views.
- The old SNP background process has been retired in Oracle9*i*. It has been replaced with a new family of processes with the queue coordinator process (CJQ0) being at the top.

Fill-in-the-Blank Questions

1. Minimal I/O recovery just applies the redo entries that pertain to the ________________ at the time of the failure.
2. You can specify the mean time to recover for the instance with the _________________________ parameter.
3. Flashback enables you to query the database as of a certain ____________ or a certain ______________ in the past.
4. LogMiner enables you to view and analyze the redo logs by querying the ________________ view.
5. Prior to Oracle9*i*, the redo logs did not record the original DDL statement; instead, they recorded a set of ______________ statements.

6. The log application service _______________ the archived redo logs to the standby database; this action synchronizes the _______________ database with the _______________ database.

7. A _______________ operation is a planned role transition where you do not have to reinstantiate either database.

8. The _______________ data availability mode assures you that the primary and secondary databases are synchronized at all times.

9. The user can perform _______________ operations on the base table while the online index rebuilding is in progress.

10. The first step in adding a new master without quiescing is to _______________ a new master site by invoking the _______________ procedure, which is part of the _______________ package.

Chapter Questions

1. In a failover situation:

A. The primary database must be instantiated.

B. The standby database must be instantiated.

C. Both the primary and standby databases must be instantiated.

D. Neither database has to be instantiated.

2. When the database is started, and the initialization parameter JOB_QUEUE_PROCESSES is set to 0 (zero):

A. All pending jobs in the job queue are executed immediately and there will be zero pending jobs.

B. The job queue coordinator (CJQ0) is started immediately (zero seconds).

C. The job queue coordinator (CJQ0) is not started.

D. The jobs in the job queue are deleted and there will be zero jobs remaining in the job queue.

3. The range of values for the FAST_START_MTTR_TARGET is:

A. 0 to 1,000

B. 0 to 10,000

C. 0 to 3,600

D. There is no specific range.

4. **To flashback to a database state at a certain time in the past, you use the following procedure in the DBMS_FLASHBACK package:**

   A. `FLASHBACK_TO_TIME`

   B. `ENABLE_AT_TIME`

   C. `FLASHBACK_TO`

   D. `GO_BACK_TO`

5. **In Oracle9*i*, the redo logs do NOT:**

   A. Track the original DDL statement.

   B. Track the associated DML statements.

   C. Enable you to recover from a table drop or truncate operation.

   D. Empower you to chart the evolution of the schema.

6. **A row in an IOT:**

   A. Has a stable location—it is not subject to change.

   B. Moves around only if and when you change the sort order.

   C. Moves around when you rebuild the index.

   D. Moves around to maintain the sort order.

7. **To update logical ROWIDs for the secondary index, *iot_product_sec_ix*, in an IOT, you use the following statement:**

   A. ALTER INDEX `iot_product_sec_ix` UPDATE BLOCK REFERENCES;

   B. ALTER INDEX `iot_product_sec_ix` REBUILD BLOCK REFERENCES;

   C. ALTER INDEX `iot_product_sec_ix` UPDATE LOGICAL ROWIDS;

   D. ALTER INDEX `iot_product_sec_ix` REBUILD LOGICAL ROWIDS;

8. In the context of changing server parameters with the `ALTER SYSTEM` statement, which of the following values is not valid for the SCOPE option?

A. MEMORY

B. INSTANCE

C. BOTH

D. SPFILE

9. When you specify a new master site, it is tracked in the following view:

A. DBA_NEW_MASTERS

B. DBA_NEW_SITES

C. DBA_NEW_REPLICATION_MASTER

D. DBA_REPSITES_NEW

10. To use the RECOVER command to recover a database through SCN 12743, use the following statement:

A. `DBMS_REPCAT.THROUGH_SCN(12743)`

B. `RECOVER DATABASE UNTIL CHANGE 12743;`

C. `RECOVER DATABASE UNTIL SCN 12743;`

D. `DBMS_REPCAT.RECOVER_TO_SCN(12743)`

Fill-in-the-Blank Answers

1. dirty blocks
2. FAST_START_MTTR_TARGET
3. time, system change number (SCN)
4. V$LOGMNR_CONTENTS
5. DML
6. applies, standby, primary
7. switchover
8. guaranteed protection

9. DML
10. specify, SPECIFY_NEW_MASTERS, DBMS_REPCAT

Answers to Chapter Questions

1. A. The primary database must be instantiated.

Explanation A failover operation is a role transition that occurs when you have a loss of the primary database. Most likely, the primary database has some loss of data. You configure the standby database to become the primary database to address the data needs of users while you decide how to recover the original primary database. After fixing the primary database, you must instantiate the database.

2. C. The job queue coordinator (CJQ0) is not started.

Explanation If JOB_QUEUE_PROCESSES (an initialization parameter) is set to 0 (zero), Oracle does not start a job queue coordinator process when the database is started. Since there is no job queue coordinator, none of the jobs in the job queue will be executed. If JOB_QUEUE_PROCESSES is greater than 0, it establishes the maximum number of job queue processes that can be spawned in that instance. The maximum value for JOB_QUEUE_PROCESSES is 1,000.

3. C. 0 to 3,600

Explanation You can specify the value for the FAST_START_MTTR_TARGET parameter in seconds. The permissible range of values is 0 to 3,600.

4. B. ENABLE_AT_TIME

Explanation ENABLE_AT_TIME enables Oracle Flashback for the session and enables you to access the database at a SCN that is closest to the specified time. If you know the SCN, you can use the `ENABLE_AT_SYSTEM_CHANGE_NUMBER` procedure and specify the SCN to flashback to.

5. C. Enable you to recover from a table drop or truncate operation.

Explanation The redo logs track the original DDL statement and the associated DML statements. LogMiner displays this information so you can observe the changes to the object definition and chart the evolution of the schema. You *cannot* recover from table drops and truncates since the DDL statement does not specifically delete the individual rows.

6. D. Moves around to maintain the sort order.

Explanation The row in the IOT does not have a stable location; it moves around as a leaf in the B-tree to maintain the sort order. Because of the transient nature of the location of the row in an IOT, Oracle does not allow you to alter the primary key index.

7. A. ALTER INDEX `iot_product_sec_ix` UPDATE BLOCK REFERENCES;

Explanation The logical ROWIDs in an IOT's secondary index are based on the primary key and on a best guess at the physical address via the database block address at which the row is most likely to be found.

8. B. INSTANCE

Explanation MEMORY only makes changes in memory for the current instance and not in the SPFILE; therefore, the value does not persist. SPFILE only makes changes to the SPFILE and not in memory, and therefore not to the current instance. BOTH makes changes to both the instance and the SPFILE.

9. D. DBA_REPSITES_NEW

Explanation When you specify a new master site by invoking SPECIFY_NEW_MASTERS, Oracle tracks these potential new master sites in two data dictionary views: DBA_REPSITES_NEW and DBA_REPEXTENSION.

10. B. `RECOVER DATABASE UNTIL CHANGE 12743;`

Explanation When adding a new master without quiescing and performing change-based recovery, you can use either the RECOVER command or the Recovery Manager's (RMAN) DUPLICATE command. The `RECOVER` statement in the answer will perform a change-based recovery through SCN 12743.

CHAPTER 3

Manageability Enhancements

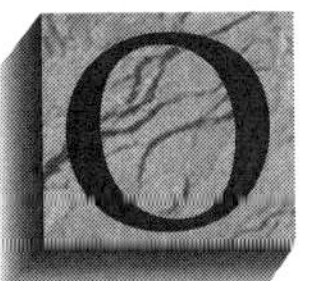

nce the database has been installed and implemented, a primary function of the database administrator (DBA) is to keep the database running at optimum efficiency. The DBA performs this function by managing specific attributes of a variety of logical objects in the Oracle database. Some of the tasks the DBA performs are

- Managing data segment space to maximize space utilization and to prevent row migration.
- Managing index segments and rebuilding them when they become unusable or adversely affect the performance.
- Managing rollback segments and ensuring that there is adequate space for transactions.
- Monitoring SGA usage and tuning the SGA for better performance.

Oracle9*i* greatly enhances the manageability of these objects; in fact, Oracle performs many of these tasks automatically. In this chapter, we will discuss the following Oracle9*i* manageability enhancements:

- Database Resource Manager
- Segment management
- Scalable session management
- File management
- Tablespace management
- Database workspace management
- Memory management
- Backup and recovery [Recovery Manager (RMAN) management enhancements]
- Oracle Enterprise Manager (OEM)

Database Resource Manager

The Database Resource Manager gives the Oracle Database Server a greater degree of control over resource management than the operating system (OS) would. Because the OS does not know about the architecture of the database server, it is inefficient in managing resources that pertain to the database. You can administer the Database Resource Manager with procedures within the

DBMS_RESOURCE_MANAGER and DBMS_RESOURCE_MANAGER_PRIVS packages. You need the ADMINISTER_RESOURCE_MANAGER privilege in order to administer the Database Resource Manager. You can also administer the Database Resource Manager via the graphic user interface (GUI)-based Oracle Enterprise Manager (OEM). The Database Resource Manager addresses this problem.

The Database Resource Manager was first introduced in Oracle8*i*; it was enhanced in Oracle9*i*. Two of these enhancements are

- Automatically detecting and preempting long-running operations
- Automatically limiting resource consumption

Automatically Detecting and Preempting Long-Running Operations

You can specify the maximum estimated time to complete (in seconds) for an operation by assigning a value to the MAX_EST_EXEC_TIME parameter; the default value for this parameter is UNLIMITED. Oracle will estimate the time the operation will table will take. If the SWITCH_ESTIMATE parameter is set to TRUE, and if Oracle's estimate is greater than the value specified by MAX_EST_EXEC_TIME, Oracle will return an error and the operation will not be not started. If the SWITCH_ESTIMATE parameter is FALSE, Oracle will start the operation even if Oracle's estimate is greater than the value specified by MAX_EST_EXEC_TIME; Oracle will only switch groups based on other criteria being met.

A resources consumer group, with multiple plan directives allocating resources to the group, could have more than one plan directive with a MAX_EST_EXEC_TIME parameter. In this situation, the Database Resource Manager takes the conservative approach; it uses the lowest value for MAX_EST_EXEC_TIME.

The MAX_EST_EXEC_TIME parameter enables the Database Resource Manager to anticipate long-running jobs and to prevent these jobs from running and therefore from excessively consuming system resources.

Automatically Limiting Resource Consumption

The primary purpose of the Database Resource Manager is to manage the allocation of system resources among the various user sessions based on criteria specified by the administrator. The Database Resource Manager accomplishes this mission by switching the session from one resource consumer group to the next whenever preestablished criteria are met. The SWITCH_GROUP parameter specifies the group to which the session will be switched.

One of the resources that you can allocate among sessions is central processing unit (CPU) utilization. However, the Database Resource Manager only enforces CPU utilization when the sessions do not get the resources that were specified.

Here are the major steps for specifying a Database Resource Manager solution. The first step is to *create a pending area*. A pending area is a staging area where you can specify your resource solution and validate it before you submit it to be implemented. You must create a pending area before you can either create a new plan or update an existing plan; otherwise, it will result in a "pending area not active" error.

You create a pending area with the following statement:

```
DBMS_RESOURCE_MANAGER.CREATE_PENDING_AREA();
```

Then you must *create a resource plan*. A resource plan is associated with resource plan directives, each of which specifies which resources are allocated to a resource consumer group. We will define a plan for the accounting application; the name of the plan is ACTG_PLAN.

You can create a resource plan with the following statement:

```
DBMS_RESOURCE_MANAGER.CREATE_PLAN(
  PLAN    => 'ACTG_PLAN',
  COMMENT => 'Plan for Accounting Application'
);
```

The other optional parameters are as follows:

- **ACTIVE_SESS_POOL_MTH** Specifies the method for managing the resources for the active session pool.
- **CPU_MTH** Specifies the method for allocating CPU resources among the groups.
- **PARALLEL_DEGREE_LIMIT_MTH** Specifies the resource allocation method to effect a specified degree of parallel operations within a give resource consumer group.
- **QUEUEING_MTH** Specifies the queuing resource allocation method.

Then you must *create resource consumer groups*. A resource plan can have many resource consumer groups, each of which represents a group of sessions that has a common set of resource requirements.

Let's assume we are defining three resource consumer groups for the ACTG_PLAN resource plan: ACTG_INT (Interactive), ACTG_BATCH, and HI_RES (High Resource).

You can create the ACTG_INT group with the following statement:

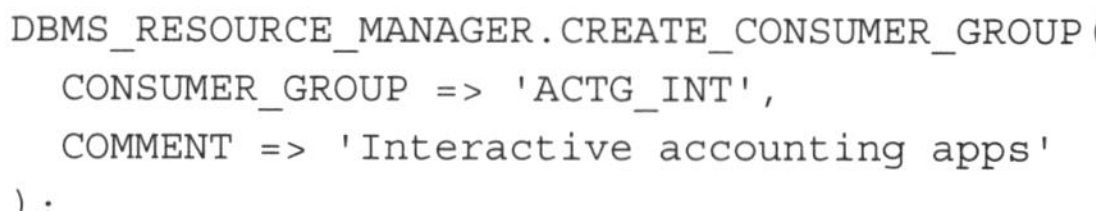

```
DBMS_RESOURCE_MANAGER.CREATE_CONSUMER_GROUP(
  CONSUMER_GROUP => 'ACTG_INT',
  COMMENT => 'Interactive accounting apps'
);
```

Besides these user-defined resource consumer groups, Oracle defines two default groups that you cannot change or delete. These Oracle supplied groups are as follows:

- **DEFAULT_CONSUMER_GROUP** This is the default initial group for users and sessions that have not been assigned an initial group.
- **OTHER_GROUPS** You must specify a resource directive for this group in any active resource plan. You cannot assign the OTHER_GROUPS group directly or explicitly to a user or session; this group is used for users and sessions that are assigned to a group that is not organized under the currently active plan.

Then you must *create the resource plan directives*. Resource plan directives associate a resource consumer group with a resource plan and specify the resources that must be allocated to the group. For example, the CPU_P1 parameter specifies the percentage of CPU allocated at the first level.

Prior to Oracle9*i*, the resources that were allocated for a transaction were not released until the transaction was complete. If an active session could not access an additional resource because it was being utilized by another transaction, it would result in an error. Also, new transactions would have to wait forever for other transactions to complete and release needed resources. This obviously had an adverse effect on performance.

Oracle9*i* gives you the ability to control the maximum number of concurrently active sessions within a given resource consumer group. You can specify the maximum number of active sessions in the resource consumer group by setting the ACTIVE_SESS_POOL_P1 parameter; the default for this parameter is UNLIMITED. This in turn controls the amount of resources that a consumer group can use; it improves your ability to manage resources.

When an incoming session cannot be executed within a resource consumer group because the active session pool is full (it has the specified maximum number of sessions), the incoming session is assigned to a queue. All parallel operations are considered to be just one session. When an active session completes, it frees up a slot, and the resource manager then schedules the session at the top of the queue to be executed.

You can also specify that a job in the queue should abort after it has waited for execution for a specified timeout period. You can specify the time in seconds that a session should wait in the queue before aborting by setting the QUEUEING_P1 parameter; the default for this parameter is UNLIMITED.

This active session pool enables you to control the amount of resource consumption and the amount of paging. The active session pool also enables you to accomplish the performance requirements of the Service Level Agreements (SLAs).

You can get information about the queue by querying V$SESSION and V$RSRC_CONSUMER_GROUP views. Oracle9*i* has added the CURRENT_QUEUE_DURATION column to the V$SESSION view that tells you how long a session has been waiting in the queue. If the session is not in the queue, this column will contain a zero. Oracle9*i* has added the QUEUE_LENGTH column to the V$RSRC_CONSUMER_GROUP view that tells you the number of queued sessions in a consumer group.

Sometimes, an active session has to wait for a resource to be freed up by another session. Oracle frees up resources by switching an active session to the group specified by the SWITCH_GROUP parameter if it has been active for more than the time specified by the SWITCH_TIME parameter in seconds. The SWITCH_TIME parameter specifies the amount of time a session can execute before it must be switched to another group. The default for the SWITCH_GROUP parameter is NULL; the default for the SWITCH_TIME parameter is UNLIMITED. When a session completes its operations, it is switched back to its original group. If the group has multiple plan directives, it takes the conservative approach and uses the most restrictive SWITCH_GROUP and SWITCH_TIME parameters.

In the context of the automatic switching of sessions in a group, Oracle gives you the SWITCH_ESTIMATE parameter to specify if Oracle should preempt operations that are estimated to take too long to run before they even start.

Oracle9*i* also gives you the UNDO_POOL parameter to specify the maximum size (in kilobytes) of the undo space that the group can use, which in turn sets a limit on the amount of undo entries corresponding to the consumer group. The default for the UNDO_POOL parameter is UNLIMITED. Once the undo space consumption has exceeded that specified by the UNDO_POOL parameter, you can continue to retrieve information with the SELECT statement, but you cannot perform any more DML operations (INSERT, UPDATE, or DELETE) because the group cannot use more undo space for the corresponding undo entries.

Oracle9*i* has added the CURRENT_UNDO_CONSUMPTION column to the V$RSRC_CONSUMER_GROUP view that tells you the amount of undo space consumed by the consumer group.

Table 3-1 summarizes the resource allocation requirements for the three groups that you specified earlier.

You can create the resource plan directive for the ACTG_INT resource consumer group as follows:

```
DBMS_RESOURCE_MANAGER.CREATE_PLAN_DIRECTIVE(
  PLAN => 'ACTG_PLAN',
  GROUP_OR_SUBPLAN => 'ACTG_INT',
  COMMENT => 'For interactive accounting applications',
  CPU_P1 => 75,
  SWITCH_ESTIMATE => TRUE,
  MAX_EST_EXEC_TIME => 1800,
  ACTIVE_SESS_POOL_P1 => 50,
  QUEUEING_P1 => 300,
  UNDO_POOL => 600);
```

You can change the resource allocations at any time by invoking the UPDATE_PLAN_DIRECTIVE in the DBMS_RESOURCE_MANAGER package.

As discussed a few paragraphs earlier, you must ensure that you have specified a resource plan directive for the OTHER_GROUPS Oracle-supplied group. Here is an example:

```
DBMS_RESOURCE_MANAGER.CREATE_PLAN_DIRECTIVE(
  PLAN => 'ACTG_PLAN',
  GROUP_OR_SUBPLAN => 'OTHER_GROUPS',
  COMMENT => 'You must specify a directive',
  CPU_P8 => 100);
```

	ACTG_INT	**ACTG_BATCH**	**HI_RES**
CPU_P1	75%	50%	100%
Switching			
■ SWITCH_GROUP			Actg_Plan
■ SWITCH_TIME			10
■ SWITCH_ESTIMATE	TRUE		TRUE
MAX_EST_EXEC_TIME	1,800		2,400
Active Session Pool			
■ ACTIVE_SESS_POOL_P1	50		7
■ QUEUEING_P1	300		120
UNDO_POOL	600K	100K	200K

TABLE 3-1. *Resource Allocation Requirements*

The other parameters are omitted to specify that OTHER_GROUPS has unlimited access to those resources.

Once you have created the directives, you must *validate the plan* in the staging area. You do this with the following statement:

```
DBMS_RESOURCE_MANAGER.VALIDATE_PENDING_AREA();
```

If no directives have been specified for the OTHER_GROUPS consumer group in this active plan, you will get the following error during this validation:

```
ORA-29382: validation of pending area failed
ORA-29377: consumer group OTHER_GROUPS is not part of top-plan ACTG_PLAN
```

The final step is to implement the plan by submitting the plan in the staging area:

```
DBMS_RESOURCE_MANAGER.SUBMIT_PENDING_AREA();
```

This step commits the changes you have made in the pending area and clears the pending area of all the entries. You could also have cleared the pending area at any time in the process by invoking the CLEAR_PENDING_AREA procedure in the DBMS_RESOURCE_MANAGER package.

For Review

1. Be familiar with the process to build a resource plan.
2. You must know about the procedures in the DBMS_RESOURCE_MANAGER package that you can use to build a resource plan.
3. You must know the purpose served by some common parameters such as SWITCH_TIME.

Exercises

1. **You build a resource plan in a staging area called the**

   A. Scratch pad

   B. Building area

   C. Temporary file

   D. Pending area

2. **The SWITCH_GROUP parameter specifies**

   A. The maximum time the session can spend in one group before it has to be switched out.

   B. The group to which the session will be switched once it meets preestablished criteria.

   C. That this consumer group is a switchable resource group.

   D. That this group is to toggle between the ON and OFF states.

Answer Key
1. D. **2.** B.

Segment Management

Oracle performs space allocation and management for storing information in the database (see Figure 3-1).

The smallest logical unit for data storage is the *datablock*, which directly corresponds to physical space on the disk. The administrator can specify the datablock size by setting the initialization parameter DB_BLOCK_SIZE. Oracle requests a number of contiguous blocks from the OS, collectively called an *extent*. A *segment* is a set of extents. Oracle allocates one extent of additional space when the extents in a segment are full (see Figure 3-2). Since space is allocated one extent at a time, there is a high probability that the extents will not be contiguous.

Prior to Oracle8*i*, the DBA had to manually monitor and fix segment management problems. Oracle8*i* introduced locally managed tablespaces to automate extent management. Oracle9*i* has added enhancements that perform many management tasks automatically. Also, Oracle9*i* has introduced additional types of segments to provide more options for data management.

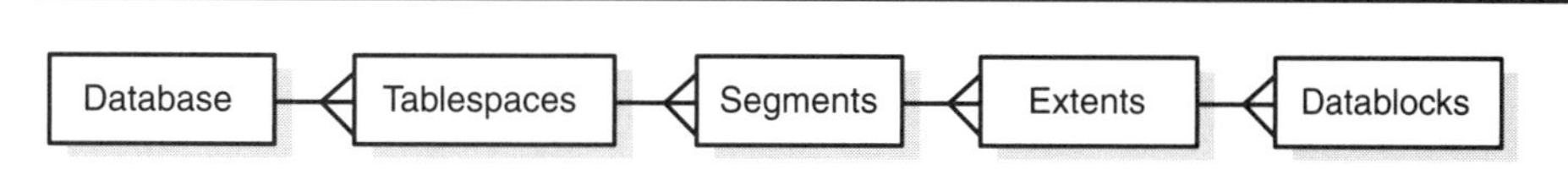

FIGURE 3-1. *Space management architecture*

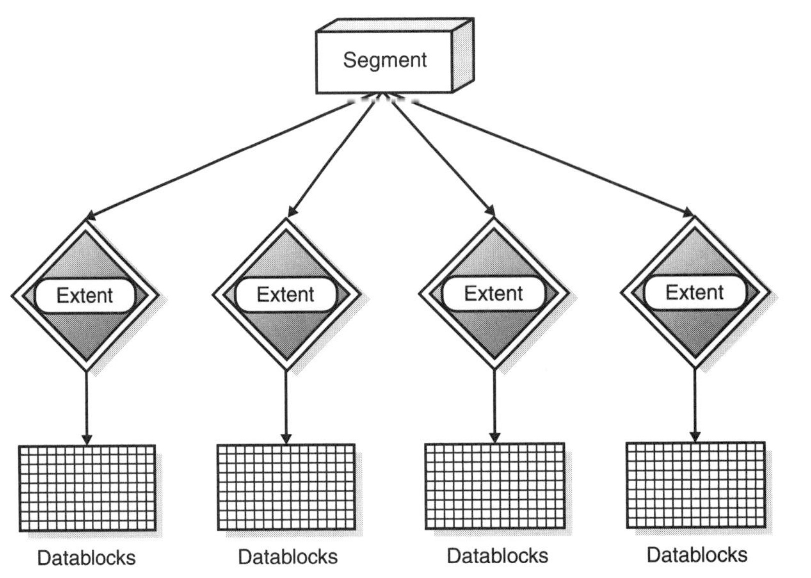

FIGURE 3-2. *Segments, extents, and datablocks*

This section discusses the following Oracle9*i* enhancements to segment management:

- Automatic global index management
- External tables
- List partitions
- Metadata Application Programming Interface (API)
- Automatic segment space management
- Bitmap join indexes

Automatic Global Index Management

The partitioning of tables was introduced in Oracle8; it enabled Oracle to split a single table into smaller segments for data storage. You can specifically manage each partition; for example, you can place each partition in its own tablespace and therefore on its own separate disk. This allows you to build tables with a large number of records, such as in a data warehouse application. You can also create indexes on partitioned tables. You can create either a global index that is partitioned independent of the table's partitioning scheme or a local index whose partitioning is linked to the partitioning scheme of the table.

You can perform a number of DDL operations on the partitions in a partitioned table. For example, you can split or drop a partition. These partition DDL operations will flag the index partitions associated with the data partitions referenced by the query as UNUSABLE, and you will have to rebuild the indexes. Rebuilding a local index is not a serious issue, since Oracle only rebuilds the local index related to that partition; all other local indexes for other partitions will continue to be VALID. On the other hand, when you initiate an action to rebuild a global index, Oracle flags the entire index as UNUSABLE and rebuilds the entire index. Rebuilding the entire index is a very expensive operation.

Oracle9*i* overcomes this problem by giving you the option to update global indexes as Oracle performs the partition DDL. This feature is not applicable to local indexes, domain indexes, index-organized tables (IOTs), or to indexes that were UNUSABLE prior to the start of the partition DML. You can invoke this capability by using the optional clause `UPDATE GLOBAL INDEXES`, as shown in this example:

```
ALTER TABLE <table_name>
  DROP PARTITION <partition_name>
  UPDATE GLOBAL INDEXES
```

If the `UPDATE GLOBAL INDEXES` clause is not specified, it defaults to `INVALIDATE GLOBAL INDEXES`, which is the mode reflected by previous Oracle versions. You can use this clause with the ADD, COALESCE, DROP, EXCHANGE, MERGE, MOVE, SPLIT, and TRUNCATE partition DDL commands.

Here are some advantages of automatically maintaining global indexes during DDL:

- The indexes are available throughout the execution of the partition DDL operation.
- It is more straightforward; the partition DDL also rebuilds the indexes.
- You do not have to discover UNUSABLE indexes and initiate rebuild operations explicitly.

External Tables

External tables are read-only tables whose data resides in an external OS flat file, and whose definition is stored inside the database. You can query the data in an external table as if it were a regular database table.

You can create external tables by specifying the ORGANIZATION EXTERNAL clause in your CREATE TABLE statement.

Let's consider an OS file *bookteam.dat* with the following data:

```
129,"Athena","Acq. Editor"
158,"Dan","Author"
109,"Jeremy","Manager"
131,"Lisa","Acq. Editor"
114,"Molly","Copy Editor"
```

You must first develop the specification for the external file using a format that is similar to the control file specification in SQL*Loader. The following code shows you how you can specify the external file. The first step is to create the directory objects for the OS directories that contain the data sources, and for the bad record and log files. Directories were available in previous versions of Oracle. You can specify directories as follows:

```
CONNECT / AS SYSDBA
CREATE OR REPLACE DIRECTORY data_dir AS 'c:\extfiles\data';
CREATE OR REPLACE DIRECTORY log_dir AS 'c:\extfiles\log';
CREATE OR REPLACE DIRECTORY bad_dir AS 'c:\extfiles\bad';
```

Then you need to grant the required privileges to those directories as follows:

```
GRANT READ ON DIRECTORY data_dir TO scott;
GRANT WRITE ON DIRECTORY log_dir TO scott;
GRANT WRITE ON DIRECTORY bad_dir TO scott;
```

The next step is to create the definition for the external file as follows:

```
CONNECT scott/tiger;
CREATE TABLE emp_ext
(
  empnum  NUMBER(3),
  empname VARCHAR2(15),
  title   VARCHAR2(14)
)
 ORGANIZATION EXTERNAL
 (
  TYPE ORACLE_LOADER
  DEFAULT DIRECTORY data_dir
  ACCESS PARAMETERS
  (
    badfile bad_dir:'bookteam.bad'
    logfile log_dir:'bookteam.log'
    records delimited by newline
```

```
    fields terminated by ',' optionally enclosed by '"'
    missing field values are null
    (
     empnum, empname, title
    )
  )
  LOCATION ('bookteam.dat')
 )
PARALLEL
REJECT LIMIT UNLIMITED;
```

The PARALLEL clause enables a parallel query on the data sources. The REJECT LIMIT clause specifies that there is no limit to the number of errors that can occur during a query of the external data. You have defined the external table; you can query this external table just as you would any regular Oracle table.

When you query the external table, ORACLE_LOADER is the default access driver. Here is an example of an external query:

```
ALTER SESSION ENABLE PARALLEL DML;
SELECT * FROM emp_ext;
```

The results of this query will be as follows:

```
EMP EMPNAME         TITLE
--- --------------- -------------
129 Athena          Acq. Editor
158 Dan             Author
109 Jeremy          Manager
131 Lisa            Acq. Editor
114 Molly           Copy Editor
```

You can change the access parameters with the ALTER TABLE command. You can also add, modify, or drop columns by altering the table. You can also remove external tables with the DROP TABLE, but this command only removes the metadata from the data dictionary; the external OS file that contains the data is not deleted. You can delete the OS file by issuing an OS command.

Some candidates for external tables are

- External source data that are used just one time.
- Online Analytical Processing (OLAP) applications that use external data on a very infrequent basis.
- External data that have large amounts of data and are queried very rarely.

Some limitations with external tables are as follows:

- This is a read-only table; you cannot perform DML operations.
- You cannot generate Indexes on external tables.
- Oracle's security can by bypassed because you can access the data via the OS.

You can obtain information about external tables from the DBA_EXTERNAL_TABLES and DBA_EXTERNAL_LOCATIONS data dictionary views. DBA_EXTERNAL_TABLES data dictionary view provides information about the attributes of the external tables in the database, while DBA_EXTERNAL_TABLES provides information about the name and location of the flat file that contains the external data.

List Partitions

The partitioning of tables was introduced in Oracle 8, and only range partitioning was available. Partitioning was enhanced in 8*i* to include hash partitioning. Oracle9*i* has introduced a new partitioning technique called list partitioning.

List partitioning enables you to partition a table's data based on discrete column values; it gives you explicit control over how rows map to partitions. This differs from range partitioning where a range of values is associated with a partition, and from hash partitioning where you had no control over the row-to-partition mapping.

The following example shows how you can create a table with list partitions:

```
CREATE TABLE concert
(
  concert_num  CHAR(5),
  artist       VARCHAR2(20),
  city         VARCHAR2(20),
  state        CHAR(2),
  concert_date DATE
)
 STORAGE(INITIAL 40K NEXT 10K)
 TABLESPACE concert_tbs1
 PARTITION BY LIST (state)
 (
  PARTITION east_concert
    VALUES ('MA', 'NY', 'MD', 'VA', 'NJ')
    STORAGE (INITIAL 10K NEXT 20K PCTINCREASE 50)
    TABLESPACE concert_tbs2,
  PARTITION west_concert
```

```
    VALUES ('CA', 'OR', 'WA', 'CO')
    PCTFREE 30 NOLOGGING,
  PARTITION south_concert
    VALUES ('TX', 'KY','TN', 'AR','AL'),
  PARTITION central_concert
    VALUES ('OH', 'IL', 'IA')
);
```

You can specify storage parameters for each partition. If you do not specify storage partitions at the partition level, they will default to storage characteristics for the table. When creating list partitions, you cannot specify MAXVALUE as the upper limit for the partition. If you insert a row whose state data value is not a valid state, Oracle will return an error.

Once a list partition table is created, you can use the ALTER TABLE statement to ADD, MODIFY, SPLIT, MERGE, or DROP partitions.

The following statement demonstrates how you can add a new partition to a list-partitioned table:

```
ALTER TABLE concert
  ADD PARTITION island_concert
        VALUES ('HI', 'PR')
        STORAGE (INITIAL 20K NEXT 10K) TABLESPACE concert_tbs4;
```

The values that specify the partition that you are adding must not exist in any other partition of the table. You can also specify physical storage attributes and logging options when adding partitions. If omitted, the partition storage parameters default to the table storage parameters. If a local index exists for this table, then a new local index partition is also added when you add partitions to the table.

You can also merge list partitions; the partitions do not have to be adjacent. The resulting partition consists of all the data from the original two partitions:

```
ALTER TABLE concert
 MERGE PARTITIONS west_concert, island_concert
  INTO PARTITION  wide_west_concert
         PCTFREE 25 STORAGE(MAXEXTENTS 18);
```

The resulting wide_west_concert partition is comprised of the set that represents the union of these two partition value lists:

```
('CA', 'OR', 'WA', 'CO', 'HI', 'PR')
```

You can also modify the definition of the partitions in a list-partitioned table. The following statement adds values to an existing partition:

```
ALTER TABLE concert
  MODIFY PARTITION central_concert
    ADD VALUES ('MI', 'MO');
```

The values that you are adding must not exist in any other partition's value list.

You can use the following statement to drop values from an existing partition value list:

```
ALTER TABLE concert
  MODIFY PARTITION east_concert
   DROP VALUES ('NJ');
```

You cannot remove values from a list partition if there are data corresponding to the partition values being deleted. You must delete the rows that contain these values before you can remove the values from the partition list. To drop all the values of a partition, you must use the DROP PARTITION clause.

Here are some limitations with the list-partitioned tables:

- List partitioning is supported for heap tables only. IOTs do not support this feature.
- Multicolumn partitioning is not supported.
- You cannot specify MAXVALUE. You can specify a NULL value.
- The set of values that specifies a partition cannot be empty; it must contain at least one value.
- The string comprising the list of values for a partition must not exceed 4KB.

Metadata Application Programming Interface (API)

Prior to Oracle9*i*, you had three options for documenting the objects in an existing database. The first option was to query the various tables in the data dictionary to obtain information about an object. This option was wieldy; it required a number of Structured Query Language (SQL) statements, it needed to be changed as new objects were added to the database, and you had to keep up with Oracle's enhancements to the DDL. A second option was to use Oracle's Export/Import utilities. You had to set the parameter ROWS=N for the export operation and SHOW=Y for the import operation. This option required you to perform a significant amount of editing to generate the documentation. A third option was to

Procedure	Description
CLOSE	Releases the resources and closes the handle generated by the OPEN procedure.
FETCH	Returns the metadata for objects specified by OPEN, SET_FILTER, and SET_COUNT.
GET_DDL	Returns metadata as DDL.
GET_QUERY	Returns the text of the query used in the FETCH.
GET_XML	Returns metadata as XML.
OPEN	Specifies the type of object to be retrieved, the version of its metadata, and the object model.
SET_COUNT	Specifies the maximum number of objects to be retrieved in one invocation.
SET_FILTER	Specifies selection criteria for retrieving the objects. For example, you could restrict it to the object name or schema name.
SET_PARSE_ITEM	Enables output parsing by specifying an object attribute to be parsed and returned.

TABLE 3-2. *Some Procedures in the DBMS_METADATA Package*

use the `OCIDescribeAny` interface. This option did not retrieve all the metadata; besides, it was not scalable.

Oracle9*i* has introduced a new package called DBMS_METADATA that enables you to retrieve all the attributes of the database object from the data dictionary with one invocation. Table 3-2 summarizes some procedures in this package.

The following example demonstrates the use of the GET_DDL function:

```
SQL>CONNECT hr/hr;
SQL>SELECT dbms_metadata.get_ddl('TABLE', 'LOCATIONS')
  2*  FROM dual;

DBMS_METADATA.GET_DDL('TABLE','LOCATIONS')
-------------------------------------------------------


  CREATE TABLE "HR"."LOCATIONS"
   (    "LOCATION_ID" NUMBER(4,0),
```

```
        "STREET_ADDRESS" VARCHAR2(40),
        "POSTAL_CODE" VARCHAR2(12),
        "CITY" VARCHAR2(30) CONSTRAINT "LOC_CITY_NN" NOT NULL ENABLE,
        "STATE_PROVINCE" VARCHAR2(25),
        "COUNTRY_ID" CHAR(2),
         CONSTRAINT "LOC_ID_PK" PRIMARY KEY ("LOCATION_ID")
  USING INDEX PCTFREE 10 INITRANS 2 MAXTRANS 255
  STORAGE(INITIAL 65536 NEXT 1048576 MINEXTENTS 1 MAXEXTENTS 2147483645
PCTINCREASE 0
  FREELISTS 1 FREELIST GROUPS 1 BUFFER_POOL DEFAULT) TABLESPACE "EXAMPLE"
ENABLE,
         CONSTRAINT "LOC_C_ID_FK" FOREIGN KEY ("COUNTRY_ID")
  REFERENCES "HR"."COUNTRIES" ("COUNTRY_ID") ENABLE NOVALIDATE
   ) PCTFREE 10 PCTUSED 40 INITRANS 1 MAXTRANS 255 LOGGING
  STORAGE(INITIAL 65536 NEXT 1048576 MINEXTENTS 1 MAXEXTENTS 2147483645
PCTINCREASE 0
  FREELISTS 1 FREELIST GROUPS 1 BUFFER_POOL DEFAULT) TABLESPACE "EXAMPLE"
```

Oracle returns the DDL generated by this query as a LONG datatype. You could also use the GET_XML package to get the output as Extensible Markup Language (XML), as opposed to DDL. By default, most functions in the DBMS_METADATA package return information in XML. You can specify an Extensible Style Language-Transformation (XSL-T) style sheet to transform the XML output into American National Standards Institute (ANSI) Standard DDL. You specify this in the TRANSFORM parameter for GET_DDL.

Automatic Segment Space Management

Prior to Oracle9*i*, you managed space utilization within a datablock with the PCTFREE and PCTUSED parameters. The addresses of datablocks that were available for storing new rows of data were added to the freelists maintained in the segment header. The PCTFREE parameter specified the percentage of the block that had to be reserved for updates to rows of data in that block. A low value for PCTFREE improves performance for INSERTS, but necessitates frequent row migrations for UPDATES and DELETES, while a high value improves performance for UPDATES and DELETES, but uses up additional blocks when adding new data. Once the datablock is full per the PCTFREE parameter, Oracle would not add new data to the block until the percentage of the block utilization drops below the PCTUSED parameter. A low value for the PCTUSED parameter improves performance for UPDATES and DELETES, but results in using more datablocks for INSERTS, while a high value improves space utilization for INSERTS, but could cause migrations and chaining for UPDATES and DELETES.

Oracle9*i*'s automatic segment space management maintains information about datablock space utilization in bitmaps, as opposed to freelists. Every automatically space-managed segment maintains a set of bitmap blocks (BMBs) for tracking and managing the utilization of blocks within that segment. These bitmaps are stored in blocks other than the blocks that contain the data, and other than the segment header that points to the blocks containing the bitmaps. When you insert a new row, the server process looks up the bitmap to locate a block into which the row can be inserted. Whenever a block becomes more or less full, the bitmap is updated accordingly. This eliminates the need to specify the PCTUSED, FREELISTS, and FREELIST GROUPS parameters.

Creating an Automatically Space-Managed Segment

To create automatically space-managed segments, the tablespace must be locally managed and you must use the SEGMENT SPACE MANAGEMENT clause introduced in Oracle9*i*. You can set the SEGMENT SPACE MANAGEMENT to MANUAL to specify freelist segments, or you can set it to AUTO for automatic space management segments. The following example shows the creation of a tablespace with automatically space-managed segments:

```
CREATE TABLESPACE pers_tbs
  DATAFILE 'C:\ORACLE\ORADATA\ORCL\PERSTBS.DBF' SIZE 30M
  EXTENT MANAGEMENT LOCAL
  SEGMENT SPACE MANAGEMENT AUTO;
```

In this case, there is no need to specify PCTUSED, FREELISTS, and FREELIST GROUPS parameters. Even if you specify them, they are ignored. You can only specify automatic SEGMENT SPACE MANAGEMENT at the tablespace level. Oracle9*i* has added a new column named SEGMENT_SPACE_MANAGEMENT to the DBA_TABLESPACES data dictionary view that tracks whether the space utilization is AUTO or MANUAL:

```
SQL> select tablespace_name,segment_space_management
  2  from dba_tablespaces;

TABLESPACE_NAME                SEGMEN
------------------------------ ------
SYSTEM                         MANUAL
UNDOTBS                        MANUAL
CWMLITE                        MANUAL
DRSYS                          MANUAL
EXAMPLE                        MANUAL
INDX                           MANUAL
TEMP                           MANUAL
TOOLS                          MANUAL
USERS                          MANUAL
PERS_TBS                       AUTO
```

The following example shows you how to create an automatically space-managed table:

```
CREATE TABLE myemployee
(
 empid    NUMBER(2),
 empname  VARCHAR2(15),
 hiredate DATE
)
 TABLESPACE PERS_TBS;
```

If you specify PCTUSED, FREELIST, and FREELIST_GROUPS parameters, they will be ignored because this is an automatic space-managed table.

The DBMS_SPACE Package

Oracle9*i* has enhanced the DBMS_SPACE package by adding the SPACE_USAGE procedure to obtain information about the free blocks in automatically space-managed (ASM) segments. You can use the SPACE_USAGE procedure to determine the number of blocks below the High Water Mark (HWM) with free space ranges of 0 to 25 percent (HS1), 25 to 50 percent (HS2), 50 to 75 percent (HS3) and 75 to 100 percent (HS4). The following example demonstrates the use of the SPACE_USAGE procedure:

```
DECLARE
   fb25 NUMBER;
   fb50 NUMBER;
   fb75 NUMBER;
   fb100 NUMBER;
   fby   NUMBER;
   fblk  NUMBER;
   fs1by NUMBER;
   fs2by NUMBER;
   fs3by NUMBER;
   fs4by NUMBER;
   ublk  NUMBER;
   uby   NUMBER;

BEGIN
   dbms_space.space_usage(segment_owner=>'SCOTT',
                          segment_name=>'MYEMPLOYEE',
                          segment_type=>'TABLE',
                          unformatted_blocks=>ublk,
                          unformatted_bytes=>uby,
                          fs1_blocks=>fb25,
                          fs2_blocks=>fb50,
                          fs3_blocks=>fb75,
```

```
                              fs4_blocks=>fb100,
                              fs1_bytes=>fs1by,
                              fs2_bytes=>fs2by,
                              fs3_bytes=>fs3by,
                              fs4_bytes=>fs4by,
                              full_blocks=>fblk,
                              full_bytes=>fby);

   dbms_output.put_line('Blocks with free space below 25% :' ||fb25);
   dbms_output.put_line('Blocks with free space below 50% :' ||fb50);
   dbms_output.put_line('Blocks with free space below 75% :' ||fb75);
   dbms_output.put_line('Blocks with free space below 100% :' ||fb100);
END;
/
```

Here are the results when you execute this procedure:

```
Blocks with free space below 25% :0
Blocks with free space below 50% :3
Blocks with free space below 75% :1
Blocks with free space below 100% :9
```

Using this procedure on a non-ASM segment will result in an error. You can obtain additional details about the SPACE_USAGE procedure in the Oracle Supplied PL/SQL Packages and Types Reference Manual.

The DBMS_REPAIR Package

You use the ALTER TABLE statement to change the PCTFREE value for both FREELIST segments (manual space-managed) and ASM segments. In the case of automatic space-managed tables, the ALTER TABLE command does not update the BMBs. Hence, these blocks may not track the true current status of the datablocks. Oracle9*i* has added a new procedure called SEGMENT_FIX_STATUS to the DBMS_REPAIR package to fix this problem. Here are the parameters for this procedure:

```
DBMS_REPAIR.SEGMENT_FIX_STATUS
(
 segment_owner  IN VARCHAR2,
 segment_name   IN VARCHAR2,
 segment_type   IN BINARY_INTEGER DEFAULT TABLE_OBJECT,
 file_number    IN BINARY_INTEGER DEFAULT NULL,
 block_number   IN BINARY_INTEGER DEFAULT NULL,
 status_value   IN BINARY_INTEGER DEFAULT NULL,
 partition_name IN VARCHAR2 DEFAULT NULL,
);
```

Here is an example of how you can use this procedure:

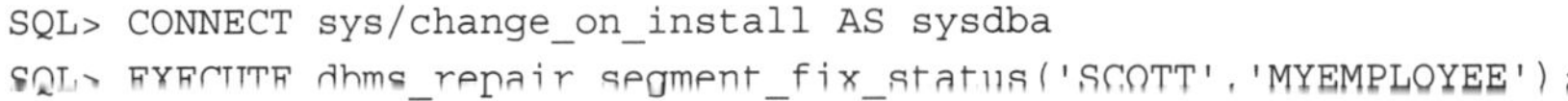

```
SQL> CONNECT sys/change_on_install AS sysdba
SQL> EXECUTE dbms_repair.segment_fix_status('SCOTT','MYEMPLOYEE');
```

Migration Issues

The technology of automatic space management segments is introduced in Oracle9*i*. The COMPATIBLE init.ora parameter must be set to 9.0.0 or higher to use this feature. There is no explicit method to convert tablespaces from FREELIST segments' tablespaces to automatic space-managed segments. You must first create a tablespace with SEGMENT SPACE MANAGEMENT set to AUTO and then move objects into this tablespace. You can move tables with the ALTER TABLE . . . MOVE, CREATE TABLE . . . AS SELECT, or EXPORT/IMPORT operations. Besides regular tables, you can automatically segment space-managed indexes, IOTs, and large objects (LOBs).

Bitmap Join Indexes

Prior to Oracle9*i*, you could create bitmap indexes on a single table. Bitmap indexes are very useful in data warehousing environments for low-cardinality columns. Oracle9*i* extends this concept to a bitmap join index that optimizes the joining of two or more tables. A bitmap join index is a space- and performance-efficient technique. By predetermining associations, bitmap join indexes eliminate the large volumes of data generated with Cartesian products performed in a join operation. For every value in a join column of a table, a bitmap join index stores the ROWIDs of corresponding rows in one or more join tables. To create the bitmap join index, you must specify the join condition, as shown here:

```
CREATE BITMAP INDEX emp_dept_bji
    ON emp(e.job)
  FROM emp e, dept d
 WHERE e.deptno = d.deptno
```

Bitmap join indexes are excellent candidates for star schemas in data warehouses to improve join query performance. Bitmap join indexes are much more space-efficient than materialized join views, an alternative for materializing joins in advance because materialized join views do not compress the ROWIDs of the fact tables.

Oracle9*i* has added a new column called JOIN_INDEX to the DBA_INDEXES data dictionary view to identify if an index is based on a join condition. Oracle9*i* also introduces a new data dictionary view, DBA_JOIN_IND_COLUMNS, to display the join condition for a bitmap join index.

Restrictions

Here are some restrictions with bitmap join indexes:

- Parallel DML is currently only supported on the fact table. When you perform parallel DML on a participating dimension table, Oracle will mark the index as unusable.
- Only one table can be updated concurrently by different transactions.
- One table cannot appear more than one time in the join condition; in other words, you cannot use a self-join.
- You cannot reference an IOT or a temporary table.
- The columns in the index must all be columns of the dimension tables.
- The dimension table join columns must be either primary key columns or they must have unique constraints.
- If a dimension table has a composite primary key, each column in the composite primary key must be involved in the join. In other words, you cannot specify a join on just a part of the primary key.

For Review

1. You must know about the impact of using partitioning DDL with local and global indexes on partitioned tables.
2. You must be able to create and use external tables.
3. You must be able to create and modify a list-partitioned table.
4. You must know how to use the metadata API to obtain comprehensive information about a database object.
5. You must have the ability to create automatically space-managed segments. You must be familiar with using the DBMS_SPACE package to review the free blocks in your automatically space-managed segments.
6. You must be able to explain and create bitmap join indexes.

Exercises

1. **UPDATE GLOBAL INDEXES**

   A. Is a command that will immediately update all global indexes.

   B. Is a command that will update all global indexes after a predetermined period of time.

C. Is a qualifier that specifies that Oracle must update the global index when it performs DML against the table.

D. Is a qualifier that specifies that Oracle must update the global index as it performs partition DDL.

2. An external table

A. Is a regular Oracle table that is read-only.

B. Is a table whose data resides in an OS file.

C. Is a regular Oracle table that is resident in an external Oracle server.

D. Is a table that you create by using SQL*Loader to load data from an external operating file.

Answer Key
1. D. **2.** B.

Scalable Session Management

Oracle9*i* enhances the scalability of the database server to address the ever-increasing needs of client/server and Internet applications. Some new features introduced in Oracle9*i*, as it relates to the DBA's ability to implement and manage a scalable database solution, are as follows:

- Oracle Shared Server
- External procedure agents
- Multithreaded heterogeneous service (HS) agents
- OCI connection pooling
- Core "Oracle kernel" library

The Oracle Shared Server

You can configure the Oracle server as a dedicated server or a shared server. The *dedicated server architecture* requires a dedicated server process for each user connection.

The Oracle *shared server architecture* enables you to share one server process with multiple user sessions. An idle server process from a server process pool services a user session from a user request queue. The shared server architecture requires the following components:

- A network listener process
- At least one dispatcher process
- At least one shared server process

When a client initiated a shared server connection to the database in previous versions of Oracle, the listener had to obtain the least loaded dispatcher's address and communicate it to the client; then the client had to make another network call to contact the dispatcher process and get the connection confirmed. This increased network communication activity slowed down the connection process. In previous versions, the shared server connection was called the multithreaded server (MTS).

When a client initiates a shared server connection to the database in Oracle9*i*, the listener uses the *direct handoff* wherever possible. This connection process requires fewer network calls and, accordingly, less overhead (see Figure 3-3).

When the listener receives the request from the client for a shared server connection, it locates the address of the least loaded dispatcher process. In previous versions, the next step would have been to pass this address back to the client for the client to contact the dispatcher again over the network. Instead, in Oracle9*i*'s direct handoff method, the listener hands the connection request to the dispatcher. The dispatcher communicates directly with the client to establish a connection without the need for the additional network calls that were required in previous versions.

You can monitor the performance of the shared server and dispatcher graphically using the Performance Manager in the Oracle9*i* Enterprise Manager. Oracle9*i* has enhanced the Performance Manager to use automated agent-based monitoring along with real-time graphical charts and historical trend analysis. You can monitor the performance of each shared server, dispatcher, and listener. You can also display the code being executed in each session, and you can obtain recommendations for tuning each shared server. Figures 3-4 and 3-5 are some sample screen shots of the performance manager.

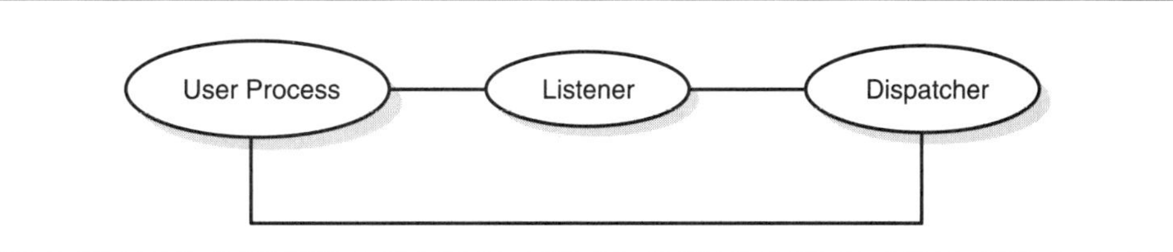

FIGURE 3-3. *The direct handoff connection process*

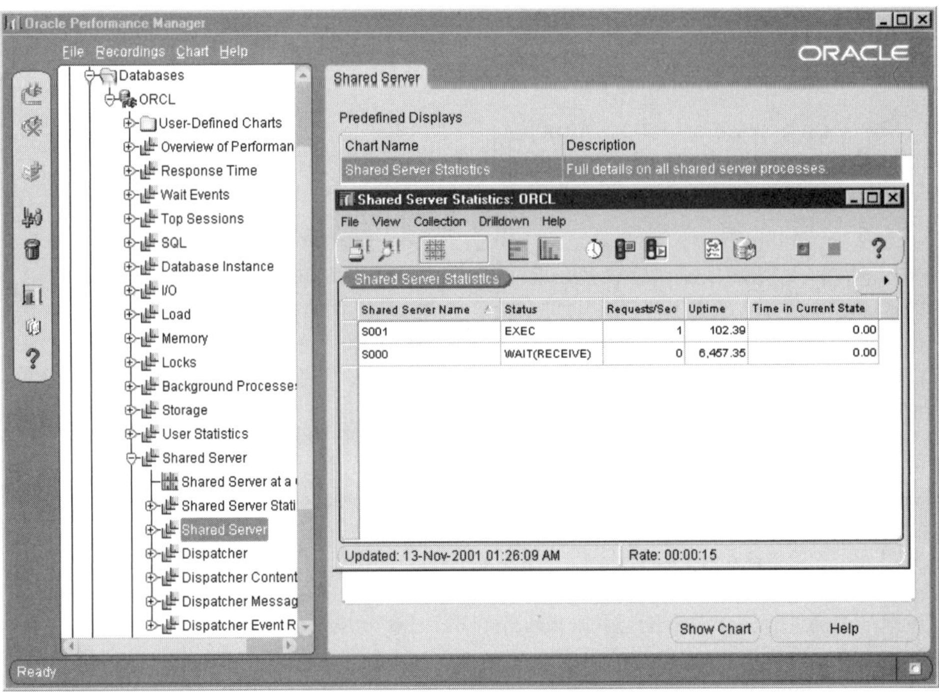

FIGURE 3-4. *Shared server performance*

External Procedure Agents

PL/SQL is the default procedural language for developing database applications. Although PL/SQL is a very powerful language for SQL-oriented transaction processing, it is not adequate for complex computational tasks because of the functionality of language and because of performance. A language such as C would greatly improve the functionality and the performance. If you create procedures in other languages and execute them on the client side, you are likely to have increased network traffic because of an increase in requests for database access.

Oracle8 overcame these problems by introducing external procedures, which enable you to create C functions as PL/SQL bodies. In other words, you can call C functions from PL/SQL. An external procedure is an external language procedure that is stored in a Dynamic Link Library (DLL), or in a libunit if you are using a Java class method.

Oracle8*i* further enhanced external procedures with the call specification special purpose interface. It enables you to call the external procedure (C function)

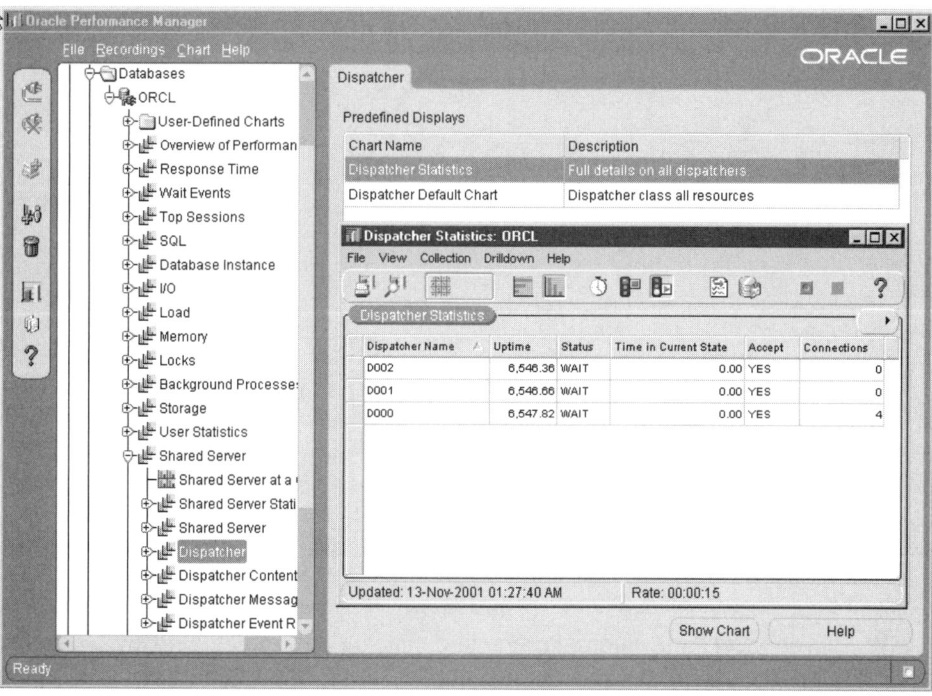

FIGURE 3-5. *Dispatcher performance*

from other languages (SQL or PL/SQL). All external procedures reference the EXTPROC default agent; Oracle establishes one EXTPROC process for every client calling one external procedure.

Oracle9*i* improves performance by establishing only one external procedure process for all clients calling one external procedure. Oracle9*i* enables you to create application-specific agents in DLLs, which you can identify in LISTENER.ORA. Because the agents are database links, you can also execute procedures on remote nodes.

Oracle9*i* has added the CREATE LIBRARY command to create external procedure agents. The general syntax of this command is as follows:

```
CREATE LIBRARY [schema_name.]library_name
  {IS | AS} 'file_path'
  [AGENT 'agent_link'];
```

In this syntax specification, file_path is the fully referenced file name, and agent_link is the name of the database link. If you omit the agent name specification, Oracle will default to EXTPROC.

Here is an example of creating a database link:

```
CREATE OR REPLACE DATABASE LINK my_agent_link
 USING 'my_tns_alias';
```

Here is an example of how you can create a library:

```
CREATE OR REPLACE LIBRARY my_utils
    IS '${my_ep_lib}\utils.so'
 AGENT 'my_agent_link';
```

In this example, my_ep_lib is an environment variable referencing the path where the external procedure files are placed on the server. You can invoke an external procedure agent that is stored in the library my_utils by referencing the database link my_agent_link. Because my_agent_link is associated with my_tns_alias when you create the link, and my_agent_link is associated with my_ep_lib when you create the library, my_tns_alias now points to the environment variable my_ep_lib on the server.

When you invoke the external procedure that you have created, PL/SQL alerts a listener process that will spawn a session-specific agent. The listener hands off this connection to the agent, and the agent gets the name of the DLL from PL/SQL. Then the agent loads the DLL and runs the external procedure. Finally, the agent passes any values that are returned by the external procedure back to your PL/SQL. The agent remains active throughout the Oracle session, even after the completion of the external procedure. This was not the case in previous versions, where the agent was terminated when the session logs out. By keeping the agent alive, the agent is invoked only once no matter how many calls are made. Thus, there is only one procedure agent running for a number of procedure calls.

Multithreaded Heterogeneous Service (HS) Agents

You can encounter a variety of heterogeneous database systems in an enterprise business environment, spanning the spectrum from legacy systems to state-of-the-art technologies. Coordinating the different applications and separate components of applications that are running on each of these databases is no small task. For example, you must concern yourself with maintaining transaction consistency and integrity. Oracle introduced HS agents to address these issues. When you use an HS agent, the Oracle server connects to the other databases, retrieves the data, and provides it to the optimizer that uses Oracle's default mechanism of executing the statement. The HS agent operation is similar to connecting to a remote Oracle database using a database link.

Prior to Oracle9*i*, the HS agent architecture was dedicated in nature; it consumed a significant amount of resources because it started an agent for each user session and for each database link. This concept is similar to the dedicated server architecture, where you need a server process for each session. This requires more system resources even though many of these processes might be idle at a given point of time. HS was called transparent gateway prior to Oracle8*i*.

Oracle9*i* has introduced multithreaded HS agent architecture, and its concept is similar to the shared server architecture. It uses a pool of shared agent processes. The tasks requested by the user sessions are put into a queue and are picked up by the first available multithreaded agent.

The multithreaded HS agent architecture has three kinds of threads:

- A single monitor thread
- Several dispatcher threads
- Several task threads

Monitor Thread

The multithreaded HS agent process first starts the monitor thread. The task of the monitor thread is to manage listener communications, monitor agent process loads, and start and stop dispatcher and task threads. This thread registers all the dispatcher threads with the listener; it also sends the load information of the dispatchers to the appropriate listeners. This enables the listeners to assign these new connections to the least loaded dispatcher. If a thread should die, the monitor process purges memory.

Dispatcher Thread

The dispatcher thread is responsible for communications with the Oracle server and for sending task requests to the task threads. These threads accept incoming connections and task requests from Oracle servers, and the threads place these requests on a queue for a task thread to pick up. Once the task thread picks up the requests and places the results on the queue, the dispatcher thread sends these results of the request back to the server that issued the request. Once a user session establishes a connection with a dispatcher, all requests from that session use the same dispatcher for the life of that session.

Task Thread

Typically, there are many more task threads than dispatcher threads. Task threads behave much like shared server processes. They pick up the pending requests from the queue, complete the task by performing necessary operations, and place the results returned by the task on the queue for the dispatcher process to pick up.

Table 3-3 describes some initialization parameters for you to configure the multithreaded HS agent initialization

OCI Connection Pooling

Connection pooling enables you to use one physical connection to service multiple user sessions. This has particular value in hosted web application servers, where many clients connect to the middle-tier web application server, and this middle-tier application has a connection to the database server. Similar to the Oracle shared server, connection pooling eliminates the need for you to establish one connection to the database server for every incoming user session. Connection pooling enhances security where the middle-tier application represents the user to the database server. Since connection pooling eliminates the need for a database connection for every user session, it enhances scalability since it consumes far fewer resources per user connection (see Figure 3-6).

You configure a connection pool with a shared pool of physical connections, which connect to a backend server pool containing the same number of dedicated server processes. OCI connection pooling operates on the middle tier; it is similar to the Oracle shared server on the database server. In the shared server architecture, a user connects to a dispatcher on the database server, and the dispatcher takes care of distributing the load on the shared server processes.

On the other hand, with OCI connection pooling you establish connections to a dedicated server process, but OCI connection pooling shares this pool of physical

Parameter	Description
max_dispatchers	The maximum number of dispatchers.
tcp_dispatcher	The number of dispatchers listening on tcp; the others will use ipc.
max_task_threads	The number of task threads.
listener_address	The listener address that is later needed for registration.
shutdown_address	The address used for shutdown messages from agtctl; this is the utility used to start and stop the multithreaded HS agent process.

TABLE 3-3. *Multithreaded HS Agent Initialization Parameters*

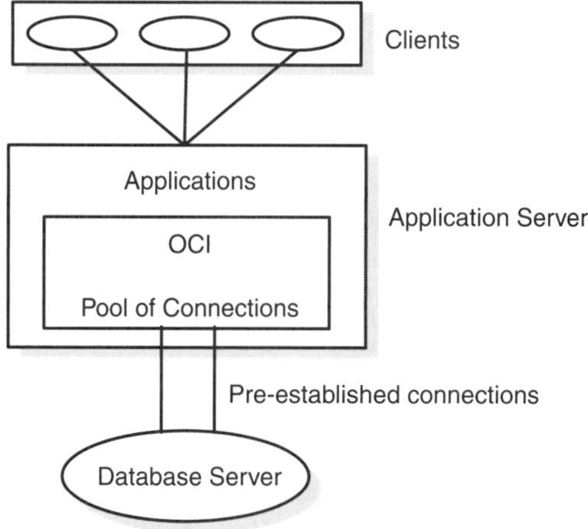

FIGURE 3-6. *The concept of connection pooling*

connections to service the various user sessions that require the database access. OCI connection pooling is responsible for monitoring user needs for database access, disconnecting the physical database connection from the user session when not required so that the same physical connection can be used by another user session. If all physical connections are busy, a new connection is added dynamically to the pool until a maximum number is reached and unused connections are released.

You can establish OCI connection pooling with the following steps:

1. Allocate the pool handle using `OCIHandleAlloc()`.
2. Creating a connection pool using `OCIConnectionPoolCreate()`.
3. Log on to the database using `OCILogon2()`.

Now that OCI connection pooling has been established, user sessions can access the database.

You can terminate the OCI connection pool with the following steps:

1. Log off from the database using `OCILogoff()`.
2. Destroy the connection pool using `OCIConnectionPoolDetroy()`.
3. Release the pool handle using `OCIHandleFree()`.

You can find a description of various parameters in the Oracle Call Interface Programmer's Guide.

The Core Oracle Kernel Library

Oracle9*i* reduces the average size of the kernel library modules, making the kernel more modular, and it also reduces the dependency between the different modules. The reduction of the dependencies makes these modules more self-contained; this self-contained feature improves memory utilization because the modules require less memory and because the number of links is reduced. The reduced module size improves memory utilization.

For Review

1. You must understand the difference between the dedicated server and the Oracle shared server architectures. You must also be able to describe the activities in a direct handoff connection process.
2. You must know about external procedures and about establishing a library for external procedures.
3. You must be familiar with multithreaded HS agents and with the different types of threads.
4. You must be able to explain the process to establish OCI connection pooling.

Exercises

1. **The Oracle shared server architecture enables you to**
   - **A.** Share one role with multiple users.
   - **B.** Share one server process with multiple user sessions.
   - **C.** Share one user with multiple roles.
   - **D.** Share one user session with multiple server processes.
2. **Multithreaded HS agents enable you to**
   - **A.** Join Oracle tables from heterogeneous applications running on one Oracle server.
   - **B.** Coordinate users logged in to Oracle servers at different locations.
   - **C.** Service and maintain the Oracle server at regular intervals.
   - **D.** Coordinate applications running on a variety of databases.

Answer Key
1. B **2.** D.

File Management

Oracle9*i* introduces Oracle-Managed Files (OMFs) to manage OS files; the DBA managed these files manually in previous versions. The DBA does not have to specify filenames while creating databases, tablespaces, and redo log groups, and they do not have to delete files that are not needed anymore, such as datafiles corresponding to dropped tablespaces. With Oracle9*i*, the DBA configures the database in terms of database objects like tablespaces without having to be concerned about OS filenames. Oracle creates the data files, redo log files, and control files automatically using standard file system interfaces. You can specify the locations for these OMFs by setting initialization parameters.

Although OMFs are particularly useful for test databases and for file systems on RAID disks, OMFs do not help when using raw devices because you cannot use OMFs with raw devices.

OMFs can coexist with non-OMFs. In other words, the use of an OMF does not affect existing databases where you have to explicitly specify and manage OS files.

In this section, you will learn about

- Creating and managing OMFs
- Automatically deleting non-OMFs using SQL
- Default temporary tablespaces

Creating and Managing OMFs

Oracle9*i* gives you two new initialization parameters, DB_CREATE_FILE_DEST and DB_CREATE_ONLINE_LOG_DEST_n, to specify the location where Oracle will create and manage OMFs. The DB_CREATE_FILE_DEST parameter specifies the location where data files and temp files should be created, while the DB_CREATE_ONLINE_LOG_DEST_n parameter specifies the location where Oracle should create the online redo log files and control files. If you do not specify the DB_CREATE_ONLINE_LOG_DEST_n parameter, the redo log and control files are created in the location specified by the DB_CREATE_FILE_DEST parameter. The directories referenced by these parameters must already exist. If you do not set these parameters either in init.ora or dynamically with the ALTER command, Oracle will not create OMF files.

The DB_CREATE_ONLINE_LOG_DEST_n parameter enables the multiplexing of redo log and control files; n can take a value from 1 to 5.

Here is an example of how you can set these parameters in init.ora:

```
DB_CREATE_FILE_DEST          = 'd:\oracle\oradata\hr_data'
DB_CREATE_ONLINE_LOG_DEST_1 = 'd:\oracle\oradata\hr_redo'
DB_CREATE_ONLINE_LOG_DEST_2 = 'd:\oracle\oradata\hr_redo'
```

You are not forced to use an OMF just because the parameters are configured in init.ora. After setting these init.ora parameters, you can create the database as follows:

```
CREATE DATABASE hr_db;
DEFAULT TEMPORARY TABLESPACE hr_temp_tbsp;
UNDO TABLESPACE undo_tbsp;
```

This example shows that you do not have to specify the data files, log files, and temp files when you create the temporary or UNDO tablespaces. Oracle will create two control files, the first one in the location specified by the DB_CREATE_ONLINE_LOG_DEST_1 parameter and the other in the location specified by DB_CREATE_ONLINE_LOG_DEST_2. Oracle will create two redo log groups with two members each; one member from each group is created in the locations specified by DB_CREATE_ONLINE_LOG_DEST_1 and DB_CREATE_ONLINE_LOG_DEST_2.

Oracle will also create a data file for the SYSTEM tablespace and another data file for the UNDO tablespace in the location specified by DB_CREATE_FILE_DEST. Oracle will further create a tempfile associated with the default temporary tablespace in the location specified by DB_CREATE_FILE_DEST. The size of data files and redo log files is 100MB for each OMF file. The data files are auto extensible with the maximum size set to unlimited.

Naming Conventions for OMF Files

Oracle will use the following naming conventions when it creates the OMF files:

Datafile	ora_%t_%u.dbf
Tempfile	ora_%t_%u.tmp
Redo log file	ora_%g_%u.log
Control file	ora_%u.ctl

In this naming convention, %t represents the tablespace name, %u is a unique 8-character string, and %g stands for the redo log group number.

Dynamically Setting OMF Parameters

Once you create the database, you can set or change these parameters dynamically with the ALTER SYSTEM or ALTER SESSION commands. Here is an example of how you can dynamically set or change these parameters:

```
ALTER SYSTEM
  SET db_create_file_dest = 'd:\oracle\oradata\hr_data';

ALTER SYSTEM
  SET db_create_online_log_dest_1 = 'd:\oracle\oradata\hr_redo';

ALTER SYSTEM
  SET db_create_online_log_dest_2 = 'd:\oracle\oradata\hr_redo';
```

Using OMF with Existing Databases

You can use OMFs in already existing databases by using the CREATE CONTROLFILE, CREATE TABLESPACE, ALTER TABLESPACE, and ALTER DATABASE commands to add log files. The following example shows how you can create tablespaces using OMFs:

```
CREATE TABLESPACE test_tbsp;
```

Oracle will *create a locally managed tablespace*, TEST_TBSP, with a 100MB OMF data file in the location specified by the DB_CREATE_FILE_DEST parameter.

You can increase the space for this tablespace with the ADD DATAFILE clause, as shown in the following example:

```
ALTER TABLESPACE test_tbsp
  ADD DATAFILE;
```

You can *add a data file* of any size by explicitly specifying the size, as shown here:

```
ALTER TABLESPACE test_tbsp
  ADD DATAFILE SIZE 200M;
```

Similarly, you can create OMF temp files when you create the temporary tablespace.

You can *remove tablespaces* that have OMFs in the same way you would remove tablespaces with non-OMFs. With non-OMF files, you have to separately go to the OS environment and remove these files. With OMFs, the OS files are automatically removed when you drop the tablespace:

```
DROP TABLESPACE test_tbsp;
```

Similarly, if a temporary tablespace is dropped, Oracle automatically removes the associated tempfiles.

There is no change in the ALTER DATABASE and ALTER TABLESPACE commands if you want to rename data files. Also, the data files have to be physically copied before renaming them, as in the case of non-OMFs. The difference is that the old OMF is deleted after renaming the file.

You can *create a new online redo log group*, as shown here:

```
ALTER DATABASE ADD LOGFILE;
```

This command *creates a new online redo log group* with a member logfile in each of the locations specified by the DB_CREATE_ONLINE_LOG_DEST_n parameters. The size of each logfile member is 100MB. You can specify a different size for the logfile as follows:

```
ALTER DATABASE ADD LOGFILE SIZE 50M;
```

You can drop a redo log group just the same way you drop a redo log group with non-OMFs. With non-OMFs, you have to manually delete the files in the OS environment. With OMFs, Oracle automatically deletes the associated files from the OS.

```
ALTER DATABASE DROP LOGFILE GROUP 4;
```

The CREATE CONTROLFILES statement *creates a control file* in the locations designated in the CONTROL_FILES initialization parameter. If you have not specified the CONTROL_FILES initialization parameter, Oracle will create the files in the location specified by DB_CREATE_ONLINE_LOG_DEST_n. If this parameter has not been specified, Oracle will create the control files in the location specified by DB_CREATE_FILE_DEST. If either of these DB_CREATE . . . parameters is specified, Oracle will create OMF control files. If either of the DB_CREATE . . . parameters is not specified, the control file is created in a platform-specific directory.

If Oracle created OMFs and you did not have a SPFILE, you must create an init.ora entry for the CONTROL_FILES parameter before you restart the instance. If you have a SPFILE, Oracle will create an entry for the CONTROL_FILES parameter automatically in the SPFILE.

If you specify NORESETLOGS and the online redo logs are OMFs, you must provide the filenames for the OMF logs in the LOGFILE specification when you create the control file using the CREATE CONTROLFILE command. Keep in mind that these filenames were created by Oracle when it created the OMF redo log files.

Once the OMF control files are created, Oracle interacts with both the OMF and non-OMF control files in the same manner. The backup, restore, and recovery operations for both OMF and non-OMF files are the same.

Oracle9*i* does not provide you with an additional column in any data dictionary view to display OMF-specific information.

Automatically Deleting Non-OMF Files Using SQL

In previous versions, Oracle only removed file pointers from the control file when you dropped tablespaces and tempfiles. You had to delete the OS files manually. Oracle9*i* introduces new clauses to the DROP TABLESPACE and ALTER DATABASE TEMPFILE statements to specify that Oracle should delete the OS files automatically when it deletes file pointers from the control file.

You can drop the tablespace and the segments in the tablespace with the following command:

```
DROP TABLESPACE test_tbsp
  INCLUDING CONTENTS;
```

You can drop the tablespace and the segments, and also delete the OS datafiles with the following command:

```
DROP TABLESPACE test_tbsp
  INCLUDING CONTENTS AND DATAFILES;
```

To also drop referential integrity constraints from foreign or primary keys of tables outside the tablespace that references primary keys of tables inside the tablespace, add the CASCADE CONSTRAINTS option as used in the following statement:

```
DROP TABLESPACE test_tbsp
  INCLUDING CONTENTS AND DATAFILES
  CASCADE CONSTRAINTS;
```

You can drop the tempfiles with the following command:

```
ALTER DATABASE
  TEMPFILE 'd:\oracle\oradata\hr_temp\temp1.dbf' DROP
  INCLUDING DATAFILES;
```

Oracle deletes the tempfiles definition in the database and automatically deletes the OS tempfiles. Oracle does not delete the tablespace.

When deleting either datafiles or tempfiles, Oracle will send a message to the alert log as it deletes each file. The command will be successful even if the OS is unable to delete the files, and Oracle will send the error message to the alert log file. Additionally, Oracle will not generate redo entries when it deletes OS files.

Default Temporary Tablespaces

When you create users, you can specify a TEMPORARY TABLESPACE clause in the CREATE USER command to specify the tablespace to be used for sort operations. If you omit the TEMPORARY TABLESPACE clause, Oracle defaults to the SYSTEM tablespace for sort operations. The use of the SYSTEM tablespace for sorts is not recommended.

Oracle9*i* introduces the DEFAULT TEMPORARY TABLESPACE clause; users for whom you did not specify a TEMPORARY TABLESPACE would default to the DEFAULT TEMPORARY TABLESPACE, instead of cluttering up the SYSTEM tablespace.

You can specify the DEFAULT TEMPORARY TABLESPACE clause when you create the database, as shown in the following example:

```
CREATE DATABASE test
  DATAFILE 'd:\oracle\oradata\hr_data\sys01.dbf' SIZE 100M
  LOGFILE  'd:\oracle\oradata\hr_redo\redo01.dbf' SIZE 5M,
           'd:\oracle\oradata\hr_redo\redo02.dbf' SIZE 3M
  DEFAULT TEMPORARY TABLESPACE dflt_temp_tbsp
      TEMPFILE 'd:\oracle\oradata\hr_temp\dflt_temp_tbsp01.dbf' SIZE 3M;
```

If the database already exists, you can specify the DEFAULT TEMPORARY TABLESPACE with the ALTER DATABASE command.

You must first create a temporary tablespace, as shown in the following example:

```
CREATE TEMPORARY TABLESPACE dflt_temp_tbsp
  TEMPFILE 'd:\oracle\oradata\hr_temp\dflt_temp_tbsp01.dbf' SIZE 40M;
```

Then you must designate this temporary tablespace as the DEFAULT TEMPORARY TABLESPACE, as shown in the following example:

```
ALTER DATABASE DEFAULT TEMPORARY TABLESPACE dflt_temp_tbsp;
```

You can identify the default temporary tablespace for the database by querying the DATABASE_PROPERTIES data dictionary view, as shown here:

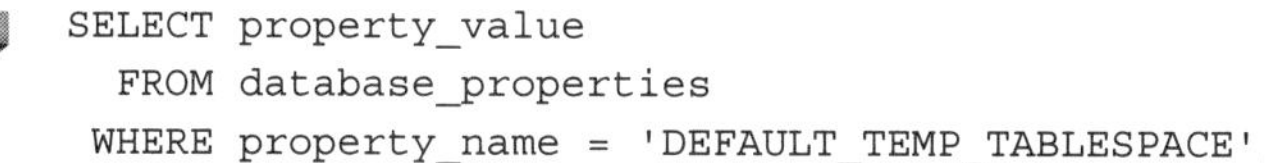

```
SELECT property_value
  FROM database_properties
 WHERE property_name = 'DEFAULT_TEMP_TABLESPACE';
```

The results of this query would be as follows:

```
PROPERTY_VALUE
-----------------------------------
DLFT_TEMP_TBSP
```

Restrictions on Default Temporary Tablespaces

The following restrictions apply to default temporary tablespaces:

- You cannot drop a default temporary tablespace until after you have created a new default temporary tablespace.
- You cannot take a default temporary tablespace offline.
- You cannot change a default temporary tablespace into a permanent tablespace.
- You cannot change a permanent tablespace into a default temporary tablespace unless it is the SYSTEM tablespace.

For Review

1. You must know how to create and manage the different kinds of OMFs.
2. You should be able to automatically delete non-OMF data files using SQL.
3. You should know how to set up a default temporary tablespace.

Exercises

1. **You can automatically delete non-OMF data files with the following SQL statement:**

   A. ALTER TABLESPACE mytbsp DROP CONTENTS AND DATAFILES

   B. DROP TABLESPACE mytbsp ALTER CONTENTS AND DATAFILES

   C. DROP TABLESPACE mytbsp INCLUDING CONTENTS AND DATAFILES

   D. ALTER TABLESPACE mytbsp DELETE CONTENTS AND DATAFILES

2. The two initialization parameters for specifying the locations for OMF files are

A. DB_CREATE_FILE_DEST and DB_CREATE_ONLINE_LOG_DEST_n

B. DB_CREATE_DATAFILE_DEST and DB_CREATE_ONLINE_LOG_DEST_n

C. DB_CREATE_FILE_DEST and DB_CREATE_REDO_LOG_DEST_n

D. DB_OMF_DATAFILE_DEST and DB_OMF_REDO_LOG_DEST_n

Answer Key

1. C. **2.** A.

Tablespace Management

An Oracle database is comprised of a number of tablespaces. Oracle defines a SYSTEM tablespace, UNDO tablespaces for undo information, and temporary tablespaces for sort operations. Oracle9*i* greatly simplifies the management of undo segments and UNDO tablespaces. This section discusses the following Oracle9*i* enhancements:

- Automatic undo management
- Creating and managing UNDO tablespaces
- Multiple block sizes within a database

Automatic Undo Management (AUM)

You can either commit or roll back database transactions. To prepare for the potential rollback of a transaction, Oracle stores the before images of the data in special purpose UNDO tablespaces. Oracle also stores pre-images of data to enhance availability and read integrity for a query running in one session while another session is performing a DML transaction. Oracle also uses the undo or rollback information to undo the uncommitted transactions if recovery should become necessary.

Traditionally, Oracle maintained this undo information in special segments called rollback segments. The DBA performed the tedious task of managing the space for these segments. The administrator had to determine the optimal number and size of the rollback segments based on the prevailing database transaction activity.

Oracle9*i* simplifies the space management of rollback segments with the introduction of automatic undo management (AUM). AUM only requires that you specify a tablespace with adequate space for the undo (rollback) segment creation; you do not have to create and size rollback segments manually. You also do not have to tune rollback segments' attributes to strike a balance between space consumption and performance via block contention.

With AUM, Oracle creates, extends, and allocates undo segments within the space available in the UNDO tablespace. AUM eliminates the need for you to explicitly assign large rollback segments for batch transactions and for you to be concerned with running out of space when different kinds of transactions occur concurrently. Oracle still uses rollback segments for storing undo information, but these segments are created and managed by Oracle. Oracle9*i*'s AUM also enables the DBA to specify the retention period for the undo information in the segment before it is overwritten. This feature gives you control over the chance of getting a Snapshot too old error.

The SYSTEM rollback segment is created automatically during database creation and is managed automatically just as it was in previous versions. You cannot take the SYSTEM rollback segment offline even though you use a special, designated UNDO tablespace. To help with migrations, it is possible for you to create UNDO tablespaces in a database that uses rollback segments; however, you must set the UNDO_MANAGEMENT parameter to AUTO in init.ora and restart the database to migrate to an AUM environment. In other words, in older databases where you did not set UNDO_MANAGEMENT to AUTO, you can create an AUM tablespace.

When performing operations with Oracle9*i*, you will typically set UNDO_MANAGEMENT to AUTO. When UNDO_MANAGEMENT is set to AUTO, you cannot use rollback segments. So for all practical purposes, both manual segments and automatic segments methods cannot coexist in one database instance for regular operations in Oracle9*i* because you are almost certain to set UNDO_MANAGEMENT to AUTO.

Creating and Managing UNDO Tablespaces

A database can have zero, one, or more UNDO tablespaces; however, AUM can only use one UNDO tablespace at a time. To implement AUM, you must perform the following tasks:

- Start the instance in the AUM mode.
- Create the UNDO tablespace.

Start the Instance in AUM Mode

Oracle9*i* introduced UNDO_MANAGEMENT, a new initialization parameter, to specify the mode for undo management. Once you set this parameter, you must start the database instance.

If you set this parameter to MANUAL (the default value), the database will use rollback segments. If you set UNDO_MANAGEMENT to AUTO, the database will use AUM and it will ignore any init.ora parameters that correspond to the manual mode. When you set UNDO_MANAGEMENT to AUTO, you can specify the UNDO tablespace that the database instance should use with the UNDO_TABLESPACE parameter. The tablespace that you specify must already exist; otherwise, Oracle will raise an error. If you did not specify this parameter, Oracle will use the first available UNDO tablespace, and if no UNDO tablespace is available, Oracle will default to the SYSTEM tablespace. Since this not a recommended practice, Oracle will send a message to the alert file.

To change from manual undo segment management mode to automatic or vice versa, you must modify the initialization parameter and restart the database instance.

Creating and Managing the UNDO Tablespace

You can either create the UNDO tablespace at database creation or after the database has been created. To create a tablespace at database creation, you must use the UNDO TABLESPACE clause in the CREATE DATABASE command as shown in the following example:

```
CREATE DATABASE aum_demo
  DATAFILE 'd:\oracle\oradata\hr_data\sys01.dbf' SIZE 100M
  LOGFILE  'd:\oracle\oradata\hr_redo\redo01.dbf' SIZE 10M,
           'd:\oracle\oradata\hr_redo\redo02.dbf' SIZE 5M
  UNDO TABLESPACE undo_tbsp
    DATAFILE 'd:\oracle\oradata\hr_redo\undo01.dbf' SIZE 80M;
```

To display the rollback segments created by Oracle, you can query the DBA_ROLLBACK_SEGS data dictionary view, as shown in the following code:

```
SELECT segment_name, tablespace_name, status
  FROM dba_rollback_segs;
```

You can obtain additional information about these rollback segments by querying DBA_SEGMENTS, as shown in the following code:

```
SELECT segment_name, tablespace_name,
       bytes, blocks, extents
  FROM dba_segments
 WHERE segment_type = 'ROLLBACK';
```

The following code shows you how to create UNDO tablespaces after you create the database:

```
CREATE UNDO TABLESPACE undo_tbsp2
    DATAFILE 'd:\oracle\oradata\hr_redo\undo02.dbf' SIZE 60M;
```

You can assign this UNDO tablespace as the new UNDO tablespace for the database instance with the following command:

```
ALTER SYSTEM
  SET UNDO_TABLESPACE = undo_tbsp2;
```

If the `undo_tbsp2` UNDO tablespace does not exist, this command will fail and Oracle will return an error.

You can use the ALTER TABLESPACE command to add, resize, or rename a datafile, bring the datafile online or take it offline. Here is an example of adding a datafile to a tablespace:

```
ALTER TABLESPACE undo_tbsp2b ADD
    DATAFILE 'd:\oracle\oradata\hr_redo\undo03.dbf' SIZE 60M
       AUTOEXTEND ON;
```

Once you start the database instance in the AUM mode, you cannot create rollback segments or manage them manually. Oracle will return an error if you attempt such operations, as shown in the following code example:

```
CREATE ROLLBACK SEGMENT rbs01;
*
ERROR at line 1:
ORA-30019: Illegal rollback Segment operation in Automatic Undo mode
```

You can drop the UNDO tablespace in the same manner as you would drop a normal tablespace, as shown in the following example:

```
DROP TABLESPACE undo_tbsp1;
```

However, you cannot drop an UNDO tablespace if it is currently being used by an instance. The statement will fail if there are any active transactions.

You must exercise caution when dropping an UNDO tablespace because the DROP TABLESPACE in the case of UNDO tablespaces performs the same function as the DROP TABLESPACE . . . INCLUDING CONTENTS. Because all the contents of the UNDO tablespace are lost, there is a chance that you may lose the data required for read-consistent images for long queries that are running. Queries that require this lost undo information will return an ORA-1555 error message. There is no risk of data loss for committed transactions; this only presents a risk for a loss of before-images that may by needed by long-running queries.

Undo Retention Period

Oracle9*i* introduced the UNDO_RETENTION initialization parameter to specify how long (in seconds) undo data must be retained in the UNDO tablespace before it is overwritten. This parameter enables you to minimize the chance that long running queries encounter the `Snapshot too old` error. UNDO_RETENTION is a dynamic parameter; you can set it with the ALTER SYSTEM command. When you specify this parameter, you must consider the size of the UNDO tablespace carefully to ensure the UNDO tablespace has an adequate amount of space to retain the undo information for a period of time specified by UNDO_RETENTION; otherwise, you are likely to get an `ORA-1555: Snapshot too old` error.

You can estimate the amount of undo space that is required with the following formula:

```
Undospace = (Undo Retention Period * Undo Blocks Per Second) + Overhead
```

The overhead should account for metadata such as bitmaps.

Oracle9*i* also provides new data dictionary views for information and statistics about undo segments. DBA_UNDO_EXTENTS contains information about the commit time for every extent in the UNDO tablespace. V$TRANSACTION contains information about undo segments, and V$ROLLSTAT contains statistics about the utilization of the undo segments in the UNDO tablespace. V$UNDOSTAT contains statistics for monitoring, tuning, and managing undo space utilization. Every row in this view represents information collected over a ten-minute interval.

Here is a sample query of V$UNDOSTAT:

```
SELECT begin_time, end_time, undotsn, undoblks,
       txncount, txntotal, maxconcurrency
  FROM V$UNDOSTAT;
```

Multiple Block Sizes Within a Database

The datablock size plays an important role in the performance of the database; smaller-sized blocks are better suited for the OLTP environment, whereas larger datablocks could enhance the performance of batch-processing or decision-support databases. Choosing a datablock size becomes an even more arduous task when you have a hybrid database, since you only have one block size in previous versions. Oracle9*i* resolves this problem by enabling you to maintain multiple block sizes in a single database. You can now create tablespaces with different block sizes to meet the requirements of OLTP and batch-processing systems. This feature also enables you to transport tablespaces between databases with different block sizes.

In previous versions, you specified the datablock size (typically 4K) with the DB_BLOCK_SIZE parameter. This parameter is called the standard block size in Oracle9*i*; it should be set to the most commonly used block size. You cannot change the size of the standard block size once the database has been created. You must recreate the database to change the default block size. The SYSTEM tablespace and the TEMPORARY tablespace can use the standard block size only.

To create tablespaces with multiple block sizes, you must first configure database buffer caches corresponding to the required block sizes. To support this feature, Oracle9*i* has introduced new initialization parameters. DB_CACHE_SIZE specifies the database buffer cache sized to the standard block size. Oracle9*i* can also support four additional block sizes; you can specify the buffer cache size corresponding to each of these block sizes with the db_nK_CACHE_SIZE parameter. In this parameter, nK stands for the nonstandard block size; n can take the following values: 2, 4, 8, 16, or 32. Here is an example of setting these initialization parameters:

```
DB_BLOCK_SIZE=4K
DB_CACHE_SIZE=20M
DB_8K_CACHE_SIZE=8M
```

In this example, the standard block size is 4K, the buffer cache size with the standard block size is 20M, and the buffer cache size with 8K blocks is set to 8M. Once you have configured the appropriate buffer cache sections, you can create tablespaces with nonstandard block sizes, as shown in the following example:

```
CREATE TABLESPACE tbsp_8k
  DATAFILE 'd:\oracle\oradata\hr_data\tbsp_8k.dbf' size 500M
  BLOCKSIZE 8k;
```

The new clause BLOCKSIZE was introduced in Oracle9*i*; it specifies the oracle block size to be used for this tablespace. If you do not specify the BLOCKSIZE, Oracle defaults to the standard block size. Oracle9*i* has also added a new column BLOCK_SIZE to the DBA_TABLESPACES data dictionary view to obtain the block size used by each tablespace.

Restrictions

- SYSTEM and temporary tablespaces cannot be of a nonstandard block size.
- All the partitions of a partitioned table must be housed in tablespaces with the same block size.

For Review

1. AUM relieves the DBA from the arduous task of managing the rollback segments manually.

2. UNDO tablespaces can be created either at database creation or after the database has been created.
3. Oracle9*i* enables you to create tablespaces with different block sizes. Before you can do this, you must configure subbuffer caches corresponding to the different block sizes.

Exercises

1. **Which of the following statements are correct with regards to AUM?**
   - **A.** UNDO tablespaces can be switched using the ALTER SYSTEM command.
   - **B.** UNDO tablespaces can be switched using the ALTER DATABASE command.
   - **C.** UNDO tablespaces can be created at database creation.
   - **D.** Rollback segments can't be created manually.
2. **Which of the following parameters must be set to create a tablespace with a nonstandard block size?**
   - **A.** db_block_size
   - **B.** db_cache_size
   - **C.** db_nK_cache_size
   - **D.** db_keep_cache_size

Answer Key
1. A, D. **2.** C.

Database Workspace Management

The Oracle database management system, as we traditionally know it, has great features to support concurrency and consistency across transactions. Oracle typically locks the rows being updated until the transaction is either committed or rolled back. These capabilities are more than adequate for databases with short-duration transactions or with long-running transactions executed by a limited number of users that are totally independent of the activity in other user sessions.

But when we have to support long-running transactions that could take hours or even days to complete, these standard transaction integrity techniques might prove insufficient. All user sessions will have to endure an unacceptably long wait for a lock on a row to be released by another user session. Also, it is next to impossible to keep a domain of data that you are analyzing constantly, while other users are performing DML operations that change this domain of data.

The Workspace Manager provides you with a virtual workspace where the domain of data is constant, even though other user changes may be altering the data in this domain. Additionally, the Workspace Manager enables you to return to this domain of data at a future point in time. This section presents the following enhancements in Oracle9*i* as they relate to the Workspace Manager:

- The Workspace Manager concept
- Creating and managing workspaces
- The workspace administrator role
- Export and import considerations for workspaces

The Workspace Manager Concept

A workspace is a virtual database facility that enables you to maintain multiple versions of one row of data and it enables each workspace context to reference a different version of this row as compared to another workspace context. In other words, the workspace context enables you to work with one version of the database in one workspace context, and with another version of the database in another workspace context, without compromising transactional integrity across the database.

You can perform your data analysis with one version in one workspace context, while a large DML transaction runs in another context. You have total availability to your data, even throughout the operation of the DML transaction. Once the transaction has committed, you can merge the changed data with the original table. Workspace management enables you to manage one or more such workspaces. When you create a database with the Database Configuration Assistant (DBCA), the Workspace Manager will be automatically installed. When you create a database with your own script, you must install Workspace Manager yourself. You can install Workspace Manager by connecting as user SYS and running ORACLE_HOME\rdbms\admin\OWMINST.PLB.

The Workspace Manager enables you to version-enable a table, which enables you to maintain multiple versions of a row in that table. The table is the fundamental unit for the Workspace Manager. When you make changes to a row in a regular table, the data is overwritten. When you make changes to a row of a version-enabled table, Oracle creates and maintains a new version of that row. Version-enabling a table can consume a large amount of space because the database has to maintain multiple versions of a row.

Creating and Managing Workspaces

Oracle9*i* has introduced DBMS_WM, a new package to enable you to create and manage workspaces. The steps to effecting workspaces are as follows:

1. Version-enable tables.
2. Create workspaces.
3. Grant privileges.
4. Access the workspace.
5. Resolve conflicts between the original rows and versioned rows.
6. Refresh/merge workspaces.
7. Disable versioning tables.
8. Remove workspaces.

Version-Enable Tables

Let's assume that you have a table called ORDER with the following structure:

```
Name                Null?     Type
-----------------   --------  ------------
ID                  NOT NULL  NUMBER
ORD_DATE                      DATE
AMOUNT                        NUMBER
```

You can use the ENABLEVERSIONING subprogram in the DBMS_WM package to version-enable this table, as shown in the following example:

```
EXECUTE dbms_wm.enableversioning('order');
```

By default, the DBA role has been granted the WM_ADMIN_ROLE role to execute procedures in the DBMS_WM package. Optionally, you can provide a second parameter to specify the version of the table that you want to maintain. When you version-enable a table, Oracle changes the table name by adding a suffix, `_LT`. Oracle also creates additional tables, views, triggers, and indexes to track the different versions of rows. For example, Oracle creates a new table to maintain information about rows that are synchronized after it resolves conflicts. Oracle generates the name of this table by taking the original name of the version-enabled table and adding a suffix, _AUX. In our example, the name of the table will be ORDER_AUX.

The versioning of tables is subject to the following restrictions:

- The table must have a primary key.
- Only the owner of the table or a user with the WM_ADMIN_ROLE can version-enable that table. By default, the DBA role is granted the WM_ADMIN_ROLE. The WM_ADMIN_ROLE has all the Workspace Manager privileges.
- You cannot version-enable SYS tables.
- You cannot perform DDL operations on version-enabled tables.
- You cannot version-enable object tables and IOTs.
- You cannot version-enable tables that contain LONG columns.
- You cannot add referential integrity constraints on a version-enabled table.
- The table name of the table to be version-enabled cannot be more than 25 characters long.

Create Workspaces

You use the CREATE_WORKSPACE procedure to create a workspace. Oracle creates this workspace in a tree hierarchy under the current workspace. By default, Oracle will create this workspace within the LIVE workspace.

You can identify the current workspace with the following code:

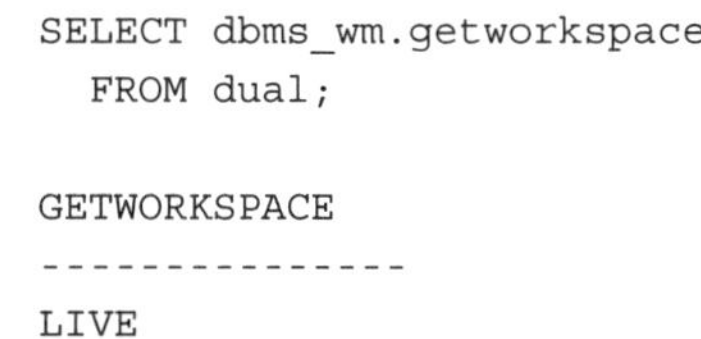

```
SELECT dbms_wm.getworkspace
  FROM dual;

GETWORKSPACE
---------------
LIVE
```

Any workspace you create will become a child workspace of this LIVE workspace. We will connect as the SYSDBA to acquire the WM_ADMIN_ROLE with the following statement:

```
CONNECT sys/<password> AS sysdba
```

You can then create a new workspace, as shown in the following example:

```
EXECUTE dbms_wm.createworkspace('phase1_orders_ws');
```

The following considerations apply to the creation of a workspace:

- The name of the workspace is case-sensitive.
- You need the WM_ADMIN_ROLE role or you will need the CREATE_WORKSPACE or CREATE_ANY_WORKSPACE privilege.
- You do not automatically enter or access the workspace when you create the workspace.

Grant Privileges

The next step is to grant privileges to the users of this workspace. For example, you can grant users or roles the privilege to *access* the workspace, *create* a workspace, *remove* a workspace, *merge* workspaces, and *rollback* workspaces. The following example demonstrates how you can grant the `access` privilege on workspace `phase1_orders_ws` to the user `athena`:

```
EXECUTE
dbms_wm.grantworkspacepriv('ACCESS_WORKSPACE','phase1_orders_ws','athena');
```

The first parameter specifies the privileges being granted. You must separate multiple privileges with a comma. The second parameter specifies the workspace on which you are granting these privileges. The third parameter specifies the user to whom you are granting these privileges.

You can use the GRANTSYSTEMPRIV procedure to grant system-level workspace privileges such as ACCESS_ANY_WORKSPACE and CREATE_ANY_WORKSPACE.

You can revoke this privilege with the following statement:

```
EXECUTE
dbms_wm.revokeworkspacepriv('ACCESS_WORKSPACE','phase1_orders_ws','athena')
;
```

Access the Workspace

The default login is the LIVE workspace. You can access any workspace by invoking the GOTOWORKSPACE procedure, as shown in the following example:

```
EXECUTE dbms_wm.gotoworkspace('phase1_orders_ws');
```

You can perform queries and DMLs on the ORDER table just as you would with a regular table. Workspace management is transparent to the user.

Modifications that you perform in this workspace will not be available to other user sessions until the workspace is merged with its parent. Oracle accomplishes this by maintaining different versions of the same row; you just have access to the versions that correspond to your workspace. Oracle still uses the default short-transaction-locking mechanism for the version of the row that you are updating.

Locks Workspace Manager enables you to apply additional locks on current and previous versions of the rows to eliminate conflicts between the parent and versioned records. You can implement an exclusive lock to prevent users from modifying the previous versions of the rows, or you can implement a shared lock to allow users in the same workspace to share the current and previous versions of the rows. You use the SETLOCKINGON procedure from the DBMS_WM package to specify the session-level locking method, the SETWORKSPACELOCKINGMODEON to specify the row-level locking method, and the LOCKROWS method to specify access to parent and versioned rows.

Freeze a Workspace You can freeze a workspace to disallow changes to rows in the version-enabled tables, as shown in the following example:

```
EXECUTE dbms_wm.freezeworkspace('phase1_orders_ws', 'READ_ONLY');
```

You can reverse this process as follows:

```
EXECUTE dbms_wm.unfreezeworkspace('phase1_orders_ws');
```

Other Workspace Operations The DBMS_WM package also provides procedures for performing other operations. For example, the CREATESAVEPOINT procedure enables you to create savepoints in the current workspace, the ROLLBACKTOSP procedure enables you to roll back changes to a particular savepoint in the workspace, and ROLLBACKTABLE enables you to roll back changes on a single table.

The concept of savepoints in workspaces is very similar to that of normal transactional savepoints, but some differences exist. For example, although workspace-managed savepoints do not consume space, modifications to rows after the savepoint creation results in a new version of the row. Also, Oracle creates explicit savepoints to facilitate partial rollbacks in workspaces, and Oracle creates implicit savepoints when you create a new workspace.

Resolve Conflicts Between the Original Rows and the Versioned Rows

When one row is modified in two or more workspaces, you will have more than two versions besides the original row, and these rows are in conflict since you have to decide which change will prevail. You must resolve these conflicts before you can refresh workspaces (apply changes from the parent workspace to the child) or merge workspaces (apply changes made in the child workspace to its parent). Oracle will raise an error if you attempt to either merge or refresh different versions of data where conflicts exist.

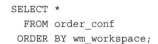

```
EXECUTE dbms_wm.refreshworkspace('phase1_orders_ws');

ORA-20056: conflicts detected for workspace: 'phase1_orders_ws' in table:
'USER_WM.PARENT_TAB'
ORA-06512: at "SYS.LT", line 4248
ORA-06512: at "SYS.LT", line 4235
ORA-06512: at line 1
```

You can display the conflicts by querying a view called <tablename>_CONF, as shown in the following example:

```
SELECT *
  FROM order_conf
 ORDER BY wm_workspace;

WM_WORKSPACE                ID ORD_DATE      AMOUNT WM_
------------------ ---------- --------- ---------- ---
BASE                         1 10-NOV-01       1000 NO
BASE                         2 11-OCT-01       1500 NO
BASE                         3 14-JUL-01       2500 NO
BASE                         4 18-NOV-01       2300 NO
BASE                         5 23-APR-01       3200 NO
LIVE                         1 10-NOV-01       4000 NO
LIVE                         2 11-OCT-01       4000 NO
LIVE                         4 18-NOV-01       4000 NO
LIVE                         5 23-APR-01       4000 NO
LIVE                         3 14-JUL-01       4000 NO
PHASE1_ORDERS_WS             1 10-NOV-01       3000 NO
PHASE1_ORDERS_WS             2 11-OCT-01       3000 NO
PHASE1_ORDERS_WS             5 23-APR-01       3000 NO
PHASE1_ORDERS_WS             4 18-NOV-01       3000 NO
PHASE1_ORDERS_WS             3 14-JUL-01       3000 NO
```

The query results show the BASE (or original) values before the data was modified in any of the workspaces. The rows with the workspaces named LIVE and PHASE1_ORDERS_WS display the data rows modified in these workspaces. This query also displays the modified data.

You must resolve these conflicts manually with the RESOLVECONFLICTS procedure before you can either refresh the child version data from the parent version data or merge the child version of the data with the parent. Here is an example for resolving conflict:

```
EXECUTE dbms_wm.beginresolve('phase1_orders_ws');
EXECUTE dbms_wm.resolveconflicts('phase1_orders_ws', 'order',
                                 'id in (1,2,3,4,5)', 'PARENT');
COMMIT;
EXECUTE dbms_wm.commitresolve('phase1_orders_ws');
```

The first line prepares the environment for conflict resolution, the second command performs conflict resolution, the third command commits pending short-term transactions, and the fourth statement commits the changes as a result of the resolved conflicts.

Now that you have resolved the rows in conflict, the following query confirms this fact:

```
SELECT *
  FROM order_conf
 ORDER BY wm_workspace;

no rows selected
```

Refresh/Merge Workspace

Now that you have resolved data conflicts, you can either merge or refresh the different versions of data. You are refreshing the workspace when you copy the parent workspace to the child workspace. You must resolve conflicts prior to refreshing or merging.

You can invoke the RefreshWorkspace procedure to refresh all the data and REFRESHTABLE to refresh data for a single table. You cannot refresh the LIVE workspace; it is the topmost workspace in the hierarchy and does not have a parent workspace to refresh from.

Merging is done when you apply modifications from the child workspace to the parent workspace. Again, you must resolve conflicts before merging. You can invoke MERGEWORKSPACE to merge all data or invoke MERGETABLE to merge just one table:

```
EXECUTE dbms_wm.mergeworkspace('phase1_orders_ws');
```

The previous command merges the changes in the `phase1_orders_ws` workspace to its parent workspace, which is the LIVE workspace in our example. The MergeWorkspace procedure has two optional parameters: one to specify whether a savepoint has to be created in the parent workspace before merging and one to specify if the workspace should be removed after the merge. Because we did not specify the optional parameters in our example, the database does not create any savepoint in the LIVE workspace before the merge, and it does not remove the workspace after the merge.

Disable Versioning Tables

Once you have completed your versioned operations, you must disable the versioning on the tables to minimize the possibility of creating unnecessary rows. This action also gets rid of the overhead of maintaining additional indexes, views, and triggers. You invoke the DISABLEVERSIONING procedure to perform this action, as shown here:

```
EXECUTE dbms_wm.disableversioning('order');
```

You either must be the owner of the table or a user with the WM_ADMIN_ROLE to perform this task. This command will fail if you have modified data in the table. If you want to execute this command regardless, you must specify that you want to FORCE it by providing the second argument, which is an optional argument. If the FORCE parameter is TRUE, it will force changes to be discarded in the child workspace table before disabling versioning for the table. This action does not remove either the workspace hierarchy or the savepoints you established.

Remove the Workspace

The final step is to remove the workspace using the REMOVEWORKSPACE procedure, as shown here:

```
EXECUTE dbms_wm.removeworkspace('phase1_orders_ws');
```

This code rolls back the data in the workspace and deletes the workspace definition from the database. You must invoke the REMOVEWORKSPACETREE procedure to remove all the workspaces in a hierarchy.

The Workspace Administrator Role

Privileges in the Workspace Manager are distinct from the regular privileges in Oracle. You have the following workspace-level privileges: ACCESS_WORKSPACE, CREATE_WORKSPACE, REMOVE_WORKSPACE, MERGE WORKSPACE, and ROLLBACK_WORKSPACE. You also have the following system-level privileges: ACCESS_ANY_WORKSPACE, CREATE_ ANY_WORKSPACE, REMOVE_ ANY_WORKSPACE, MERGE_ ANY_WORKSPACE, and ROLLBACK_ ANY_WORKSPACE.

The Workspace Manager provides the WM_ADMIN_ROLE role that contains all the workspace-level and system-level privileges that you can grant to the user. Oracle grants the WM_ADMIN_ROLE role to the DBA role.

You can assign workspace-level privileges and system-level privileges to a user with the GrantWorkspacePriv and the GrantSystemPriv procedures, respectively. You use the RevokeWorkspacePriv and the RevokeSystemPriv procedures to revoke privileges.

Export and Import Considerations for Workspaces

You can perform exports and imports on version-enabled databases much the same as you would with regular databases; however, you must take the following restrictions into consideration:

- The target database for the import must have Workspace Manager installed, it should only contain the LIVE workspace, and it should not contain any version-enabled tables.
- You can only export or import the entire database in the case of version-enabled databases. You cannot perform exports or imports on just the schema, tables, partitions, or workspaces.
- You must set the IGNORE parameter to Y for imports.
- You cannot perform an ownership change of objects using FROMUSER and TOUSER parameters.

For Review

1. Workspace management enables different users to modify a table and still use their own version of the data until these changes are merged with the original table.
2. The DBMS_WM package contains procedures to enable workspace management.
3. The WM_ADMIN_ROLE role contains all privileges to perform any workspace management task.
4. You can either merge changes to the table with the parent, or you can discard these changes.

Exercises

1. **The unit for workspace management is**

   A. User schema

   B. Table

   C. Package

   D. Materialized view

2. When importing the data with workspace management, the IGNORE parameter shall be set to

A. Y

B. N

C. The parameter doesn't affect the import

D. Workspace_Tables

Answer Key
1. B. **2.** A.

Memory Management

Oracle uses a *shared SQL area* within the shared pool of the system global area (SGA) and a *private SQL area* to execute the user's SQL statements. Oracle stores the parse tree and the execution plan for an SQL statement in the shared SQL area. When other users execute the same SQL statement, Oracle reuses the tree and execution plan in the shared SQL area; each user will continue to have a private SQL area. When Oracle encounters a new statement, it allocates additional memory from the shared pool for the statement's tree and execution plan to be stored in the shared SQL area. If there is no shared pool space, Oracle will deallocate statements from the shared SQL area based on a modified Least Recently Used (LRU) algorithm, and the parse trees and execution plans for these statements will no longer be available for reuse. The ability to reuse the parse trees and execution plans in a shared SQL area saves memory for new statements, enhances reuse and memory management time by minimizing the deallocation of SQL statements in the shared SQL area, and saves memory.

When a user connects to the database server, Oracle spawns a server process and organizes memory to manage data and control information related to the server process. This organized memory is called the Program Global Area (PGA). This memory area cannot be shared by other server processes; it contains user-session-specific information, such as bind information for the SQL statements, and works areas to take care of sort requirements and joins.

This section discusses the following Oracle9*i* enhancements to optimize memory management:

- The automatic and dynamic sizing of SQL working areas
- Views and columns for SQL execution memory management
- Allocating and tracking memory for dynamic SGA

Automatic and Dynamic Sizing of SQL Working Areas

Prior to Oracle9*i*, the DBA was responsible for setting the values of the various parameters that maintained limits for the different work areas. These parameters are SORT_AREA_SIZE, HASH_AREA_SIZE, CREATE_BITMAP_AREA_SIZE, and BITMAP_MERGE_AREA_SIZE; they are collectively addressed as the *_AREA_SIZE parameters. Setting these parameters was a critical and arduous task for the DBA. If the DBA specified the wrong values for these parameters, the applications would degrade in performance.

For example, the SORT_AREA_SIZE parameter specifies the memory to be used for a sort. Larger values facilitate better performance for large sorts; you realize this efficiency at the expense of memory consumption. Smaller values divide the sort into smaller sort runs with intermediate results written into temporary segments on disk. Performance is severely degraded since disk I/O is significantly slower than memory. The default values for the *_WORK_AREA parameters are adequate for standard OLTP applications; they have to be modified to tune data warehousing and decision-supporting systems where data access volume is bulky.

Oracle9*i* (9.0.1) has introduced enhancements to automatically manage these work areas. PGA memory is organized into two parts: tunable memory for SQL areas and non-tunable memory for everything else. Oracle9*i*'s automatic work management only tunes the tunable part of PGA memory.

Oracle9*i* has also introduced additional parameters to enable automatic work area management. These parameter values can be changed dynamically to enable the DBA to switch between automatic and manual modes of managing SQL work areas. PGA_AGGREGATE_TARGET is a new instance-level parameter that specifies the total memory in KB, MB, or GB for the PGA of all the sessions combined. This is a dynamic parameter; you can set this parameter with the ALTER SYSTEM command. The default value for this parameter is 0; this 0 value specifies that automatic work area management be disabled. Setting this parameter to a nonzero value enables automatic work area management; the range of possible values is

10MB to 4TB. The following example shows you how to set the PGA_AGGREGATE_TARGET parameter to 10MB:

```
ALTER SYSTEM
  SET pga_aggregate_target=10M;

System altered.
```

Oracle9*i* gives you a second parameter, WORKAREA_SIZE_POLICY, to specify the work-area-sizing mechanism. This is a dynamic parameter that you can set with the ALTER SYSTEM or ALTER SESSION commands. If you set WORKAREA_SIZE_POLICY to AUTO, Oracle automatically sizes the appropriate work area, but also ensures that the total PGA memory for the instance does not exceed the PGA_AGGREGATE_TARGET parameter value. You must set PGA_AGGREGATE_TARGET to a nonzero value before you set WORKAREA_SIZE_POLICY to AUTO. If you do not observe this sequence, Oracle gives you the following error message:

```
ORA-04032: pga_aggregate_target must be set before switching to auto mode
```

When the value of WORKAREA_SIZE_POLICY is set to MANUAL, the behavior is the same as it was in previous versions of the database where you had to set the *_WORK_AREA parameters manually.

Here is an example of how you can specify the WORKAREA_SIZE_POLICY parameter:

```
ALTER SYSTEM
  SET workarea_size_policy = auto;

System altered.
```

Views and Columns for SQL Execution Memory Management

Oracle9*i* adds the following new columns to the V$PROCESS view:

Column	Description
PGA_USED_MEM	PGA memory is being used by the process.
PGA_ALLOC_MEM	PGA memory is currently allocated by the process.
PGA_MAX_MEM	Maximum PGA memory is allocated by the process.

The following query provides information from the V$PROCESS view:

```
SELECT username, pid, program, pga_used_mem, pga_alloc_mem, pga_max_mem
  FROM v$process;
```

Oracle9*i* also has added new statistics in V$SYSSTAT, V$SESSTAT, and V$MYSTAT. V$SYSSTAT contains system statistics, V$SESSTAT contains user session statistics, and V$MYSTAT contains information about the current session.

The following query is an example of retrieving session-wide statistics for the work areas from these views:

```
SELECT SN.name, ST.value, SE.username
  FROM v$sesstat ST, v$statname SN, v$session SE
 WHERE SN.name LIKE 'workarea%'
   AND ST.statistic# = SN.statistic#
   AND ST.sid = SE.sid;
```

The results of this query are as follows:

```
NAME                                         VALUE USERNAME
----------------------------------- ---------- ------------
workarea memory allocated                       28 SCOTT
workarea memory allocated                       68 SYS
workarea executions - optimal                   12 SCOTT
workarea executions - optimal                   27 SYS
workarea executions - onepass                    0 SCOTT
workarea executions - onepass                    0 SYS
workarea executions - multipass                  0 SCOTT
workarea executions - multipass                  0 SYS
```

In this example, *workarea memory allocated* represents the total PGA allocated to a session. The *workarea executions* represent how PGA memory is utilized. The *optimal* qualifier specifies the number of times workarea operations are performed in memory, *onepass* provides an indication of disk usage, and *multipass* is an indication of the number of times a single operation is written to disk. A value for multipass should be 0, and a nonzero value is a strong indicator that the PGA memory is too small; you must increase the value of PGA_AGGREGATE_TARGET to improve the performance.

Oracle9*i* also gives you V$SQL_WORKAREA_USAGE for the current usage of work areas and V$PGASTAT for instance-level PGA utilization.

Allocating and Tracking Memory for Dynamic SGA

Prior to Oracle9*i*, SGA size parameters were static parameters. Once you tuned SGA, you had to restart the instance and the instance was temporarily unavailable to the user.

Oracle9*i* has enhanced the nature of these SGA parameters; they are now dynamic. You can change the values of the shared pool and the buffer cache without restarting the database instance. The Oracle9*i* dynamic SGA concept enables you to take memory from one area of the SGA and allocate it to another area as needed while the database instance is up and running. Additionally, the unit of memory allocation for SGA is a granule in Oracle9*i*. The size of a granule is 4MB if the SGA at startup is less than 128MB; it will be 16MB otherwise. So the sizes of different components of SGA should be multiples of these granule sizes.

Oracle9*i* also introduces SGA_MAX_SIZE, a new static parameter that enables the DBA to start with a smaller SGA and dynamically increase it to the maximum value specified by SGA_MAX_SIZE. If you do not set SGA_MAX_SIZE or if you set it to a value less than the initial SGA size, you cannot increase the SGA size later.

You can change the sizes of the SGA components dynamically with the ALTER SYSTEM command. The following command dynamically changes the size of the shared pool:

```
ALTER SYSTEM
  SET shared_pool_size = 32M;

System altered.
```

When you change any SGA component size, the new SGA size should not exceed the value specified by the SGA_MAX_SIZE parameter. You can display the amount of memory allocated to a shared pool by querying V$SGASTAT. Just like earlier versions, you tune the shared pool depending upon the hit ratios of the library cache and the dictionary cache. Oracle9*i* enables you to change the size of the shared pool dynamically.

Oracle9*i* introduces DB_CACHE_SIZE, DB_KEEP_CACHE_SIZE, and DB_RECYCLE_CACHE_SIZE to dynamically manage the buffer cache, the largest component of the SGA. The corresponding static parameters DB_BLOCK_BUFFERS, BUFFER_POOL_KEEP, and BUFFER_POOL_KEEP from previous versions have been deprecated, but they are still available for backward compatibility. DB_CACHE_SIZE specifies the size of the default buffer cache size; you cannot set this parameter to 0. Oracle9*i* also gives you the DB_nK_CACHE_SIZE parameters to configure buffer pools with various block sizes; the value of n can be 2, 4, 8, 16, or 32. The tuning methodology is still the same; you reduce physical reads and increase logical reads. You can get these statistics from V$SYSSTAT.

The following example shows how you can dynamically change the default buffer cache:

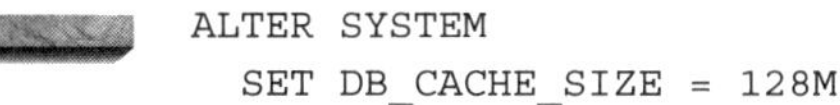

```
ALTER SYSTEM
  SET DB_CACHE_SIZE = 128M;
```

Oracle9*i* introduces a new approach to determine how the buffer cache is being used and how much memory has to be added or released from the buffer cache for optimal performance. This approach consists of the following three steps:

1. You must instruct Oracle to gather statistics on the buffer cache by setting the value of the DB_CACHE_ADVICE parameter to ON. The default value for this parameter is OFF. DB_CACHE_ADVICE can take on a third value, READY, which specifies that memory is allocated, but it does not gather statistics. The activity of collecting statistics affects the performance of the system. DB_CACHE_ADVICE is a dynamic parameter and can be changed to ON using ALTER SYSTEM command, as shown here:

```
ALTER SYSTEM
  SET DB_CACHE_ADVICE = ON;
```

2. The second step is to display the statistics gathered by querying the new dynamic performance view, V$DB_CACHE_ADVICE. This view contains information about the physical reads for the different cache sizes. Each row in the view shows statistics for one cache size. The ESTD_PHYSICAL_READ_FACTOR provides the ratio of the number of estimated reads to the number of actual reads. For each buffer pool, this view shows statistics for 20 different sample sizes that range from 10 to 200 percent of the existing buffer pool size. This view also contains an estimate of the percentage of physical reads as compared to the actual buffer pool size in the ESTD_PHYSICAL_READ_FACTOR column. Here is a sample query:

```
SELECT id, name, block_size, buffers_for_estimate
       estd_physical_reads, estd_physical_read_factor;
```

3. The third step is to increase the buffer cache size if warranted by your observations in the second step.

For Review

1. Oracle9*i* automatically manages the SQL work areas by tuning the *_AREA_SIZE parameters
2. You can dynamically change SGA memory parameters.

Exercises

1. **Which two parameters must you configure to instruct Oracle to automatically tune SQL workareas?**
   - **A.** SHARED_POOL_SIZE
   - **B.** PGA_AGGREGATE_TARGET
   - **C.** SORT_AREA_SIZE
   - **D.** WORKAREA_SIZE_POLICY
2. **The default value for PGA_AGGREGATE_TARGET parameter is**
   - **A.** 0
   - **B.** 10MB
   - **C.** 4TB
   - **D.** 128MB

Answer Key

1. B, D. **2.** A.

Backup and Recovery

Oracle9*i* introduces many enhancements to the manageability and reliability of backup and recovery operations. This section discusses the following new features:

- Recovery Manager (RMAN) manageability and reliability enhancements
- Trial recovery
- Miscellaneous RMAN enhancements

Recovery Manager (RMAN) Manageability and Reliability Enhancements

Oracle9*i* has added many new features to the RMAN utility to make it more manageable and reliable. These features make it easier to write the command syntax and reduce the time required to restore and recover database files. In this topic, we will discuss the following features:

- Persistent configuration
- Backup of archivelogs
- Restartable backups
- Block Media Recovery (BMR)

Persistent Configuration

Oracle9*i*'s new CONFIGURE command enables you to configure various backup, restore, and recover parameters that are persistent across RMAN sessions. We will now discuss some RMAN settings that you can configure.

Retention Policy You can use the CONFIGURE command to specify a *redundancy policy* that establishes the number of backups files and control files you want to retain. Here is an example:

```
CONFIGURE RETENTION POLICY TO REDUNDANCY 3;
```

Alternatively, you can use the CONFIGURE command to specify a *recovery window policy* that establishes the number of days the backups are to be retained.

Here is an example of a weekly backup system:

```
CONFIGURE RETENTION POLICY TO RECOVERY WINDOW OF 7 DAYS;
```

The redundancy policy and the recovery window policy are mutually exclusive.

You can use the DELETE OBSOLETE command to eliminate backups and copies that are no longer needed for media recovery, based on the retention policy you have specified.

Automatic Channel Configuration and Allocation You can use the CONFIGURE command to establish a persistent number of channel settings. You can configure the channel information to specify the target device type, which is the target location for backups. The RMAN command becomes minimal because RMAN automatically allocates these channels when you issue a BACKUP, RESTORE, or a COPY command within RMAN. For example, you can just issue a BACKUP DATABASE command without any additional clauses:

```
CONFIGURE CHANNEL DEVICE TYPE DISK
   FORMAT 'd:\backup\bkup_%d_%s_%p';
```

In the file name, %d will be substituted with the name of the database, %s with the backup set number, and %p with the piece number in the backup set.

Configure the Default Device Type You can configure the default device type to be used for backups:

```
CONFIGURE DEFAULT DEVICE TYPE TO DISK;
```

You can remove the options you specified and return it to the default values with the following command:

```
CONFIGURE DEFAULT DEVICE TYPE CLEAR;
```

The RMAN Prompt You can execute the BACKUP and RESTORE commands directly from the RMAN prompt. This eliminates the need to always perform these tasks within the RUN command.

Automatic Backup of Control Files You can configure control files to be automatically backed up whenever a BACKUP command is used without specifying the INCLUDING CONTROL FILE option.

Backup Optimization You can configure backup optimization to be either ON or OFF as follows:

```
CONFIGURE BACKUP OPTIMIZATION ON;
```

Backup optimization is also enabled if you run BACKUP DATABASE or BACKUP ARCHIVELOG with the ALL or LIKE options.

If it is ON, RMAN skips the files for which a backup already exists on the same device with the same header status. The same header status implies that no modifications were made to the data in those files since the last backup. This feature is useful for archivelog backups; in this case, the archivelog files that are already backed up can be skipped.

Excluding Tablespaces You can use the CONFIGURE command to exclude tablespaces that need not be backed up every time. This eliminates the need to specify that read-only tablespaces should not be backed up every time. Here is an example:

```
CONFIGURE EXCLUDE FOR TABLESPACE hr_tbsp;
```

You can start including the hr_tbsp tablespace in your backups with the following command:

```
CONFIGURE EXCLUDE FOR TABLESPACE hr_tbsp CLEAR;
```

Backup of Archivelogs

You can use the new PLUS ARCHIVELOG clause to specify that archivelogs that have not been backed up are included with the data backup. Here is an example:

```
BACKUP DATAFILE 2 PLUS ARCHIVELOG;
```

This command performs a log switch, backs up the online log, backs up the archived logs, performs another log switch, and then backs up the remaining logs. RMAN looks at multiplexed archive files as potential alternatives if the files in the first location have some corruptions.

Restartable Backups

Oracle9*i* has added another new clause to the BACKUP statement, NOT BACKED UP [SINCE TIME . . . .]. This clause specifies that Oracle should only back up files that have not been backed up since a particular date and time. The following code demonstrates one way of using this clause:

```
BACKUP DATABASE NOT BACKED UP SINCE TIME 'sysdate - 7';
```

You can use this clause to restart the backup process when it fails after completing a part of the backup; this clause only backs up the files that were missed by the first backup that failed. This clause enables you to reduce the time required for the backup; otherwise, you would have to perform a full backup again. If you omit the SINCE TIME option, files that have never been backed up become candidates for backup.

Oracle9*i* also optimizes the restoration of files from a backup; files whose file headers match the headers of the files in the backup sets are not restored. This keeps you from restoring files that have already been restored in the case of a restore operation that fails midway. This enables you to optimize the time required for the restoration process.

Block Media Recovery (BMR)

BMR enables you to back up specific blocks in a datafile without taking the database offline. The default backup method is datafile media recovery. You use the new BLOCKRECOVER statement to perform BMR.

Datablocks can become corrupted due to various reasons during normal database operations. Oracle writes information about the datablock corruption into the alert log file and the user trace files. In previous versions, you had to restore and recover the entire file by applying the redo required from the archived log files, even though just one single block was corrupted. A considerable amount time is consumed to restore and recover the entire file.

Oracle9*i* introduces BMR to enable you to restore and recover just those blocks that are corrupted. You can determine the corrupt blocks from trace files or from V$BACKUP_CORRUPTION and V$COPY_CORRUPTION views. Also, because you do not have to take the datafile or the database offline to restore and recover blocks with BMR, database availability is greatly enhanced. Also, because the entire data file does not have to be restored, the Mean Time To Recover (MTTR) is minimized. The general syntax for performing BMR is as follows:

```
BLOCKRECOVER DATAFILE d1 BLOCK b1[,b2...]
             [DATAFILE d2 BLOCK b3[,b4...]]...
```

The following restrictions apply to BMR:

- You can only perform BMR from the RMAN interface; you cannot do this from SQLPLUS.
- You can only perform a complete recovery of a block.
- Corrupted blocks are not available to users until the block has been fully recovered.
- You can only perform a block media recovery from a full backup; you cannot do this from incremental backups.

Trial Recovery

The intent of user-managed recovery operations is to successfully perform the desired recovery operation. Occasionally, however, recovery sessions fail to completely recover the database, and some files are left in an inconsistent state. These situations require you to start the restore and recover operations all over again from scratch.

Oracle9*i* contains a new recovery mechanism called trial recovery, which enables the DBA to anticipate such problems before performing the recovery. You can mark the datablocks that cannot be recovered as corrupted, and you can perform trial recovery to determine if additional problems exist.

Performing trial recovery is similar to the normal recovery. You use the following command to initiate trial recovery:

```
RECOVER DATABASE ... TEST;
```

You will be prompted for the redo log just as if it were a normal recovery. The difference between regular recovery and trial recovery is that data is not written to the files and changes are only recorded in the buffers. Trial recovery writes any errors encountered into the alert log file.

Once the trial recovery is completed, all the effects of trial recovery are nullified except for the problem datablock information written into the alert log file, and the database is still in a consistent state.

If many blocks are corrupted, you can set the database in read-only mode and open the reset logs. If the corrupt blocks are few, you can perform a recovery that ignores the corrupt blocks but recovers the rest, as shown in the following statement:

```
RECOVER DATABASE ALLOW 2 CORRUPTION;
```

The ALLOW n CORRUPTION option was introduced in Oracle9*i*.

Miscellaneous RMAN Enhancements

Oracle9*i* introduces the following enhancements that enable better maintenance of the recovery catalog:

- Oracle9*i* adds the new clause RECOVERY WINDOW <n> to the REPORT OBSOLETE command to specify that the command must report obsolete backups that are not required to keep the database recoverable within a particular window of time. In other words, this command considers the obsolete backups before the most recent backup prior to the start of the time specified. Here is an example:

  ```
  REPORT OBSOLETE RECOVERY WINDOW 7 DAYS;
  ```

  You can use the DELETE OBSOLETE command to delete these obsolete backups. The RECOVERY WINDOW clause and the REDUNDANCY clause are mutually exclusive.

  Oracle9*i* also adds the RECOVERY WINDOW <n> clause to the REPORT NEED BACKUP command:

  ```
  REPORT NEED BACKUP RECOVERY WINDOW 7 DAYS;
  ```

- Oracle9*i* unifies the LIST, CHANGE, CROSSCHECK, and DELETE EXPIRED commands and makes their syntax similar.
- You can use the CROSSCHECK command to check if backup sets or file copies exist.
- The LIST command has been enhanced; now you can specify either BY BACKUP or BY FILE output orientation. The BY BACKUP option is the default.

```
LIST BACKUP;
LIST BACKUP BY FILE;
```

- Oracle9*i* adds a SHOW command to display the RMAN session configuration. Some of the items you can display are RETENTION POLICY, EXCLUDE (tablespaces), DATAFILE BACKUP COPIES, ARCHIVELOG BACKUP COPIES, DEVICE TYPE, DEFAULT DEVICE TYPE, CHANNEL, and SNAPSHOT CONTROLFILE. You can specify the whole configuration with the keyword ALL, as shown here:

```
SHOW ALL;
```

- In Oracle9*i*, RMAN can back up tablespaces with different block sizes using a single command.
- NOCATALOG is the default in Oracle9*i*. You do not have to explicitly specify either CATALOG or NOCATALOG.

For Review

1. You must know about the many Oracle9*i* enhancements that improve RMAN manageability and reliability.
2. You must be able to describe BMR and show how it decreases MTTR and increases availability.
3. You can be able to discuss trial recovery (user-managed recovery) to anticipate problem blocks.

Exercises

1. **Which of the following recoveries can only be performed from the RMAN interface and not the SQL*Plus interface?**

   A. Complete database recovery

   B. Tablespace recovery

C. Block Media Recovery (BMR)

D. Partial recovery

2. **Which of the following commands is not an RMAN command?**

A. LIST

B. CROSSCHECK

C. CHANGE

D. ALTER

Answer Key
1. C. **2.** D.

Oracle Enterprise Manager (OEM)

The OEM has been enhanced in Oracle9*i* and improves the DBA's ability to manage the database. Some of these enhancements are

- A new console look and feel
- A standalone mode for the console
- Integrated OEM functionality
- HTML reports
- User-defined events

New Console Look and Feel

The OEM console provides a GUI interface for administering the database. The console has a two-pane interface to implement a master-detail control configuration (see Figure 3-7).

The left pane is the navigator pane. The navigator is a hierarchical list of target objects such as events, jobs, databases, nodes, groups, and listeners. The navigator also lists the child objects that these target objects are comprised of. You can expand an object to see the child objects or you can collapse them to hide the child objects. You select an object in the navigator pane by clicking it, and the OEM displays the information about that object in the detail pane on the right. Typically, this information is a datasheet with multiple columns that lists details about various

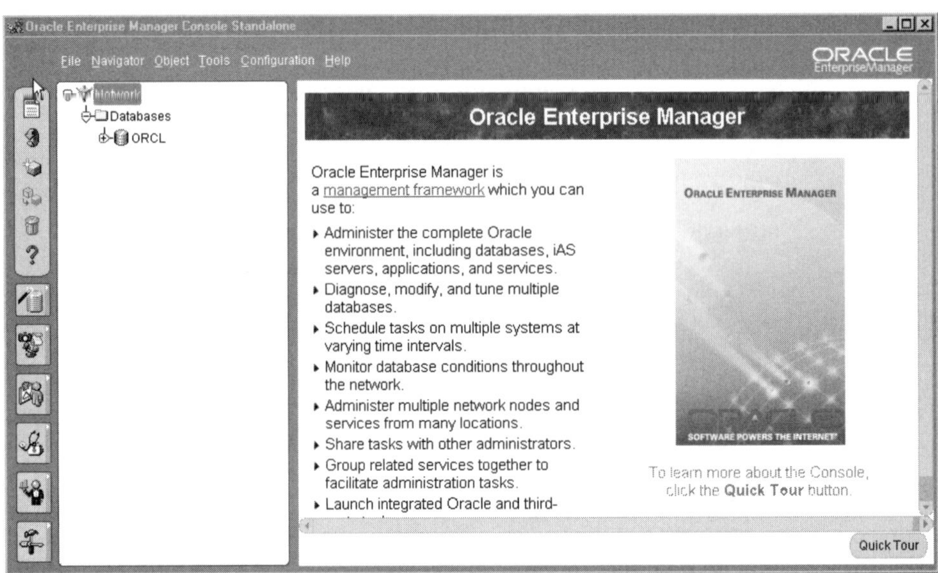

FIGURE 3-7. *The two-pane interface of the OEM console*

attributes of the object. This information could also be a property sheet that lists the properties and values of the selected object.

For example, if you expand the Databases folder object, you will see the databases that you have. If you expand one of these database objects, you will see some child objects such as Instance, Schema, Security, and Storage. If you expand Instance, you will see child objects and folders such as Configuration, Stored Configuration, Sessions, Locks, In-Doubt Transactions, Resource Consumer Groups, Resource Plans, and Resource Plan Schedule. You can also manage these features of the instance.

If you select the database object, you will see detailed information about the database object for this instance (see Figure 3-8). You will see a traffic light to display the status of the database; you can start the database or shut it down on this screen. The detail pane will also display information such as the host name, the instance name, the instance start time, and the archive log mode.

Standalone Mode for the Console

When launching the OEM Console or other OEM applications, you will have to choose to either start the console in the standalone mode or to login to the Oracle Management Server (OMS), a middle-tier application (see Figure 3-9).

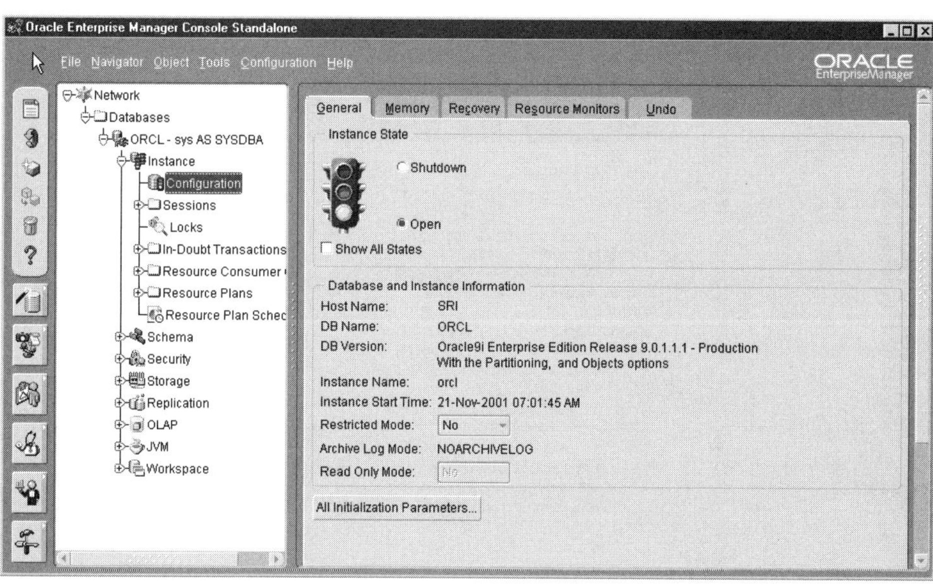

FIGURE 3-8. *The database object within the instance*

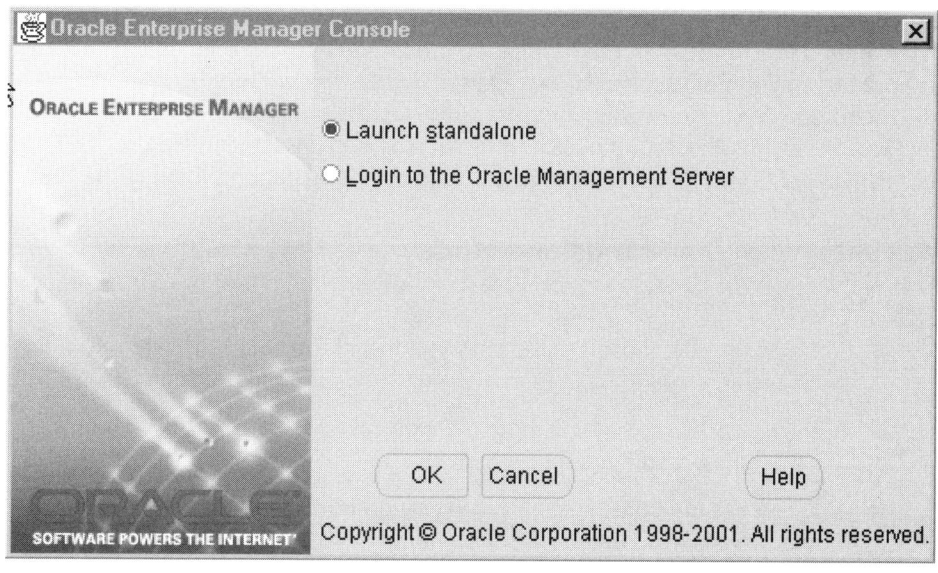

FIGURE 3-9. *The choice between a standalone and an OMS login*

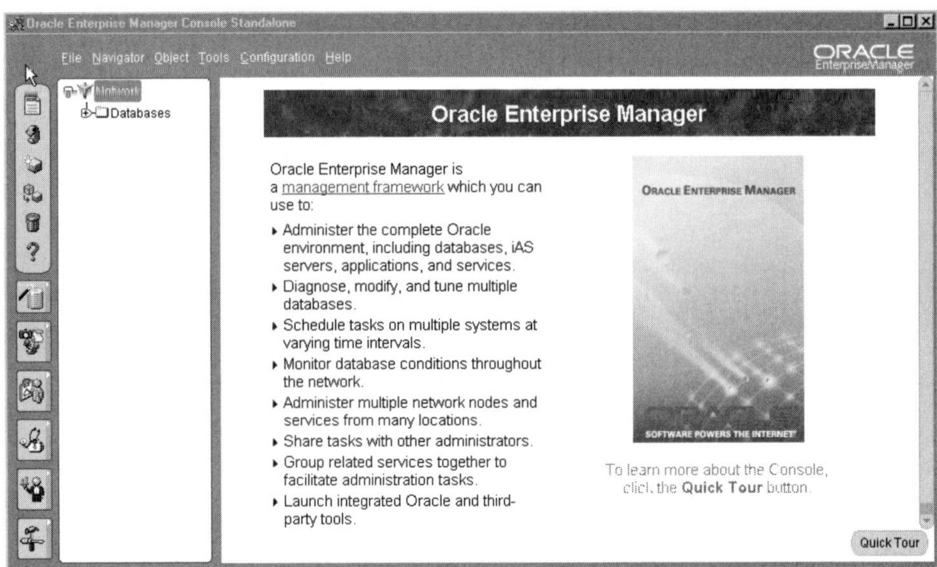

FIGURE 3-10. *The console in the standalone mode*

The standalone mode enables you to use the OEM console even if the OMS is not installed or not available in your database configuration (see Figure 3-10). You have limited functionality in the standalone mode; the console only enables you to connect to and administer the database target object. You will not be able to discover nodes with the Intelligent Agent in the standalone mode.

To administer other target object types such as HTTP web servers, jobs, and events, you will have to close the console, then start it again, and login to the OMS.

Advantages of the Standalone Mode

Some advantages of standalone mode are as follows:

- You can use the console as soon as you install the database right out of the box.
- You can use the console without the existence or availability of the OMS in your database configuration.
- You can use the console even when you do not have the Intelligent Agent operational in your database environment.

- You are directly connected to the target object, even though you can only connect to the database object. This direct connection is in contrast with having access to many target object types via a connection to the OMS.

Restrictions in the Standalone Mode

Some restrictions of the standalone mode are as follows:

- You can only connect to and administer the database object type. You cannot administer other object types such as HTTP web servers, events, and jobs.
- You cannot share administrative information among many administrators.
- You cannot utilize the backup and data management tools.
- You cannot generate and publish enterprise, web-enabled reporting.
- You cannot run the client console within a web browser.
- The Oracle Management Pack for Oracle applications does not support the standalone mode.

The Standalone Repository

Some integrated applications in the console require a standalone repository. This standalone repository is different and separate from the repository used by the OMS. Some of these applications are

- Oracle SQL Analyze
- Oracle Expert
- Oracle Index Tuning Wizard
- Oracle Change Manager
- Oracle Tablespace Manager

Oracle will prompt you to create this single-user standalone repository and will prompt you for the user who will own this repository. Oracle recommends that you create a new user because the user requires distinct roles and privileges, and it recommends that you create a new tablespace because the repository needs distinct tablespace attributes.

Integrated OEM Functionality

The OEM in Oracle9*i* was enhanced to provide support for the new features that were introduced in the Oracle9*i* database. Some of these supported features are

- Server Parameter File (SPFILE)
- Automatic Undo Management (AUM)
- Default temporary tablespace
- Multiple block sizes
- Buffer cache sizing advisor
- Instance recovery MTTR
- Unicode specification
- Online table reorganization
- Materialized view enhancements

Server Parameter File (SPFILE)

You need the SYSDBA or SYSOPER privilege in order to create a SPFILE. To create a SPFILE from a PFILE using the OEM, you must first expand the Databases folder, then expand one of the databases, and proceed to expand the instance object. You should see the configuration object under the instance object (see Figure 3-11).

Click the Configuration folder object and click Import spfile within the Object Menu option. As an alternative, you can right-click the Configuration object and then click **Import spfile** (see Figure 3-12).

You must specify the PFILE and the SPFILE, both of which must reside on the same machine as the database server. You can either type in the full path for the source PFILE, or you can click the Local Browse button and select the PFILE. Similarly, you can either type in the full path for the target SPFILE, or you can click the Local Browse button and specify the SPFILE. Then click OK.

Create a PFILE from a SPFILE You can also create a PFILE from an SPFILE by performing a similar set of operations. The only difference is that you would select **Export spfile** instead of **Import spfile**.

Modify SPFILE Parameters You can edit the database configuration and modify all the parameter values. If you change a **configured** parameter value, the change is stored in the parameter file on the server and it will persist to the next database restart. If you change a dynamic parameter value, the change will be in effect immediately, and the change will be stored to the SPFILE on the server (see Figure 3-13).

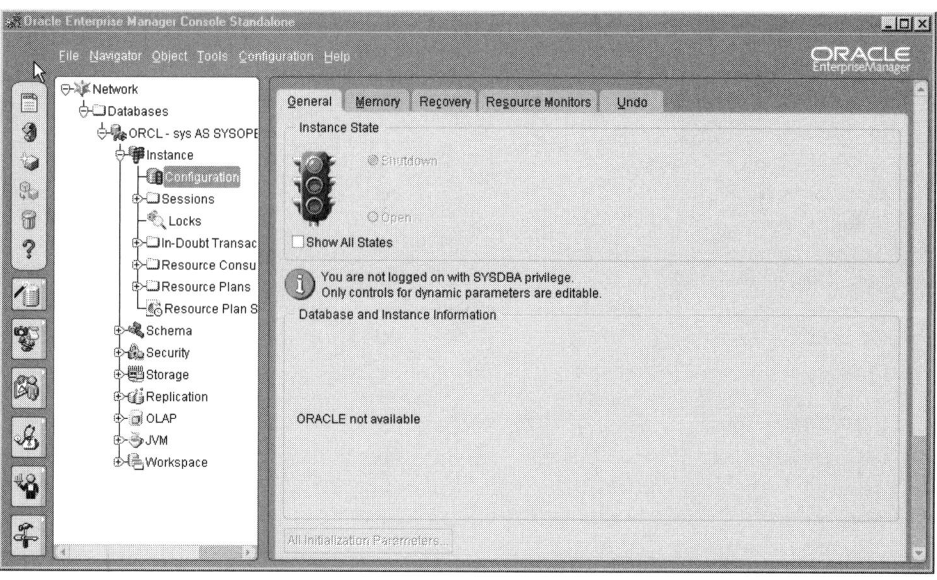

FIGURE 3-11. *The instance object in the OEM*

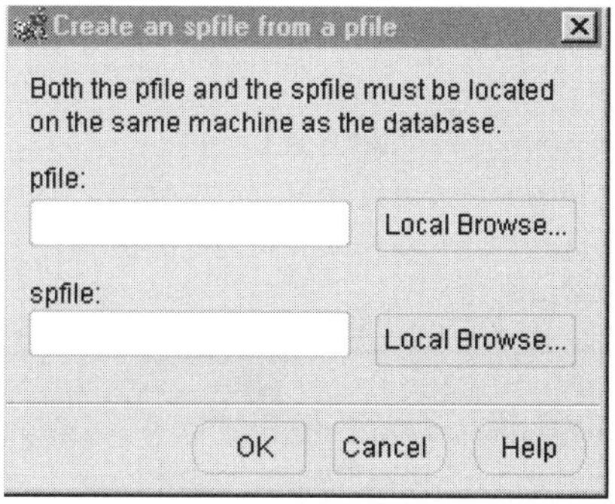

Create an spfile from a pfile

Both the pfile and the spfile must be located on the same machine as the database.

pfile: Local Browse...

spfile: Local Browse...

OK Cancel Help

FIGURE 3-12. *The "Import a pfile into an spfile" dialog box*

If you change a dynamic **running** parameter value, the change takes effect immediately, but it is not saved to the SPFILE. The change will be lost if you restart the database.

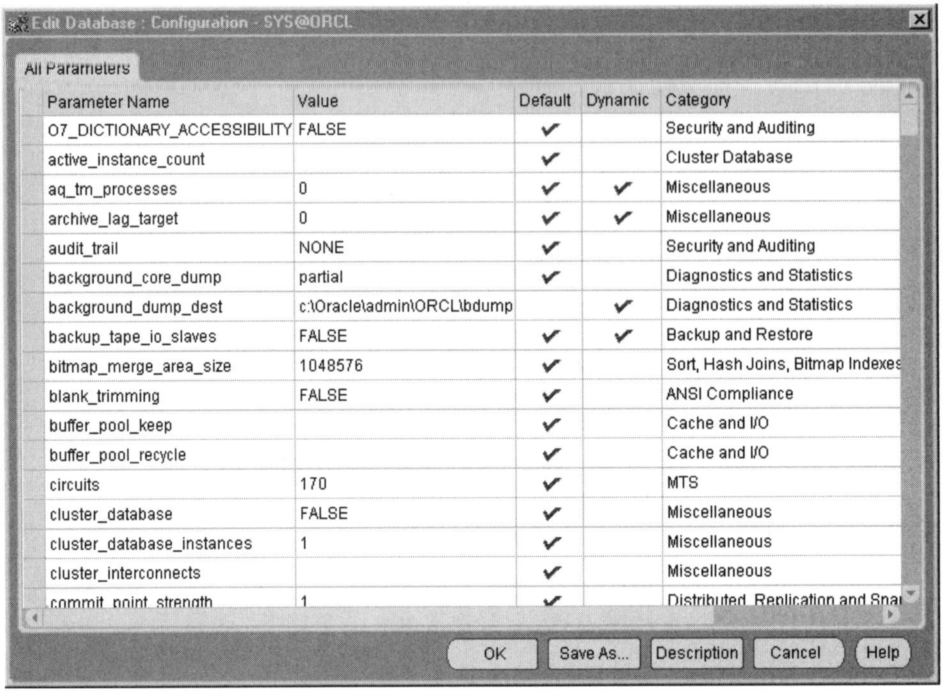

Edit Database : Configuration - SYS@ORCL

All Parameters

Parameter Name	Value	Default	Dynamic	Category
O7_DICTIONARY_ACCESSIBILITY	FALSE	✔		Security and Auditing
active_instance_count		✔		Cluster Database
aq_tm_processes	0	✔	✔	Miscellaneous
archive_lag_target	0	✔	✔	Miscellaneous
audit_trail	NONE	✔		Security and Auditing
background_core_dump	partial	✔		Diagnostics and Statistics
background_dump_dest	c:\Oracle\admin\ORCL\bdump		✔	Diagnostics and Statistics
backup_tape_io_slaves	FALSE	✔	✔	Backup and Restore
bitmap_merge_area_size	1048576	✔		Sort, Hash Joins, Bitmap Indexes
blank_trimming	FALSE	✔		ANSI Compliance
buffer_pool_keep		✔		Cache and I/O
buffer_pool_recycle		✔		Cache and I/O
circuits	170	✔		MTS
cluster_database	FALSE	✔		Miscellaneous
cluster_database_instances	1	✔		Miscellaneous
cluster_interconnects		✔		Miscellaneous
commit_point_strength	1	✔		Distributed, Replication and Snap

OK | Save As... | Description | Cancel | Help

FIGURE 3-13. *Instance parameters*

Automatic Undo Management (AUM)

One new feature of Oracle9*i* is AUM, a new alternative to rollback segments. The administrator only has to allocate undo entries to a single UNDO tablespace, which Oracle manages automatically.

To view the details about the UNDO tablespace, select the configuration object within the instance object in the Navigator pane and then select the Undo tab on the Details pane. The Undo tab was introduced in the Enterprise Manager provided with Oracle9*i*. You will see the current UNDO tablespace name and the retention period for undo entries.

You can specify if the database should use and manage rollback segments or have the database automatically manage undo entries in an UNDO tablespace by setting the UNDO_MANAGEMENT initial parameter. The OEM can let you know if the database is operating in the AUM mode.

In the Create Tablespace dialog box, you can specify that this tablespace should be an UNDO tablespace by selecting the Undo option.

Default Temporary Tablespace

Oracle stores temporary data in a temporary tablespace. The temporary tablespace requires a lower overhead than regular tablespaces. If a user is not assigned a temporary tablespace specifically, he or she will be assigned this default temporary tablespace.

To specify the default temporary tablespace, you must select a database, expand the storage object, expand the tablespaces object, and click the DEFTEMP object in the Navigator pane (see Figure 3-14).

When you specify a tablespace, you must check the Default Temporary Tablespace option.

Multiple Block Sizes

Oracle9*i* enables you to specify a standard block size and up to five other block sizes. The additional block sizes are essential in an Exact, Transform, and Load (ETL) transaction when moving data from an OLTP database to an OLAP data warehouse. When you create a new tablespace within the OEM, you can select the block size for that tablespace from a drop-down list.

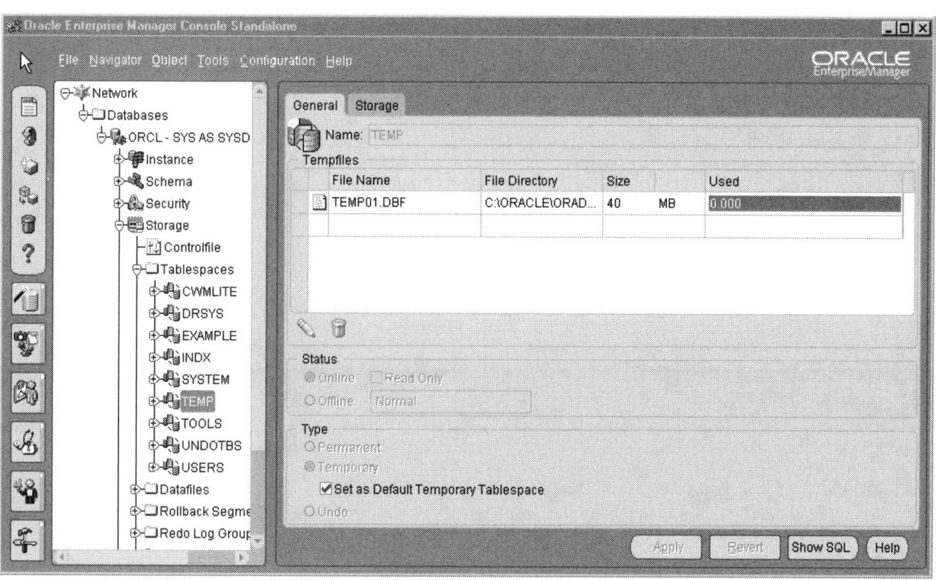

FIGURE 3-14. *Managing tablespaces*

Buffer Cache Sizing Advisor

You can query the V$DB_CACHE_ADVICE view to get cache data, which you can use to determine the optimum size of the cache. You can use OEM to get a graphical depiction of the cache by clicking the Memory tab for the Configuration object and then clicking Cache Buffer Size Advice. Figure 3-15 displays the relative change in physical reads against the cache buffer size.

Although the graph contains a lot of information for the optimal sizing of the cache, you can move your mouse over the graph and OEM will display a text message to help you understand the graph. For example, the text message could read, "If you set the cache to 10M, the physical reads will increase by 3 percent."

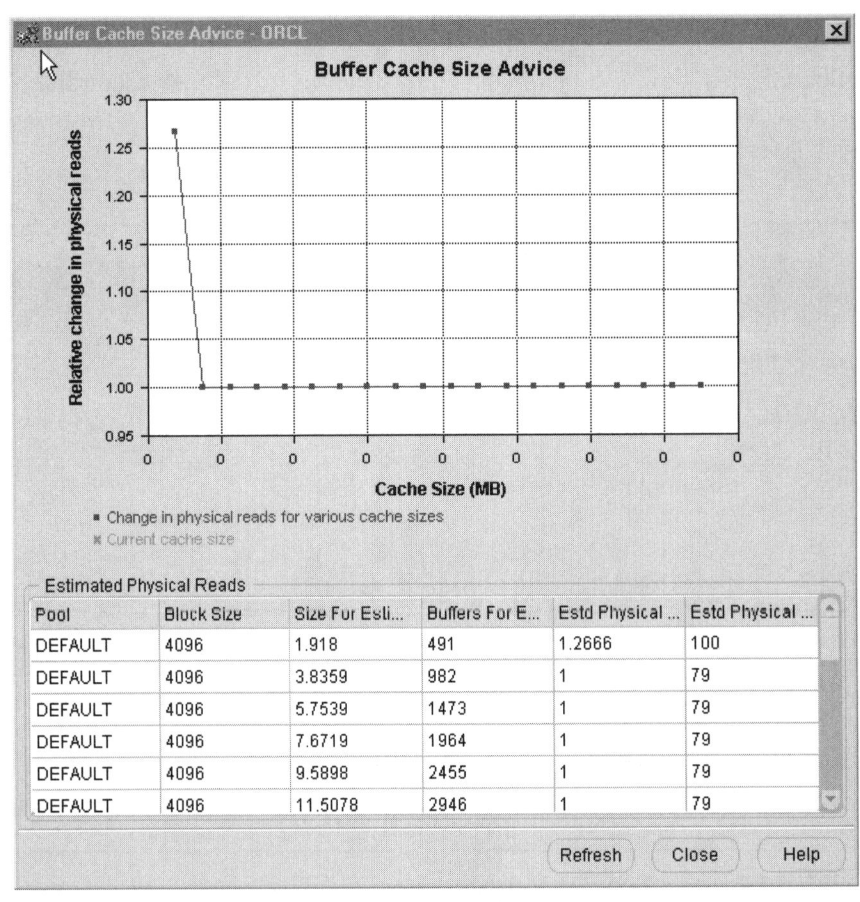

Pool	Block Size	Size For Esti...	Buffers For E...	Estd Physical ...	Estd Physical ...
DEFAULT	4096	1.918	491	1.2666	100
DEFAULT	4096	3.8359	982	1	79
DEFAULT	4096	5.7539	1473	1	79
DEFAULT	4096	7.6719	1964	1	79
DEFAULT	4096	9.5898	2455	1	79
DEFAULT	4096	11.5078	2946	1	79

FIGURE 3-15. *Buffer cache size advice*

Instance Recovery MTTR

To specify and manage instance recovery, select the configuration object under the instance object in the Navigator pane, and then select the Recovery tab in the Details pane on the right.

When you specify a value for "The desired mean time to recover," the FAST_START_MTTR_TARGET parameter will change. This parameter specifies the desired time within which you would like the instance to automatically recover after a failure. This parameter has been discussed in Chapter 2.

Unicode Specification

Unicode is a universal character-representation, 16-bit coding that enables you to represent characters in any language, as opposed to the 8-bit ASCII coding that only represents the English language characters.

When you use Unicode for character representation, you must specify the character encoding that is to be used. For example, you have the 16-bit encoding system UTF-16 and the 8-bit, multibyte encoding system UTF-8. OEM enables you to specify the Unicode encoding system when you create a table. You can find more information about Unicode in Chapter 5.

Online Table Reorganization

To enhance availability, Oracle9*i* provides the capability of performing table reorganizations online. See Chapter 2 for additional information about online table reorganization and for restrictions that must be met in order to perform this function.

The Oracle Tuning Pack, an optional add-on to the Enterprise Manager, provides a Reorg Wizard that can perform online table reorganizations, among other capabilities. The OEM console, the OMS, and the Intelligent Agent must be available in order to use the Reorg Wizard.

Materialized View Enhancements

The Summary Advisor Wizard analyzes workload data in order to recommend which materialized views you must create, retain, or get rid of. The Enterprise Manager lets you know the areas of the operations the materialized views support.

HTML Reports

The Enterprise Manager has a central reporting framework to enable you to design, select, customize, generate, schedule, and publish predefined and user-defined HTML reports to a web site. This reporting framework is integrated into all the OEM applications. You can generate and publish these reports either as needed or on a fixed schedule.

The reporting framework comes with a rich variety of predefined reports, such as reports about the configuration, the alerts, the events, and the storage. You can generate reports about the whole configuration or about an object in the configuration.

Generating a Database Configuration HTML Report

The first step is to expand the database object and select a database in the Navigator pane.

To initiate the creation of a report, you can either click the Create Report button on the toolbar, or you can select the Create Report option in the Object menu. You can also right-click the database object and click the Create Report option in the popup menu.

Now specify the elements of the report that you would like to display in your report. Then click OK to generate the report.

User-Defined Events

One feature that you have via the Oracle Diagnostics Pack is the capability to create custom scripts that monitor conditions that you specify. Once you have created your user-defined event, you can integrate them into the Events framework within the Enterprise Manager.

Components of User-Defined Events

Your custom scripts are made up of the following three components:

- The first software component *monitors the condition* that interests you. For example, you could monitor the amount of free space, or the percent of the tablespace that is used.
- The second software component *evaluates the results* of the first component. The OEM Event framework evaluates the values against the threshold and critical levels.
- The third software component sends the results of the evaluation to the Event framework using XML tags. The result returned should either be the value of the item monitored or it should represent the status.

You can send a value to the Event framework with the following statement:

```
print "<oraresult>340</oraresult>"
```

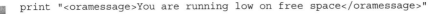

This statement sends a value of 340 to the Event framework.

You can specify the notification message with the following statement if the event is triggered:

```
print "<oramessage>You are running low on free space</oramessage>"
```

For Review

1. You should know about the advantages and the restrictions of using the standalone mode for the OEM console.
2. You should be familiar with the OEM functionality that supports the new features of Oracle9*i*.
3. You should be aware that you can generate HTML reports. You should also know about user-defined events.

Exercises

1. **While the OEM is operating in the standalone mode**
   - **A.** You are connected to the OMS.
   - **B.** You are not connected to the OMS.
   - **C.** You can manage database objects.
   - **D.** You can manage events.

Answer Key
1. B. C.

Chapter Summary

This chapter explores the various enhancements to manageability in Oracle9*i*.

The *Database Resource Manager* manages the distribution of resources based on preestablished criteria. The Database Resource Manager estimates the length that an operation will run, and it will prevent an operation from starting if it exceeds a specified value (specified via the MAX_EST_EXEC_TIME parameter).

When a session meets preestablished criteria, the session is switched to another group specified by the SWITCH_GROUP parameter. If the session waits in the queue for a time equal to the value specified by QUEUE_P1, the session will abort or timeout.

Oracle9*i* enhances the *scalability of user sessions* by sharing user processes with many user sessions, by sharing a database session with many user sessions, by sharing agent processes, by sharing external procedure agent processes, and by modularizing the Oracle Core Library.

Oracle9*i* introduces the concept of *Oracle-Managed Files* (OMF) to assume the task of managing OS files from the database administrator.

Oracle9*i* introduces *Automatic Undo Management* (AUM), which you implement by specifying the UNDO_MANAGEMENT parameter, creating an UNDO tablespace, and assigning it to the database. Oracle automatically manages the undo segments in the UNDO tablespaces. To cater to the needs of diverse applications, Oracle enables you to create tablespaces with multiple block sizes within a single database.

Oracle9*i* introduces the *Workspace Manager* to enable different users to have different versions of a row in the version-enabled table. This enables users to make changes to the table without interfering with other users that may be performing data analysis.

Oracle9*i* has made many enhancements to improve the manageability and reliability of backup and recover operations. Oracle9*i* introduces the BLOCKRECOVER command to perform block media recovery (BMR). Oracle9*i* also introduced trial recovery to anticipate problem blocks prior to actually performing the recovery.

You can start the *Oracle Enterprise Manager* (OEM) console in standalone mode, that is, without logging in to the OMS. The functionality in the standalone mode is limited to the database object.

You can use, design, modify, generate, and publish HTML reports on a Web site either on demand or on a fixed schedule. You can create user-defined events that you can integrate into the OEM Event framework.

Two-Minute Drill

1. Database Resource Manager

- You can specify the MAX_EST_EXEC_TIME.
  - If the estimated execution time for the operation exceeds this parameter value, the operation will not be started.
  - The SWITCH_ESTIMATE must be set to TRUE for the MAX_EST_EXEC_TIME parameter to take effect.
  - You can disable this parameter from taking effect by setting the SWITCH_ESTIMATE to FALSE.
- To build a resource plan, you
  - Build a resource plan in a pending area.
  - Create a resource plan.
  - Create the resource consumer groups.

- Create the resource plan directives. You need to have a resource management plan before you can build these directives.
- Validate the plan.
- Submit the plan to implement it.

2. **Segment management**
   - You can use the UPDATE GLOBAL INDEXES to specify that Oracle should update the global index as it performs partitioning DDL.
   - External tables enable you to query data in OS flat files just as you would query a regular Oracle table.
   - You can create list-partitioned tables where the partitions are based on a list of discrete column values.
   - You can use the DBMS_METADATA package to obtain information about a database object.
   - Automatic segment space management tracks datablock space utilization in bitmap blocks (BMBs).
   - Bitmap join indexes optimize a join operation by building a bitmap index on multiple tables.
3. **Scalable session management**
   - The Oracle shared server enables one server process to service many user sessions. It also optimizes the connection process.
   - OCI connection pooling enables one database connection from a middle-tier application to service many user sessions. This is particularly useful in web-hosted applications.
   - External procedures have been enhanced to enable one external procedure agent process to service many calls to that external procedure.
   - Multithreaded heterogeneous service (HS) agents establish a dynamic pool of shared agent processes.
4. **File management**
   - Oracle-Managed Files (OMFs) eliminate the need for DBAs to specify filenames when creating tablespaces and temporary tablespaces.
   - You can delete non-OMF files directly with an SQL statement, as opposed to going to the OS environment to delete files.

- If you create users without specifying the temporary tablespace, Oracle9*i* defaults to the default temporary tablespace that you specify for the database.

5. **Tablespace management**
    - You implement Automatic Undo Management (AUM) by setting the UNDO_MANAGEMENT parameter to AUTO and specifying the UNDO tablespace in the UNDO_TABLESPACE parameter.
    - Oracle takes care of numbers and sizes of undo segments.
    - You cannot implement AUM and manually managed rollback segments at the same time within the instance.
    - You must set db_nK_cache_size in order to create tablespaces with nonstandard block sizes.
6. **Workspace management**
    - The unit for implementing workspaces is a table.
    - You must version-enable tables, create workspaces, and grant privileges to users; then users can access the workspace.
    - The default workspace is LIVE.
    - You have to explicitly navigate to the child workspaces.
    - You must resolve conflicts in data before merging the child workspace with the parents.
    - When merging the child workspace with the parent, the changes in the child can be applied to the parent or you can force them to be discarded.
    - You can disable workspace management by disabling the versioning of tables and removing the workspace.
7. **Backup and recovery (Recovery Manager [RMAN])**
    - RMAN has many enhancements to improve manageability and reliability.
    - RMAN parameters are persistent across sessions.
    - Oracle9*i* has optimized RMAN backup and restore operations.
    - Block Media Recovery (BMR) decreases mean time to recover (MTTR) and increases availability.

- You can use trial recovery (user-managed recovery) to anticipate problems prior to actually performing the database recovery.
- Oracle9*i* has enhanced the REPORT and LIST commands to enable better recovery catalog maintenance.

8. **Oracle Enterprise Manager (OEM)**
   - OEM has a new look with two panes: the Navigator pane and the Details pane.
   - OEM can be used in standalone mode without logging into an Oracle Management Server (OMS).
   - Logging into an OMS gives you additional functionality.
   - Enhancements were made to support the new features of the Oracle9*i* database.
   - OEM Has a reporting framework to design, select, customize, generate, schedule, and publish predefined and user-defined HTML reports to a web site.
   - You can create custom scripts (user-defined events) and integrate them into the Events framework.

Fill-in-the-Blanks

1. If the ________________ parameter is set to ____________, and if Oracle's estimate of the time that the operation will take is greater than the value specified by MAX_EST_EXEC_TIME, Oracle will return an error and the operation will not be started.
2. You ___________ administer HTTP web servers when the OEM console is in the standalone mode.
3. If you do not specify the UPDATE GLOBAL INDEXES clause, it defaults to _____________ GLOBAL INDEXES.
4. A shared server architecture requires a _________ _________ process, at least one ________ process, and at least one ________ ________ process.
5. The default size for Oracle-managed data files and redo log files is _________.
6. The parameter used to specify the time period before which undo data should not be overwritten is _____________.

7. The parameter used to specify a buffer cache with a standard block size is __________.
8. The role required to perform all Workspace Manager tasks is __________.
9. When a user connects to the database, by default the user is in the ________ workspace.
10. You must add the _______ option to the RECOVER DATABASE command to perform trial recovery.
11. The ______ command is used to display RMAN configuration settings.

Chapter Questions

1. **The final step in building a resource plan is to implement the plan in the pending area with the following command:**

   A. IMPLEMENT_PLAN

   B. SUBMIT_PLAN

   C. FINALIZE_PLAN

   D. USE_PLAN

2. **When you rebuild a global index on a partitioned table, Oracle will**

   A. Rebuild the whole index.

   B. Rebuild only the indexes that are marked as UNUSABLE.

   C. Not rebuild the index.

   D. Rebuild the partitioned table first and then rebuild the index.

3. **When the listener receives the request from a client for a shared server connection, the first step is for the listener to**

   A. Locate the address of the most loaded dispatcher.

   B. Locate the address of the shared server process.

   C. Locate the address of the least loaded dispatcher.

   D. Locate the address of a peer listener.

4. **You create a connection pool by using which procedure?**

   A. `OCIMakeConnectionPool`

   B. `OCICreateConnectionPool`

C. `OCIConnectionPoolNew`

D. `OCIConnectionPoolCreate`

5. **To add an OMF data file to a tablespace, which of the following would you use?**

A. ALTER TABLESPACE mytbsp ADD DATAFILE

B. ALTER TABLESPACE mytbsp CREATE DATAFILE

C. ALTER DATABASE ADD DATAFILE TO TABLESPACE mytbsp

D. ALTER TABLESPACE mytbsp ADD OMF_DATAFILE

6. **The parameter used to set the database in the AUM mode is**

A. rollback_segments

B. undo_management

C. undo_suppress_errors

D. transaction_per_rollback_segment

7. **Which of the following tablespaces are not candidates for nonstandard block sizes?**

A. Index tablespace

B. User tablespace

C. SYSTEM tablespace

D. Temporary tablespace

8. **During custom database creation, the script file to be run to install the Workspace Manager utility is**

A. Orapwdmg.sql

B. Prvtutil.plb

C. Catproc.sql

D. Owminst.plb

9. **To apply the changes in the parent workspace to the child workspace, you should use the following DBMS_WM procedure:**

A. MergeWorkspace

B. ResolveConflicts

C. RefreshWorkspace

D. MergeTable

10. Which of the following statements is true once the trial recovery is completed?

A. The changes to the buffers are written to the data files.

B. The buffer changes are written to a temporary file.

C. The buffer changes are not written to any files.

D. The buffer changes are displayed on the console.

11. Which of the following statements is not correct in case of BMR?

A. It can be performed from the SQLPLUS interface.

B. It can be performed from the RMAN interface.

C. Only complete recovery is possible.

D. It can be performed only from a full backup.

Fill-in-the-Blank Answers

1. SWITCH_ESTIMATE, TRUE
2. cannot
3. invalidate
4. network listener, dispatcher, shared server
5. 100MB
6. undo_retention
7. db_cache_size
8. WM_ADMIN_ROLE
9. LIVE
10. TEST
11. SHOW

Answers to Chapter Questions

1. B. SUBMIT_PLAN

Explanation Once you build your plan in the pending area, you must validate the plan. The final step is to implement the plan by invoking the SUBMIT_PLAN in the DBMS_RESOURCE_MANAGER package.

2. A. Rebuild the whole index.

Explanation When you initiate an action to rebuild a global index, Oracle flags the entire index as UNUSABLE and rebuilds the entire index. Rebuilding the entire index is obviously a rather resource-intensive and expensive operation.

3. C. Locate the address of the least loaded dispatcher.

Explanation When the listener receives the request from the client for a shared server connection, it locates the address of the least loaded dispatcher process. In previous versions, the next step would have been to pass this address back to the client for it (the client) to contact the dispatcher again over the network. Instead, in Oracle9*i*'s direct handoff method, the listener hands the connection request to the dispatcher. The dispatcher communicates directly with the client to establish a connection without the need for the additional network calls that were required in previous versions.

4. D. `OCIConnectionPoolCreate`.

Explanation When establishing an OCI connection pool, the first step is to allocate a pool handle using `OCIHandleAlloc`, the next step is to create a connection pool using `OCIConnectionPoolCreate`, and the third step is to log into the database using `OCILogon2`.

5. A. ALTER TABLESPACE mytbsp ADD DATAFILE

Explanation You use the ALTER TABLESPACE command to add a datafile to the tablespace. Obviously, this statement assumes that you have already created the tablespace.

6. B. undo_management

Explanation The UNDO_MANAGEMENT initialization parameter should be set to AUTO to start the database in the AUM mode. Parameters such as ROLLBACK_SEGMENTS and TRANSACTION_PER_ROLLBACK_SEGMENT do not affect the AUM mode because they are associated with the manual rollback segment mode. You can use the parameter UNDO_SUPPRESS_ERRORS to suppress errors that were raised when rollback segments are managed manually in the AUM mode.

7. C, D. SYSTEM tablespace, Temporary tablespace

Explanation SYSTEM and temporary tablespaces should always use the standard block size represented by DB_BLOCK_SIZE.

8. D. Owminst.plb

Explanation You can create a custom database by connecting as a SYS user and running OWMINST.PLB. This file is available in the ORACLE_HOME\rdbms\admin folder.

9. C. RefreshWorkspace

Explanation You refresh the workspace when the parent workspace is copied to the child workspace. You must resolve data conflicts before refreshing the workspace. You can invoke the *RefreshWorkspace* procedure to refresh all the data and invoke *RefreshTable* to refresh a single table.

10. C. The buffer changes are not written to any files.

Explanation Once the trial recovery is completed, all the effects of trial recovery are nullified except for the messages written into the alert log file.

11. A. It can be performed from SQLPLUS interface.

Explanation The following restrictions apply to BMR:

- BMR can be performed only from the RMAN interface, not from SQLPLUS.
- Only complete recovery is possible.
- BMR is suitable when a fewer number of blocks are to be recovered.
- BMR is possible from full backup only, not from incremental backups.

CHAPTER 4

Performance and Scalability Enhancements

erformance and scalability are critical to enterprise-wide database solutions that are deployed on the Web, where hundreds of thousands of users can attempt to interact with the database. Oracle9*i* introduces a number of significant enhancements to performance and scalability.

The first part of this chapter focuses on a number of performance-related enhancements in Oracle9*i*. The second part of this chapter describes scalability enhancements specific to Real Application Clusters (RACs).

Performance Enhancements

Database solutions have become more comprehensive and the number of users has increased exponentially with the improved connectivity of the Internet. The increased user community competes for common resources; this can result in severe performance problems. Oracle9*i* has introduced various enhancements to greatly improve performance, some of which are as follows:

- Index monitoring
- Skip scan index access
- Cursor sharing
- Cached execution plans
- First rows optimization
- Gathering system statistics

Index Monitoring

Indexes are the logical structures associated with tables and other objects, such as clusters, that provide Structured Query Language (SQL) statements with a faster data access path to the table. Oracle defines several indexes to enhance the speed of data access. Some of these indexes are

- B-tree indexes (the default)
- B-tree cluster indexes
- Hash cluster indexes
- Global and local indexes
- Reverse key indexes

- Bitmap indexes (These are compact; they work best for columns with a small set of values.)
- Function-based indexes
- Domain indexes

When Oracle performs a full-table scan, it scans all blocks below the high watermark sequentially and reads each row. The full-table scan is generally used when you want to retrieve data from most of the rows in the table. When Oracle performs an index scan, it searches the index for the index column values specified in the SQL statement. If the SQL statement requires some columns that are not in the index, Oracle uses the ROWID obtained from the index to locate relevant rows. Index scans improve performance when you are retrieving a small portion of the rows of the table.

When you execute an SQL statement, the cost-based optimizer steers the SQL statement execution away from nonselective indexes. Even though the index is not used, Oracle continues to maintain the indexes. These indexes constitute an overhead on memory, I/O, and CPU resources because the index has to be updated for DML operations. The Rules Based Optimizer (RBO) has been retained in Oracle9*i* for backward compatibility and the default mode is still CHOOSE.

To mitigate this problem, Oracle9*i* provides the capability to monitor index utilization. If it is determined that an index is not being used, it can be dropped, thus eliminating unnecessary statement overhead. You can review the utilization information and drop indexes that are not being used in order to improve performance.

You can start the process of monitoring and collecting index utilization statistics by using the following statement:

```
ALTER INDEX part_ix MONITORING USAGE;
```

You can stop the process of monitoring and collecting index utilization statistics by using the following statement:

```
ALTER INDEX part_ix NOMONITORING USAGE;
```

You can query the V$OBJECT_USAGE view to review the index utilization data. If the index has been used within the period of time it was monitored, the USED column within this view will contain a YES value; it will contain a NO otherwise.

This view also tracks the start and stop times of the monitoring period for the index in the START_MONITORING and END_MONITORING columns respectively. If the monitoring activity is still ongoing, the MONITORING column will contain a

YES; it will contain a NO otherwise. When you start the utilization monitoring for an index, Oracle resets the information in the V$OBJECT_USAGE view for that index.

You can query the dba_indexes and dba_ind_columns data dictionary views, as you did in earlier versions of Oracle, to obtain information about the indexes that have been created for a table. You can obtain the expressions for function-based indexes by querying the DBA_IND_EXPRESSIONS view. You can obtain information about the blocks in the segment, the number of leaf rows, and the number of leaf blocks gathered during the last ANALYZE INDEX . . . VALIDATE STRUCTURE by querying the INDEX_STATS view. You can get the corresponding information about the number of index keys by querying the INDEX_HISTOGRAM view.

Skip Scan Index Access

Prior to Oracle9*i*, the Oracle optimizer would use the composite index in the execution plan only if you referenced the index prefix column in the where clause of your SQL statement. The optimizer would not use the composite index if you omitted the index prefix column in your SQL statement.

Although you could create an index on the nonprefix index columns to provide faster data access in this situation, it adds a significant overhead when Oracle has to update multiple indexes during DML operations. Oracle9*i* addresses this problem by enhancing the optimizer's data access technology. The optimizer will now use the composite index even if you omitted the index prefix column in your SQL statement. You can thus have faster data access without having to create an additional index.

Oracle uses *skip scan* technology to scan composite indexes when your SQL statement does not include the index prefix column. Although you can use skip scanning for the default B-tree index, you cannot use skip scanning for bitmap indexes, domain indexes, function-based indexes, and for reverse keys. Oracle9*i* also supports skip scanning for cluster indexes and descending index scans, and with the CONNECT BY clause of the SQL statement.

The skip scan algorithm first determines the domain of distinct values for the index prefix column and then cycles through each distinct value in the domain. For each distinct value, Oracle performs regular index scans. In effect, Oracle treats the composite index search as a number of smaller subindex searches to retrieve ROWIDs; one subindex search is performed for each distinct value within the index prefix column. This technology functions as if you issued a sequence of SQL statements, with each statement specifying a single value for the index prefix column.

Although skip scanning is not as fast as a full-index scan, skip scanning is faster than a full-table scan, since it is faster to scan index blocks than to scan the table's data blocks. The efficiency of skip scanning increases as the domain of distinct values for the prefix index column decreases. The optimizer uses the data distribution statistics of the prefix index column to determine whether skip scanning would be more efficient than full-table scanning or other possible data access paths. Skip scanning will be used only if the Cost-Based Optimizer (CBO) is being used.

Cursor Sharing

It is common for applications to execute the same SQL statements over and over again. Oracle introduced cursor sharing as far back as version 7 to provide you with the capability to share statements that are exactly the same. When parsing a statement, Oracle verifies if a totally identical statement exists in the shared SQL pool. If it does exist, Oracle will use (or share) the statement in the shared pool. If the executing statement differs from the existing statement in the shared pool even in the smallest detail, Oracle will not share the statement. You can enable cursor sharing by setting the initialization parameter named CURSOR_SHARING to EXACT, which is the default value.

With shared cursors, application processes executing the same statement can share compiled statements in memory that are the same. Shared cursors enhance performance by reducing memory and CPU utilization, and by eliminating the time to optimize and determine execution plans. CURSOR_SHARING is a dynamic parameter that you can set with either of the following commands:

```
ALTER SYSTEM
  SET cursor_sharing = EXACT;
```

or

```
ALTER SESSION
  SET cursor_sharing = EXACT;
```

However, it is common that applications execute statements that are pretty much the same, but differ only in the literals. Oracle8*i* introduced the FORCE option for cursor sharing to enable you to share execution plans among similar statements. You would have had to determine a separate execution plan for each similar statement if you did not have Oracle8*i*'s FORCE option. You could enable this capability to share execution plans by setting the initialization parameter named CURSOR_SHARING to FORCE.

Let's consider an INVOICE table that tracks invoices; the primary key for this table is INVOICE_ID. The SALESPERSON_ID column is a foreign key in this table that references the SALESPERSON_ID column in the SALESPERSON table.

Let's compare the following queries that use the primary key:

```
SELECT invoice_id, invoice_date, salesperson_id, amount
  FROM invoice
 WHERE invoice_id = 73;
```

and

```
SELECT invoice_id, invoice_date, salesperson_id, amount
  FROM invoice
WHERE invoice_id = 298;
```

These queries are similar queries; they only differ in the literal values *73* and *298*. If you set cursor sharing to FORCE, Oracle will always use the same execution plan for both statements. The use of one execution plan does not introduce any risk in this example; it is a safe approach for the optimizer since you either have no rows or just one row to access regardless of the literal value you specify.

Let's compare the following queries that use the foreign key:

```
SELECT invoice_id, invoice_date, salesperson_id, amount
  FROM invoice
 WHERE salesperson_id = 27;
```

and

```
SELECT invoice_id, invoice_date, salesperson_id, amount
  FROM invoice
 WHERE salesperson_id = 319;
```

These queries are similar queries; they only differ in the literal values *27* and *319*. If you set cursor sharing to FORCE, Oracle8*i* always uses the same execution plan for both statements. Let's examine this scenario to determine whether the use of one execution plan for both queries constitutes a potential performance risk.

Let's assume that statistics are available for the invoice table, and that the histogram statistics accessed by the optimizer show that only two invoices (rows) have a salesperson_id of 27 and that 45,000 invoices (rows) have a salesperson_id of 319. Let's also assume that the invoice table has a total of 100,000 rows. The use of the same execution plan, however, introduces a significant performance risk; it is not a safe approach since it is definitely not optimal for both queries since there is such a disparity in the number of rows corresponding to these values. It would be more advisable for the optimizer to consider the histogram statistics as it determines the execution plan.

Oracle9*i* has enhanced cursor sharing to enable you to control this risk with a third value, SIMILAR, for the CURSOR_SHARING parameter. When you specify SIMILAR, Oracle only uses the execution plan if is certain that the execution plan does not have any association with the specific literal value.

You can enable similar statements to share the same SQL execution plan by setting CURSOR_SHARING to either FORCE or SIMILAR. The FORCE parameter value forces similar statements to share the SQL area without considering the possibility that one execution plan may not be appropriate for all cases of similar statements where just the literal value is different.

When you specify SIMILAR, Oracle first checks the shared pool to see if there is an identical statement in the shared pool. If Oracle does not find an identical statement, Oracle searches for a similar statement in the shared pool. If Oracle finds a similar statement in the shared pool, Oracle verifies if the executable form of the cursor (the execution plan) can be used. If Oracle cannot use the executable form of the existing statement, it performs a hard parse to generate the executable form of the executing statement. The optimizer generates the execution plan based on bind variables and not the actual literal values themselves.

Cached Execution Plans

Oracle stores the execution plan of a SQL statement to enable a database administrator (DBA) to analyze the execution plan of a poorly performing SQL statement without having to rerun the query. Oracle9*i* has introduced the V$SQL_PLAN view to display the cached execution plan, the compilation environment, and the execution statistics of each variable. It also helps the database administrators to determine the actual plan of a query at the time of reported performance problem.

Table 4-1 summarizes the columns of the new V$SQL_PLAN view in Oracle9*i*.

Column	**Description**
ADDRESS	The cursor handle.
HASH_VALUE	The hash value of the cached parent statement.
CHILD_NUMBER	The number of child cursors.
OPERATION	The internal operation, such as ACCESS.
OPTIONS	The variation on the operation, such as FULL.
OBJECT_NODE	The database link for referencing the object.
OBJECT#	The object number of the table or the index.
OBJECT_NAME	The name of the table or index.
OBJECT_OWNER	The schema owner.
OPTIMIZER	The current mode of the optimizer for the first row of the plan.

TABLE 4-1. *The New V$SQL_PLAN View Columns*

Column	Description
ID	A number assigned to each step in the execution plan.
PARENT_ID	The ID of the next execution step that uses the output of the current step.
DEPTH	The level of the operation in the tree.
POSITION	The order of processing for operations with the same PARENT_ID.
COST	The cost-based cost estimate. This is NULL for rule-based optimization.
CARDINALITY	The cost-based estimate of the number of rows.
BYTES	The cost-based estimate of the number of bytes.
OTHER	Other information.
OTHER_TAG	A description of the items in the OTHER column.
PARTITION_START	The starting partition.
PARTITION_STOP	The ending partition.

TABLE 4-1. *The New V$SQL_PLAN View Columns* (Continued)

All columns in the PLAN_TABLE view are also in the V$SQL_PLAN view with the exception of the LEVEL column. The ADDRESS, HASH_VALUE, CHILD_NUMBER, and DEPTH columns are in the V$SQL_PLAN view, but not in the PLAN_TABLE. You can join the V$SQL_PLAN view with the V$SQLAREA view using the ADDRESS and HASH_VALUE columns to obtain cursor-specific information. You can join the V$SQL_PLAN view with the V$SQL view using the ADDRESS, HASH_VALUE, and CHILD_NUMBER columns to obtain child-cursor-specific information.

Oracle9*i* also adds the PLAN_HASH_VALUE column to the V$SQL view that contains the hash value of the SQL plan for this cursor. You can use this value to determine if two SQL plans are the same.

First Rows Optimization

The CBO generates alternative data access execution plans and determines the least-cost alternative. The CBO uses statistics about various database objects and any hints you specify to determine the least-cost data access path. The cost represents anticipated resource consumption such as memory and CPU. The three common alternative data access paths are a full-table scan, index-based access, and ROWID-based access.

You can establish the mode and the goal for the optimization by setting the OPTIMIZER_MODE and OPTIMIZER_GOAL initialization parameters. The possible values for the OPTIMIZER_MODE parameter are RULE, ALL_ROWS, CHOOSE (the default), FIRST_ROWS, and FIRST_ROWS_n.

The RULE value specifies that the optimizer is to use rule-based optimization. The ALL_ROWS value specifies that the optimizer uses cost-based optimization for the least resource utilization. The CHOOSE value specifies that the optimizer is to use cost-based optimization if statistics are available; it must use rule-based optimization otherwise. If set to CHOOSE, Oracle will use the CBO if any of the objects used in processing the SQL statement have statistics generated.

The FIRST_ROWS parameter value specifies that the optimizer use a combination of cost- and rule-based heuristics optimization to retrieve a certain number of the first rows. It is quite likely that the heuristics generate an execution plan that is more expensive than a plan that can be generated without the heuristics. FIRST_ROWS is available in Oracle9*i* for backward compatibility.

Oracle9*i* has introduced the FIRST_ROWS_n parameter value that specifies cost-based optimization for retrieving the first set of rows in the shortest period of time. The value of *n* represents the number of rows to be returned. The possible values for *n* are 1, 10, 100, and 1000.

You can use FIRST_ROWS_n as shown in the following code:

```
ALTER SESSION
  SET OPTIMIZER_MODE = FIRST_ROWS_100;
```

You can set the OPTIMIZER_GOAL parameter to any value that you can assign to the OPTIMIZER_MODE parameter. The OPTIMIZER_GOAL parameter can override the optimizer approach specified by OPTIMIZER_MODE for a session. Here is an example that uses the OPTIMIZER_GOAL parameter:

```
ALTER SESSION
  SET OPTIMIZER_GOAL = FIRST_ROWS_10;
```

You can also specify an optimizer hint in a single SQL statement; the FIRST_ROWS(n) hint will override the values specified by both the OPTIMIZER_GOAL and OPTIMIZER_MODE parameters. The value of *n* in the FIRST_ROWS(n) hint can be any positive integer, so the FIRST_ROWS(n) hint gives you more flexibility to specify any number of rows for retrieval. If you omit *n* in the FIRST_ROWS(n) hint, the optimizer will resort to the behavior of the old FIRST_ROWS parameter.

Here is an example of using an optimizer hint:

```
SELECT /*+ FIRST_ROWS(28) */
       invoice_id, invoice_date,
       salesperson_id, amount
  FROM invoice
 WHERE salesperson_id = 319;
```

Gathering System Statistics

You can gather statistics about the operational, storage, and data distribution characteristics for objects such as tables, columns, indexes, and partitions with the DBMS_STATS package. Operational characteristics represent statistics about system-level resources such as CPU and IO utilization. The cost-based optimizer can use these statistics to determine the most efficient sequence for joins and the optimal execution plan that has the least cost.

Since the nature of the data captured in these statistics influences the determination of the execution plan, it is critical that you gather these statistics whenever large volumes of data have changed; otherwise, statistics will be stale and will mislead the optimizer. A safe approach is to generate statistics for all relevant tables, clusters, indexes, and partitions prior to using the cost-based approach.

Also, system statistics such as CPU and I/O utilization vary depending on the workload at the time the statistics are gathered. Therefore, you must gather these statistics during a period of time that represents the desired environmental workload.

When you gather system statistics, the parsed and cached SQL statements are not invalidated; Oracle just uses the new statistics to optimize new queries. This is not true with gathering table, index, or column statistics.

Oracle9*i* has introduced the following procedures within the DBMS_STATS package:

- **GATHER_SYSTEM_STATS** Gathers statistics about the system.
- **SET_SYSTEM_STATS** Sets system statistics in the table specified in the STATTAB parameter.
- **GET_SYSTEM_STATS** Gets system statistics from the table specified in the STATTAB parameter.

You can gather system characteristics with the following statement:

```
EXECUTE DBMS_STATS.GATHER_SYSTEM_STATS ( -
   interval => 60, -
   stattab   => 'teststats', -
   statid    => 'monthend' -
);
```

The STATID parameter enables you to name your set of statistics.

Oracle9*i* has introduced a new AUTO_SAMPLE_SIZE value for the ESTIMATE_PERCENT parameter used in various procedures within the DBMS_STATS. This value enables Oracle9*i* to determine the optimum size for the ESTIMATE_PERCENT parameter.

Oracle9i introduces the following new options for the METHOD_OPT parameter in various procedures in DBMS_STATS:

- **SKEWONLY** Creates a histogram based on just the data distribution.
- **REPEAT** Creates a histogram with the same number of buckets.
- **AUTO** Creates a histogram based on data distribution and the manner in which the column is accessed by the application.

Here is an example of how you can use the AUTO_SAMPLE_SIZE value:

```
EXECUTE DBMS_STATS.GATHER_TABLE_STATS ( -
  ownname          => 'oe', -
  tabname          => 'invoice', -
  partname         => 'oe_tbsp', -
  estimate_percent => DBMS_STATS.AUTO_SAMPLE_SIZE, -
  method_opt       => 'FOR ALL COLUMNS SIZE AUTO' -
  );
```

Oracle9*i* also introduces the GATHER AUTO value for the OPTIONS parameter in various procedures in DBMS_STATS. The GATHER AUTO option is similar to executing GATHER_SCHEMA_STATS with both the GATHER STALE and GATHER EMPTY options. Here is an example with the GATHER AUTO value:

```
EXECUTE DBMS_STATS.GATHER_SCHEMA_STATS ( -
  ownname          => 'oe', -
  estimate_percent => DBMS_STATS.AUTO_SAMPLE_SIZE, -
  options          => 'GATHER AUTO' -
  );
```

The cost-based optimizer in Oracle8*i* had a number of limitations. For example, the cost model assumed that the columns were independent of one another when it determined the selectivity of multiple predicates. Oracle9*i* introduces the following enhancements to the cost model:

- Oracle9i adds the following new columns to the PLAN_TABLE:
  - **CPU_COST** The estimated CPU cost for cost-based optimization specified in seconds, null for rule-based.

- **IO_COST** The estimated I/O cost for cost-based specified in seconds, null for rule-based.
- **TEMP_SPACE** The estimated temporary space for cost-based specified In bytes, null for rule-based.

- The cost model estimates CPU utilization for SQL functions and operators.
- The cost model addresses the cost savings in caching for nested-loop joins; it also addresses index pre-fetching.

For Review

1. You must know how to start and stop index monitoring, as well as how to display the utilization information.
2. You must understand skip scan technology when using composite indexes.
3. You must know the difference between the EXACT, SIMILAR, and FORCE values for the CURSOR_SHARING parameter.
4. You must be familiar with cached execution plans and with the columns of the V$SQL_PLAN view.
5. You must be able to use the FIRST_ROWS_n parameter value to specify cost-based optimization for retrieving the first set of rows.
6. You must know about gathering system statistics that are considered by the optimizer when determining a least-cost execution plan.

Exercises

1. **Which of the following procedures was added in Oracle9*i* to collect statistics?**

   A. COLLECT_SYSTEM_STATS

   B. GATHER_SYSTEM_STATS

   C. GATHER_OBJECT_STATS

   D. COLLECT_OBJECT_STATS

2. **Skip scan technology enables you to use the composite index when**

   A. The composite index is in the shared read mode.

   B. The composite index is in the write lock mode.

   C. The prefix index column is omitted in the SQL statement.

   D. The prefix index column is specified in the SQL statement.

Answer Key
1. B. **2.** C.

Real Application Clusters (RACs)

Oracle9i has introduced RACs that enable you to start multiple instances or nodes that concurrently interact and transact with one database. The previous generation of the RAC technology was called the Oracle Parallel Server (OPS) in Oracle8*i*. The RAC configuration is a set of interconnected clusters of nodes with the database residing on a set of shared disks (see Figure 4-1). A node is one instance that runs on a set of processors, shared memory, and shared disks. A cluster is a set of loosely coupled nodes.

The Oracle RAC manages communications, control, and access between the nodes and the shared database to implement a concurrent solution that is characterized by concurrency, consistency, instance transparency, and data integrity. Instance transparency assures that you will get the same results no matter which instance executes your transactions. Each database instance has its own system global area (SGA), background processes (such as the log writer process), and the archive log. Instances within a cluster also share or have access to SGAs, control files, data files, and online redo logs throughout the cluster.

This section discusses the following topics:

- The benefits of Oracle RACs
- RAC architecture
- Resource modes and resource roles
- Cache Fusion

Benefits of Oracle RACs

The fact that many instances can concurrently interact with one database offers a number of distinct advantages. RACs offer the following benefits:

- **Performance** You can divide a task into smaller units and assign these units to different instances to be concurrently executed. You can add more nodes to improve the performance.
- **Scalability** As the number of users increases, you can add new nodes and instances to the RAC.

- **Availability** When one instance is not operational, you still have access to the remaining instances. The failure of one node does not affect any other node. The nodes are insulated from each other in the RAC.

RAC Architecture

A RAC is an organized interconnection of clusters that provide coordinated and concurrent access to a shared database, using an operating-system-dependent (OSD) layered architecture. RACs are comprised of the following components:

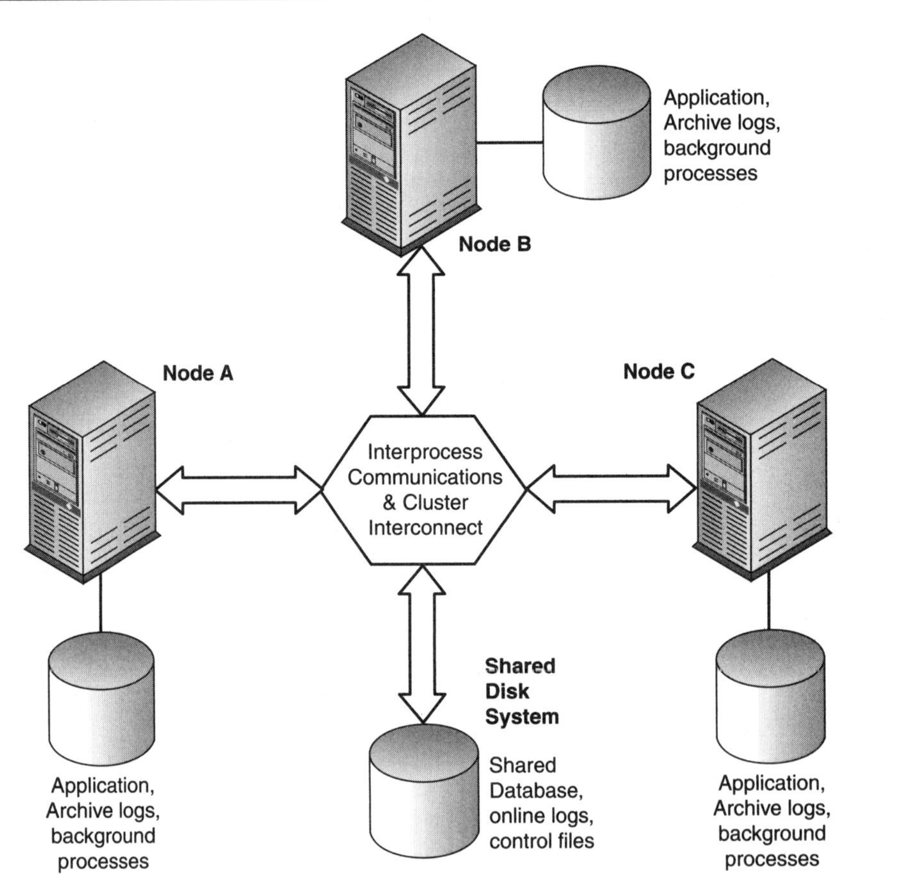

FIGURE 4-1. *The Oracle RAC configuration*

- **Cluster Manager** The Cluster Manager is the chief operating officer of the cluster. It manages node membership in the cluster, terminates (or fires) the node if it is inactive or not doing its job properly, and communicates with nodes about the status of various resources and about changes in node membership.
- **Global Cache Service (GCS)** The GCS is a fault-tolerant administrative assistant. It transparently coordinates access to the shared database and to other shared resources in the shared database. The GCS also improves load distribution by "smartly" assigning resources to instances. Other than obtaining the status of nodes in the cluster from the Cluster Manager, the GCS is independent of it.
- **Interprocess Communications (IPC) and Cluster Interconnect (CI)** The IPC is the chief of corporate communications. It provides the connectivity between the nodes, specifies asynchronous Message Oriented Middleware (MOM) to facilitate interprocess message exchange, and provides the interfaces to physically send messages across the cluster. This CI mechanism must be high speed; otherwise, cluster performance will degrade since processes are waiting for requests and responses from other processes. The IPC communications layer enables other services at higher layers, such as the GCS, to fulfill their responsibilities.
- **Shared disk subsystem** The disk subsystem is the inventory clerk. It provides concurrent access to the disk and to the database on the disk for all client nodes in the cluster. The performance of the disk subsystem is critical to the performance of the cluster since it is the common element that services all nodes. Since the disk subsystem is the single point of failure (SPOF), it is important that you engineer it for fault tolerance.

Resource Modes and Resource Roles

The GCS manages access to shared resources in the cluster. The most popular resource request by the instances is for datablocks. The GCS ensures that the different instances have appropriate access to the shared database buffer caches, even though you may have different versions of a datablock in existence. The GCS works with the Lock Management Services (LMS) to ensure that only one instance can modify a datablock at any given point in time; GCS assigns a datablock to an instance on a first-come, first-served basis only if it has the privileges to access that block. GCS provides, transmits, and synchronizes cache access on a cluster-wide basis. It also assigns the datablock to an instance on a cluster-wide basis and makes the status of caches visible to all the nodes in the cluster. An instance can *hold* a resource in one of the following modes:

- **NULL** This indicates that the instance does not have specific rights.
- **Shared** In this mode, multiple processes can read the datablock, and the holding instance cannot modify the datablock.
- **Exclusive** Here the instance has exclusive rights to modify the datablock. Other instances can only hold it in NULL mode.

These modes were available in prior versions.

Oracle9*i* has also introduced *resource roles,* in which an instance can hold a resource in either the local or global role. The *local resource role* implements the behavior of previous releases. When one instance holds a resource in the exclusive mode, other instances can only hold the resource in the NULL mode. The *global resource role* enables other instances to hold the resource in shared or NULL mode when one instance holds it in the exclusive mode.

Cache Fusion

Let's assume that one instance has changed a datablock in its cache, and another instance is requesting the data pertaining to that datablock. The requesting instance needs the current image of the datablock in the holding instance. The GCS requests the holding instance for the current image of the datablock in its cache. The GCS then provides three methods for transferring the block from the holding instance to the requesting instance:

- **Block Transfer with Forced Disk Write** Using this method, only one instance can modify a datablock at any given point in time. The holding instance writes the current image in its cache to the shared disk. The requesting instance reads the recently updated datablock on the shared disk. This was the only method available prior to Oracle8.1. The forced disk write method is not used as often, so instead you choose the newer Cache Fusion technology that significantly improves performance (see Figure 4-2).
- **Read Consistent Cache Fusion** The holding instance creates a read-consistent image in its own buffer for direct cache-to-cache transmission to the requesting instance. Because this block transfer method does not involve disk writes, it has significant gains in performance over the Forced Disk Write method. The Read Consistent Cache Fusion method was introduced in Oracle8*i*.
- **Cache Fusion Block Transfer** This is a direct cache-to-cache block transfer method introduced in Oracle9*i* to transfer either clean or dirty blocks (see Figure 4-3).

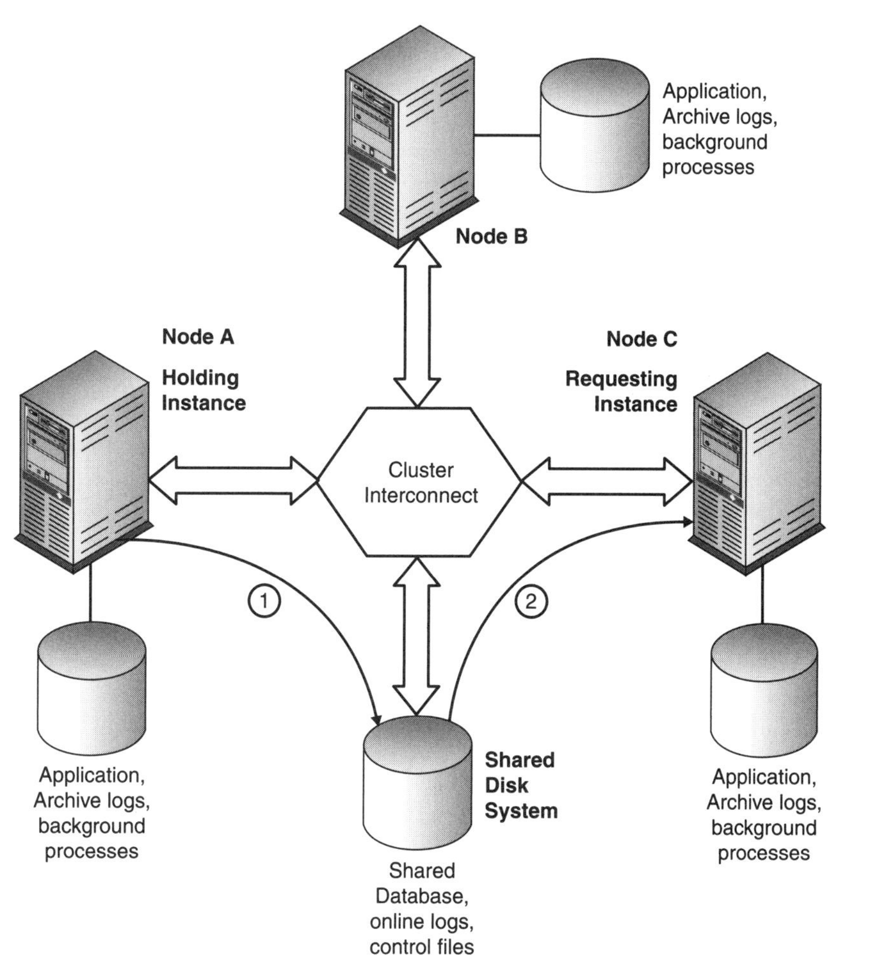

FIGURE 4-2. *The Block Transfer with Forced Disk Write method*

Shared Server-Side Initialization Parameter File

The shared server configuration of RACs significantly enhances the performance of applications and improves the availability of the cluster. In the shared server configuration, the user process connects to a dispatcher; then the dispatcher directs incoming session requests to a common queue. When the server process is available, the dispatcher connects the request to an idle dispatcher. In this clustered environment, a small number of shared servers can service a lot of database instances.

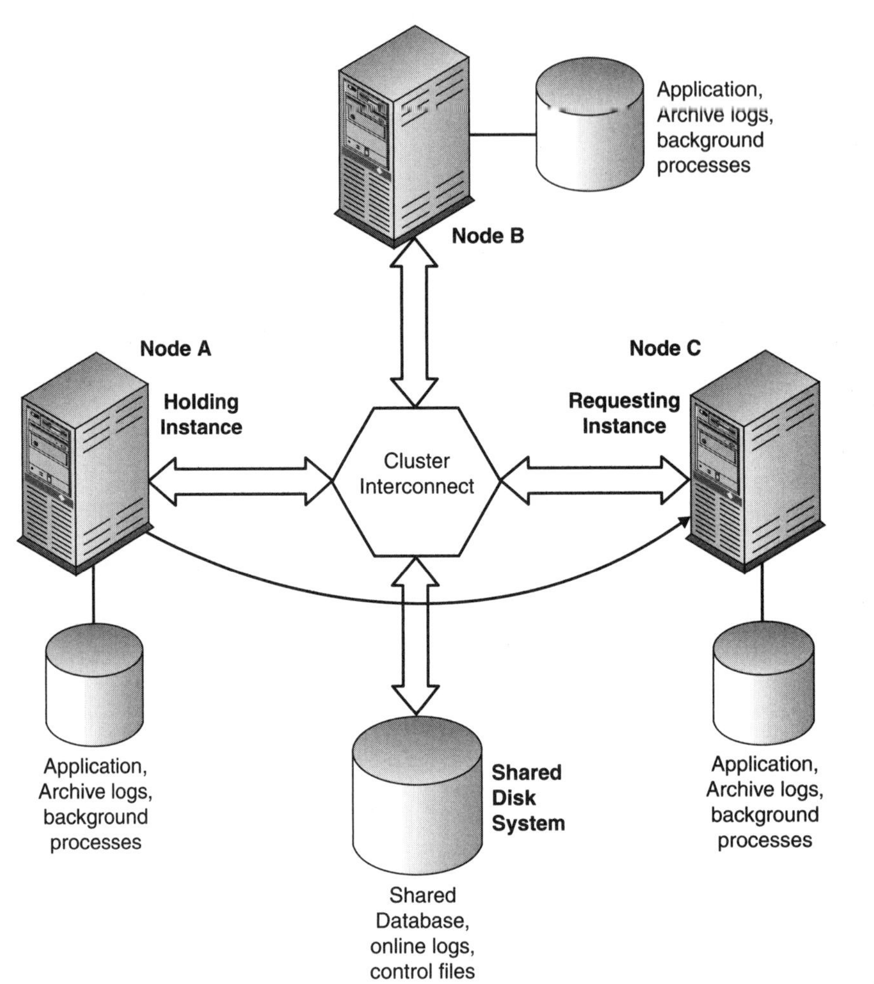

FIGURE 4-3. *The Cache Fusion Block Transfer method*

Prior to Oracle9*i*, each one of these instances required its own initialization parameter file. It was your responsibility to ensure that the appropriate parameters in these instance parameter files were the same. Besides the hassle of maintaining many files, it imposed a quality problem because it is next to impossible to keep the same information in many files consistent. DBAs addressed this problem by storing the common parameters in one file and referencing that common file in each instance file by using the IFILE initialization parameter.

Oracle9*i* overcame these problems by enabling you to store the parameters for all instances in one initialization parameter file that you can share among all instances. You can specify instance-specific parameters by prefixing the initialization parameter with the name of the instance, as shown in the following example where you have two instances named *accounting* and *marketing*:

```
accounting.processes = 50
marketing.processes  = 80
```

While you minimized the management hassle, you still have to store a copy of the initialization parameter file on each node to facilitate startup of the instances. You can avoid distributing copies by converting this initialization parameter file into a Server Parameter File (SPFILE). Then you put just the one parameter, as shown here, in the initialization parameter file for each instance:

```
spfile = oracle_home:\config\spfile
```

For Review

1. You must know the benefits of RACs.
2. You must understand how the components work together to accomplish the mission of the RACs.
3. You must know the difference between the NULL, shared, and exclusive resource modes. You must know about the local and global resource roles, and how they modify the implication of the exclusive resource mode.
4. You must know about the different ways you can transfer blocks between instances and about the advantages of Cache Fusion.
5. You must be able to specify common parameters and instance-specific parameters in one SPFILE, and to share it among all the instances in the cluster.

Exercises

1. **Which of the following components specifies the Message Oriented Middleware (MOM) protocols?**

   A. Cluster Manager

   B. Global Cache Service (GCS)

   C. Interprocess Communications (IPC) and Cluster Interconnect (CI)

   D. None of the above

2. When an instance holds a resource in the NULL mode

A. The instance deletes all the information in the resource.

B. The instance has read rights, but cannot write; other instances have no rights.

C. Only this instance can modify the datablock; other instances have no rights.

D. The instance has no specific rights.

Answer Key

1. C. **2.** D.

Chapter Summary

Indexes are logical structures associated with tables and clusters that provide SQL statements with a faster data access path. Oracle uses a variety of indexing schemes such as B-tree (the default), Hash, Bitmap, Global, and Local. Oracle9*i* enables you to *monitor index utilization* with the MONITORING USAGE clause for the ALTER INDEX command. The utilization information is available in the V$OBJECT_USAGE view.

In prior versions, Oracle would not use a composite index if you did not specify the prefix index column in the SQL statement. If you overcame this problem by creating another index, you would be increasing the overhead during DML operations. Oracle9*i* provides *skip scanning* technology that enables you to use the composite index even if the prefix index column is omitted in the SQL statement.

The Oracle database provides *shared cursors* to enhance performance by reusing the parsed and cached statement when the statement is executed again. You can enable cursor sharing by setting the CURSOR_SHARING initialization parameter to either EXACT, SIMILAR, or FORCE. Oracle9*i* introduces the SIMILAR value to specify that the database should only reuse execution plans for similar statements (statements that differ just in the literal values) when you are guaranteed that performance will never degrade when you reuse the execution plan.

Oracle9*i* provides the V$SQL_PLAN view to display the cached execution plan, the compilation environment, and execution statistics. A *cached execution plan* enables you to analyze the plan without having to rerun the SQL statement.

The FIRST_ROWS parameter uses both cost- and rule-based heuristics to optimize the retrieval of a first set of rows. Sometimes the resulting execution plan can be more expensive than a plan that is generated without the heuristic. Oracle9*i* mitigated this problem with the FIRST_ROWS_n parameter that tells the database to use cost-based optimization.

You can gather operational, storage, and data distribution characteristics for objects such as tables, columns, indexes, and partitions. Oracle9*i* gives you many enhancements to gather statistics about the system. Among these enhancements are three new procedures (GATHER_SYSTEM_STATS, GET_SYSTEM_STATS, and SET_SYSTEM_STATS) related to system statistics. You can pass these statistics to the optimizer to help it determine the lowest-cost execution plan.

Oracle Real Application Clusters (RACs) is an integrated, interconnected computing solution that enables multiple computers to share one database. The advantages of the RAC concept are performance, scalability, and availability. Oracle RAC accomplishes its mission with four components: Cluster Manager, Global Cache Service (GCS), Interprocess Communications (IPC), and the shared disk subsystem.

A database instance can hold a resource in NULL, shared, or exclusive resource mode to ensure data integrity and coherency. Oracle9*i* has introduced resource roles that can be set to either local or global. When it is local, it behaves just like it did in Oracle8*i*. If you set it to global, it adds the possibility for other instances to hold the resource in shared mode when one instance holds it in exclusive mode.

Cache Fusion eliminates the need for the holding instance to write the modified datablock to a disk and for the requesting instance to pick it up from the disk. Cache fusion transfers the block directly from the cache of the holding instance to the cache of the requesting instance. This direct memory-cache-to-memory-cache transfer enhances throughput and performance significantly because disk I/O is relatively very slow compared to memory I/O.

In prior releases, you had to create an initialization parameter file for each instance. In Oracle9*i*, you can maintain both common parameters and instance specify parameters in one server parameter file. You can reference instance specify parameters by prefixing them with the name of the instance.

Two-Minute Drill

1. Index monitoring

- Unused indexes constitute unnecessary overhead because these indexes must also be updated during DML operations.
- You can monitor index utilization with the ALTER INDEX parts_ix MONITORING USAGE statement.
- You query the V$OBJECT_USAGE view to determine whether or not an index has been used.

- You should drop unused indexes because they increase overhead when you perform DML operations.
- You can stop index monitoring with the NOMONITORING USAGE clause.

2. **Skip scan index access**
   - Prior to Oracle9*i*, the optimizer would skip a composite index if the SQL statement omitted the prefix index column.
   - If you mitigated this situation by creating an additional index, you would be introducing a significant overhead during DML operations.
   - Oracle9*i* introduces skip scanning technology that enables you to use the composite index even when the prefix index column is omitted in the SQL statement.
   - When the prefix index column is omitted, skip scanning technology treats the composite index search as a number of smaller subindex searches, one for each distinct value within the prefix index column.
3. **Cursor sharing**
   - Shared cursors enable you to reuse the parsed and cached statement when you execute the same statement over and over again.
   - You enable cursor sharing be setting the CURSOR_SHARING initialization parameter to EXACT (default), SIMILAR, or FORCE.
   - When you specify EXACT, Oracle will reuse the parsed and cached statement only if the executing statement is exactly the same as the cached statement.
   - CURSOR_SHARING is a dynamic parameter that you can also set with the ALTER SYSTEM or ALTER SESSION statement.
   - Two statements are similar when the only difference between them is in the literal values.
   - When you set CURSOR_SHARING to SIMILAR, Oracle will reuse the execution plan of a similar statement only if you are assured that the execution plan is optimal for all these similar statements.
4. **Cached execution plans**
   - You can cache the execution plan for a statement so you can analyze the execution plan later without the need to rerun the query.
   - Oracle9*i* introduces the V$SQL_PLAN view to display the cached execution plan.

- All columns in the PLAN_TABLE view are also in the V$SQL_PLAN view with the exception of the LEVEL column. The ADDRESS, HASH_VALUE, CHILD_NUMBER, and DEPT columns are in the V$SQL_PLAN view, but not in the PLAN_TABLE view.

5. **First rows optimization**

   - Prior to Oracle9*i*, the FIRST_ROWS parameter enabled you to specify the number of rows you wanted to retrieve as part of the first set of rows. The optimizer used a combination of cost-based and rule-based heuristics to determine an execution plan. Sometimes the resulting plan was much more expensive than a plan that was generated when the optimizer did not use the heuristics.
   - Oracle9*i* addresses this problem by introducing the FIRST_ROWS_n parameter value that always uses cost-based optimization to retrieve first rows. The value of *n* can be 1, 10, 100, or 1000.
   - You can use FIRST_ROWS_n using the following command:

   ```
   ALTER SESSION SET OPTIMIZER_MODE = FIRST_ROWS_100.
   ```

   - The FIRST_ROWS_n optimizer hint enables you to specify any number of rows in the first set. This hint will override the values specified in OPTIMIZER_MODE and OPTIMIZER_GOAL parameters.

6. **Gathering system statistics**

   - You can gather statistics about the storage and data distribution characteristics of database objects such as tables, columns, indexes, and partitions. The optimizer can use these statistics to determine an optimal execution plan.
   - Oracle9*i* enables you to collect operational statistics about the system. It gives you the GATHER_SYSTEM_STATS, SET_SYSTEM_STATS, and GET_SYSTEM_STATS procedures in the DBMS_STATS package.
   - Oracle9*i* has added the GATHER AUTO value for the OPTIONS parameter of various procedures in DBMS_STATS.
   - It also adds the CPU_COST, IO_COST, and TEMP_SPACE columns to the PLAN_TABLE.

7. **Real Application Clusters (RACs)**

   - RAC exploits the computing potential of multiple computers by enabling them to work together effectively as they share the computing load.

- The Cluster Manager controls cluster membership and makes all nodes aware of the status of the member clusters.
- You can add nodes to an RAC configuration to improve performance and to address the computing needs of additional users.
- Cache Fusion eliminates disk I/O and enhances read concurrency by transferring datablocks directly between the caches of instances. Cache Fusion greatly improves performance.
- In Oracle9*i*, you can store common parameters and instance-specific parameters in one SPFILE within a RAC configuration.

Fill-in-the-Blanks

1. ________ are optional logical structures associated with tables and clusters that enable SQL statements to execute more quickly against a table.
2. You can display information about index utilization by querying the ______ view.
3. Skip scanning enables you to use the __________ index even when the index prefix column is omitted in the SQL statement.
4. When you set the CURSOR_SHARING parameter to _________, Oracle will share one execution plan among all similar statements.
5. You can display the cached execution plan by querying the ________ view.
6. You can generate and manage system statistics to optimize SQL statements by executing procedures in the SQL ________ package.
7. The FIRST_ROWS_n parameter value specifies that the optimization is entirely ______ based.
8. The ____________ controls cluster membership and provides the status of all instances cluster-wide.
9. The ____________ assigns resources to requesting instances.
10. The GCS works with the _______________ to ensure that only one instance can modify a datablock at any given point in time.
11. Cache Fusion enables you to transfer datablocks directly between the _________ of the holding instance and the ________ or the requesting instance.
12. In the shared resource mode, many instances can read the _________________.

Chapter Questions

1. **The default index mechanism is**
   - **A.** B-tree index
   - **B.** B-tree hash index
   - **C.** Hash cluster index
   - **D.** Global and local index
2. **To start monitoring index utilization, you use**
   - **A.** ALTER INDEX part_ix MONITORING UTILIZATION
   - **B.** ALTER INDEX part_ix SET MONITORING = ON
   - **C.** ALTER INDEX part_ix MONITORING USAGE
   - **D.** ALTER SYSTEM SET MONITORING = ON
3. **System statistics enable the optimizer to perform**
   - **A.** Cost-based optimization
   - **B.** Rule-based optimization
   - **C.** A combination of cost-based optimization and rule-based optimization
   - **D.** Statistical sampling optimization
4. **The values that CURSOR_SHARING can take are**
   - **A.** BASIC, SIMILAR, FORCE
   - **B.** SIMILAR, ALL, BASIC
   - **C.** FORCE, SAFE, EXACT
   - **D.** SIMILAR, EXACT, FORCE
5. **The column that Oracle9*i* added to the V$SQL view is**
   - **A.** HASH_VALUE
   - **B.** COST
   - **C.** COST_ESTIMATE
   - **D.** PLAN_HASH_VALUE

6. **Oracle9*i* has introduced the following parameter value to specify the number of rows to be retrieved as part of the first set of rows:**

   A. FIRST_ROWS

   B. FIRST_ROWS_n

   C. NUMBER_OF_ROWS

   D. ROWS_n

7. **Oracle9*i* has introduced the following value for the ESTIMATE_PERCENT parameter in various DBMS_STATS procedure calls:**

   A. OPTIMUM_ESTIMATE

   B. BEST_SAMPLE_SIZE

   C. AUTO_SAMPLE_SIZE

   D. AUTO_ESTIMATE

8. **When an instance holds a resource in the shared mode, which of the following is true?**

   A. The holding instance can modify the datablock and can share this modify privilege with the other instances.

   B. The holding instance can modify the datablock, but it cannot share this modify privilege with the other instances.

   C. Many instances can read the datablock; the holding instance cannot modify the datablock.

   D. Many instances can read the datablock; the holding instance can modify the datablock.

9. **Which of the following statements is true about Cache Fusion?**

   A. Cache Fusion writes or fuses the cache to disk.

   B. Cache Fusion synchronizes or fuses the cache with the disk.

   C. Cache Fusion continuously synchronizes or fuses the caches of two instances.

   D. Cache Fusion performs a direct cache-to-cache datablock transfer.

10. **Which of the following will set an instance-specific parameter, *processes,* to *100* for the marketing *instance*?**

    A. marketing.processes = 100

    B. processes = 100 (marketing)

C. processes (marketing) = 100

D. marketing (processes) = 100

Fill-in-the-Blank Answers

1. indexes
2. V$OBJECT_USAGE
3. composite
4. FORCE
5. V$SQL_PLAN
6. DBMS_STATS
7. cost
8. Cluster Manager
9. Global Cache Service (GCS)
10. Lock Management Services (LMS)
11. cache or buffer, cache or buffer
12. datablock

Answers to Chapter Questions

1. A. B-tree index

Explanation Indexes are logical structures associated with tables and clusters that provide SQL statements a faster data access path. Oracle uses a variety of indexing schemes such as B-tree, Hash, Bitmap, Function-based, Global, and Local. The default index mechanism is the B-tree index.

2. C. ALTER INDEX part_ix MONITORING USAGE

Explanation You can start monitoring an index for usage with this statement. If an index is unused, it should be a good candidate for being dropped because it needs to be updated during DML operations even if it is not used.

3. A. Cost-based optimization

Explanation You can gather statistics about the operational, storage, and data distribution characteristics for objects such as tables, columns, indexes, and partitions with the DBMS_STATS package. Operational characteristics represent statistics about system-level resources such as CPU and I/O utilization. The cost-based optimizer can use these statistics to determine the most efficient sequence for joins and the optimal execution plan that has the least cost.

4. D. SIMILAR, EXACT, FORCE

Explanation EXACT specifies that Oracle will reuse the parsed and cached statement if the executing statement is exactly the same as the cached statement. SIMILAR specifies that Oracle will reuse the execution of a similar statement only if you can be assured that the plan will be optimal for the executing similar statement. Two statements are said to be similar if the only difference is in the specific value of the literals. FORCE specifies that Oracle will reuse the execution plan for all similar statements regardless of whether or not you may encounter some degradation.

5. D. PLAN_HASH_VALUE

Explanation Oracle9*i* has added the PLAN_HASH_VALUE column to the V$SQL view. This column contains the hash value of the SQL plan for this cursor.

6. B. FIRST_ROWS_n

Explanation Oracle9*i* has introduced the FIRST_ROWS_n parameter value that specifies cost-based optimization for retrieving the first set of rows in the shortest period of time. The value of *n* represents the number of rows to be returned. The possible values for *n* are 1, 10, 100, and 1000. You can use FIRST_ROWS_n as follows: `ALTER SESSION SET OPTIMIZER_MODE = FIRST_ROWS_100;`

7. C. AUTO_SAMPLE_SIZE

Explanation When you specify AUTO_SAMPLE_SIZE value for the ESTIMATE_PERCENT parameter in DBMS_STATS procedure calls, Oracle will determine the optimum size for the ESTIMATE_PERCENT parameter.

8. C. Many instances can read the datablock; the holding instance cannot modify the datablock.

Explanation An instance can *hold* a resource in one of the following modes:

- **NULL** This indicates that the instance does not have specific rights.
- **Shared** Here multiple processes can read the datablock; the holding instance cannot modify the datablock.
- **Exclusive** Here the instance has exclusive rights to modify the datablock. Other instances can only hold it in NULL mode.

These modes were available in prior versions.

9. D. Cache Fusion performs a direct cache-to-cache datablock transfer.

Explanation The GCS provides three methods for transferring the block from the holding instance to the requesting instance:

- **Block Transfer with Forced Disk Write** Only one instance can modify a datablock at any given point in time. The holding instance writes the current image in its cache to the shared disk. The requesting instance reads the recently updated datablock on the shared disk. This was the only method prior to Oracle8.1.
- **Read Consistent Cache Fusion** The holding instance creates a read-consistent image in its own buffer for direct cache-to-cache transmission to the requesting instance. The Read Consistent Cache Fusion method was introduced in Oracle8*i*.
- **Cache Fusion Block Transfer** This is a direct cache-to-cache block transfer method introduced in Oracle9*i* to transfer either clean or dirty blocks.

10. A. marketing.processes = 100.

Explanation Prior to Oracle9*i*, each one of these instances required its own initialization parameter file. Oracle9*i* enables you to store the parameters for all instances in one initialization parameter file that you can share among all instances. You can specify instance-specific parameters by prefixing the initialization parameter with the name of the instance, as shown in the following example where you have two instances named *accounting* and *marketing*:

```
accounting.processes = 50
marketing.processes  = 80
```

CHAPTER 5

Language Enhancements

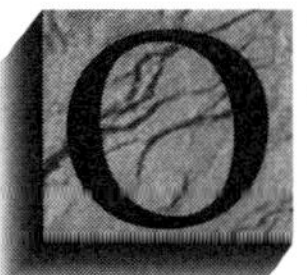

racle9*i* introduces a number of significant enhancements in the context of language. This chapter focuses on

- Enhancements to SQL
- Enhancements to globalization

Enhancements SQL

This section discusses the following Oracle9*i* enhancements to address the SQL language:

- The International Organization for Standardization/American National Standards Institute (ISO/ANSI) standardization
- Constraints
- FOR UPDATE WAIT
- Large Objects (LOBs)
- Procedural Language/SQL (PL/SQL)

ISO/ANSI Standardization

Standards bodies such as ANSI and ISO enhance the SQL language on a regular basis. The most recent official release of the SQL language is called SQL:99, and it was officially adopted in July 1999. SQL:99 represents both the ISO/IEC 9075-1:1999 and ANSI x3.135-1999 standards. Oracle9*i* introduces a number of enhancements that implement the SQL:99 standards. Some of which are as follows:

- Join statements
- CASE statements
- Scalar subqueries
- MERGE
- Analytic functions

Join Statements

Prior to Oracle9*i*, the join operation was implied; Oracle performed a join operation when you listed multiple tables after the FROM clause. Oracle9*i* implements full SQL:99 syntax, and SQL:99 syntax calls for the keyword JOIN explicitly. SQL:99 calls for the following types of joins:

- The CROSS JOIN
- Equijoin with the NATURAL JOIN keywords
- Equijoin with the USING keyword
- The ON clause
- The OUTER JOIN

The CROSS JOIN The CROSS JOIN specifies the cross product, also called a Cartesian product. The CROSS JOIN is the same operation performed when you specify two or more comma-separated tables in the FROM clause without specifying a join condition.

Let's assume you have a table called FLAVOR to track ice cream flavors, and that the table contains the following values:

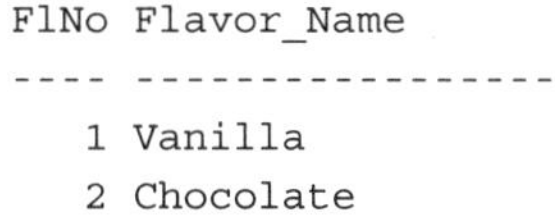

```
FlNo Flavor_Name
---- ------------------
   1 Vanilla
   2 Chocolate
   3 Strawberry
```

Let's assume you have a table called TOPPING to track the toppings, and that this table contains the following values:

```
TpNo Topping_Name
---- ------------------
   A Hot Fudge
   B Sprinkles
   C M&Ms
```

Prior to Oracle9*i*, you would use the following query to perform the CROSS JOIN and get the Cartesian product:

```
SELECT flavor_name, topping_name
  FROM flavor, topping;

FLAVOR_NAME        TOPPING_NAME
------------------ ------------------
Vanilla            Hot Fudge
Vanilla            Sprinkles
Vanilla            M&Ms
Chocolate          Hot Fudge
Chocolate          Sprinkles
Chocolate          M&Ms
```

```
Strawberry          Hot Fudge
Strawberry          Sprinkles
Strawberry          M&Ms
```

You would specify the same query using SQL:99 in Oracle9*i* with the CROSS JOIN as follows:

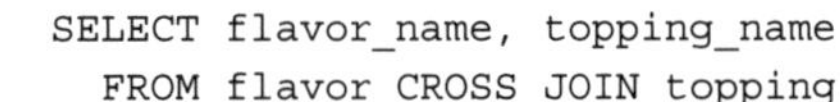

```
SELECT flavor_name, topping_name
  FROM flavor CROSS JOIN topping;

FLAVOR_NAME         TOPPING_NAME
------------------ ------------------
Vanilla             Hot Fudge
Vanilla             Sprinkles
Vanilla             M&Ms
Chocolate           Hot Fudge
Chocolate           Sprinkles
Chocolate           M&Ms
Strawberry          Hot Fudge
Strawberry          Sprinkles
Strawberry          M&Ms
```

The advantages of using the SQL:99 syntax is that you can exchange SQL queries with other databases that are SQLX:99 compliant, and you are explicitly using the keyword JOIN to specify the join operation.

Equijoin with the NATURAL JOIN Keywords The NATURAL JOIN matches rows that have equal values in all columns that have the same name. Oracle assumes that the matching columns with the same name also have the same datatype. If they have different datatypes, you will encounter an error. Depending on the datatypes of the different columns, you could get the `ORA-01722: invalid number` error. Also, the matching columns cannot be a LOB column or a collection column.

Let's consider a third table named CLIENT with the following data:

```
ClNo Client_Name        FlNo Qty
---- ------------------ ---- ---
   A Andy                  1   4
   B Beth                  1   2
   C Carol                 3   2
```

Prior to Oracle9*i*, you used the following query to perform the NATURAL JOIN:

```
SELECT client_name, flavor_name, qty
  FROM client, flavor
 where client.flno = flavor.flno;

CLIENT_NAME        FLAVOR_NAME        QTY
------------------ ------------------ ---
Andy               Vanilla              4
Beth               Vanilla              2
Carol              Strawberry           2
```

You would get the same results when you specify the same query using SQL:99 in Oracle9*i* as follows:

```
SELECT client_name, flavor_name, qty
  FROM client NATURAL JOIN flavor;
```

With the SQL:99 syntax, you do not have to specify the join condition specifically in the WHERE clause.

The following query attempts to also display the FLNO column, which is involved in the join condition:

```
SELECT client_name, flno, flavor_name, qty
  FROM client, flavor
 where client.flno = flavor.flno;
```

This query yields an "ambiguous column" error. You are forced to prefix it with the name of the table or the table alias as follows:

```
SELECT client_name, client.flno, flavor_name, qty
  FROM client, flavor
 where client.flno = flavor.flno;
```

You do not have to prefix the name of the column with the SQL:99 syntax; the following query would be valid:

```
SELECT client_name, flno, flavor_name, qty
  FROM client NATURAL JOIN flavor;

CLIENT_NAME        FLNO FLAVOR_NAME        QTY
------------------ ---- ------------------ ---
Andy                  1 Vanilla              4
Beth                  1 Vanilla              2
Carol                 3 Strawberry           2
```

The following query qualifies the FLNO column:

```
SELECT client_name, client.flno, flavor_name, qty
  FROM client NATURAL JOIN flavor;
```

This query is not valid because you are not allowed to add the table name or alias prefix with the NATURAL JOIN; it results in the following error:

```
ORA-25155:  column used in NATURAL join cannot have qualifier
```

The new syntax does not need nor does it permit a table prefix with a column in the select list.

Prior to Oracle9*i*, the following SELECT * query would yield an ambiguous column error:

```
SELECT *
  FROM client, flavor
 where client.flno = flavor.flno;
```

With SQL:99, the following SELECT * query would not yield an ambiguous column error:

```
SELECT *
  FROM client NATURAL JOIN flavor;
```

This is a valid query; it displays the FLNO column only once.

Equijoin with the USING Keyword One problem with the NATURAL JOIN specification is that it uses all the matching columns that have the same name. You can perform the equijoin on a subset of the matching columns with the USING clause.

Let's assume that you have two matching columns in the CLIENT and FLAVOR tables. The USING keyword enables you to perform an equijoin on just one of those matching columns as follows:

```
SELECT client_name, flavor_name, qty
  FROM client JOIN flavor USING (flno);

CLIENT_NAME        FLAVOR_NAME        QTY
------------------ ------------------ ---
Andy               Vanilla              4
Beth               Vanilla              2
Carol              Strawberry           2
```

You are not allowed to prefix join columns in the USING clause with the name of the table or the table alias; it will return the following error:

```
ORA-25155:  column used in NATURAL join cannot have qualifier
```

Also, you are not allowed to use LOB columns or collection columns in the USING clause for the join condition.

The ON Clause Instead of having to specify a join condition along with other criteria in the WHERE clause, the ON clause enables you to specify the join condition separate from the other criteria. Here is an example:

```
SELECT client_name, flavor_name, qty
  FROM client JOIN flavor
       ON (client.flno = flavor.flno)
 WHERE client_name IN ('Andy', 'Carol');

CLIENT_NAME        FLAVOR_NAME        QTY
------------------ ------------------ ---
Andy               Vanilla              4
Carol              Strawberry           2
```

You have greater flexibility with the ON clause than with the NATURAL JOIN or the USING clauses, which restrict you to an equijoin. The ON clause enables you to use any logical operator. You can specify any condition in the ON clause that you can include in a WHERE clause, and this includes subqueries.

The OUTER JOIN Outer joins enable you to retrieve rows that satisfy the join condition as well as rows in a table where no rows from the other table satisfy the join condition. Even when ANSI and ISO standards for outer joins did not exist, many past versions of Oracle enabled you to specify the outer join with the (+) qualifier. You could only specify one (+) qualifier to give you a left or right outer join.

In Oracle9*i*, you can use the SQL:99 specification for the outer join, where you can explicitly use the keywords OUTER JOIN instead of the not so readable (+) qualifier.

Let's assume you inserted the following row of data into the CLIENT table:

```
ClNo Client_Name        FlNo Qty
---- ------------------ ---- ---
   D David                 7   4
```

Here is the CLIENT table data:

```
ClNo Client_Name        FlNo Qty
---- ------------------ ---- ---
   A Andy                  1   4
   B Beth                  1   2
   C Carol                 3   2
   D David                 7   4
```

And here is the FLAVOR table data:

```
FlNo Flavor_Name
---- ------------------
   1 Vanilla
   2 Chocolate
   3 Strawberry
```

The fourth row in the CLIENT table (David) has a FLNO value of 7, which has no corresponding row in the FLAVOR table. The second row in the FLAVOR table (Chocolate) has an FLNO of 2, which has no corresponding row in the CLIENT table.

Here is an example of the LEFT OUTER JOIN:

```
SELECT client_name, flavor_name
  FROM client LEFT OUTER JOIN flavor
       ON (client.flno = flavor.flno);

CLIENT_NAME        FLAVOR_NAME
------------------ ------------------
Andy               Vanilla
Beth               Vanilla
Carol              Strawberry
David
```

Here is an example of the RIGHT OUTER JOIN:

```
SELECT client_name, flavor_name
  FROM client RIGHT OUTER JOIN flavor
       ON (client.flno = flavor.flno);

CLIENT_NAME        FLAVOR_NAME
------------------ ------------------
Andy               Vanilla
Beth               Vanilla
Carol              Strawberry
                   Chocolate
```

And here is an example of the FULL OUTER JOIN:

```
SELECT client_name, flavor_name
  FROM client FULL OUTER JOIN flavor
       ON (client.flno = flavor.flno);

CLIENT_NAME          FLAVOR_NAME
------------------ ------------------
Andy                 Vanilla
Beth                 Vanilla
Carol                Strawberry
David
                     Chocolate
```

You could only perform the full outer join in prior versions by using two select statements UNIONed together.

CASE Statements

You can now perform If . . . Then . . . Else logic within SQL:99 statements without having to use PL/SQL procedures. SQL:99 provides four types of CASE statements:

- The simple CASE expression
- The searched CASE expression
- The NULLIF function
- The COALESCE function

The Simple CASE Expression The simple CASE expression was available in Oracle 8.1.7 SQL only, not in PL/SQL. The simple CASE expression is very similar to the DECODE statement that uses value and substitution expression pairs. The simple CASE expression enables you to specify a number of WHEN . . . THEN . . . pairs. Here is the general format:

```
CASE expression
   WHEN comparison_expression1 THEN use_expression1
   WHEN comparison_expression2 THEN use_expression2
   WHEN comparison_expression3 THEN use_expression3
   ELSE default_use_expression
END
```

For each WHEN clause, Oracle will perform the use_expression if the CASE expression is equal to the comparison_expression. You can also specify an ELSE clause, which is a catchall clause. If none of the WHEN . . . conditions are met, the

CASE expression performs the default_use_expression specified in the ELSE clause; Oracle will give you a NULL value if you did not specify an ELSE clause. Only one use_expression will be executed; it will either be the first one associated with a true comparison_expression or it will be the default_use_expression. You cannot use the NULL literal value to specify the use_expression or a default_use_expression.

Here is an example of the simple CASE expression:

```
SELECT client_name, flavor_name, qty,
       (CASE qty
           WHEN 1 THEN 'Got to have it'
           WHEN 2 THEN 'Just a little more'
           WHEN 3 THEN 'Bring it on'
         ELSE
            'Real hungry'
         END)  AS "Whatsup!"

  FROM client NATURAL JOIN flavor;

CLIENT_NAME         FLAVOR_NAME         QTY Whatsup!
------------------- ------------------- --- ------------------
Andy                Vanilla               4 Real Hungry
Beth                Vanilla               2 Just a little more
Carol               Strawberry            2 Just a little more
```

Each CASE expression can have up to 255 arguments, and each WHEN . . . THEN . . . pair counts as 2 arguments. At the most, you can have 127 WHEN . . . THEN . . . pairs and one ELSE expression in one CASE expression. When you nest a CASE expression within another CASE expression, the nested CASE expression enables you an additional set of 255 arguments.

The Searched CASE Expression Oracle9*i* introduces the searched CASE expression. The general format for the searched CASE expression is very similar to the format of the simple CASE expression. There is one difference, however; in the WHEN clause, you compare the CASE expression to the comparison_expression to determine your course of action. In the searched CASE expression, you do not specify a CASE expression, and you specify a condition or predicate instead of a comparison_expression after the WHEN keyword. A predicate is the criteria that you are used to specifying in the WHERE clause of an SQL statement. Only one use_expression will be executed; it will either be the first one associated with a true condition or it will be the default_use_expression. Here is the general format:

```
CASE
   WHEN condition1 THEN use_expression1
   WHEN condition2 THEN use_expression2
```

```
   WHEN condition3 THEN use_expression3
   ELSE default_use_expression
END
```

Here is an example of the searched CASE expression:

```
SELECT client_name, flavor_name, qty,
       (CASE
           WHEN qty >= 4 THEN 'You must be hungry'
           WHEN UPPER(flavor_name) LIKE '%ILL%' THEN 'This is bad for you'
         ELSE
            'Have a blast!'
         END)  AS "Remarks"

  FROM client NATURAL JOIN flavor;

CLIENT_NAME        FLAVOR_NAME        QTY Remarks
------------------ ------------------ --- ------------------
Andy               Vanilla              4 You must be hungry
Beth               Vanilla              2 This is bad for you
Carol              Strawberry           2 Have a blast!
```

Even though more than one condition in the searched CASE expression may be true, Oracle stops at the first TRUE condition and performs that use_expression.

The NULLIF Function Oracle9*i* introduces the NULLIF function. The general format is

```
NULLIF(expression1, expression2)
```

If expression1 is equal to expression2, Oracle returns a NULL; otherwise, it returns *expression1*. You cannot specify the NULL literal value for expression1.

You could also use the following searched CASE expression to perform the same thing:

```
CASE
   WHEN expression1 != expression2 THEN expression1
END
```

The COALESCE Function Oracle9*i* introduces the COALESCE function. The general format is

```
COALESCE(expression1, expression2, expression3,...)
```

Oracle returns the first expression in the comma-separated list that is not a NULL. You cannot specify the NULL literal value for at least one of the expressions. If all the arguments turn out to NULL upon evaluation, Oracle will return a NULL.

You could also use the following searched CASE expression to perform the COALESCE operation with three expressions:

```
CASE
   WHEN expression1 IS NOT NULL THEN expression1
   ELSE (CASE
           WHEN expression2 IS NOT NULL then expression2
           ELSE (CASE
                   WHEN expression3 IS NOT NULL THEN expression3
                 END)
        END)
END
```

You could also use the following NVL function to perform the COALESCE operation with two expressions:

```
NVL(expression1, expression2)
```

If expression1 is nonnull, NVL returns expression1; otherwise, NVL returns expression2.

Scalar Subqueries

The scalar subquery enables you to treat the output of a subquery as a column or expression within a SELECT statement. A scalar subquery is a query that only selects one column or expression and returns just one row. If the scalar subquery does not select any rows, Oracle will use a NULL value for the output of the scalar subquery.

Prior to Oracle9*i*, you could use the scalar subquery within the SET clause of the UPDATE statement and within the VALUES list of the INSERT INTO statement. Oracle9*i* gives you greater flexibility to use the scalar subquery pretty much anywhere you can use an expression. Here are some places you cannot use the scalar subquery:

- For default column values
- As the basis for the function-based index
- As hash expressions for clusters
- In CHECK constraints for DDL statements
- In the RETURNING clause for DML statements

- In WHEN conditions for CASE statements
- In GROUP BY and HAVING clauses for SQL queries
- In CONNECT BY and START WITH clauses for SQL queries

Here is an example of using the scalar subquery to determine how many rows in the CLIENT table contain a flavor corresponding to each row in the FLAVOR table:

```
SELECT F.flno, flavor_name, (SELECT count(*)
                               FROM client C
                              WHERE C.flno = F.flno) AS "How Many Times"
  FROM flavor F;

FLNO FLAVOR_NAME        How Many Times
---- ------------------ --------------
   1 Vanilla                         2
   2 Chocolate                       0
   3 Strawberry                      1
```

MERGE

Oracle9*i* introduces the MERGE statement to enable you to retrieve rows from a source table and either update existing rows or insert new rows into a destination table. You update the row in the destination table if there is a matching row in the destination table; otherwise, you insert a new row into the destination table. You can specify the basis for the match with a condition in the ON clause. You specify the UPDATE in the WHEN MATCHED clause and you specify the INSERT in the WHEN NOT MATCHED clause.

Here is an example:

```
MERGE INTO CLIENT_MASTER CM
  USING CLIENT C
  ON    (CM.clno = C.clno AND
         CM.flno = C.flno)
  WHEN MATCHED THEN
    UPDATE SET CM.qty = CM.qty + C.qty
  WHEN NOT MATCHED THEN
    INSERT (CM.clno, CM.client_name, CM.flno, CM.qty)
     VALUES (C.clno,  C.client_name,  C.flno,  C.qty)
```

In this example, you are merging the contents of the CLIENT table into the CLIENT_MASTER table.

Analytic Functions

Analytic functions enable you to compute aggregate values for a specific group of rows. Some Oracle9*i* enhancements related to analytic functions in Oracle9*i* are

- Distribution functions
- Inverse percentile functions
- Rank functions
- Positional functions
- Histogram bucket function
- Grouping sets

Distribution Functions Oracle9*i* provides the CUME_DIST function to determine the cumulative distribution of a particular value within a set of values. The returned value will be between 0 and 1.

You can use CUME_DIST either as an aggregate function or as an analytic function. When you use CUME_DIST as an *aggregate* function, it determines the relative position of an apparent row of information within an existing group of rows. For example, use the following query to determine the relative position of an apparent CLIENT row with a quantity of 3:

```
SELECT CUME_DIST(3)
  WITHIN GROUP (ORDER BY qty) AS "Relative Position"
  FROM CLIENT;

Relative Position of QTY = 3
----------------------------
                          .5
```

This query indicates that a row that has a quantity of 3 would be the third of five rows.

CUME_DIST as an *analytic* function determines the relative position of a specific value within a group of values.

Inverse Distribution Functions Oracle9*i* introduces PERCENTILE_CONT and PERCENTILE_DISC, which are inverse distribution functions that enable you to interpolate values based on continuous and discrete distribution models, respectively. Given a percentile and a sequence, these functions will determine the interpolated value at that percentile. The interpolation ignores NULL values. The interpolated values will be between 0 and 1.

Here is an example of how you can interpolate the median quantity (*qty*) of any ice cream purchased by clients:

```
SELECT flavor_name AS "Ice Cream",
       PERCENTILE_CONT(0.5) WITHIN GROUP
             (ORDER BY qty) AS "Median Qty (Cont)"
       PERCENTILE_DIST(0.5) WITHIN GROUP
             (ORDER BY qty) AS "Median Qty (Disc)"
  FROM client
 GROUP BY flavor_name
```

Rank Functions Oracle8*i* introduced rank functions, and Oracle9*i* has enhanced them to accept a parameter to specify the analysis.

The RANK function determines the rank of a value within a set of values. You can use RANK as an aggregate function or as an analytic function.

When you use RANK as an aggregate function, it determines the rank of an apparent row value within the specified sort sequence of the row values. Here is an example:

```
SELECT RANK(3) WITHIN GROUP (ORDER BY qty) AS "Rank of Quantity"
  FROM client;

Rank of Quantity
----------------
               3
```

As an analytic function, RANK determines the rank of each row relative to the other rows. Here is an example:

```
SELECT clno, client_name, qty,
       RANK() OVER (ORDER BY qty) AS "Rank of Quantity"
  FROM client;

ClNo Client_Name       Qty Rank of Quantity
---- ----------------- --- ----------------
   B Beth                2                1
   C Carol               2                1
   A Andy                4                3
   D David               4                3
```

When you have more than one row with the same value for the basis of the ranking, the rank will skip a few consecutive numbers. The largest rank will either be the total number of rows, or the total number of rows less the number of rows with equal values at the very end.

DENSE_RANK is very similar to the RANK function. The primary difference is that DENSE_RANK does not skip numbers. The highest rank will be the number of distinct values.

Here is an example of DENSE_RANK as an aggregate function:

```
SELECT DENSE_RANK(3) WITHIN GROUP (ORDER BY qty) AS "Rank of Quantity"
  FROM client;

Rank of Quantity
----------------
               2
```

Here is an example of DENSE_RANK as an analytic function:

```
SELECT clno, client_name, qty,
       DENSE_RANK() OVER (ORDER BY qty) AS "Rank of Quantity"
  FROM client;

ClNo Client_Name       Qty Rank of Quantity
---- ----------------- --- ----------------
   B Beth                2                1
   C Carol               2                1
   A Andy                4                2
   D David               4                2
```

The PERCENT_RANK function determines the percentage rank on a scale from 0 to 1. It is determined as the RANK minus 1 divided by the number of rows.

Positional Functions Oracle9*i* gives you the FIRST and LAST functions to return the values from rows that rank as first or last respectively within a set of rows.

If you have a set of sorted groups, the FIRST and LAST functions return the values from rows that rank first or last respectively within each group within the specified sort order.

Histogram Bucket Function Oracle9*i* gives you the WIDTH_BUCKET function to divide a range for the histogram into equal intervals, and to return the number of the bucket into which a particular value falls.

Here is an example that shows how you can use the WIDTH_BUCKET function:

```
SELECT clno, client_name, qty,
       WIDTH_BUCKET(qty, 1, 10, 5) AS "Bucket Number"
  FROM client;
```

```
ClNo Client_Name        Qty Bucket Number
---- ----------------- --- -------------
   A Andy               4             2
   B Beth               2             1
   C Carol              2             1
   D David              4             2
```

The argument list for the WIDTH_FUNCTION is (expression, low_value, high_value, number_of_buckets).

Even though we specify just five buckets in the example, in reality, Oracle creates seven buckets. Of the two additional buckets that Oracle creates, bucket #0 is for values that are below the low_value of 1, while bucket #6 is for values that are above the high_value of 10.

You can get a better understanding of the WIDTH_BUCKET function by observing the following CASE expression that performs the same task:

```
SELECT clno, client_name, qty,
       (
        CASE WHEN qty < 1 THEN 0,
             WHEN qty <= 2 THEN 1,
             WHEN qty <= 4 THEN 2,
             WHEN qty <= 6 THEN 3,
             WHEN qty <= 8 THEN 4,
             WHEN qty <= 10 THEN 5,
             ELSE               6
        END
       ) AS "Bucket Number"
  FROM client;
```

Grouping Sets Although grouping sets are not functions, they are discussed with analytic functions because they specify the groups for the aggregation functions.

Oracle8*i* introduced the CUBE and ROLLUP qualifier for the GROUP BY clause. You had to perform multiple queries and perform UNION ALLs to combine the rows into one set. Oracle9*i* has enhanced the CUBE and ROLLUP qualifiers with GROUPING SETs that enable you to perform the same task with a single query.

GROUPING SETs greatly enhance the GROUP BY clause; you can specify multiple groupings of data for aggregation, and just the groupings that you are interested in. Oracle does not have to aggregate based on every combination of the expressions in the CUBE or ROLLUP operation. Hence, GROUPING SETS are more efficient. Oracle applies the groupings specified in the GROUPING SETS and combines the result with an implied UNION ALL.

The CUBE operation is a great tool for generating cross-tabulation reports; it produces subtotals along each dimension of the data cube specified by the expressions in parentheses. The number of combinations is 2 to the power of *n*, where *n* is the number of expressions specified by the CUBE. Let's consider the following clause, `GROUP BY CUBE (country, state, city)`. It generates subtotals for each of the eight faces in a three-dimensional data cube. The groups or combinations are as follows:

- Country, state, city
- Country, state
- State, city
- Country, city
- Country
- State
- City
- Grand total

Let's assume that you are only interested in the following groups:

- Country, state, city
- State, city
- Country, city

Prior to GROUPING SETs, you would have had to write three queries with a GROUP BY clause for each of the prior combinations, and then you would have had to use UNION ALL for the three queries to get all the rows. The GROUPING SET enables you to accomplish this objective in one query. Here is the clause you need to use:

```
GROUP BY GROUPING SETS
  ((country, state, city),
   (state, city),
   (country, city))
```

A *composite key* is a key that is comprised of more than one column. A *composite column* is a set of columns that is treated as one group in generating group-based aggregate information. The `GROUP BY ROLLUP (country, state, city)` clause generates the following four groupings:

- Country, state, city
- Country, state

- Country
- Grand total

You enclose columns in parentheses to use them as a composite column. For example, the `GROUP BY ROLLUP (country, (state, city))` clause treats state and city as a composite column; it results in the following three groupings:

- Country, state, city
- Country
- Grand total

Concatenated groupings enable you to specify combinations of groupings along a dimension of a cube, as opposed to a simple expression. Oracle uses the cross product of the combinations to generate groupings. You can concatenate grouping sets, cubes, and rollups. For example, the `GROUP BY GROUPING SETS (country, state), GROUPING SETS (county, city)` clause specifies the following groupings:

- Country, county
- Country, city
- State, county
- State, city

A concatenation of grouping sets enables you to

- Specify dimensions of the cube that are themselves combinations of groups, or a subcube if you will
- To generate combinations without having to specify each combination
- Interact with Online Analytical Processing (OLAP) applications where they are already used to concatenating grouping sets

Constraints

Oracle9*i* introduces the following enhancements to constraint specifications:

- Explicit index control
- Minimized foreign key locking

- Cached primary keys
- Declarative constraints on views

Explicit Index Control

In Oracle9*i*, you can explicitly create an index within a CREATE TABLE statement. Here is an example:

```
CREATE TABLE inventory
(itemid CHAR(4) CONSTRAINT inventory_pk PRIMARY KEY
                   USING INDEX (CREATE INDEX inventory_ix
                                     ON inventory(itemid)),
 item_name VARCHAR2(20),
 price NUMBER(9,2),
 quantity NUMBER(4));
```

When you DROP or DISABLE a constraint, you can explicitly tell Oracle to either KEEP the index or DROP the index. When you DROP constraints, the associated implicitly created unique indexes are dropped by default.

```
ALTER TABLE inventory
 DROP CONSTRAINT inventory_pk
 KEEP INDEX;
```

Minimized Foreign Key Locking

When you perform an update or delete operation on the primary key, Oracle places a table-level share lock on foreign keys that are not indexed. In earlier releases, Oracle would not release this share lock until the update or delete operation was completed. Oracle9*i* does not hold on to this lock until the operation is complete; instead, it releases this lock almost immediately after it has been placed. Oracle9*i* accomplishes this quick lock-release by getting a savepoint, obtaining the lock, releasing the lock, and rolling back to the savepoint if needed.

Cached Primary Keys

The verification of the existence of a matching primary key before adding a foreign key can consume a significant amount of time. Oracle9*i* addresses this performance problem by enabling you to cache the first 256 primary keys; this improves the time it takes to verify the existence of a primary key and therefore enhances performance when adding multiple foreign keys.

Oracle9*i* only caches the primary key when you have DML statements that involve many rows because the time for caching the primary key will degrade the performance of DML statements that involve a single row. This feature is automatically available.

Declarative Constraints on Views

Oracle9*i* enables you to define primary key constraints, unique constraints, and referential integrity constraints on views. Check constraints, however, are excluded.

Constraints on views are declarative constraints; Oracle does not actually enforce them. When you perform DML statements on views, Oracle assures integrity by enforcing the constraints defined on the base tables within the view.

The purpose of the declarative constraints on views is not for enforcing integrity; they are used to identify multidimensional data. Declarative constraints on views are useful in data warehousing/OLAP applications.

Because these constraints are declarative logical constraints, they are subject to the following restrictions:

- You can specify the RELY or NORELY states.
- You can specify the DISABLE NOVALIDATE state.
- You cannot specify attributes; for example, the USING INDEX clause is not allowed.
- You cannot specify actions triggered by the ON DELETE clause for foreign key constraints.
- You cannot use the EXCEPTIONS INTO clause.

Here is an example of specifying a constraint on a view:

```
CREATE VIEW vanilla_client
      (clno, client, quantity,
       CONSTRAINT vanilla_client_pk PRIMARY KEY (clno)
             RELY DISABLE NOVALIDATE) AS
SELECT clno, client_name, qty
  FROM client
 WHERE UPPER(flavor_name) = 'VANILLA';
```

FOR UPDATE WAIT

Prior to Oracle9*i*, the SELECT . . . FOR UPDATE statement only enabled you to wait until the lock was released or to exit the operation immediately with an error message when the row you were attempting to select was locked.

Oracle9*i* has enhanced the SELECT . . . FOR UPDATE statement, and you no longer have to be stuck waiting indefinitely. You can now specify the period of time in seconds that you can wait for a lock to be released.

The format is

```
SELECT...
  FROM
 WHERE...
   FOR UPDATE WAIT 10;
```

In this statement, you are specifying that you will wait ten seconds for the lock on the row to be released. This eliminates having to wait indefinitely for a lock to be released; you now have control over establishing an acceptable wait time.

You can also specify that you do not want to wait to acquire a lock by using the NOWAIT option. If a lock is not immediately available, it returns an error to indicate that you cannot acquire a lock at this time.

LOBs

To convert a LONG or a LONG RAW column to a CLOB or BLOB column respectively in Oracle8*i*, you had to first create a second table with a LOB column instead of the LONG column in the original table. Let's assume that the DDL for the original table was

```
CREATE TABLE orig_tab
(clno CHAR(4),
 client_name VARCHAR2(20),
 client_history LONG);
```

The following DDL statement creates a second corresponding table with the LOB column:

```
CREATE TABLE new_tab
(clno CHAR(4),
 client_name VARCHAR2(20),
 client_history CLOB);
```

Then you must populate the second table with data from the original table. In the process of populating the second table, you must convert the LONG or LONG RAW data in the original table into the CLOB or BLOB data in the second table. Oracle8*i* introduced the TO_LOB function that enables you to convert a LONG or a LONG RAW value to a CLOB or BLOB value respectively. Here is the SQL statement to do this:

```
INSERT INTO new_tab
 (SELECT clno, client_name, TO_LOB(client_history)
    FROM orig_tab);
```

Your next step is to DROP the *orig_tab* table, and finally you must rename the *new_tab* table to the original table name orig_tab.

Oracle9*i* simplifies the process of converting a LONG or LONG RAW column into a CLOB or BLOB column respectively. You use the ALTER TABLE . . . MODIFY statement to change a LONG or LONG RAW column into a CLOB or BLOB column respectively. Here is the statement to perform this change:

```
ALTER TABLE orig_tab MODIFY
(client_history CLOB);
```

The ALTER TABLE . . . MODIFY statement can only convert a LONG or LONG RAW to a CLOB or BLOB column respectively. It will not change a VARCHAR or a RAW column into a LOB column.

You must manually rebuild indexes, and you must drop domain indexes before starting the migration. You also have to create the index manually on the LOB column after the migration is complete. This conversion requires twice the amount of space because both the LONG and the LOB columns exist for the duration of the conversion.

For the most part, SQL functions and operators that can accept VARCHAR2 values can also handle CLOB values. All PL/SQL package functions that can accept LONG values can also handle CLOB values. Both SQL and PL/SQL functions that accept RAW values can accept BLOB values too. The PL/SQL engine performs implicit conversions from LOB to VARCHAR and RAW, and the reverse conversions also.

When changing LONG columns to LOB columns, you must keep in mind that LONG columns are allowed in clustered tables, but you cannot have LOB columns in clustered tables.

If you have replicated copies of the original table with the LONG column, you must manually change each replicated table to contain the LOB column.

PL/SQL

You can natively compile PL/SQL procedures in Oracle9*i* to improve performance. When you compile PL/SQL procedures, Oracle generates native C code, then compiles it using the C compiler on the system, and links it to the Oracle process. You must provide the C compiler; it is not packaged with Oracle. You can compile both the packages supplied by Oracle and the procedures or packages that you develop. Oracle-supplied packages are statically linked, and procedures or packages you develop are dynamically linked to the process running the Oracle executable.

To compile procedures and packages, you must perform these steps:

1. Update the Oracle-supplied makefile *spnc_makefile.mk* located in *$ORACLE_HOME:\plsql* to reflect the appropriate paths.
2. Replace the default INTERPRETED value for the PLSQL_COMPILER_FLAGS initialization parameter with the NATIVE value. You can perform this by modifying the entry in the initialization parameter file, or you can use ALTER SESSION or ALTER SYSTEM to dynamically alter the PLSQL_COMPILER_FLAGS parameter, as shown here:

   ```
   ALTER SYSTEM
     SET PLSQL_COMPILER_FLAGS = NATIVE;
   ```

3. Compile the procedure or the package of interest with one of the following options:
   - Use CREATE OR REPLACE PROCEDURE to compile the procedure.
   - Use the ALTER PROCEDURE to compile the procedure.
   - Use the ALTER PACKAGE to compile the whole package.
   - Use DROP PROCEDURE to drop the procedure and then create it again with the CREATE procedure to compile the procedure.
   - Create a database with the PLSQL_COMPILER_FLAGS initialization parameter set to NATIVE to compile all the Oracle-supplied packages. Oracle does this by starting the UTLIRP script.
4. Confirm that the procedure of interest has been NATIVE compiled by querying the USER_STORED_SETTINGS data dictionary view as follows:

   ```
   SELECT object_name, param_value
     FROM user_stored_settings
    WHERE object_name = 'SHOW_IT' AND
          param_name  = 'PLSQL_COMPILER_FLAGS'

   OBJECT_NAME PARAM_VALUE
   ----------- -----------
   SHOW_IT     NATIVE
   ```

If the procedure SHOW_IT is not compiled for native execution, it will contain INTERPRETED.

Besides the standard degradation in performance to parse interpreted code, the execution of native code is much faster because

- A jump to another location in code is accomplished by going directly to the address of a label in C, as opposed to locating the destination of the jump in interpreted code.
- Function calls to target functions in one unit are mapped to C function calls.
- Primary memory for frames is allocated from the C stack, as opposed to interpreted MCODE that uses the program global area (PGA).
- The compiled PL/SQL code is mapped in the PGA, as opposed to interpreted MCODE that is loaded entirely into the system global area (SGA).
- Compiled PL/SQL code performs exception handling via switch statements. Interpreted MCODE has to look up the exception handler table.

For Review

1. You must be able to identify and use SQL:99 enhancements to joins, such as the CROSS JOIN, the NATURAL JOIN, and the equijoin with the USING keyword, the ON clause, and the outer joins.
2. You must know about other SQL:99 enhancements such as simple CASE expressions, searched CASE expressions, the NULLIF function, and the COALESCE function.
3. You must be able to develop scalar subqueries and use the MERGE statement.
4. You must know about various analytic functions such as distribution, inverse percentile, rank, positional, and histogram bucket functions. You must be able to use grouping sets to define your own groupings for analysis and aggregation.
5. You must know about enhancements to constraints, the SELECT . . . FOR UPDATE statement, LOBs, and PL/SQL procedures/packages.

Exercises

1. **The NATURAL JOIN**

   A. Generates the Cartesian product.

   B. Requires you to explicitly specify the join condition in the WHERE clause.

C. Matches values in columns that have the same name.

D. None of the above

2. The NULLIF function

A. Returns the second argument value if the first argument evaluates to a NULL.

B. Returns a NULL if the first and the second argument are not equal.

C. Returns the first argument value if the first argument and the second argument are equal.

D. Returns a NULL if the first argument and the second argument are equal.

Answer Key

1. C. **2.** D.

Enhancements to Globalization

Oracle's Globalization Support architecture enables characters, numbers, money, time, calendar dates, and error messages to automatically adapt to the local native language and the locale. In previous releases, Globalization Support was called National Language Support (NLS). Even though NLS was changed to Globalization, you will still encounter functions and parameters whose names contain the abbreviation NLS. This section discusses the following enhancements to Globalization in Oracle9*i*:

- New date and time datatypes
- Enhancements to Unicode
- Enhancements to sorting
- The character set scanner
- Byte and character semantics
- The Locale Builder

New Date and Time Datatypes

Oracle9*i* introduces the following date- and time-related datatypes:

- TIMESTAMP
- TIMESTAMP WITH TIME ZONE
- TIMESTAMP WITH LOCAL TIME ZONE
- INTERVAL DAY TO SECOND
- INTERVAL YEAR TO MONTH

TIMESTAMP

The TIMESTAMP datatype is very much like the DATE datatype; it can store both the date and time values. Unlike the DATE datatype, you can specify the precision of the fractional seconds value in the TIMESTAMP datatype. The default is 6 digits, and you can specify a value within the range from 0 through 9.

The syntax for the TIMESTAMP datatype is

```
TIMESTAMP [ (fractional_seconds_precision) ]
```

Here is an example of using the TIMESTAMP datatype:

```
CREATE TABLE calltrack
( callnum integer,
  calltime TIMESTAMP(4)
);
```

You can use the NLS_TIMESTAMP_FORMAT initialization parameter to specify the default timestamp data format for retrieval and for the TO_CHAR and TO_TIMESTAMP conversion functions. NLS_TIMESTAMP_FORMAT is a dynamic parameter that you can change with an ALTER SESSION command. Let's say you specified the NLS_TIMESTAMP_FORMAT parameter as follows:

```
ALTER SESSION SET NLS_TIMESTAMP_FORMAT = 'MMDDYYHH24MISSFF';
```

You can insert a value using NLS_TIMESTAMP_FORMAT that you specified:

```
INSERT INTO calltrack (callnum, calltime)
 VALUES (1001, '12220123184842');
```

This value specifies 11:18:48.42 P.M. on December 22, 2001. You can also use the TIMESTAMP keyword with the following standard format:

```
TIMESTAMP 'YYYY-MM-DD HH24:MI:SS.FF'
```

So an alternative to the earlier INSERT INTO statement is

```
INSERT INTO calltrack (callnum, calltime)
 VALUES (1001, TIMESTAMP '2001-12-22 23:18:48.42');
```

TIMESTAMP WITH TIME ZONE

The TIMESTAMP WITH TIME ZONE datatype adds a slight twist to the TIMESTAMP datatype. In addition to the date and time, you can store the time zone displacement (or offset), which requires additional bytes of storage. The time zone displacement is the difference in hours and minutes between the local time and the Universal Time (Coordinated) (UTC), which formerly was the Greenwich Meridian Time (GMT).

Here is an example of using the TIMESTAMP WITH TIME ZONE datatype:

```
CREATE TABLE calltrack
( callnum integer,
  calltime1 TIMESTAMP(4) WITH TIME ZONE
);
```

TIMESTAMP WITH TIME ZONE represents *absolute* time.

You can use the NLS_TIMESTAMP_TZ_FORMAT initialization parameter to specify the default timestamp data format for retrieval and for the TO_CHAR and TO_TIMESTAMP_TZ conversion functions. NLS_TIMESTAMP_TZ_FORMAT is a dynamic parameter that you can change with an ALTER SESSION command. Let's say you specified the NLS_TIMESTAMP_TZ_FORMAT parameter as follows:

```
ALTER SESSION SET NLS_TIMESTAMP_FORMAT = 'MMDDYYHH24MISSFF TZH';
```

You can insert a value using the NLS_TIMESTAMP_TZ_FORMAT that you specified:

```
INSERT INTO calltrack (callnum, calltime1)
 VALUES (1001, '12220123184842 -8');
```

This value specifies 11:18:48.42 P.M. on December 22, 2001 and the Pacific Standard Time (PST) time zone, which is eight hours behind UTC. You can get a list of time zone names and the displacement from UTC by querying the V$TIMEZONE_NAMES view.

Let's say you specified the NLS_TIMESTAMP_TZ_FORMAT parameter to reflect the time zone region as follows:

```
ALTER SESSION SET NLS_TIMESTAMP_FORMAT = 'MMDDYYHH24MISSFF TZR';
```

You can insert a value using the time zone region specified in the NLS_TIMESTAMP_TZ_FORMAT parameter:

```
INSERT INTO calltrack (callnum, calltime1)
 VALUES (1001, '12220123184842 US/Pacific');
```

You can also use the TIMESTAMP keyword with the following standard format:

```
TIMESTAMP 'YYYY-MM-DD HH24:MI:SS.FF' AT TIME ZONE <timezone_region>
```

So an alternative to the earlier INSERT INTO statement is

```
INSERT INTO calltrack (callnum, calltime1)
 VALUES
  (1001, TIMESTAMP '2001-12-22 23:18:48.42' AT TIME ZONE 'US/Pacific');
```

TIMESTAMP WITH LOCAL TIME ZONE

The TIMESTAMP WITH LOCAL TIME ZONE datatype is also a variant of the TIMESTAMP datatype. Much like the TIMESTAMP WITH TIME ZONE datatype, TIMESTAMP WITH LOCAL TIME ZONE includes time zone information, but unlike the TIMESTAMP WITH TIME ZONE datatype, it does not store the time zone displacement in additional bytes of storage. Instead, it stores the time values normalized in terms of the database's time zone. When a user attempts to retrieve this information, the database displays the information in terms of the local time zone of the user's session.

Here is an example of the TIMESTAMP WITH LOCAL TIME ZONE datatype:

```
CREATE TABLE calltrack
( callnum integer,
  calltime2 TIMESTAMP(4) WITH LOCAL TIME ZONE
);
```

The TIMESTAMP WITH LOCAL TIME ZONE represents *relative* time.

The prior discussion about NLS_TIMESTAMP_TZ_FORMAT initialization parameter and the INSERT INTO statement within the context of the TIMESTAMP WITH TIME ZONE datatype section is applicable to the TIMESTAMP WITH LOCAL TIME ZONE datatype.

INTERVAL DAY TO SECOND

The TIMESTAMP datatypes represent a point in time, while the INTERVAL datatypes represent the duration of time. The INTERVAL DAY TO SECOND datatype can store a time interval value in terms of days, hours, minutes, and seconds. You can specify the precision for the number of days in a range from 0 to 9, the default being 2. You can also specify the precision for the fractional seconds in a range from 0 to 9, the default being 6. The general syntax is as follows:

```
INTERVAL DAY [(number_of_days_precision)]
  TO SECOND [(fractional_seconds_precision)]
```

Here is an example:

```
CREATE TABLE calltrack
( callnum integer,
  calltime1 TIMESTAMP(4) WITH TIME ZONE
  callduration INTERVAL DAY(1) TO SECOND(2)
);
```

You can use the INTERVAL keyword as shown to specify a literal value for a column of type INTERVAL DAY TO SECOND:

```
INTERVAL '<day> <hour>:<minute>:<second>.<fractional_second>'
  DAY TO SECOND
```

For example, you can insert a row of data into the *calltrack* table as follows:

```
INSERT INTO calltrack (callnum, calltime1, callduration)
 VALUES
  (1001,
   TIMESTAMP '2001-12-22 23:18:48.42' AT TIME ZONE 'US/Pacific'
   INTERVAL '2 5:25:12.11' DAY TO SECOND);
```

The TO_DSINTERVAL conversion function converts a character string into an INTERVAL DAY TO SECOND datatype.

INTERVAL YEAR TO MONTH

The INTERVAL YEAR TO MONTH datatype can store a time interval value in terms of years and months. You can specify the precision for the number of years in a range from 0 to 9, the default being 2. The general syntax is as follows:

```
INTERVAL YEAR [(number_of_years_precision)] TO MONTH
```

For example, you could track the time it took to construct highway bridges with the INTERVAL YEAR TO MONTH datatype:

```
CREATE TABLE highwaybridge
( bridgenum integer,
  constructionduration INTERVAL YEAR(1) TO MONTH
);
```

You can use the INTERVAL keyword as shown to specify a literal value for a column of type INTERVAL YEAR TO MONTH:

```
INTERVAL '<year>-<month>' YEAR TO MONTH
```

For example, you can insert a row of data into the *highwaybridge* table as follows:

```
INSERT INTO highwaybridge (bridgenum, constructionduration)
 VALUES
  (1001,
   INTERVAL '3-5' YEAR TO MONTH);
```

The TO_YMINTERVAL conversion function converts a character string into an INTERVAL YEAR TO MONTH datatype.

Enhancements to Unicode

The American Standard Code for Information Interchange (ASCII) is a 1-byte or 8-bit encoded character set. It can take on one of 256 values (0 to 255) and each value represents an English character or a special character, such as the TAB key or CTRL key. Unicode is a 2-byte or 16-bit encoded character set that can take on one of 65,536 values and can represent most characters in languages around the world. The concept of surrogate pairs enables you to encode 32-bit character codes that can encode millions of characters.

Oracle first introduced the Unicode character set in Oracle7. This included UTF8 encoding, which required two 8-bit bytes to represent a character, and UTFE, which is a variant of UTF8 for EBCDIC character sets. Oracle9*i* was enhanced to support the Unicode Standard Version 3.0; this Unicode standard does not support surrogate pairs at this time. Oracle9*i* introduced two new Unicode character sets, AL16UTF16 and AL32UTF8.

AL16UTF16 is a 2-byte, fixed-width Unicode character set, which is also referred to as UTF16 or UCS2. The ASCII English character set is assigned the first 128 values from 0 (0x00) through 127 (0x7F) in Unicode, which translates to 1 byte. Even though AL16UTF16 uses one more byte than UTF8 for ASCII character representation, it is still faster because it uses fixed-width encoding as opposed to UTF8, which uses variable-width encoding.

AL32UTF8 is an enhanced implementation of UTF8. This is an 8-bit, variable-width encoding set that uses multiple bytes to represent a Unicode character. Although UTF8 is supported in Oracle9*i* for backward compatibility and for the migration of data from earlier versions of Oracle, you should use AL32ATF8 instead of UTF8. UTFE is also supported in Oracle9*i*, but AL24UTFFSS is no longer supported in Oracle9*i*.

Enhancements to Sorting

Traditionally, we sorted a set of character strings based on the ASCII numeric value of the characters. Although this binary sort is fast and generally satisfies the sorting requirements of words in the English language, it introduces a few anomalies. The sort sequence ASCII character encoding would not be exactly the same as the sort sequence with EBCDIC coding. And assuming ASCII encoding, a binary sort of *applet, Apple, zoo, and Zebra* results in the following sequence: *Apple, Zebra, applet, and zoo*. The applet comes after the Zebra because lowercase letters have a higher ASCII code value than uppercase letters. With EBCDIC coding, the sequence would be *applet, zoo, Apple, and Zebra.*

Oracle introduced the concept of linguistic sorting, which enables you to look up the sorting value of the character in the alphabet instead of using the encoding value from the character encoding system. You can specify the sort sequence to be used by setting the NLS_SORT initialization parameter. Prior to Oracle9*i*, the linguistic sort sequence gave you two values for each character; the first was a major sorting value and the second was a minor sorting value. Oracle would compare the minor sorting values only after it discovered that the major sorting values for two characters matched. Oracle used these two-level sort values to group letters with the same base character together.

For example, lowercase *a* has a major value of 15 and a minor value of 5, while an uppercase *A* has a major value of 15 and a minor value of 10. The lowercase *ä* (a with an umlaut) has a major value of 15 and a minor value of 15, while an uppercase *Ä* has a major value of 15 and a minor value of 20. The sort sequence recognizes that *a, A, ä,* and *Ä* are the same character with just a difference of case or diacritics and will therefore be grouped together by having a major sort value of 15. Within this group, you can distinguish one character from the next with the minor sort.

Oracle9*i* enables you to have up to four sort values for each character to enable a four-level linguistic sort. Oracle9*i* maintains these sort values in Unicode to enable sorting various global character sets. This four-level sort also enables you to perform multilingual sorts where you can sort many language character sets within one sort operation.

Within each character set, the primary sort value distinguishes one base character from another, so *a, A, ä,* and *Ä* have the same primary sort value. The secondary sort value distinguishes one diacritical mark from another. For example, *ä* and *Ä* have the same secondary sort value. The third sort value distinguishes case; it distinguishes between *ä* and *Ä*, and between *a* and *A*. Just as you could in previous versions of Oracle, you specify the linguistic sort definitions by setting the NLS_SORT initialization parameter.

Oracle9*i* also enables the following special considerations for performing sorts on global character sets:

- **Contracting characters** In most languages, a single character is the primitive basis for the sort. In some languages, multiple characters serve as one primitive element for sorting. For example, in Spanish, the characters *ch* form a single primitive element in a sort operation.
- **Expanding characters** This is the reverse of the contracting characters. Here one character may have to be treated as a string of characters in a sort operation. For example, the ō must be treated as a string *oe* for sorting in some languages.
- **Ignoring characters** Some characters can be ignored in some sorts. For example, the hyphen (-) can be ignored in English. The words *email* and *e-mail* should be grouped together.
- **Swapping characters** In some languages such as Thai, you must swap some characters before determining the sort sequence.
- **Reverse secondary sorting** In French, base characters are sorted left to right (L-R), while accents are sorted right to left (R-L).

Oracle9*i* also introduces the sort definitions shown in Table 5-1.

The Character Set Scanner

You can encounter some data truncation, data loss, and data corruption when migrating from one character set to another.

When you declare a CHAR or VARCHAR2 datatype, you specify the precision in bytes. Let's assume the data was in the WE8MSWIN1252 single-byte encoding character set, so each byte corresponds to a single character. If you had 20 bytes, you can store 20 characters. If you were migrating to the AL32UTF8 multibyte, variable-width character set, some characters can use two bytes. If you had 20 bytes, you may just be able to store 10 to 14 characters. If you migrate the data without first changing the column width, you will encounter data truncation.

If the target character set is not a superset of the source character set, some characters in the source will not have corresponding characters in the target

Sort Definition	Description
BIG5	Traditional Chinese.
CANADIAN_M	Canadian French sort: reverse secondary, expanding characters.
CYRILLIC_M	Cyrillic sort.
DANISH_M	Danish sort.
FRENCH_M	French sort: reverse secondary sort.
GBK	Simplified Chinese.
GENERIC_M	Based on ISO 14651: Unicode canonical equivalence.
HKSCS	Hong Kong Supplementary Character Set.
JAPANESE_M	Japanese sort.
KOREAN_M	Korean sort: Hangul characters precede Hanja characters. Hangul uses Unicode binary sort, and Hanja uses pronunciation.
SCHINESE_PINYIN_M	Simplified Chinese Pin Yin sort.
SCHINESE_STROKE_M	Simplified Chinese: the number of strokes is primary, and radical is secondary.
SPANISH_M	Spanish sort: special contracting characters.
TCHINESE_RADICAL_M	Traditional Chinese sort: radical is primary, and the number of strokes is secondary.
TCHINESE_STROKE_M	Traditional Chinese sort: the number of strokes is primary, and radical is secondary.
THAI_M	Thai sort-swap characters.

TABLE 5-1. Oracle9*i* Sort Definitions

character set. These characters may be replaced with a standard character such as the question mark (?). This results in data corruption and data loss.

Depending on the source and target character sets, Oracle performs its own conversions. If you have two user machines that are set to different languages, Oracle could perform different conversions on each of the user machines resulting in a character set mismatch.

Oracle9*i* provides you with the Character Set Scanner (csscan) utility that scans the data to discover potential problems with character set migrations. The scanner utility scans the data in CHAR, VARCHAR2, LONG, CLOB, NCHAR, NVARCHAR2, and NCLOB. The scanner verifies the following:

- That the data in the target database can fit into the column's data size.
- That the data in the source can be mapped without being replaced in the target database.
- That the data can be correctly converted particularly when dealing with differences in byte sizes and fixed/variable byte encoding systems

After the scan operation, the Character Set Scanner generates an *.out* file that captures the screen log, a *.txt* file that contains a summary of the scanning operations, and a *.err* file that contains potential problems that were discovered.

You can invoke the scanner in one of three modes:

- The *Full Database scan* verifies all tables for all users in the database. You perform this by adding a switch FULL=Y.
- The *User scan* verifies all tables for a given user. You must set FULL=N and set USER=Y.
- The *Table scan* verifies a single table that you specify. You must set FULL=N, USER=N, and TABLE=highwaybridge.

Here is a sample invocation of the scanner for a Full Database scan:

```
csscan sys/pw FULL=Y TOCHAR=AL32UTF8 PROCESS=10
```

Byte and Character Semantics

You specify the precision for a CHAR or VARCHAR2 datatype in bytes. For a single-byte, character-encoding character set such as the WE8MSWIN1252, each byte corresponds to a single character. If you have 20 bytes, you can store 20 characters. On the contrary, some characters can use two bytes with the AL32UTF8 multibyte, variable-width character set. If you have 20 bytes, you may just be able to store 10 to 14 characters.

To store the same number of characters (20), you would have to determine the number of bytes required, and then define the column with the recalculated number of bytes. Oracle9*i* mitigates this problem by enabling you to specify byte or character semantics with the NLS_LENGTH_SEMANTICS initialization parameter.

With a single-byte system, it does not matter whether you set the semantics to character or to byte, because one byte corresponds to one character in this system. When you specify character semantics, the database will reserve the number of bytes needed to store the characters when using multibyte systems. With byte semantics, you must calculate the bytes needed and specify how many. Thus, character semantics make it easier for you to work with multibyte systems.

NLS_LENGTH_SEMANTICS does not have any influence or effect on SYS and SYSTEM tables. You can specify the semantics by setting the NLS_LENGTH_SEMANTICS as follows:

```
ALTER SESSION SET NLS_LENGTH_SEMANTICS = CHAR;
```

Alternatively, you can specify the semantics within the column definition as follows:

```
CREATE TABLE test1
(
  first_name CHAR(15 BYTE),
  last_name  CHAR(15 CHAR)
);
```

The *first_name* column uses byte semantics, while the *last_name* column uses character semantics.

You can specify the semantics within the SQL*Loader control file by adding the following clause:

```
LENGTH SEMANTICS CHAR
```

The Locale Builder

Oracle9*i* introduces the Locale Builder, which is a GUI tool used to modify existing locales or to define new locales, even though it is strongly recommended that you do not modify the Oracle-supplied definitions. The Locale Builder maintains this information in *.nlt* files and *.nlb* files, which are binary versions of the corresponding *.nlt* files. You can define the language, the territory, the character set, the linguistic sort definitions, and special linguistic considerations such as reverse secondary sorting. The good news is that you can do all this without having to explore the NLS data definition formats within the *.nlt* files that contain these definitions.

Assuming that you have defined a path for ORACLE_HOME:\ocommon\nls, you start the Locale Builder by invoking the following executable:

```
lbuilder
```

Here are some tasks that you can perform with the Locale Builder:

- Set month names and day names for languages
- Define the default date format to be used for a territory

- Specify the default language and the default language sort
- Specify replacement characters when converting between character sets
- Define the linguistic sort order

For Review

1. You must be able to use the new date and time datatypes and be able to specify the corresponding literal values.
2. You must know about the enhancements to Unicode such as the ALT32UTF8 character set.
3. You must know about the Oracle9*i* enhancements to linguistic sorting. You must also understand the special considerations in performing linguistic sorts such as reverse secondary sorting.
4. You must be able to describe the potential problems that could arise when migrating from one character set to another. You must also know about the Character Set Scanner utility and how it addresses these potential problems.
5. You must know the difference between byte semantics and character semantics.
6. You must know some tasks that you can perform with the Locale Builder.

Exercises

1. **The datatype to specify date and time information in order to include fractional seconds is**

   A. DATE TO SECOND

   B. DATE_X

   C. TIMESTAMP TO SECOND

   D. TIMESTAMP

2. **Reverse secondary sorting tells Oracle to**

   A. Use the secondary sort sequence specified in NLS_SORT2.

   B. Perform the sort for the second time in reverse to confirm the first sort. For example, if the first sort was ASC, then the second sort should be DESC.

C. Traverse characters from right to left for the secondary-level sort if the primary-level sort traversed characters from left to right.

D. If the ORDER BY clause specifies more than one expression, the sort on the second expression must be the reverse of the first expression. For example, if one was ASC, the other must be DESC.

Answer Key

1. D. **2.** C.

Chapter Summary

Oracle9*i* introduces a number of enhancements to give you compliance with the ISO and ANSI SQL:99 standards. Oracle9*i* includes a variety of joins including the CROSS JOIN, the NATURAL JOIN, and the equijoin specified with the USING keyword, the ON clause, and the OUTER JOIN. Oracle9*i* also includes a variety of CASE operations that includes the simple CASE expression, the searched CASE expression, the NULLIF function, and the COALESCE function. Oracle9*i* enhances the scalar subquery, which can be used in most places where an expression is used. The MERGE statement enables you to retrieve rows from one table and either update existing rows or insert new rows into a second table. Oracle9*i* also gives you a number of analytic functions such as distribution functions, inverse percentile functions, rank functions, positional functions, and histogram bucket functions. GROUPING SETS greatly enhance the GROUP BY clause; you can specify multiple groupings of data for data analysis and aggregation.

Oracle9*i* introduces a number of enhancements to constraints. You can explicitly create an index within a CREATE TABLE statement. Oracle9*i* performs minimal table-level share locking on foreign keys that are not indexed when performing update or delete operations on the primary key. Oracle9*i* optimizes the addition of foreign keys by enabling you to cache the first 256 primary keys. You can identify multidimensional data by placing declarative primary key constraints, unique constraints, and referential integrity constraints on views.

Prior to Oracle9*i*, the SELECT . . . FOR UPDATE statement forced you to either wait indefinitely for the lock to be released or not to wait at all as it returned an error message. Oracle9*i* enhances this statement; you can now specify the interval of time that you are willing to wait.

In Oracle8*i*, the migration of a LONG or LONG RAW column to a CLOB or BLOB column respectively was an involved process. Oracle9*i* simplifies this migration; you can now perform the migration with a simple ALTER TABLE . . . MODIFY statement.

You can compile both Oracle-supplied PL/SQL packages and procedures, as well as the procedures that you create for native execution. Native compilation gives you significant performance savings.

Oracle9*i* introduces three new datatypes to enable you to store date, time, and fractional seconds information. Two of these three can also track time zone information. Oracle9*i* also introduces two new datatypes to track the length of time intervals.

Oracle9*i* offers enhancements to comply with Unicode Standard Version 3.0. It has introduced two new Unicode-character-encoding systems.

You can perform up to four levels of linguistic sorting to accommodate the needs of almost all international languages. Oracle9*i* provides a Character Set Scanner to identify potential problems as part of a migration to another character set. Oracle also gives you a GUI Locale Builder tool to modify territory, language, character set, and linguistic sort definitions.

Oracle9*i* enables you to specify byte or character semantics to simplify and clarify your intent within DDL CREATE and ALTER TABLE statements.

Two-Minute Drill

- ISO/ANSI SQL:99 standardization
  - Joins
    - The CROSS JOIN performs the cross product that is also called the Cartesian product.
    - The NATURAL JOIN performs an equijoin; it matches rows that have values in all columns that have the same name.
    - In an equijoin, you can specify which of the same-named columns should participate in the join condition with the USING keyword.
    - You can use the ON keyword to specify any predicate separate from the criteria in the WHERE clause.
    - You can explicitly specify a LEFT, RIGHT, or FULL OUTER JOIN operation.
  - CASE statements
    - The simple CASE expression was available in Oracle8*i*; it is very similar to the DECODE statement that uses value and substitution expression pairs.
    - Oracle9*i* introduces the searched CASE expression to specify a condition or predicate and a corresponding substitution expression.

- The NULLIF function returns a NULL if the two expressions are equal; otherwise, it will return the first expression.
- The COALESCE function returns the first expression in the list that is not a NULL.

- The *scalar subquery* enables you to treat the output of a subquery as a column or expression within a select statement. Prior to Oracle9*i*, you could use the scalar subquery within the SET clause of the UPDATE statement and the VALUES list of the INSERT INTO statement. Oracle9*i* gives you greater flexibility to use the scalar subquery in most places where you can use an expression.
- The MERGE statement enables you to retrieve rows from one table and either update existing rows or insert them, if they are new, into a second table.
- Analytic functions
    - **Distribution functions** The CUME_DIST function, for example, determines the cumulative distribution of a particular value within a set of values.
    - **Inverse distribution functions** The PERCENTILE_CONT and PERCENTILE_DISC interpolate values are based on continuous and discrete distribution models respectively.
    - **Rank functions** The RANK function determines the rank of a value within a set of values. The DENSE_RANK function is similar to the RANK functions; however, it does not skip numbers as the RANK function does when you encounter identical values. The PERCENT_RANK function determines the percentage rank on a scale from 0 to 1.
    - **Positional functions** The FIRST and LAST functions return the values that rank as first or last respectively within a set of rows.
    - **Histogram bucket function** The WIDTH_BUCKET function divides a range for the histogram into equal intervals and returns the number of the bucket into which the specified value falls.
    - **Grouping sets** Grouping sets enable you to enhance the GROUP BY clause; you can specify just those multiple groupings of data that you are interested in.

- Constraints
  - You can explicitly create an index within a CREATE TABLE statement.
  - Oracle9*i* minimizes the duration of locking on unindexed foreign keys when performing an update or delete operation on the primary key.
  - You can cache the first 256 primary keys to improve performance when adding a foreign key.
  - You can define declarative primary key constraints, unique constraints, and referential integrity constraints on views; check constraints are excluded.
- You can specify the period of time in seconds that you can wait for a lock to be released.
- Oracle9*i* simplifies the process of converting a LONG or a LONG RAW column into a CLOB or BLOB column respectively. You can perform that action with a simple ALTER TABLE . . . MODIFY statement.
- You can improve performance significantly by compiling PL/SQL statements into native C code first.
- New date and time datatypes
  - The TIMESTAMP datatype is much like the DATE datatype; you can store date and time values. Unlike the DATE datatype, you can specify the precision of the fractional seconds value.
  - The TIMESTAMP WITH TIMEZONE adds a twist to the TIMESTAMP datatype; you can store the time zone displacement.
  - The TIMESTAMP WITH LOCAL TIMEZONE normalizes the time in terms of the database's time zone.
  - The INTERVAL DAY TO SECOND datatype enables you to store an interval of time in terms of days, hours, minutes, and seconds.
  - The INTERVAL YEAR TO MONTH stores a time interval in terms of years and months.
- Oracle has added the AL16UTF16 and the AL32UTF8 Unicode character encoding sets.
- Oracle9*i* enables you to implement four levels of linguistic sorts. You can also specify special considerations such as contracting characters and reverse secondary sorting.

- The Character Set Scanner identifies potential problems such as data truncation, data loss, data truncation, and data corruption when migrating from one character set to another.
- You can specify the NLS_LENGTH_SEMANTICS to be either BYTE or CHAR. This parameter interprets the precision of CHAR and VARCHAR2 columns in DDL statements as either bytes or characters accordingly. This eliminates the need for you to recalculate the precision when the bytes per character change in a migration. An example would be going from a single-byte UTF8 to a multibyte, variable-width AL32UTF8.
- The Locale Builder is a GUI tool that enables you to modify or specify definitions for language, territory, character set, linguistic sort, and special linguistic considerations.

Fill-in-the-Blanks

1. The ____________ performs an equijoin by matching rows with equal values in all columns that have the same name.
2. The _________ keyword enables you to specify a criteria or condition separate from the other criteria in the WHERE clause.
3. The ________ ________ statement is very similar to the DECODE statement; you can specify value and substitution value pairs.
4. The __________ function returns the first expression in the list that is not NULL.
5. The __________ function determines the cumulative distribution of a particular specified value within a set of values.
6. The ________ function determines the rank of a specified value without skipping numbers.
7. The ___________ datatype enables you to store the time zone displacement along with the date and time values.
8. The time zone displacement is the difference between the local time zone and the _____________, which was formerly known as the ____________.
9. The _____________ and ___________ datatypes enable you to track the duration or the length of a period of time.
10. Oracle9*i* introduces two new Unicode character-encoding sets: ________ and ________.

Chapter Questions

1. Which of the following statements is correct, given that flavor_name and topping_name are columns in the flavor and topping tables respectively?

A.
```
SELECT flavor_name, topping_name
  FROM flavor CROSS JOIN topping USING (flno);
```

B.
```
SELECT flavor_name, topping_name
  FROM flavor CROSS JOIN WITH topping;
```

C.
```
SELECT flavor_name, topping_name
  FROM flavor AND topping (CROSS JOIN);
```

D.
```
SELECT flavor_name, topping_name
  FROM flavor CROSS JOIN topping;
```

2. The NATURAL JOIN

A. Performs a Cartesian product.

B. Matches rows with equal values in some columns that have the same name.

C. Matches rows with equal values in all columns that have the same name.

D. Matches rows based on the user-specified condition or predicate.

3. Which of the following statements is correct?

A.
```
SELECT flavor_name, topping_name
  FROM client JOIN flavor USING (flno);
```

B.
```
SELECT flavor_name, topping_name
  FROM client CROSS JOIN flavor USING (flno);
```

C.
```
SELECT flavor_name, topping_name
  FROM client, flavor JOIN USING (flno);
```

D.
```
SELECT flavor_name, topping_name
  FROM client JOIN flavor USING (flno = flno);
```

4. Which of the following is the correct syntax for a left outer join?

A.
```
SELECT client_name, flavor_name
  FROM LEFT JOIN client, flavor
    ON (client.flno = flavor.flno);
```

B.
```
SELECT client_name, flavor_name
  FROM LEFT OUTER JOIN client, flavor
    ON (client.flno = flavor.flno);
```

C.
```
SELECT client_name, flavor_name
  FROM client LEFT JOIN flavor
    ON (client.flno = flavor.flno);
```

D.
```
SELECT client_name, flavor_name
  FROM client LEFT OUTER JOIN flavor
    ON (client.flno = flavor.flno);
```

5. The TIMESTAMP datatype

A. Is the same as the DATE datatype.

B. Is a variant of the DATE datatype. In addition to storing date and time information, you can specify the precision for the fractional seconds.

C. Is a variant of the DATE datatype. In addition to storing date and time information, you can specify the precision for the fractional minutes.

D. Is reserved for and restricted to system actions such as auditing.

6. Oracle9*i* introduced the following new Unicode character encoding sets:

A. AL16UTF8 and AL32UTF8

B. AL16UTF16 and AL32UTF16

C. AL16UTF16 and AL32UTF8

D. AL16UTF16 and AL32UTF32

Fill-in-the-Blank Answers

1. NATURAL JOIN
2. ON
3. simple, CASE
4. COALESCE
5. CUME_DIST
6. DENSE_RANK
7. TIMESTAMP WITH TIME ZONE

8. Universal Time (Coordinated) (UTC), Greenwich Meridian Time (GMT)
9. INTERVAL DAY TO SECOND, INTERVAL YEAR TO MONTH
10. AL16UTF16, AL32UTF8

Answers to Chapter Questions

1. D.
```
SELECT flavor_name, topping_name
  FROM flavor CROSS JOIN topping;
```

Explanation The CROSS JOIN specifies the cross product also called the Cartesian product. The CROSS JOIN does not need a condition or predicate, and it does not require columns with the same name. It just matches every row from the first table with every row in the second table. You specify the CROSS JOIN instead of the comma that separates the two tables in the FROM clause.

2. C. Matches rows with equal values in all columns that have the same name.

Explanation The NATURAL JOIN performs an equijoin. It identifies all columns that have the same name in both tables and matches the rows that have equal values in all those columns.

3. A.
```
SELECT flavor_name, topping_name
  FROM flavor JOIN topping USING (flno);
```

Explanation The NATURAL JOIN uses all the columns that have the same name. Sometimes this can present a problem; you may want to use some but not all of these columns in the join condition. The USING clause solves this problem; it helps you limit the join condition to just some of these columns with the same name.

4. D.
```
SELECT client_name, flavor_name
  FROM client LEFT OUTER JOIN flavor
    ON (client.flno = flavor.flno);
```

Explanation Outer joins enable you to retrieve rows that satisfy the join condition as well as rows in a table where no rows from the other table satisfy the join condition. Even when ANSI and ISO standards for outer joins did not exist, many past versions of Oracle enabled you to specify the outer join with the (+) qualifier. You could only specify one (+) qualifier to give you a left or a right outer join.

In Oracle9*i*, you can use the SQL:99 specification for the outer join, where you can explicitly use the keywords OUTER JOIN instead of the not-so-readable (+) qualifier. You can also specify LEFT OUTER JOIN instead of the comma that separates the tables in the FROM clause.

5. B. Is a variant of the DATE datatype. In addition to storing date and time information, you can specify the precision for the fractional seconds.

Explanation The TIMESTAMP datatype is very much like the DATE datatype; it can store both the date and time values. Unlike the DATE datatype, you can specify the precision of the fractional seconds value in the TIMESTAMP datatype. The default is 6 digits, and you can specify a value within the range from 0 through 9.

6. C. AL16UTF16 and AL32UTF8

Explanation AL16UTF16 is a 2-byte, fixed-width Unicode character set that is also referred to as UTF16 or UCS2. The ASCII English character set is assigned the first 128 values from 0 (0x00) through 127 (0x7F) in Unicode, which translates to 1 byte. Even though AL16UTF16 uses one more byte than UTF8 for ASCII character representation, it is still faster because it is a fixed-width encoding as opposed to UTF8, which uses variable-width encoding.

AL32UTF8 is an enhanced implementation of UTF8. This is an 8-bit, variable-width encoding that uses multiple bytes to represent a Unicode character. Although UTF8 is supported in Oracle9*i* for backward compatibility and for the migration of data from earlier versions of Oracle, you should use AL32ATF8 instead of UTF8. UTFE is also supported in Oracle9*i*, but AL24UTFFSS is no longer supported in Oracle9*i*.

PART II

Oracle9*i* Certified Professional New Features Practice Exams

CHAPTER 6

OCP Oracle9*i* Upgrade Exam: New Features for Administrators

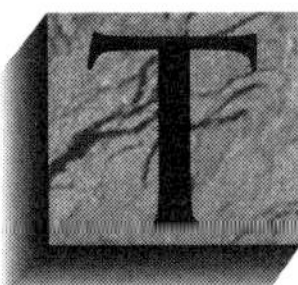

he Oracle9*i* Upgrade exam focuses on the new features of Oracle9*i*. To successfully pass this exam, you need to be proficient in security enhancements, availability enhancements, manageability enhancements, performance and scalability enhancements, and Structured Query Language (SQL) and globalization enhancements.

Practice Exam I

1-1. Which of the following Server Manager commands is supported in SQL*Plus?

A. STARTUP

B. SET DATEWIDTH

C. SET CHARWIDTH

D. SET RETRIES

1-2. In Oracle9*i*, which of the following passwords does the DBCA utility use for the SYSTEM account when creating a new database?

A. change_on_install

B. sys

C. It prompts you for a password.

D. manager

1-3. What is `p.pwd` in the following statement to create a role?

```
CREATE ROLE r1 IDENTIFIED USING p.pwd;
```

A. The password for the role

B. The procedure to authenticate the role

C. An alternative name for the role

D. None of the above

1-4. Which two of the following statements are true in the case of the Global Application Context?

A. It uses connections pooling.

B. A separate session is created for each user.

C. An existing session is reused.

D. None of the above

1-5. One Oracle9*i* enhancement to LogMiner is

A. The DBMS_LOGMNR_D Package

B. Tracking DDL commands

C. Creating a dictionary file

D. Tracking DML commands

1-6. Which of the following conditions do not have to be met in order to add new masters without quiescing?

A. All master sites in the replication configuration must be at Oracle 9.0.0 or higher.

B. The master group to which you are adding the new master must be replicating in the asynchronous mode.

C. You must have enough space for rollback segments or undo tablespace to support the export.

D. The master group to which you are adding the new master must be replicating in the synchronous mode.

1-7. Which of the following is a parameter to specify the target mean-time-to-recover for the instance recovery?

A. FAST_START_IO_TARGET

B. FAST_START_MTTR_TARGET

C. LOG_CHECKPOINT_TIMEOUT

D. INSTANCE_RECOVER_MTTR_TARGET

1-8. To use the Flashback feature, the database should be using

A. Either automatic or manual undo management

B. Manual undo management (rollback segments)

C. Automatic undo management

D. None of the above

1-9. Which of the following conditions can Resumable Space Allocation (RSA) not correct?

A. Out of space

B. Disk crash

C. Maximum extents reached

D. Space quota exceeded

1-10. Which two of the following values can the new Oracle9*i* import parameter, STATISTICS, take?

A. ALWAYS

B. NEVER

C. NONE

D. ALL

1-11. Which of the following is not a component of the Data Guard Broker?

A. The Data Guard Scheduler

B. The Data Guard Command Line Interface

C. The Data Guard Monitor

D. The Data Guard Manager

1-12. Which of the following is/are the parameter(s) used to specify the standby database when configuring a Data Guard solution?

A. DG_DEST_2

B. DG_STANDBY_2

C. LOG_ARCHIVE_DEST_2

D. LOG_DEST_2

1-13. Which of the following is not a requirement that must be met in order to perform the switchover operation?

A. You can have up to two active SQL sessions on the instance in which you are performing the switchover.

B. You must have an active Oracle Net connection between the primary database and the standby database.

C. The online redo logs and control files of the primary database must be available.

D. The standby database must be in the Archivelog mode.

1-14. When rebuilding an index online, which of the following statements is true if DML operations are performed that affect the index?

A. The old index entries are changed immediately.

B. The new index entries are changed immediately.

C. DML operations are not allowed on the table while the index is being rebuilt online.

D. The updates are journalled in an index-organized table (IOT).

1-15. Which one of the following integrity constraints is mandatory for a table to be redefined online?

A. Primary key

B. Unique

C. Referential integrity

D. Not null

1-16. Which of the following statements is the correct statement to validate the structure of a table with the online Analyze command?

A. `ANALYZE TABLE product ONLINE VALIDATE STRUCTURE;`

B. `ANALYZE TABLE product VALIDATE STRUCTURE ONLINE;`

C. `VALIDATE STRUCTURE ANALYZE TABLE product ONLINE;`

D. `ANALYZE TABLE product STRUCTURE VALIDATE ONLINE;`

1-17. Which of the following statements about the SPFILE is not true?

A. It is a binary file that serves as a storage facility for initialization parameters.

B. It is maintained by the Oracle database server.

C. It makes the initialization parameters persistent between database shutdown and startups.

D. It can be manually edited with a text editor.

1-18. To specify the maximum estimated time for an operation to complete (in seconds), which of the following parameters do you assign a value to?

A. MAX_EST_EXEC_TIME

B. MAX_EST_TIME

C. MAX_EST_ TIME_TO_COMPLETE

D. MAX_ EXEC_TIME

1-19. What is the first step when you specify a Database Resource Manager solution?

A. Create a resource plan

B. Create a plan directive

C. Create a pending area

D. Create a resource consumer group

1-20. Which of the following is not a required component of the Oracle Shared Server architecture?

A. A network listener process

B. At least one dispatcher process

C. At least one resource directive

D. At least one shared server process

1-21. Which of the following statements is not true about the threads in the Multithreaded Heterogeneous Service Agent Architecture?

A. It has several task threads

B. It has several dispatcher threads

C. It has a single monitor thread

D. It has a single server manager thread

1-22. Which of the following statements specifies that Oracle should update global indexes as it performs the partition DDL?

A.
```
ALTER TABLE <table_name>
 DROP PARTITION <partition_name>
 WITH UPDATE GLOBAL INDEXES
```

B.
```
ALTER TABLE <table_name>
 DROP PARTITION <partition_name>
 UPDATE GLOBAL INDEXES
```

C.
```
ALTER TABLE <table_name>
 UPDATE GLOBAL INDEXES WITH
 DROP PARTITION <partition_name>
```

D.
```
ALTER TABLE <table_name>
 UPDATE GLOBAL INDEXES AND
 DROP PARTITION <partition_name>
```

1-23. Which of the following operations are allowed on external tables?

A. Insert

B. Update

C. Delete

D. Select

1-24. In which version of Oracle was hash partitioning introduced?

A. 7

B. 8

C. 8*i*

D. 9*i*

1-25. Which of the following statements is false when documenting database objects prior to Oracle9*i*?

A. You can query the various data dictionary views to obtain information about an object.

B. Using Oracle's Export/Import utilities, you must set the parameter ROWS=N for the export operation and SHOW=Y for the import operation.

C. Use procedures in the DBMS_METADATA package.

D. Use the `OCIDescribeAny` interface.

1-26. Which of the following statements must be true for automatic segment space management?

- **A.** The Segment Management clause can be specified with the CREATE TABLE command with no other requirements.
- **B.** The Segment Management clause can be specified with the CREATE TABLESPACE command and the tablespace must be dictionary managed.
- **C.** The Segment Management clause can be specified with the CREATE TABLESPACE command and the tablespace must be locally managed.
- **D.** In Oracle9*i*, the space within each block of a segment is always automatically managed and hence there is no need to specify any Segment Management clause.

1-27. Which of the following packages do you use to obtain information about the free blocks in automatically space-managed segments?

- **A.** DBMS_SPACE
- **B.** DBMS_BLOCKS
- **C.** DBMS_FREE
- **D.** DBMS_SEGMENTS

1-28. Which of the following statements is not true for a bitmap join index?

- **A.** Only one table can be updated concurrently by different transactions if the indexed column is being modified.
- **B.** One table cannot appear more than one time in the join condition.
- **C.** You cannot reference an index-organized table or a temporary table.
- **D.** This feature was introduced in Oracle8*i*.

1-29. Which of the following statements must be true in order to version-enable a table?

- **A.** The table must have a primary key.
- **B.** The table can contain a LONG datatype column.
- **C.** After version enabling a table, DDL operations can be performed on it.
- **D.** An index-organized table can be version-enabled.

1-30. You can access any workspace by

A. Invoking the SETTOWORKSPACE procedure

B. Invoking the GOTOWORKSPACE procedure

C. Invoking the ASSIGNWORKSPACE procedure

D. Invoking the ACCESSWORKSPACE procedure

1-31. Which of the following statements is not true about Oracle-Managed Files (OMF)?

A. You do not have to specify filenames when creating databases, tablespaces, and redo log groups.

B. You have to delete unnecessary files such as datafiles corresponding to dropped tablespaces.

C. You can specify the locations for these OMFs by setting initialization parameters.

D. Oracle names and creates the data files, redo log files, and control files automatically.

1-32. Which initialization parameter specifies the location of Oracle-managed datafiles?

A. DB_OMF_DIRECTORY_n

B. DB_CREATE_ONLINE_LOG_DEST

C. DB_CREATE_FILE_DEST

D. DB_OMF_FILES_n

1-33. When dropping tablespaces with non-OMF files, which clause do you add to also drop referential integrity constraints from foreign or primary keys of tables outside the tablespace that reference primary keys of tables inside the tablespace?

A. INCLUDING EXTERNAL REFERENCES

B. CASCADE EXTERNAL CONSTRAINTS

C. INCLUDING REFERENCES

D. CASCADE CONSTRAINTS

1-34. Which of the following commands can you use to associate a default temporary tablespace with a database?

A. CREATE DATABASE

B. CREATE TEMPORARY TABLESPACE

C. CREATE TABLESPACE

D. CREATE DEFAULT TEMPORARY TABLESPACE

1-35. Which of the following statements are true about automatic undo management (AUM)?

A. AUM gives you a GUI interface to analyze redo logs.

B. AUM automatically archives redo entries to a mirror site.

C. AUM performs the space management of rollback segments.

D. AUM automatically develops the undo information for DDL statements.

1-36. Automatic undo management (AUM) can use

A. One undo tablespace at a time

B. Up to five undo tablespaces at a time

C. Unlimited tablespaces

D. AUM does not use tablespaces

1-37. Which of the following is not an initialization parameter to configure multiple block sizes?

A. DB_BLOCK_BUFFERS

B. DB_CACHE_SIZE

C. DB_nk_CACHE_SIZE

D. DB_BLOCK_SIZE

1-38. What new clause for the CREATE TABLESPACE command did Oracle9*i* introduce to specify the block size to be used for the tablespace?

A. USE BLOCKSIZE

B. SET BLOCKSIZE

C. BLOCKSIZE

D. None of the above

1-39. Which of the following options is a new Oracle9*i* instance-level parameter that specifies the total memory for the Program Global Area (PGA) of all sessions combined?

A. DBA_PGA_MEM

B. PGA_AGGREGATE_TARGET

C. DBA_AGGREGATE_TARGET

D. PGA_MEMORY

1-40. Which of the following are not new columns that Oracle9*i* added to V$PROCESS?

A. PGA_USED_MEM

B. PGA_ALLOC_MEM

C. PGA_MAX_MEM

D. PGA_TOTAL_MEM

1-41. The unit of memory allocation for dynamic SGA is

A. KB

B. Module

C. DB_BLOCK_SIZE

D. Granule

1-42. Which new command did Oracle9*i* introduce to configure various backup, restore, and recover parameters that are persistent across RMAN sessions?

A. RMANCONFIG

B. CONFIGURE

C. RMANPARAM

D. RMANPERSIST

1-43. Which two of the following tasks does Oracle9*i*'s new recovery mechanism called Trial Recovery enable you to do?

A. Perform recovery operations without committing the operations so you can roll back if the need arises.

B. Perform recovery operations that give you estimates of the time to complete before you begin the actual recovery operations.

C. Only records data in the buffers as opposed to writing the data to files.

D. Anticipate problems before performing the recovery.

1-44. The new Oracle9*i* RECOVERY WINDOW clause and the REDUNDANCY clause are

A. Mutually exclusive

B. Independent of each other

C. Are not clauses of the same command

D. Can accomplish the same job

1-45. Which of the following tasks can you perform if you have invoked the Oracle Enterprise Manager (OEM) console in the standalone mode?

A. You can administer the database.

B. You can administer HTTP web servers.

C. You can administer events and jobs.

D. You can utilize the backup and data management tools.

1-46. Which of the following is not a component of a user-defined event?

A. A component to monitor the condition of interest

B. A component that evaluates the results of the first component

C. A component that generates reports that can be published on the Web

D. A component that sends the results of the evaluation to the Event framework using XML tags

1-47. Which of the following views contains information about index utilization?

A. DBA_INDEXES

B. DBS_OBJECTS

C. V$OBJECT_USAGE

D. V$SYSSTAT

1-48. In which version of Oracle was cursor sharing introduced?

A. 7

B. 8

C. 8*i*

D. 9*i*

1-49. Which of the following views was introduced in Oracle9*i* to display cached execution plans?

A. V$SQLAREA

B. V$SQL_TEXT

C. V$LIBRARYCACHE

D. V$SQL_PLAN

1-50. Which new columns did Oracle9*i* not add to the PLAN_TABLE?

A. CPU_COST

B. IO_COST

C. TEMP_SPACE

D. OPERATION

1-51. Which of the following is not an alternative for the Global Cache Service (GCS) to transfer the block from the holding instance to the requesting instance?

A. Block Transfer with Forced Disk Write

B. Block Transfer with Cache Fusion

C. Read Consistent Cache Fusion

D. Cache Fusion Block Transfer

1-52. Which statement is true about the initialization parameter file in the Oracle Real Application Clusters (RAC) implementation?

A. A separate parameter file has to be maintained for each instance.

B. A parameter file is not sharable.

C. You use the `<INSTANCE_NAME>.<PARAMETER> = VALUE` notation for instance-specific parameters.

D. No special changes are required to the parameter file; it is always sharable.

1-53. Which line in the following SELECT statement causes an error?

```
SELECT client_name, client.flno, flavor_name, qty
  FROM client NATURAL JOIN flavor
WHERE qty > 3
ORDER BY client_name;
```

A. Line 1

B. Line 2

C. Line 3

D. Line 4

1-54. Which of the following statements is true in the context of explicit index control in Oracle9*i*?

A. Oracle will always DROP the index when you DROP a constraint.

B. Oracle will always KEEP the index when you DROP a constraint.

C. You can explicitly tell Oracle to either KEEP the index or DROP the index when you DROP a constraint.

D. Oracle will always DISABLE the index when you DROP a constraint.

1-55. To what value must you set the PLSQL_COMPILER_FLAGS parameter to compile PL/SQL code into native C code?

A. INTERPRETED

B. NATIVE

C. FAST

D. COMPILED

1-56. Which statement is not true about the TIMESTAMP datatype?

A. You can store the date.

B. You can store the time.

C. You can specify the precision of the fractional seconds.

D. There is no TIMESTAMP datatype.

1-57. AL16UTF16 is

A. A 2-byte, fixed-width Unicode character set

B. A 8-bit, fixed-width Unicode character set

C. A 2-byte, variable-width Unicode character set

D. A 4-byte, fixed-width Unicode character set

1-58. Which mode can you not invoke the Character Set Scanner in?

A. Full Database scan

B. User scan

C. Table scan

D. Character Set scan

1-59. Which datatype enables you to specify the offset of the time from the Greenwich Meridian Time (GMT)?

A. TIMESTAMP WITH TIME ZONE

B. TIMESTAMP

C. DATE

D. INTERVAL YEAR TO MONTH

1-60. Which statements are true when comparing the ON clause with the NATURAL JOIN?

A. You have greater flexibility with the ON clause than with the NATURAL JOIN.

B. You have greater flexibility with the NATURAL JOIN than with the ON clause.

C. The NATURAL JOIN and the ON clause are exactly the same statement.

D. One is a join operation; the other is not.

Practice Exam 2

2-1. Which of the following is a privileged connection that was deprecated in Oracle9*I*?

A. CONNECT DBA

B. CONNECT AS DBA

C. CONNECT AS INTERNAL

D. CONNECT INTERNAL

2-2. To which of the following values does Oracle9*i* set the 07_DICTIONARY_ACCESSIBILITY parameter?

A. YES

B. NO

C. TRUE

D. FALSE

2-3. Oracle9*i* enables you to associate multiple policies with a table when implementing a virtual private database. When multiple policies are specified on a table, which of the following statements is correct?

A. Data access is granted if any one of the policies is satisfied.

B. Data access is granted when at least 50 percent of the policies are satisfied.

C. Data access is granted only when all policies are satisfied.

D. None of the above

2-4. Which of the following do you use to implement partitioned fine-grained access control?

A. Passwords

B. Privileges

C. Roles

D. Policy groups

2-5. The view that you query to review the DDL/DML redo entries is

A. V$LOGMNR_CONTENTS

B. V$LOGMNR_LOGS

C. V$LOGMNR_DICTIONARY

D. V$LOGMNR_PARAMETERS

2-6. Which of the following restrictions must be true when you add new masters without quiescing?

A. You cannot add a new master to the group until the previous add new master operation is completed.

B. You can add a new master to the group before the previous add new master operation is completed.

C. You can add a new master to the group once the previous add new master operation reaches the percent specified by the PREV_MASTER_PERCENT parameter.

D. None of the above

2-7. Which of the following parameters used to manage instance recovery prior to Oracle9*i* was retired in Oracle9*i*?

A. LOG_CHECKPOINT_INTERVAL

B. LOG_CHECKPOINT_TIMEOUT

C. FAST_START_IO_TARGET

D. DB_BLOCK_MAX_DIRTY_TARGET

2-8. Which of the following statements can you use while in the Flashback mode?

A. DML statements

B. DDL statements

C. Select statements

D. All of the above

2-9. To perform custom operations when a resumable operation is suspended, you

A. Use the AFTER SUSPEND clause in the CREATE OR REPLACE PROCEDURE statement.

B. Use the WHEN SUSPENDED clause in the CREATE OR REPLACE PROCEDURE statement.

C. Use the AFTER SUSPEND clause in the CREATE OR REPLACE TRIGGER statement.

D. Use the WHEN SUSPENDED clause in the CREATE OR REPLACE TRIGGER statement.

2-10. Which of the following are new Oracle9*i* parameters for performing exports and imports?

A. RESUMABLE_TIME

B. RESUMABLE_TIMEOUT

C. EXPORT_TIMEOUT

D. EXPORT_TIME

2-11. Which of the following is the process your local Data Guard Manager or Data Guard Command Line Interface (CLI) needs to communicate with in order to interact with an Oracle instance or obtain information about the instance?

A. The Data Guard Communicator (DGC) process

B. The Data Guard Scheduler (DGS) process

C. The Data Guard Network (DNET) process

D. The Data Guard Monitor (DMON) process

2-12. Which of the following statements specifies that the archive transmission for the standby database named 'friday' must be performed synchronously (SYNC)?

A. `LOG_ARCHIVE_DEST_n = 'SERVICE=friday LGWR SYNC'`

B. `LOG_ARCHIVE_DEST_n = 'SERVICE=friday ARCHIVER=LGWR TRANS=SYNC'`

C. `LOG_ARCHIVE_ n = 'SERVICE=friday LGWR SYNC'`

D. `LOG_ARCHIVE_DEST_n = 'SERVICE=friday LGWR SYNC'`

2-13. Which of the following statements is true in a database switchover operation?

A. There is no loss of data and you must instantiate both databases.

B. There is no loss of data and you must instantiate either database.

C. There is no loss of data and you do not have to instantiate either database.

D. There is some loss of data.

2-14. Which of the following is the statement to rebuild an existing index "product_description_ix"?

A. `REBUILD INDEX product_description_ix ONLINE;`

B. `ALTER INDEX product_description_ix REBUILD ONLINE;`

C. `ONLINE REBUILD INDEX product_description_ix ONLINE;`

D. `ALTER INDEX product_description_ix ONLINE REBUILD;`

2-15. Which one of the following statements is a requirement for a table to be redefined online?

A. The table cannot be part of a cluster.

B. The table can have a BFILE column.

C. The table can have a LONG column.

D. The table can have user-defined types.

2-16. While the validating table structure with the online Analyze command is in progress, which of the following statements is true?

A. You can perform DML operations.

B. You can perform DDL operations.

C. You can perform TRUNCATE operations.

D. None of the above

2-17. Which of the following must you do in order to view the contents of the server parameter file?

A. You query the V$SPPARAMETER view.

B. You invoke the DBMS_SPFILE.DISPLAY_PARAMETERS procedure.

C. You query the V$SPFILE view.

D. You invoke the DBMS_SPFILE.SHOW_PARAMETERS procedure.

2-18. Which of the following statements is true if the SWITCH_ESTIMATE parameter is set to TRUE, and if Oracle's estimate is greater than the value specified by MAX_EST_EXEC_TIME?

A. Oracle will display an error and perform the operation.

B. Oracle will return an error and the operation will not be not started.

C. Oracle will not return an error; the operation will not be not started.

D. None of the above

2-19. Which two of the following are the Oracle-defined default resource consumer groups that you cannot change or delete?

A. DEFAULT_RESOURCE_CONSUMER_GROUP

B. DEFAULT_CONSUMER_GROUP

C. DEFAULT_GROUPS

D. OTHER_GROUPS

2-20. In Oracle9*i*, when the listener receives the request from the client for a shared server connection, it locates the address of the least loaded dispatcher process and then

A. Passes this address back to the client, so the client can contact the dispatcher over the network

B. Passes this address back to the client, so the client can contact the server over the network

C. Passes the connection request to the dispatcher

D. None of the above

2-21. Which of the following statements is true about the Multithreaded Heterogeneous Service Agent architecture in Oracle9*i*?

- **A.** It uses an agent for each user session.
- **B.** It uses an agent for each database link.
- **C.** It uses a pool of shared agent processes.
- **D.** It uses a pool of shared agent processes for every different database.

2-22. Which of the following statements is true if you do not specify the `UPDATE GLOBAL INDEXES` clause in the partition DDL statement?

- **A.** It defaults to `IGNORE GLOBAL INDEXES`.
- **B.** It defaults to `INVALIDATE GLOBAL INDEXES`.
- **C.** It defaults to `VALIDATE GLOBAL INDEXES`.
- **D.** None of the above.

2-23. Which of the following is true when creating external tables?

- **A.** You specify the ORGANIZATION EXTERNAL TABLE clause in the CREATE TABLE statement.
- **B.** You specify the ORGANIZATION EXTERNAL clause in the CREATE TABLE statement.
- **C.** You specify the ORGANIZATION EXTERNAL OS FILE clause in the CREATE TABLE statement.
- **D.** You specify the ORGANIZATION OS FILE clause in the CREATE TABLE statement.

2-24. Which two of the following statements are true in the case of list partitioning?

- **A.** You cannot use list partitioning with Index Organized Tables (IOTs).
- **B.** You cannot merge list partitions.
- **C.** You cannot add new list partitions.
- **D.** You cannot specify MAXVALUE.

2-25. Which of the following tasks does the GET_DDL procedure in the DBMS_METADATA package enable you to do?

- **A.** It gets you a history of all the DDL statements performed in the database.
- **B.** It gets you the DDL statements used to create the tables and views.
- **C.** It returns the metadata as DDL.
- **D.** None of the above.

2-26. Which of the following data dictionary views should be queried to determine if the segment space management is automatic or manual?

- **A.** DBA_TABLESPACES
- **B.** DBA_OBJECTS
- **C.** DBA_TABLES
- **D.** DBA_SEGMENTS

2-27. Which of the following clauses of the CREATE TABLESPACE statement do you use to create a tablespace with automatically space-managed segments?

- **A.** AUTOMATIC SEGMENT SPACE MANAGEMENT
- **B.** AUTOMATIC SPACE MANAGED SEGMENTS
- **C.** SEGMENT SPACE MANAGEMENT AUTO
- **D.** SPACE MANAGEMENT AUTO

2-28. Which of the following statements enables you to determine if an index is based on a join condition?

- **A.** You query the COLUMN_NAME column in the DBA_JOIN_INDEXES data dictionary.
- **B.** You query the JOIN_INDEX column in the DBA_INDEXES data dictionary.
- **C.** You invoke the SHOW_JOIN_INDEX package in the DBMS_INDEXES package.
- **D.** You invoke the SHOW_COLUMNS package in the DBMS_JOIN_INDEXES package.

2-29. Which procedure do you use to version-enable a table?

- **A.** The VERSIONENABLE subprogram in the DBMS_WM package
- **B.** The ENABLEVERSIONING subprogram in the DBMS_WORKSPACE package
- **C.** The VERSIONENABLE subprogram in the DBMS_ WORKSPACE package
- **D.** The ENABLEVERSIONING subprogram in the DBMS_WM package

2-30. Which of the following privileges do you not need in order to create a workspace?

- **A.** The CREATE_WORKSPACE role
- **B.** The CREATE_WORKSPACE privilege
- **C.** The WM_ADMIN_ROLE role
- **D.** The CREATE_ANY_WORKSPACE privilege

2-31. Which of the following is true about Oracle-Managed Files (OMFs)?

- **A.** OMF enables you to refer to table data stored in OS files just like you would regular tables.
- **B.** OMF enables you to refer to table and column definitions stored in OS files just like you would query the data dictionary.
- **C.** OMF enables you to archive rarely used information in OS files and refer to them just like you would regular table data.
- **D.** OMF manages operating system files such as datafiles corresponding to tablespaces.

2-32. Which statements are true when dropping a tablespace that uses OMF files?

- **A.** The tablespace is dropped, but the datafiles are not deleted from the disk.
- **B.** The tablespace is dropped and the datafiles are deleted from the disk.
- **C.** You cannot drop a tablespace that uses OMF files.
- **D.** None of the above.

2-33. Which of the following is not true when you run the following SQL statement?

```
ALTER DATABASE
  TEMPFILE 'd:\oracle\oradata\hr_temp\temp1.dbf' DROP
  INCLUDING DATAFILES;
```

A. Oracle deletes the tempfiles definition in the database.

B. Oracle deletes the OS tempfiles.

C. Oracle deletes the tablespace.

D. Oracle sends a message to the alert log.

2-34. What is the purpose of a default temporary tablespace?

A. This is a tablespace outside the firewall for temporary or anonymous users on the Web.

B. This is a tablespace for users that were not assigned a tablespace.

C. This is the temporary tablespace for users that were not assigned a temporary tablespace.

D. None of the above.

2-35. When using automatic undo management (AUM), what is the appropriate action to minimize the "Snapshot Too Old" error?

A. Create a large rollback segment.

B. Set the UNDO_RETENTION parameter appropriately.

C. Create a large temporary tablespace for additional rollback segment space.

D. This is not an AUM error.

2-36. Which two of the following parameters enable you to specify automatic undo management (AUM)?

A. ROLLBACK_SEGMENTS

B. UNDO_MANAGEMENT

C. TRANSACTIONS_PER_ROLLBACK_SEGEMNT

D. UNDO_TABLESPACE

2-37. What is the maximum number of different block sizes that are supported in Oracle9*i*?

A. One

B. Five

C. Six

D. Unlimited

2-38. Which statement is true if you do not specify the BLOCKSIZE?

A. Oracle defaults to the maximum block size (32K).

B. Oracle defaults to the minimum block size (2K).

C. Oracle defaults to the standard block size.

D. Oracle defaults to the median block size (8K).

2-39. Which of the following statements is true when specifying work area management and work area sizing?

A. You must set PGA_AGGREGATE_TARGET to a nonzero value before you set WORKAREA_SIZE_POLICY to AUTO.

B. You must set WORKAREA_SIZE_POLICY to AUTO before you set PGA_AGGREGATE_TARGET to a nonzero value.

C. You must set PGA_AGGREGATE_TARGET to AUTO before you set WORKAREA_SIZE_POLICY to a nonzero value.

D. The sequence does not matter.

2-40. Which of the following is not a new view to which Oracle9*i* added process statistics?

A. V$SESSTAT

B. V$MYSTAT

C. V$PROCSTAT

D. V$SYSSTAT

2-41. The parameter used to size the dynamic database buffer cache is

A. DB_CACHE_SIZE

B. DB_BLOCK_BUFFERS

C. BUFFER_POOL_KEEP

D. BUFFER_POOL_RECYCLE

2-42. The redundancy policy and the recovery window policy are?

A. Independent of each other.

B. They are ANDed.

C. They are ORed.

D. Mutually exclusive.

2-43. Which of the following statements is incorrect in the context of block media recovery?

A. You cannot do this from SQL*PLUS.

B. You can only perform complete recovery of a block.

C. Corrupted blocks are not available to users until the block has been fully recovered.

D. You can perform block media recovery from incremental backups.

2-44. Which of the following statements are true about Recovery Manager (RMAN)?

A. RMAN cannot back up tablespaces with different block sizes using a single command.

B. RMAN can back up tablespaces with different block sizes using a single command.

C. RMAN cannot back up tablespaces in an instance that uses different block sizes.

D. None of the above.

2-45. Which of the following statements is not true about the Oracle Enterprise Manager's (OEM) central reporting framework?

A. This reporting framework is integrated into all the OEM applications.

B. You can generate and publish these reports either as needed or on a fixed schedule.

C. You can generate reports about the whole configuration, but not about an object in the configuration.

D. You can design, select, customize, generate, schedule, and publish predefined and user-defined HTML reports to a web site.

2-46. How do you display the OEM tab to view details about the undo tablespace?

A. Select the Configuration object within the Instance object in the Navigator pane, and then select the Undo tab on the Details pane.

B. Select the Database object within the Instance object in the Navigator pane, and then select the Undo Tablespace tab on the Details pane.

C. Select the Configuration object within the Instance object in the Navigator pane, and then select the Undo Tablespace tab on the Details pane.

D. Select the Performance Manager object within the Instance object in the Navigator pane, and then select the Undo tab on the Details pane.

2-47. Which of the following statements start the process of monitoring and collecting index utilization statistics?

A. `ALTER INDEX part_ix MONITOR USAGE;`

B. `ALTER INDEX part_ix START MONITORING;`

C. `ALTER INDEX part_ix START MONITORING USAGE;`

D. `ALTER INDEX part_ix MONITORING USAGE;`

2-48. In what version of Oracle was the FORCE option for cursor sharing introduced to enable you to share execution plans among similar statements?

A. 7

B. 8

C. 8*i*

D. 9*i*

2-49. Which column did Oracle9*i* add to the V$SQL view?

A. EXECUTION_PLAN

B. PLAN_HASH_VALUE

C. CACHE_USAGE

D. PLAN_CACHE_INDEX

2-50. Which package contains the GATHER_SYSTEM_STATS and the GET_SYSTEM_STATS procedures?

A. DBMS_STATS

B. DBA_STATS

C. SYSTEM_STATS

D. OBJECT_STATS

2-51. Which method for transferring the block from the holding instance to the requesting instance was available prior to Oracle 8.1?

A. Block Transfer with Forced Disk Write

B. Block Transfer with Cache Fusion

C. Read Consistent Cache Fusion

D. Cache Fusion Block Transfer

2-52. Which of the following is not true about shared server-side initialization parameter files in Real Application Clusters (RACs)?

A. You can store the parameters for all instances in one initialization parameter file.

B. You can share one initialization parameter file among many instances.

C. You cannot share one initialization parameter file among many instances.

D. You can specify instance-specific parameters by prefixing the initialization parameter with the name of the instance.

2-53. Which of the following statements is not true when using the NATURAL JOIN?

A. Tables used in the NATURAL JOIN can have a pair of columns that have the same name.

B. Tables used in the NATURAL JOIN can have any number of pairs of columns with the same names.

C. You are not required to have columns in both tables with the same name, but the datatype of at least one pair of columns must be the same.

D. You cannot qualify columns with the table names or aliases.

2-54. When verifying the existence of a matching primary key before adding a foreign key, you

A. Cannot cache primary keys

B. Cache up to 64 primary keys

C. Cache up to 256 primary keys

D. Cache up to 512 primary keys

2-55. Which data dictionary view tells you if a PL/SQL code unit has been compiled in the interpreted mode or native mode?

A. DBA_OBJECTS

B. DBA_SOURCE

C. DBA_STORED_SETTINGS

D. DBA_VIEWS

2-56. Which statement is true about the TIMESTAMP WITH TIME ZONE datatype?

A. It represents *absolute* time.

B. In addition to the date and time, you can store the time zone displacement (or offset), which requires additional bytes of storage.

C. In addition to the date and time, you can store the time zone displacement (or offset) without consuming additional bytes of storage.

D. You can use the NLS_TIMESTAMP_TZ_FORMAT initialization parameter to specify the default timestamp data format for retrieval.

2-57. AL32UTF8 is an enhanced implementation of

A. UTF16

B. UTF32

C. UTF8

D. AL16UTF16

2-58. The Character Set Scanner utility (CSSCAN) enables you to

A. Scan in new character sets and create a font

B. Discover potential problems with character set migrations

C. Perform Optical Character Recognition (OCR) tasks

D. Manage the character sets or fonts

2-59. What is the maximum number of rows that a scalar subquery can return?

A. 1

B. 10

C. 100

D. 1,000

2-60. Which of the following statements is not true in the context of the simple CASE expression?

A. Each CASE expression can have up to 255 arguments.

B. It enables you to specify a number of WHEN . . . THEN . . . pairs.

C. The nested CASE expression enables you to have an additional set of 255 arguments.

D. Each WHEN . . . THEN . . . pair counts as one argument.

Practice Exam 3

3-1. Which of the following utilities can you not use to perform administrative tasks in Oracle9*i*?

A. RMAN

B. Server Manager

C. OEM

D. SQL*Plus

3-2. The OEM tool that enables you to manage security policies is

A. Security Manager

B. Security Policy Manager

C. Virtual Private Database Manager

D. Policy Manager

3-3. When implementing fine-grained access control, which of the following packages helps you to create and maintain policy groups?

A. DBMS_FGA

B. DBMS_RLS

C. DBMS_SESSION

D. DBMS_LOCK

3-4. Oracle9*i*'s fine-grained auditing enables you to audit the

A. SELECT statement

B. INSERT INTO statement

C. UPDATE statement

D. DDL statements

3-5. Which of the following statements is false when working with the LogMiner utility?

A. You can extract data dictionary information to an operating system file.

B. You can extract data dictionary information to redo log files.

C. You can use LogMiner without a data dictionary.

D. You cannot use LogMiner without a data dictionary.

3-6. Which of the following restrictions are true when you add new masters without quiescing?

A. You can only add one new master site at a time at a master site.

B. You can only add two new master sites at a time at a master site.

C. You can only add five new master sites at a time at a master site.

D. The maximum number of new master sites that you can add at a time at a master site is the number specified in the NEW_MASTERS parameter.

3-7. Which two of the following are columns that were added to V$INSTANCE_RECOVERY?

A. FAST_START_MTTR_TARGET

B. TARGET_MTTR

C. FAST_START_ESTIMATED_MTTR

D. ESTIMATED_MTTR

3-8. Which of the following procedures must you invoke to enable Flashback for the session and to access the database at the system change number (SCN) that is closest to the specified time?

A. DBMS_FLASHBACK.ENABLE_AT_SYSTEM_CHANGE_NUMBER

B. DBMS_FLASHBACK.ENABLE_AT_NEAREST_SCN

C. DBMS_FLASHBACK.ENABLE_AT_SCN

D. DBMS_FLASHBACK.ENABLE_AT_TIME

3-9. Which of the following statements would you use to set the session in the resumable mode?

A. ALTER SESSION ENABLE RESUMABLE;

B. ALTER SESSION SET RESUMABLE;

C. ALTER SESSION SET RESUMABLE = TRUE;

D. None of the above

3-10. Which of the following is a new Oracle9*i* import-related parameter?

A. RECALCULATE

B. EXPORT_STATISTICS

C. ANALYZE

D. STATISTICS

3-11. Which of the following is not a function performed by the Log Application service?

A. It automatically applies archived redo logs.

B. It archives the redo logs from the primary database onto each standby database.

C. It automatically recovers archive gaps.

D. It automatically delays the application of archived redo logs.

3-12. Assuming that the standby database is available, which of the following statements is true about the Guaranteed Protection mode?

A. It is zero data divergence, but not zero data loss.

B. It is zero data loss, but not zero data divergence.

C. It is both zero data divergence and zero data loss.

D. It is neither zero data divergence nor zero data loss.

3-13. Which of the following values in the SWITCHOVER_STATUS column of the V$DATABASE view tells you that it is possible to switchover a primary database to a standby?

A. READY FOR STANDBY

B. TO STANDBY

C. TO SWITCHOVER

D. READY FOR SWITCHOVER

3-14. Which of the following statements is not true?

A. The online rebuilding of indexes was introduced in Oracle8*i*.

B. Oracle9*i* performs online index rebuilding of reverse key indexes and function-based indexes.

C. Oracle9*i* performs online index rebuilding of bitmap or partitioned local and global indexes.

D. Oracle9*i* performs online index rebuilding of compressed indexes on tables and of key compressed indexes on index organized tables (IOT).

3-15. To verify that a table can be redefined online

A. You query the `can_redef_table` column in the `v$dbms_redefinition` view.

B. You query the `ok_to_redefine` column in the `v$dbms_redefinition` view.

C. You invoke the `ok_to_redefine` procedure in the `dbms_redefinition` package.

D. You invoke the `can_redef_table` procedure in the `dbms_redefinition` package.

3-16. Which of the following statements is not true when you use the ANALYZE command with the VALIDATE STRUCTURE option?

A. You verify the structural integrity of a table.

B. You verify the structural integrity of a materialized view.

C. You verify the structural integrity of a cluster.

D. You verify the structural integrity of a database.

3-17. When you specify SCOPE = MEMORY when changing server parameters with the ALTER SYSTEM statement, which of the following statements is true?

A. You make changes in memory for the current instance and also to the SPFILE; the changes persist.

B. You only makes changes in memory for the current instance and not the SPFILE; the changes do not persist.

C. You make changes in memory for the current instance and set up the changes in a memory queue to be later applied to the SPFILE; the changes persist most of the time.

D. None of the above.

3-18. When a resources consumer group with multiple plan directives allocates resources to the group and has more than one plan directive with a MAX_EST_EXEC_TIME parameter, which of the following statements is true?

A. It uses the MAX_EST_EXEC_TIME of the plan directive that was created first.

B. It uses the lowest value for MAX_EST_EXEC_TIME.

C. It uses the highest value for MAX_EST_EXEC_TIME.

D. It uses the average value for MAX_EST_EXEC_TIME.

3-19. Which of the following is the Oracle9*i* parameter that controls the maximum number of concurrently active sessions within a given resource consumer group?

A. ACTIVE_SESS_POOL_P1

B. ACTIVE_SESSIONS_POOL_P1

C. ACTIVE_SESSIONS_P1

D. ACTIVE_POOL_P1

3-20. Which of the following statements is not true about the Oracle Shared Server architecture?

A. The server polls the clients in a round-robin fashion to determine if a client has a request.

B. You can share one server process with multiple user sessions.

C. An idle server process from a server process pool services a user session from a user request queue.

D. A client initiates a shared server connection to the database.

3-21. Which two of the following statements is true about the monitor thread?

A. It registers all the dispatcher threads with the listener.

B. It accepts incoming connections and task requests from Oracle servers.

C. It picks up the pending requests from the queue.

D. It sends the load information of the dispatchers to the appropriate listeners.

3-22. Which of the following is not an advantage of automatically maintaining global indexes during partition DDL?

A. The indexes are available throughout the execution of the partition DDL operation.

B. It is more straightforward; the partition DDL also rebuilds the indexes.

C. It is more efficient; the partition DDL only rebuilds the local index related to that partition.

D. You do not have to discover UNUSABLE indexes and initiate rebuild operations explicitly.

3-23. When defining an external table, what does the REJECT LIMIT clause specify?

A. There is no limit on the number of columns that you can have in an external table.

B. There is no limit on the number of rows that you can have in an external table.

C. There is no limit on the number of errors that can occur during a query of the external data.

D. None of the above.

3-24. Which of the following statements is incorrect when you add a new partition to a list-partitioned table?

A. The values that specify the partition that you are adding must not exist in any other partition of the table.

B. If omitted, the partition storage parameters default to that of the nearest partition.

C. If a local index exists for this table, then a new local index partition is also added.

D. You can specify physical storage attributes and logging options when adding partitions.

3-25. Which of the following tasks does the OPEN procedure in the DBMS_METADATA package not enable you to do?

A. It enables you to open the external file that contains the metadata.

B. It enables you to specify the type of object to be retrieved.

C. It enables you to specify the version of its metadata.

D. It enables you to specify the object model.

3-26. Which package do you have to use to reset the bitmap blocks in the case of automatic segment space-managed tables if the PCTFREE parameter value is changed?

A. DBMS_SPACE

B. DBMS_REPAIR

C. DBMS_DDL

D. DBMS_SQL

3-27. Which of the following statements is true if you specify PCTUSED, FREELIST, and FREELIST_GROUPS parameters in an automatic space-managed table?

A. The parameters will be ignored.

B. Automatic space management will be turned off and the parameters will be used.

C. The parameters will be used.

D. None of the above.

3-28. Which of the following data dictionary views did Oracle9*i* introduce to display the join condition for a bitmap join index?

A. DBA_JOIN_IND_COLUMNS

B. DBA_JOIN_INDEX_COLUMNS

C. DBA_IND_COLUMNS

D. DBA_JOIN_COLUMNS

3-29. When you version-enable a table, what suffix does Oracle add to name of the table?

A. _VE

B. _EV

C. _TL

D. _LT

3-30. Which role do you require in order to invoke the procedures in the DBMS_WM package?

A. CONNECT

B. RESOURCE

C. WM_ADMIN_ROLE

D. SELECT_CATALOG_ROLE

3-31. Which of the following is not true about Oracle-Managed Files (OMFs)?

A. OMF file management can manage file systems on RAID disks.

B. You can use OMF with raw devices.

C. You can specify the locations for OMF files by setting initialization parameters.

D. OMF files can coexist with non-OMF files.

3-32. If you do not specify the DB_CREATE_ONLINE_LOG_DEST_n parameter, where are the redo logs and control files created?

A. $ORACLE_OMF

B. $ORACLE_HOME

C. DB_CREATE_FILE_DEST

D. DB_OMF_FILES

3-33. Which statement also removes the datafiles when dropping tablespaces that do not use OMF files?

A. `DROP TABLESPACE <tablespace_name> INCLUDING CONTENTS;`

B. `DROP TABLESPACE <tablespace_name> INCLUDING DATAFILES;`

C. `DROP TABLESPACE <tablespace_name> INCLUDING CONTENTS AND DATAFILES;`

D. `DROP TABLESPACE <tablespace_name> WITH DATAFILES;`

3-34. Which of the following is true when you designate the DEFAULT TEMPORARY TABLESPACE in a CREATE or ALTER DATABASE command?

A. You do not have to create the TEMPORARY TABLESPACE; it is automatically created when you designate it.

B. You must first create the TEMPORARY TABLESPACE before you designate it.

C. You can create the TEMPORARY TABLESPACE after you designate it.

D. None of the above.

3-35. Which of the following statements is true in the context of automatic undo management (AUM)?

A. You have to create rollback segments manually; they are tracked automatically.

B. You have to manually create rollback segments of at least two different sizes.

C. You must set the OPTIMAL_AUM parameter.

D. You must create a tablespace with sufficient space and specify that as the undo tablespace.

3-36. Once you start the database instance in automatic undo management (AUM) mode

A. You can create rollback segments manually, but you cannot manage them manually.

B. You can create rollback segments and manage them manually.

C. You cannot create rollback segments or manage them manually.

D. You cannot create rollback segments manually, but you can manage them manually.

3-37. To which data dictionary view did Oracle9*i* add a new column BLOCK_SIZE to obtain the block size used by each tablespace?

A. V$DBA_BLOCK_SIZES

B. V$DBA_TABLESPACES

C. DBA_BLOCK_SIZES

D. DBA_TABLESPACES

3-38. Which two of the following are tablespaces that cannot be of a nonstandard block size?

A. The SYSTEM tablespace.

B. The ORADATA tablespace.

C. There are no such restrictions on tablespaces.

D. Temporary tablespaces.

3-39. Which initialization parameter do you use to enable automatic work area management?

A. SORT_AREA_SIZE

B. SORT_AREA_RETAINED_SIZE

C. PGA_AGGREGATE_TARGET

D. WORKAREA_SIZE_POLICY

3-40. Which view does Oracle9*i* provide for the current usage of work areas?

A. V$SQL_CURRENT_WORKAREA_USAGE

B. V$SQL_WORKAREA_USAGE

C. V$SQL_WORKAREA_CURRENT_USAGE

D. DBA_WORKAREA_USAGE

3-41. The DBA can start with a smaller SGA and dynamically increase it subject to the maximum of

A. 10 TB

B. SGA_MAX

C. 100 TB

D. SGA_MAX_SIZE

3-42. Which new clause did Oracle9*i* add to the BACKUP command to specify that archivelogs that have not been backed up should be included with the data backup?

A. PLUS ARCHIVELOG

B. WITH ARCHIVELOG

C. ARCHIVELOG

D. UNARCHIVED ARCHIVELOG

3-43. Which clause has Oracle9*i* added to the RECOVER command to perform a recovery that ignores the corrupt blocks but recovers the rest?

A. IGNORE CORRUPTIONS

B. IGNORE n CORRUPTION

C. ALLOW n CORRUPTIONS

D. ALLOW n CORRUPTION

3-44. Which two of the following are LIST command enhancements?

A. BY BACKUP

B. BY DATE

C. BY FILE

D. BY BLOCK

3-45. When the parameter DB_CACHE_ADVICE is set to ON to gather the statistics for the buffer cache usage, which view should you query to determine the optimum size of the buffer cache?

A. V$DB_OBJECT_CACHE

B. V$SYSSTAT

C. V$DB_CACHE_ADVICE

D. V$BUFFER_POOL_STATISTICS

3-46. When you create a new tablespace within the OEM,

A. You select the block size for that tablespace from a drop-down list.

B. You must specify the block size via an ALTER TABLESPACE command.

C. You cannot create a new tablespace within the OEM.

D. None of the above.

3-47. Which two of the following are the values that the USED column of the V$OBJECT_USAGE view contains at the end of an index-monitoring session?

- **A.** KEEP or DELETE
- **B.** The number of times the index was referenced
- **C.** OFTEN, RARELY, or NONE
- **D.** YES or NO

3-48. Which cursor sharing option has Oracle9*i* introduced for the CURSOR_SHARING initialization parameter?

- **A.** SIMILAR
- **B.** FORCE
- **C.** EXACT
- **D.** None of the above

3-49. Which of the following statements is true in the context of cached execution plans in Oracle9*i*?

- **A.** All columns in the PLAN_TABLE view are also in the V$SQL_PLAN view with the exception of the LEVEL column.
- **B.** The V$SQL_PLAN view has complete one-to-one correspondence with the PLAN_TABLE view.
- **C.** All columns in the V$SQL_PLAN view are also in the PLAN_TABLE view with the exception of the LEVEL column.
- **D.** The ADDRESS, HASH_VALUE, CHILD_NUMBER, and DEPTH columns are in the PLAN_TABLE view but not in the V$SQL_PLAN view.

3-50. Which option does Oracle9*i* not introduce for the method_opt parameter in various procedures in DBMS_STATS?

- **A.** SKEWONLY
- **B.** REPEAT
- **C.** MANUAL
- **D.** AUTO

3-51. Which method for transferring the block from the holding instance to the requesting instance is introduced in Oracle9*i*?

A. Block Transfer with Forced Disk Write

B. Block Transfer with Cache Fusion

C. Read Consistent Cache Fusion

D. Cache Fusion Block Transfer

3-52. Which of the following statements is true in the context of a shared server configuration prior to Oracle9*i*?

A. Each instance requires its own initialization parameter file.

B. Many instances can share one initialization parameter file.

C. You cannot have instance-specific parameters in a shared initialization parameter file.

D. None of the above.

3-53. Which clause can you use to specify the join columns as separate from the other criteria when joining two tables that don't have a common column name?

A. WHERE

B. ON

C. FILTER

D. JOIN CONDITION

3-54. Which two of the following statements are false in Oracle9*i*?

A. You can define primary key constraints on views.

B. You can define referential integrity constraints on views.

C. You cannot define any constraints on views because a view is read only.

D. You can define check constraints on views.

3-55. Which of the following statements are true about the TO_LOB function?

A. It can only convert a LONG value to a CLOB value.

B. It can only convert a LONG RAW value to a BLOB value.

C. It converts a LONG value to a CLOB value and a LONG RAW value into a BLOB value.

D. It converts both a LONG value and a LONG RAW value to a CLOB value.

3-56. Which of the following statements is true about the INTERVAL DAY TO SECOND datatype?

A. You can just store days and seconds.

B. The precision for the days ranges from 1 through 10.

C. The datatype stores a time interval value in terms of days, hours, minutes, and seconds.

D. The precision for the days ranges from 1 through 10.

3-57. Oracle9*i* was enhanced to support

A. The Unicode Standard Version 2.0

B. The Unicode Standard Version 3.0

C. The Unicode Standard Version 4.0

D. The Unicode Standard Version 2001

3-58. Which of the following is not a task performed by the Character Set Scanner?

A. It verifies that the data in the target database can fit into the column's data size.

B. It verifies that the data in the source can be mapped without being replaced in the target database.

C. It verifies that the data can be correctly converted particularly when dealing with differences in byte sizes and fixed/variable byte-encoding systems.

D. It scans in new fonts to create a font or character set.

3-59. Which statement is correct in the case of skip scan index access?

A. The optimizer would not use the composite index if you omitted the index prefix column in your SQL statement.

B. The index is used even if the index prefix column in the concatenated index is not used in the select statement.

C. The index scans of the single column indexes are skipped.

D. The single column primary key index scan is skipped.

3-60. Which of the following statements is true in the case of the new NULLIF function in Oracle9*i*?

A. If expression1 is not equal to expression2, Oracle will return a NULL; otherwise, it will return *expression1*.

B. If expression1 is greater than expression2, Oracle will return a NULL; otherwise, it will return *expression1*.

C. If expression1 is less than expression2, Oracle will return a NULL; otherwise, it will return *expression1*.

D. If expression1 is equal to expression2, Oracle will return a NULL; otherwise, it will return *expression1*.

Answers to Practice Exam I

1-1. A. STARTUP

Explanation The Server Manager utility is deprecated in Oracle9*i*. You can use SQL*Plus to issue STARTUP and SHUTDOWN commands and to perform most Server Manager line-mode scripts. However, you should expect to modify your Server Manager scripts to adapt them to SQL*Plus.

The Server Manager commands SET CHARWIDTH and SET DATEWIDTH that change the width of all character and date columns are not supported by SQL*Plus. In SQL*Plus, the `COLUMN colname FORMAT` command does not set the widths of all columns of a specified type; it only sets the width of the one specific column that is named. An example of the SQL*Plus command is `COLUMN city FORMAT A15`.

The Server Manager commands SET MAXDATA and SET RETRIES are not available in SQL*Plus and there are no SQL*Plus equivalents; you must remove these commands.

1-2. C. It prompts you for a password.

Explanation Prior to Oracle9*i*, the installer assigned the SYS and SYSTEM user accounts the default passwords of CHANGE_ON_INSTALL and MANAGER respectively. You were responsible to change the password when you completed the installation. In Oracle9*i*, the DBCA will prompt you for the passwords for the SYS and SYSTEM accounts when installing a new database.

1-3. B. Procedure to authenticate the role

Explanation You have been familiar with using passwords for authentication. Once an unauthorized person knows the password, they can gain access. Oracle9*i* has introduced secure application roles that use a procedure for authentication. For example, this procedure can verify if you are authorized to access the database from a particular URL. The syntax for creating such a role is

```
CREATE ROLE <role_name> IDENIFIED USING <procedure_name>;
```

1-4. A, C. A: It uses connections pooling. C: An existing session is reused.

Explanation You implement the global application context when using the application server in Web-based applications where it is common for thousands of users to connect to the database. Establishing a separate connection for each user on the Web can require significant overhead because the Web is stateless. You can also implement user-based, fine-grained access control in middle-tier applications where a single application user connects to the database and interacts with the database on behalf of the end users. When the number of users is small, there is no need to reuse an existing connection to the database.

On the Web, when hundreds of users connect to the middle tier, there will be a need to reuse an existing connection to the database. Oracle9*i* provides a facility for connection pooling, where many connections to the middle tier can share application contexts. This concept of enabling many connections to share and reuse application contexts is called the Global Application Context. This concept of pooling connections results in highly scalable applications.

1-5. B. Tracking DDL commands

Explanation Prior to Oracle9*i*, DDL statements were recorded as a set of DML statements. Oracle 9*i* records the original DDL statement in the redo logs, and LogMiner lists this DDL statement followed by the set of generated DML statements.

1-6. D. The master group to which you are adding the new master must be replicating in the synchronous mode.

Explanation One of the conditions that must be met is that the master group to which you are adding the new master must be replicating in the asynchronous mode. The synchronous mode is not a required condition to be met.

1-7. B. FAST_START_MTTR_TARGET

Explanation In Oracle9*i*, you can specify the target mean-time-to-recover for instance recovery by assigning the initialization parameter FAST_START_MTTR_TARGET a value between 0 and 3,600 seconds. When you set this parameter to 0, Oracle9*i* will not use this parameter to manage instance recovery time.

1-8. C. Automatic undo management

Explanation One requirement in order to use Flashback is that you must use automatic undo management as opposed to the older technique of rollback segments.

1-9. B. Disk crash

Explanation You have an *out of space* error when you cannot get any more extents for various database objects in a table space. You have a *maximum extents reached* error when the number of extents in various database objects exceeds the maximum extents that you have specified for the object. You have a *space quota exceeded* error when you exceed the space quota that was assigned to you in the tablespace.

1-10. A, C. A: ALWAYS C: NONE

Explanation Oracle9*i* introduces the new import parameter STATISTICS. The options for this parameter are as follows:

- **ALWAYS** Always import database optimizer statistics. This is the default.
- **NONE** Do not import or recalculate the database optimizer statistics.
- **SAFE** Import the database optimizer stats only if they are nonquestionable.
- **RECALCULATE** Recalculate the statistics; do not import them.

1-11. A. The Data Guard Scheduler

Explanation The *Data Guard Manager* is a GUI component of the Data Guard framework, which is included in the Oracle Enterprise Manager (OEM). It enables you to establish and manage the Data Guard configuration by pointing and clicking. The *Data Guard Command Line Interface* (CLI) enables you to use text commands to establish, manage, and monitor the Data Guard configuration. The *Data Guard Monitor* is the component of the Data Guard Broker that is responsible for actually managing and monitoring the configuration.

1-12. C. LOG_ARCHIVE_DEST_2

Explanation You specify the standby database named 'friday' with the following entry in the primary database's initialization parameter file:

```
LOG_ARCHIVE_DEST_2 = 'SERVICE=friday'
```

You use the SERVICE parameter to specify the database based on the Oracle Net service name. This service name must have an associated database system identifier (SID).

1-13. A. You can have up to two active SQL sessions on the instance in which you are performing the switchover.

Explanation You can have only one active SQL session on the instance in which you are performing the switchover. You must terminate all other sessions.

1-14. D. The updates are journalled in an index-organized table (IOT).

Explanation The index rebuilding operation builds a new index based on the information in the existing or old index. The user can still perform DML operations on the data table; the old index is still helping to enhance the performance of the DML operations. If changes are made to the table that affect the old index table, the updates that should be made to the old index are not actually made to it; instead, they are journalled in an IOT. Once the new index generation is completed, the rebuild operation will merge the journal table entries into the new index, associate the new index with the table, and get rid of the old index.

1-15. A. Primary key

Explanation One requirement for an online table redefinition is that the table must have a primary key. If this requirement is violated, you will get the following error:

```
ORA-12089: cannot online redefine table "OE"."PRODUCT2" with no primary key.
```

1-16. B. `ANALYZE TABLE product VALIDATE STRUCTURE ONLINE;`

Explanation You can use the ANALYZE command with the VALIDATE STRUCTURE option to verify the structural integrity of a table, index, materialized view, or cluster.

1-17. D. It can be manually edited with a text editor.

Explanation You should not manually edit the SPFILE with a text editor; you will corrupt the file if you do so. This corruption will keep the new instance from starting and will cause the existing instance to crash.

1-18. A. MAX_EST_EXEC_TIME

Explanation You can specify the maximum estimated time to complete (in seconds) for an operation by assigning a value to the MAX_EST_EXEC_TIME parameter; the default value for this parameter is UNLIMITED.

1-19. C. Create a pending area

Explanation To specify a Database Resource Manager solution, you must first create a pending area. A pending area is a staging area where you can specify your resource solution and validate it before you submit it to be implemented. You must create a pending area before you can either create a new plan or update an existing plan; otherwise, it will result in a "pending area not active" error.

1-20. C. At least one resource directive

Explanation The resource plan directive is needed for database resource management and not for the Oracle Shared Server architecture.

1-21. D. It has a single server manager thread.

Explanation The monitor thread manages listener communications, monitors agent process loads, and starts and stops dispatcher and task threads. The dispatcher threads accept incoming connections and task requests from Oracle servers, and place these requests on a queue for a task thread to pick up. The task threads pick up the pending requests from the queue, complete the task by performing necessary operations, and place the results returned by the task on the queue for the dispatcher process to pick up.

1-22. B.
```
ALTER TABLE <table_name>
  DROP PARTITION <partition_name>
  UPDATE GLOBAL INDEXES
```

Explanation You can update global indexes as you perform the partition DDL by using the optional clause `UPDATE GLOBAL INDEXES` of the partition DDL statement.

1-23. D. Select

Explanation External tables are read-only tables. As such, DML operations (Insert, Update, and Delete) are not allowed on these types of tables.

1-24. C. 8*i*

Explanation The partitioning of tables was introduced in Oracle 8, and only range partitioning was available. Partitioning was enhanced in 8*i* to include hash partitioning. Oracle9*i* introduced a new partitioning technique called list partitioning.

1-25. C. Use procedures in the DBMS_METADATA package

Explanation The DBMS_METADATA package was introduced in Oracle9*i*.

1-26. C. The Segment Management clause can be specified with the CREATE TABLESPACE command and the tablespace must be locally managed.

Explanation You must use the SEGMENT SPACE MANAGEMENT clause introduced in Oracle9*i* to create automatic space-managed segments and the tablespace must be locally managed. You can set the SEGMENT SPACE MANAGEMENT to MANUAL to specify freelist segments or you can set it to AUTO for automatic space management segments.

1-27. A. DBMS_SPACE

Explanation Oracle9*i* enhanced the DBMS_SPACE package by adding the SPACE_USAGE procedure to obtain information about the free blocks in automatically space-managed segments.

1-28. D. This feature was introduced in Oracle8*i*.

Explanation Bitmap join indexes are introduced in Oracle9*i*. The other options are restrictions on utilizing bitmap join indexes.

1-29. A. The table must have a primary key.

Explanation Here are some restrictions in order to version-enable a table: The table must have a primary key, you cannot perform DDL operations on version-enabled tables, you cannot version-enable tables that contain LONG columns, and you cannot version-enable object tables or IOTs.

1-30. B. Invoking the GOTOWORKSPACE procedure

Explanation You can access any workspace by invoking the GOTOWORKSPACE procedure in the DBMS_WM package.

1-31. B. You have to delete unnecessary files such as datafiles corresponding to dropped tablespaces.

Explanation Oracle deletes these files.

1-32. C. DB_CREATE_FILE_DEST

Explanation Oracle9*i* gives you two new initialization parameters, DB_CREATE_FILE_DEST and DB_CREATE_ONLINE_LOG_DEST_n, to specify the location where Oracle creates and manages OMF files.

1-33. D. CASCADE CONSTRAINTS

Explanation This clause also drops referential integrity constraints from foreign or primary keys of tables outside the tablespace that reference primary keys of tables inside the tablespace.

1-34. A. CREATE DATABASE

Explanation Oracle9*i* introduces the DEFAULT TEMPORARY TABLESPACE clause in the CREATE DATABASE or ALTER DATBASE commands.

1-35. C. AUM performs the space management of rollback segments.

Explanation With automatic undo management, Oracle creates, extends, and allocates undo segments within the space available in the undo tablespace.

1-36. A. One undo tablespace at a time

Explanation A database can have zero, one, or more undo tablespaces; however, automatic undo management can only use one undo tablespace at a time.

1-37. A. DB_BLOCK_BUFFERS

Explanation Oracle9*i* introduces new initialization parameters to create tablespaces with multiple block sizes. DB_CACHE_SIZE specifies the database buffer cache size to the standard block size. You can specify the buffer cache size corresponding to each of these block sizes with the DB_nK_CACHE_SIZE parameter. DB_BLOCK_SIZE is the standard block size in Oracle9*i*; it should be set to the most commonly used block size.

1-38. C. BLOCKSIZE

Explanation Oracle9*i* introduces the BLOCKSIZE clause to specify the block size to be used for the tablespace.

1-39. B. PGA_AGGREGATE_TARGET

Explanation PGA_AGGREGATE_TARGET is a new Oracle9*i* instance-level parameter that specifies the total memory in KB, MB, or GB for the PGA of all sessions combined.

1-40. D. PGA_TOTAL_MEM

Explanation PGA_USED_MEM is the PGA memory being used by the process. PGA_ALLOC_MEM is the PGA memory currently allocated by the process. PGA_MAX_MEM is the maximum PGA memory allocated by the process.

1-41. D. Granule

Explanation The unit of memory allocation for SGA is a granule in Oracle9*i*. The size of a granule is 4MB if the SGA at startup is less than 128MB; it will be 16MB otherwise. The sizes of different components of SGA should be multiples of the granule size.

1-42. B. CONFIGURE

Explanation Oracle9*i*'s new CONFIGURE command enables you to configure various backup, restore, and recover parameters that are persistent across RMAN sessions. For example, you can use the CONFIGURE command to specify a *redundancy policy* that establishes the number of backup and control files you want to retain.

1-43. C, D. C: Only records data in the buffers as opposed to writing data to files. D: Anticipate problems before performing the recovery

Explanation Occasionally, recovery sessions fail to completely recover the database, and some files are left in an inconsistent state. Trial Recovery enables you to anticipate such problems before performing the recovery. The difference between regular recovery and trial recovery is that data is not written to the files and changes are only recorded in the buffers.

1-44. A. Mutually exclusive

Explanation You can use the CONFIGURE command to specify a *redundancy policy* that establishes the number of backup files and control files you wish to retain. Here is an example:

```
CONFIGURE RETENTION POLICY TO REDUNDANCY 3;
```

Alternatively, you can use the CONFIGURE command to specify a *recovery window policy* that establishes the number of days the backups are to be retained. Here is an example for a weekly backup system:

```
CONFIGURE RETENTION POLICY TO RECOVERY WINDOW OF 7 DAYS;
```

The redundancy policy and the recovery window policy are mutually exclusive.

1-45. A. You can administer the database.

Explanation You can only connect to and administer just the database object type. You cannot administer other object types such as HTTP web servers, events, and jobs. You cannot utilize the backup and data management tools.

1-46. C. A component that generates reports that can be published on the Web

Explanation The Enterprise Reporting Framework generates reports that can be published on the Web.

1-47. C. V$OBJECT_USAGE

Explanation You query the V$OBJECT_USAGE view to review index utilization data. If the index has been used within the period of time it was being monitored in, the USED column within this view will contain a YES value; otherwise, it will contain a NO.

1-48. A. 7

Explanation Oracle introduced cursor sharing as far back as version 7 to provide you with the capability to share statements that are exactly the same.

1-49. D. V$SQL_PLAN

Explanation Oracle stores the execution plan of a SQL statement to enable a DBA to analyze the execution plan of a poorly performing SQL statement without having to rerun the query. Oracle9*I* has Introduced the V$SQL_PLAN view to display the cached execution plan, the compilation environment, and the execution statistics of each variable.

1-50. D. OPERATION

Explanation Oracle9*i* has added the CPU_COST, IO_COST, and TEMP_SPACE columns to the PLAN_TABLE. The OPERATION column existed in prior versions of Oracle.

1-51. B. Block Transfer with Cache Fusion

Explanation The GCS provides three alternatives for transferring the block from the holding instance to the requesting instance. The alternatives are Block Transfer with Forced Disk Write, Read Consistent Cache Fusion, and Cache Fusion Block Transfer.

1-52. C. You use the <INSTANCE_NAME>.<PARAMETER>=VALUE notation for instance-specific parameters.

Explanation Oracle9*i* enables you to store the parameters for all instances in one initialization parameter file that you can share among all instances in Oracle Real Application Clusters (RAC) implementation. You can specify instance-specific parameters by prefixing the initialization parameter with the name of the instance.

1-53. A. Line 1

Explanation The NATURAL JOIN matches rows that have equal values in columns in both tables that have the same name. Line 1 of the select statement causes the following error because you cannot qualify columns with the tablename or an alias when using the ANSI standard NATURAL JOIN:

```
ORA-25155:  column used in NATURAL join cannot have qualifier
```

1-54. C. You can explicitly tell Oracle to either KEEP the index or DROP the index when you DROP a constraint.

Explanation When you DROP or DISABLE a constraint, you can explicitly tell Oracle to either KEEP the index or DROP the index. When you DROP constraints, the associated implicitly created unique indexes are dropped by default.

1-55. B. NATIVE

Explanation You can compile PL/SQL procedures in Oracle9*i* to improve performance by replacing the default value (INTERPRETED) for the

PLSQL_COMPILER_FLAGS initialization parameter with NATIVE. When you compile PL/SQL procedures, Oracle generates native C code, then compiles it with the C compiler on the system, and links it to the Oracle process.

1-56. D. There is no TIMESTAMP datatype.

Explanation The TIMESTAMP datatype is very much like the DATE datatype; it can store both the date and time values. Unlike the DATE datatype, you can specify the precision of the fractional seconds value in the TIMESTAMP datatype. The default is six digits, so you can specify a value within the range from 0 through 9.

1-57. A. A 2-byte, fixed-width Unicode character set

Explanation AL16UTF16 is a 2-byte, fixed-width Unicode character set that is also referred to as UTF16 or UCS2.

1-58. D. Character Set scan

Explanation You can invoke the scanner in one of three modes:

- The *Full Database scan* verifies all tables for all users in the database. You perform this by adding a switch FULL=Y.
- The *User scan* verifies all tables for a given user. You must set FULL=N and set USER=Y.
- The *Table scan* verifies a single table that you specify. You must set FULL=N, USER=N, and TABLE=highwaybridge.

1-59. A. TIMESTAMP WITH TIME ZONE

Explanation The TIMESTAMP WITH TIME ZONE adds a slight twist to the TIMESTAMP datatype. In addition to the date and time, you can store the time zone displacement (or offset), which requires additional bytes of storage. The time zone displacement is the difference in hours and minutes between the local time and the Universal Time (Coordinated) (UTC), which formerly was the Greenwich Meridian Time (GMT).

1-60. A. You have greater flexibility with the ON clause than with the NATURAL JOIN.

Explanation You have greater flexibility with the ON clause than with the NATURAL JOIN or the USING clauses, which restrict you to an equijoin. The ON clause enables you to use any logical operator. You can specify any condition in the ON clause that you can include in a WHERE clause, and this includes subqueries.

Answers to Practice Exam 2

2-1. D. CONNECT INTERNAL

Explanation Previous versions of Oracle used CONNECT INTERNAL and CONNECT INTERNAL/PASSWORD to authenticate database administrator connections to the database. CONNECT INTERNAL and CONNECT INTERNAL/PASSWORD are not supported in Oracle9*i*. If you attempted to use the CONNECT INTERNAL in Oracle9*i*, you will get the ORA-09275 Oracle error "CONNECT INTERNAL is not a valid DBA connection."

Instead of the CONNECT INTERNAL, you can use the SYSDBA or the SYSOPER privileges. The SYSOPER privilege is a subset of the SYSDBA privilege. To perform administrator tasks such as starting and stopping databases, you can use either the SYSDBA or SYSOPER privileges. To create a database, you need the SYSDBA privilege.

2-2. D. FALSE

Explanation Oracle set the parameter 07_DICTIONARY_ACCESSIBILITY to TRUE in previous versions of Oracle. This enabled anyone who had the ANY privilege to use this privilege on the Data Dictionary.

Oracle9*i* enhances security by setting this parameter to FALSE by default in order to limit access to just the SYSDBA privileged connections.

2-3. C. Data access is granted only when all policies are satisfied.

Explanation Oracle9*i* enables you to associate several policies with a table or view. In such a case, Oracle takes a conservative approach; every policy must be satisfied before you are granted access to the data. Oracle will not grant you access to the table even if just one policy is not satisfied. This is an all or nothing deal; there is an implicit AND between the policies.

2-4. D. Policy groups

Explanation When you set up many policies against a table, you must satisfy all these policies to gain access to the table. Although this maximizes security, it presents a problem for your application. The accessible rows for your application may be restricted because of the security requirement policies of other applications.

Oracle gives you the ability to combine a number of security policies into a security policy group, which you can associate with an application context (also called the "driving" application context). When you access a table or view, Oracle refers to the driving application context to identify the associated security policy group; Oracle then enforces all the policies in the associated security policy group.

2-5. A. V$LOGMNR_CONTENTS

Explanation You just query V$LOGMNR_CONTENTS to review and analyze the redo entries in the redo log files. When you query V$LOGMNR_CONTENTS, you can see DDL under the OPERATION column and the DDL statement itself under the SQL_REDO column. To determine which redo logs are being analyzed, you can query the V$LOGMNR_LOGS view.

2-6. A. You cannot add a new master to the group until the previous add new master operation is completed.

Explanation You cannot add a new master to the group until the previous add new master operation is completed. To verify if the previous add new master is completed, look for the master group in the view `DBA_NEW_REPSITES`. If you do not find it, it means that the add-master operation is completed. If you found the entry, it means that the operation is still underway, and you need to wait.

2-7. D. DB_BLOCK_MAX_DIRTY_TARGET

Explanation The DB_BLOCK_MAX_DIRTY_TARGET parameter specifies the maximum number of dirty data blocks that you can have in the buffer cache. This parameter has been retired in Oracle9*i*.

2-8. C. Select statements

Explanation You can query the data corresponding to the SCN at a specified time. You cannot perform any DML or DDL statements while in the flashback mode.

2-9. C. Use the AFTER SUSPEND clause in the CREATE OR REPLACE TRIGGER statement.

Explanation Oracle provides you with the AFTER SUSPEND system event to enable you to perform custom operations whenever an operation is suspended. You can specify a trigger that contains your custom code at either the database or schema level to respond to the AFTER SUSPEND system event. The SQL code within the AFTER SUSPEND trigger is autonomous and it is not resumable.

2-10. B. RESUMABLE_TIMEOUT

Explanation Oracle9*i* also introduces the following new parameters for performing exports and imports:

- **RESUMABLE** Enables or disables resumable space allocation.
- **RESUMABLE_NAME** Identifies the resumable operation when you query the USER_RESUMABLE or DBA_RESUMABLE views.

- **RESUMABLE_TIMEOUT** Specifies the time period within which the situation that suspended the operation must be resolved.
- **FLASHBACK_SCN** Specifies that the export or import enables Flashback and applies to data that are relevant to that SCN.
- **FLASHBACK_TIME** Specifies that the export or import enables Flashback and applies to data that is relevant to the SCN that is closest to the time specified.

2-11. D. The Data Guard Monitor (DMON) process

Explanation The DMON is the component of the Data Guard Broker that is responsible for actually managing and monitoring the configuration. Oracle initiates a DMON process on each site in the Data Guard configuration. When your local Data Guard Manager or CLI needs to interact with an Oracle instance or obtain information about the instance, it communicates with the DMON process on the server where the instance is running. The DMON processes maintain information about the configuration in a binary file on the site it monitors.

2-12. A. `LOG_ARCHIVE_DEST_n = 'SERVICE=friday LGWR SYNC'`

Explanation You can specify that the archive transmissions be performed synchronously (SYNC) or asynchronously (ASYNC) for that archive destination with respect to the primary database. If you specify SYNC, the log writer will transmit to the remote archive destinations concurrently with adding entries to the online redo log on the primary database. Control is returned only after the redo logs reach the archive destination; hence, the performance of the primary database can be adversely impacted. If you specify ASYNC, control is returned immediately.

2-13. C. There is no loss of data and you do not have to instantiate either database.

Explanation You perform the switchover operation deliberately; you take the primary database offline so you can perform maintenance functions, and you transition a standby database to function as the primary database so users can enjoy continued access to their databases even while you perform maintenance functions.

2-14. B. `ALTER INDEX product_description_ix REBUILD ONLINE;`

Explanation You use the ALTER INDEX . . . statement to rebuild an index online.

2-15. A. The table cannot be part of a cluster.

Explanation Here are some requirements for redefining a table online: The table cannot have a BFILE column or a LONG column, LOB columns are allowed, and the table cannot have user-defined types.

2-16. A. You can perform DML operations.

Explanation Oracle9*i* enables you to perform this VALIDATE command online. In other words, you can perform DML operations against the object while the ANALYZE command is validating the command.

2-17. A. You query the V$SPPARAMETER view.

Explanation Because Oracle does not want you to edit the SPFILE with a text editor, they provide the V$SPPARAMETER view to display the contents of the server parameter file.

2-18. B. Oracle will return an error and the operation will not be not started.

Explanation If the SWITCH_ESTIMATE parameter is set to TRUE, and if Oracle's estimate is greater than the value specified by MAX_EST_EXEC_TIME, Oracle will return an error and the operation will not be not started. If the SWITCH_ESTIMATE parameter is FALSE, Oracle will start the operation even if Oracle's estimate is greater than the value specified by MAX_EST_EXEC_TIME; Oracle will only switch groups based on other criteria being met.

2-19. B, D. B: DEFAULT_CONSUMER_GROUP D: OTHER_GROUPS

Explanation DEFAULT_CONSUMER_GROUP is the default initial group for users and sessions that have not been assigned an initial group, while OTHER_GROUPS is used for users and sessions that are assigned to a group that is not organized under the currently active plan. You must specify a resource directive for OTHER_GROUPS in any active resource plan.

2-20. C. Passes the connection request to the dispatcher

Explanation In previous versions, the next step would have been to pass this address back to the client for the client to contact the dispatcher again over the network. Instead, in Oracle9*i*'s direct handoff method, the listener hands the connection request to the dispatcher. The dispatcher communicates directly with the client to establish a connection without the need for the additional network calls that were required in previous versions.

2-21. C. It uses a pool of shared agent processes.

Explanation Prior to Oracle9*i*, the HS agent architecture was dedicated in nature; it consumed a significant amount of resources because it started an agent for each user-session and for each database link. Oracle9*i* introduces Multithreaded HS Agent architecture. The concept is similar to the Shared Server architecture, and it uses a pool of shared agent processes.

2-22. B. It defaults to `INVALIDATE GLOBAL INDEXES`.

Explanation If the `UPDATE GLOBAL INDEXES` clause is not specified, it defaults to `INVALIDATE GLOBAL INDEXES`, which is the mode reflected by previous Oracle versions.

2-23. B. You specify the ORGANIZATION EXTERNAL clause in the CREATE TABLE statement.

Explanation You can create external tables by specifying the ORGANIZATION EXTERNAL clause in your CREATE TABLE statement.

2-24. A, D. A: You cannot use list partitioning with Index Organized Tables (IOTs). D: You cannot specify MAXVALUE.

Explanation The limitations of list partitioning are that it is applicable to heap tables only, it is not applicable to IOTs, and you cannot specify MAXVALUE. You can perform the Add, Modify, Drop, Merge, and Split DDL operations on list partitions.

2-25. C. It returns the metadata as DDL.

Explanation GET_DDL returns the metadata as DDL, as opposed to GET_XML, which returns the metadata as XML.

2-26. A. DBA_TABLESPACES

Explanation Oracle9*i* added a new column named SEGMENT_SPACE_MANAGEMENT to the DBA_TABLESPACES data dictionary view that tracks whether the space utilization is AUTO or MANUAL.

2-27. C. SEGMENT SPACE MANAGEMENT AUTO

Explanation You can set the SEGMENT SPACE MANAGEMENT to MANUAL to specify freelist segments or you can set it to AUTO for automatic space management segments.

2-28. B. You query the JOIN_INDEX column in the DBA_INDEXES data dictionary.

Explanation Oracle9*i* has added a new column called JOIN_INDEX to the DBA_INDEXES data dictionary view to identify if an index is based on a join condition.

2-29. D. ENABLEVERSIONING subprogram in the DBMS_WM package

Explanation You can use the ENABLEVERSIONING subprogram in the DBMS_WM package to enable versioning the ORDER table, as shown in the following example:

```
EXECUTE dbms_wm.enableversioning('order');
```

2-30. A. The CREATE_WORKSPACE role

Explanation There is no CREATE_WORKSPACE role. You need the WM_ADMIN_ROLE role or you will need the CREATE_WORKSPACE or CREATE_ANY_WORKSPACE privilege to create a workspace.

2-31. D. OMF manages operating system files such as datafiles corresponding to tablespaces.

Explanation OMF specifies filenames while creating databases, tablespaces, and redo log groups. OMF also deletes these files when they are no longer needed, such as when you drop the corresponding tablespace.

2-32. B. The tablespace is dropped and the datafiles are deleted from the disk.

Explanation Oracle also removes the OS files when a tablespace with OMF files is dropped.

2-33. C. Oracle deletes the tablespace.

Explanation Oracle deletes the tempfiles definition in the database and automatically deletes the OS tempfiles. Oracle does not delete the tablespace.

2-34. C. This is the temporary tablespace for users that were not assigned a temporary tablespace.

Explanation Oracle9*i* introduces the DEFAULT TEMPORARY TABLESPACE, and users for whom you did not specify a TEMPORARY TABLESPACE would default to the DEFAULT TEMPORARY TABLESPACE instead of cluttering up the SYSTEM tablespace.

2-35. B. Set the UNDO_RETENTION parameter appropriately.

Explanation AUM enables the DBA to specify the retention period for the undo information in the segment before it is overwritten. This feature gives you control over the chance of getting a 'Snapshot too old' error.

2-36. B, D. B: UNDO_MANAGEMENT D: UNDO_TABLESPACE

Explanation Oracle9*i* introduces UNDO_MANAGEMENT, a new initialization parameter, to specify the mode for undo management. When you set UNDO_MANAGEMENT to AUTO, you must specify the undo tablespace that the database instance should use with the UNDO_TABLESPACE parameter.

2-37. C. Six

Explanation Oracle9*i* can support the standard block size plus five other block sizes; you can specify the buffer cache size corresponding to each of these block sizes with the db_nK_CACHE_SIZE parameter. In this parameter, nK stands for the nonstandard block size, and n can take the following values: 2, 4, 8, 16, or 32.

2-38. C. Oracle defaults to the standard block size

Explanation If you do not specify the BLOCKSIZE, Oracle defaults to the standard block size.

2-39. A. You must set PGA_AGGREGATE_TARGET to a nonzero value before you set WORKAREA_SIZE_POLICY to AUTO.

Explanation You must set PGA_AGGREGATE_TARGET to a nonzero value before you set WORKAREA_SIZE_POLICY to AUTO. If you do not observe this sequence, Oracle gives you the following error message:

```
ORA-04032: pga_aggregate_target must be set before switching to auto mode
```

2-40. C. V$PROCSTAT

Explanation V$SYSSTAT contains system statistics, V$SESSTAT contains user session statistics, and V$MYSTAT contains information about the current session.

2-41. A. DB_CACHE_SIZE

Explanation Oracle9*i* introduces DB_CACHE_SIZE, DB_KEEP_CACHE_SIZE, and DB_RECYCLE_CACHE_SIZE to dynamically manage the buffer cache.

2-42. D. Mutually exclusive

Explanation The *redundancy policy* establishes the number of backup files and control files you want to retain. The *recovery window policy* establishes the number of days the backups are to be retained. They are mutually exclusive.

2-43. D. You can perform block media recovery from incremental backups.

Explanation The following restrictions apply to block media recovery:

- You can only perform block media recovery from the RMAN interface; you cannot do this from SQL*PLUS.
- You can only perform complete recovery of a block.
- Corrupted blocks are not available to users until the block has been fully recovered.
- You can only perform block media recovery from a full backup; you cannot do this from incremental backups.

2-44. B. RMAN can back up tablespaces with different block sizes using a single command.

Explanation This is an Oracle9*i* enhancement.

2-45. C. You can generate reports about the whole configuration, but not about an object in the configuration.

Explanation This statement is false. You can generate reports about the whole configuration or about an object in the configuration.

2-46. A. Select the Configuration object within the Instance object in the Navigator pane, and then select the Undo tab on the Details pane.

Explanation To view the details about the undo tablespace, select the Configuration object within the Instance object in the Navigator pane, and then select the Undo tab on the Details pane. The Undo tab was introduced in the Enterprise Manager provided with Oracle9*i*. You will see the current undo tablespace name and the retention period for undo entries.

2-47. D. `ALTER INDEX part_ix MONITORING USAGE;`

Explanation You can start the process of monitoring and collecting index utilization statistics by using the following statement:

```
ALTER INDEX part_ix MONITORING USAGE;
```

2-48. C. 8*i*

Explanation It is common that applications execute statements that are pretty much the same, but differ only in the literals. Oracle8*i* introduced the FORCE option for cursor sharing to enable you to share execution plans among similar statements that differ just in the literals.

2-49. B. PLAN_HASH_VALUE

Explanation Oracle9*i* also adds the PLAN_HASH_VALUE column to the V$SQL view that contains the hash value of the SQL plan for this cursor. You can use this value to determine if two SQL plans are the same.

2-50. A. DBMS_STATS

Explanation Oracle9*i* introduces the GATHER_SYSTEM_STATS, SET_SYSTEM_STATS, and GET_SYSTEM_STATS procedures in the DBMS_STATS package.

2-51. A. Block Transfer with Forced Disk Write

Explanation Only one instance can modify a datablock at any given point in time. The holding instance writes the current image in its cache to the shared disk. The requesting instance reads the recently updated datablock on the shared disk. This was the only method prior to Oracle 8.1.

2-52. C. You cannot share one initialization parameter file among many instances.

Explanation Oracle9*i* enables you to store the parameters for all instances in one initialization parameter file that you can share among all instances. You can specify instance-specific parameters by prefixing the initialization parameter with the name of the instance.

2-53. C. You are not required to have columns in both tables with the same name, but the datatype of at least one pair of columns must be the same.

Explanation The tables should have columns with the same name in both tables. You can have any number of pairs of commonly named columns. You must have at least one pair of columns with the identical name and datatype.

You are not allowed to add the table name or alias prefix with the NATURAL JOIN; it results in the following error:

```
ORA-25155:  column used in NATURAL join cannot have qualifier
```

The new syntax does not need nor does it allow a table prefix with a column in the select list.

2-54. C. Cache up to 256 primary keys

Explanation The verification of the existence of a matching primary key before adding a foreign key can consume a significant amount of time. Oracle9*i* addresses this performance problem by enabling you to cache the first 256 primary keys; this improves the time it takes to verify the existence of a primary key.

2-55. C. DBA_STORED_SETTINGS

Explanation You can query the USER_STORED_SETTINGS or DBA_STORED_SETTINGS data dictionary views to confirm that a procedure has been NATIVE compiled or INTERPRETED.

2-56. C. In addition to the date and time, you can store the time zone displacement (or offset) without consuming additional bytes of storage.

Explanation The TIMESTAMP WITH TIME ZONE adds a slight twist to the TIMESTAMP datatype. In addition to the date and time, you can store the time zone displacement (or offset), which requires additional bytes of storage. The time zone displacement is the difference in hours and minutes between the local time and the Universal Time (Coordinated) (UTC), which formerly was the Greenwich Meridian Time (GMT).

2-57. C. UTF8

Explanation AL32UTF8 is an enhanced implementation of UTF8. This is an 8-bit, variable-width encoding that uses multiple bytes to represent a Unicode character. Although UTF8 is supported in Oracle9*i* for backward compatibility and for the migration of data from earlier versions of Oracle, you should use AL32ATF8 instead of UTF8.

2-58. B. To discover potential problems with character set migrations

Explanation Oracle9*i* provides you with the Character Set Scanner (CSSCAN) utility that scans the data to discover potential problems with character set migrations. The scanner utility scans the data in CHAR, VARCHAR2, LONG, CLOB, NCHAR, NVARCHAR2, and NCLOB.

2-59. A. 1

Explanation The scalar subquery enables you to treat the output of a subquery as a column or expression within a SELECT statement. A scalar subquery is a query that only selects one column or expression and returns just one row.

2-60. D. Each WHEN . . . THEN . . . pair counts as one argument.

Explanation The simple CASE expression is very similar to the DECODE statement that uses value and substitution expression pairs. The simple CASE expression allows you to specify a number of WHEN . . . THEN . . . pairs. Each CASE expression can have up to 255 arguments, and each WHEN . . . THEN . . . pair counts as two arguments. At the most, you can have 127 WHEN . . . THEN . . . pairs and one ELSE expression in one CASE expression. When you nest a CASE expression within another CASE expression, the nested CASE expression allows you an additional set of 255 arguments.

Answers to Practice Exam 3

3-1. B. Server Manager

Explanation The Server Manager utility has been deprecated in Oracle9*i*. Instead, you use the SQL*Plus utility to perform the tasks that you previously performed with the Server Manager. You can also use the Oracle Enterprise Manager (OEM) to perform various administrative tasks and the RMAN to perform backup and recovery tasks.

3-2. D. Policy Manager

Explanation The Oracle Policy Manager is a GUI tool used to create and manage security policies; it is part of the OEM. The Security Manager enables you to create and manage users.

3-3. B. DBMS_RLS

Explanation To establish fine-grained access control, you must create policy groups and associate them with application context. The DBMS_RLS package contains a number of interfaces that enable you to work with policy groups. For example, you create a policy group with the CREATE_POLICY_GROUP interface. You can add a security policy to an existing security policy group by using the ADD_GROUPED_POLICY interface. You add a driving application context to an existing policy group with the ADD_POLICY_CONTEXT interface. DBMS_FGA is used for fine-grained auditing, DBMS_SESSION is used to manage session-related activities, and DBMS_LOCK is used to manage locks on tables.

3-4. A. SELECT statement

Explanation Prior to Oracle9*i*, value-based auditing was possible with before and after triggers for the INSERT, UPDATE, and DELETE operations. Oracle9*i* extended the concept of the fine-grained access control to the auditing function to enable you to audit SELECT operations. When a user attempts to access data that the user does not have authorization to access, the SELECT operation is unsuccessful. Oracle9*i* can specifically audit just the successful operations or the unsuccessful operations. In other words, fine-grained access control can audit attempts to access information even if the information itself was not accessed.

3-5. D. You cannot use LogMiner without a data dictionary.

Explanation You can extract the data dictionary to a flat file or to the redo log files by using the BUILD procedure in the DBMS_LOGMNR_D package. If LogMiner can access a dictionary, it translates the object identifiers and datatypes to give you the name of the object and the external data formats. Without a dictionary, LogMiner returns the object identifier and hex data representations.

3-6. A. You can only add one new master site at a time at a master site.

Explanation You can only add one new master site at a time at a master site. You can add another master site separately and after the previous add new master has completed.

3-7. B, D. B: TARGET_MTTR D: ESTIMATED_MTTR

Explanation Oracle9*i* adds the following three columns to V$INSTANCE_RECOVERY:

- **TARGET_MTTR** The user's setting for the FAST_START_MTTR_TARGET parameter.
- **ESTIMATED_MTTR** The mean time to recover (MTTR) that is estimated based on the number of dirty blocks and the number of redo log blocks.
- **CKPT_BLOCK_WRITES** The number of data blocks that were written by the checkpoint write operation.

3-8. D. DBMS_FLASHBACK.ENABLE_AT_TIME

Explanation Invoke DBMS_FLASHBACK.ENABLE_AT_TIME to enable Flashback for the session and to access the database at the system change number (SCN) that is closest to the specified time. You also have the option of invoking DBMS_FLASHBACK.ENABLE_AT_SYSTEM_CHANGE_NUMBER to enable Flashback for the session and to access the database at the specified SCN.

3-9. A. ALTER SESSION ENABLE RESUMABLE;

Explanation You will need the RESUMABLE system privilege to perform this operation.

3-10. D. STATISTICS

Explanation Export places the ANALYZE statement in the dump file if statistics were requested to enable you to recalculate the database optimizer statistics for the table. Import uses the precalculated statistics that are in the dump file, as opposed to using the ANALYZE statement written by Export, to generate statistics.

If you did not want to import precalculated statistics or the questionable statistics, you influenced the Import in Oracle8*i* with the ANALYZE statement and the RECALCULATE_STATISTICS parameter. Oracle9*i* introduces the new import parameter STATISTICS.

3-11. B. It archives the redo logs from the primary database onto each standby database.

Explanation The *Log Transport service* archives the redo logs from the primary database onto each standby database. The *Log Application service* performs the other three tasks.

3-12. C. It is both zero data divergence and zero data loss.

Explanation Guaranteed Protection mode is the most conservative of the Data Availability modes. It assures that the primary and standby databases are totally synchronized at all times. The transaction on the primary database is not committed until there is a confirmation that the log writer on the primary database site has transmitted the transaction, and that it has been applied on at least one standby database in the Data Guard configuration.

3-13. B. TO STANDBY

Explanation You can verify the possibility for a switchover by looking at the SWITCHOVER_STATUS in the V$DATABASE view. If the column contains the string 'TO STANDBY', it is possible that you can switch the primary database to a standby database.

3-14. C. Oracle9*i* performs online index rebuilding of bitmap or partitioned local and global indexes.

Explanation The online rebuilding of indexes was introduced in Oracle8*i* to reduce the locking, but it had a lot of limitations. Oracle9*i* has extended this online index rebuilding capability to reverse key indexes, function-based indexes, key compressed indexes on tables, and key compressed indexes on index organized tables (IOTs). Oracle9*i* does not currently support online index rebuilding for bitmap or partitioned local and global indexes.

3-15. D. You invoke the `can_redef_table` procedure in the `dbms_redefinition` package.

Explanation The first step in redefining a table online is to verify that the table can be redefined online by invoking the `can_redef_table` procedure in the `dbms_redefinition` package.

3-16. D. You verify the structural integrity of a database.

Explanation You can use the ANALYZE command with the VALIDATE STRUCTURE option to verify the structural integrity of a table, index, materialized view, or cluster.

3-17. B. You only make changes in memory for the current instance and not the SPFILE; the changes do not persist.

Explanation You change server parameters with the ALTER SYSTEM statement. Optionally, you can specify the scope of the change as follows:

- **MEMORY** Only makes changes in memory for the current instance and not the SPFILE; the changes do not persist.
- **SPFILE** Makes changes only in the SPFILE and not in the instance; the specified changes will persist.
- **BOTH** Makes changes to both the instance and the SPFILE; the changes will persist.

3-18. B. It uses the lowest value for MAX_EST_EXEC_TIME.

Explanation The Database Resource Manager takes a conservative approach; it uses the lowest value for MAX_EST_EXEC_TIME.

3-19. A. ACTIVE_SESS_POOL_P1

Explanation You can specify the maximum number of active sessions in the resource consumer group by setting the ACTIVE_SESS_POOL_P1 parameter; the default for this parameter is UNLIMITED.

3-20. A. The server polls the clients in a round-robin fashion to determine if a client has a request.

Explanation The server does not poll the clients; instead a client initiates a shared server connection to the database.

3-21. A, D. A: It registers all the dispatcher threads with the listener. D: It sends the load information of the dispatchers to the appropriate listeners.

Explanation The monitor thread registers all the dispatcher threads with the listener; it also sends the load information of the dispatchers to the appropriate listeners. The dispatcher threads accept incoming connections and task requests from Oracle servers. The task threads pick up the pending requests from the queue.

3-22. C. It is more efficient; the partition DDL only rebuilds the local index related to that partition.

Explanation The `UPDATE GLOBAL INDEXES` clause also rebuilds the *global* index as it performs the partition DDL.

3-23. C. There is no limit on the number of errors that can occur during a query of the external data.

Explanation The REJECT LIMIT clause specifies that there is no limit on the number of errors that can occur during a query of the external data.

3-24. B. If omitted, the partition storage parameters default to that of the nearest partition.

Explanation List partitioning enables you to partition a table's data based on discrete column values, it gives you explicit control over how rows map to partitions. This differs from range partitioning where a range of values is associated with a partition, and from hash partitioning where you had no control over the row to partition mapping. You can specify storage parameters for each partition. If you do not specify storage partitions at the partition level, they will default to storage characteristics for the table.

3-25. A. It enables you to open the external file that contains the metadata.

Explanation The OPEN procedure enables you to specify the type of object to be retrieved, the version of its metadata, and the object model.

3-26. B. DBMS_REPAIR

Explanation You can use the ALTER TABLE statement to change the PCTFREE value for FREELIST segments (manual space managed). In the case of automatic space-managed tables, the ALTER TABLE command does not update the bitmaps blocks (BMB); hence, these blocks may not track the true current status of the data blocks. Oracle9*i* has added a new procedure called SEGMENT_FIX_STATUS to the DBMS_REPAIR package to fix this problem.

3-27. A. The parameters will be ignored.

Explanation If you specify PCTUSED, FREELIST, and FREELIST_GROUPS parameters, they will be ignored because this is an automatic space-managed table.

3-28. A. DBA_JOIN_IND_COLUMNS

Explanation Oracle9*i* introduces a new data dictionary view, DBA_JOIN_IND_COLUMNS, to display the join condition for a bitmap join index.

3-29. D. _LT

Explanation When you version-enable a table, Oracle changes the table name by adding a suffix `_LT`.

3-30. C. WM_ADMIN_ROLE

Explanation The WM_ADMIN_ROLE role contains all the workspace-level and system-level privileges that you can grant to the user. By default, the DBA role has been granted the WM_ADMIN_ROLE role to execute procedures in the DBMS_WM package.

3-31. B. You can use OMF with raw devices.

Explanation OMF does not help when using raw devices since you cannot use an OMF with raw devices.

3-32. C. DB_CREATE_FILE_DEST

Explanation The DB_CREATE_FILE_DEST parameter specifies the location where data files and temp files should be created, while the DB_CREATE_ONLINE_LOG_DEST_n parameter specifies the location where Oracle should create the online redo log files and control files. If you do not specify the DB_CREATE_ONLINE_LOG_DEST_n parameter, the redo log and control files are created in the location specified by the DB_CREATE_FILE_DEST parameter.

3-33. C. `DROP TABLESPACE <tablespace_name> INCLUDING CONTENTS AND DATAFILES;`

Explanation Answer A drops a tablespace and its contents, but not the datafiles, and the syntax is not valid in answers B and D. Answer C drops a tablespace, its contents, and the corresponding datafiles.

3-34. B. You must first create the TEMPORARY TABLESPACE before you designate it.

Explanation You must first create the TEMPORARY TABLESPACE and then you can designate this TEMPORARY TABLESPACE as the DEFAULT TEMPORARY TABLESPACE.

3-35. D. Create a tablespace with sufficient space and specify that as the undo tablespace.

Explanation Oracle9*i* simplifies the space management of rollback segments with the introduction of automatic undo management (AUM). AUM only requires you to specify a tablespace with adequate space for the undo (rollback) segment creation; you do not have to create and size rollback segments manually.

3-36. C. You cannot create rollback segments or manage them manually.

Explanation Once you start the database instance in the AUM mode, you cannot create rollback segments or manage them manually. Oracle will return the following error if you attempt such operations:

```
ORA-30019: Illegal rollback Segment operation in Automatic Undo mode
```

3-37. D. DBA_TABLESPACES

Explanation Oracle9*i* has added a new column, BLOCK_SIZE, to the DBA_TABLESPACES data dictionary view to obtain the block size used by each tablespace.

3-38. A, D. A: The SYSTEM tablespace. D: Temporary tablespaces.

Explanation SYSTEM and temporary tablespaces cannot be of a nonstandard block size.

3-39. C. PGA_AGGREGATE_TARGET

Explanation PGA_AGGREGATE_TARGET is a new instance-level parameter that specifies the total memory in KB, MB, or GB for the Program Global Area (PGA) of all sessions combined. Setting this parameter to a nonzero value enables Automatic Work Area management; the range of possible values is 10 MB to 4 TB. Oracle9*i* gives you a second parameter, WORKAREA_SIZE_POLICY, to specify the work area sizing mechanism.

3-40. B. V$SQL_WORKAREA_USAGE

Explanation Oracle9*i* gives you V$SQL_WORKAREA_USAGE for the current usage of work areas and V$PGASTAT for instance-level PGA utilization.

3-41. D. SGA_MAX_SIZE

Explanation Oracle9*i* introduces SGA_MAX_SIZE, a new static parameter that enables the DBA to start with a smaller SGA and dynamically increase it, subject to the maximum value specified by SGA_MAX_SIZE. If you do not set SGA_MAX_SIZE or if you set it to a value less than the initial SGA size, you cannot increase the SGA size later.

3-42. A. PLUS ARCHIVELOG

Explanation You can use the new PLUS ARCHIVELOG clause to specify that archivelogs that have not been backed up are included with the data backup. Here is an example:

```
BACKUP DATAFILE 2 PLUS ARCHIVELOG;
```

3-43. D. ALLOW n CORRUPTION

Explanation If many blocks are corrupted, you can set the database in read-only mode and open the reset logs. If the corrupt blocks are few, you can perform a recovery that ignores the corrupt blocks but recovers the rest, as shown in the following statement:

```
RECOVER DATABASE ALLOW 2 CORRUPTION;
```

3-44. A, C. A: BY BACKUP C: BY FILE

Explanation The LIST command was enhanced; you now can specify either BY BACKUP or BY FILE output orientation. The BY BACKUP option is the default.

3-45. C. V$DB_CACHE_ADVICE

Explanation You can query the V$DB_CACHE_ADVICE view to get data about the cache that you can use to determine the optimum size of the cache. You can use OEM to get a graphical depiction of the cache by clicking the Memory tab for the Configuration object and then clicking Cache Buffer Size Advice.

3-46. A. You select the block size for that tablespace from a drop-down list.

Explanation When you create a new tablespace within the OEM, you can select the block size for that tablespace from a drop-down list.

3-47. D. YES or NO

Explanation If the index was used within the period of time it was monitored in, the USED column within the V$OBJECT_USAGE view will contain a YES value; otherwise, it will contain a NO.

3-48. A. SIMILAR

Explanation The use of the same execution plan sometimes introduces a significant performance risk. For example, the use of the same execution plan is not a safe approach because it is definitely not optimal for queries that have a disparity in the number of rows corresponding to the specified literal values. It would be more advisable for the optimizer to consider the histogram statistics as it determines the execution plan. Oracle9*i* has enhanced cursor sharing to enable you to control this risk with a third value, SIMILAR, for the CURSOR_SHARING parameter. When you specify SIMILAR, Oracle only uses the execution plan if it is certain that the execution plan does not have any association with the specific literal value.

3-49. A. All columns in the PLAN_TABLE view are also in the V$SQL_PLAN view with the exception of the LEVEL column.

Explanation All columns in the PLAN_TABLE view are also in the V$SQL_PLAN view with the exception of the LEVEL column. The ADDRESS, HASH_VALUE, CHILD_NUMBER, and DEPTH columns are in the V$SQL_PLAN view but not in the PLAN_TABLE.

3-50. C. MANUAL

Explanation Oracle9*i* introduced the following new options for the method_opt parameter in various procedures in DBMS_STATS:

- **SKEWONLY** Creates a histogram based on just the data distribution
- **REPEAT** Creates a histogram with the same number of buckets
- **AUTO** Creates a histogram based on data distribution and the manner in which the column is accessed by the application

3-51. C. Read Consistent Cache Fusion

Explanation The holding instance creates a read-consistent image in its own buffer for direct cache-to-cache transmissions to the requesting instance. Because this block transfer method does not involve disk writes, it has significant gains in performance over the Forced Disk Write method. The Read Consistent Cache Fusion method was introduced in Oracle8*i*.

3-52. B. Many instances can share one initialization parameter file.

Explanation Oracle9*i* enables you to store both common parameters for all instances and instance-specific parameters in one initialization parameter file that you can share among all instances.

3-53. B. ON

Explanation Instead of having to specify a join condition along with other criteria in the WHERE clause, the ON clause enables you to specify the join condition separate from the other criteria.

3-54. C, D. C: You cannot define any constraints on views because a view is read only. D: You can define check constraints on views.

Explanation Oracle9*i* enables you to define primary key constraints, unique constraints, and referential integrity constraints on views; check constraints are excluded. Constraints on views are declarative constraints; Oracle does not actually enforce these constraints. When you perform DML statements on views, Oracle assures integrity by enforcing the constraints defined on the base tables within the view.

3-55. C. It converts a LONG value to a CLOB value and a LONG RAW value into a BLOB value.

Explanation Oracle8*i* introduced the TO_LOB function that enables you to convert a LONG or a LONG RAW value to a CLOB or BLOB value respectively.

3-56. C. Stores a time interval value in terms of days, hours, minutes, and seconds

Explanation The TIMESTAMP datatype represents a point in time, while the INTERVAL datatype represents a duration of time. The INTERVAL DAY TO SECOND datatype can store a time interval value in terms of days, hours, minutes, and seconds. You can specify the precision for the number of days in a range from 0 to 9, the default being 2. You can also specify the precision for the fractional seconds in a range from 0 to 9, the default being 6.

3-57. B. The Unicode Standard Version 3.0

Explanation Oracle9*i* has been enhanced to support the Unicode Standard Version 3.0; this Unicode standard does not support surrogate pairs at this time. Oracle9*i* has introduced two new Unicode character sets, AL16UTF16 and AL32UTF8.

3-58. D. It scans in new fonts to create a font or character set.

Explanation Oracle9*i* provides you with the Character Set Scanner (CSSCAN) utility to scan data to discover potential problems with character set migrations. The scanner verifies the following:

- That the data in the target database can fit into the column's data size.
- That the data in the source can be mapped without being replaced in the target database.
- That the data can be correctly converted particularly when dealing with differences in byte sizes and fixed/variable byte encoding systems.

3-59. B. The index is used even if the index prefix column in the concatenated index is not used in the select statement.

Explanation Prior to Oracle9*i*, the Oracle Optimizer used the composite index in the execution plan only if you referenced the index prefix column in the where clause of your SQL statement. Oracle9*i* addresses this problem by enhancing the optimizer's data access technology by introducing Skip Scan Index Access. The optimizer will now use the composite index even if you omit the index prefix column in your SQL statement.

3-60. D. If expression1 is equal to expression2, Oracle will return a NULL; otherwise, it will return *expression1*.

Explanation If expression1 is equal to expression2, Oracle will return a NULL; otherwise, it will return *expression1*. You cannot specify the NULL literal value for expression1.

Glossary

he following terms are relevant to the various Oracle9*i* enhancements discussed in this book.

- **07_DICTIONARY_ACCESSIBILITY** The initialization parameter that either enables anyone who has the ANY privilege to be granted the privilege on the Data Dictionary or precluded access to the Data Dictionary.
- **ANALYZE** A statement to analyze a table, index, or cluster to gather information about the object or to validate the object.
- **ANALYZE . . . VALIDATE STRUCTURE** Enables you to verify the structural integrity of a table, index, materialized view, or cluster.
- **Application-specific predicate** Uses application context to return an application-specific security policy to establish a secure application context.
- **Archived redo log** Oracle can archive online redo log files before they are reused. The archived files are called archived redo logs. You can set the mode for the redo logs to ARCHIVELOG to archive filled redo logs before reuse, or you can choose the NOARCHIVELOG mode to just reuse them without archiving them.
- **Archive log gap** You have an archive log gap whenever the primary database archives the online redo log, but it is not archived to the standby database.
- **ASCII** The American Standard Code for Information Interchange (ASCII) is a 1-byte or 8-bit encoded character set that can take on one of 256 values (0 to 255); each value represents an English character or a special character such as the TAB key or CTRL character. On the other hand, Unicode is a 2-byte or 16-bit encoded character set that can take on one of 65,536 values and can represent most of the language characters of the world.
- **Audit column** If you specify the audit column, the audit is not triggered even if the audit condition is met, unless the audit column is referenced in the query. If you do not specify an audit column, Oracle9*i* treats all columns as audit columns.
- **Automatic segment space management** Maintains information about data block space utilization in bitmaps as opposed to freelists. Every automatically space managed segment maintains a set of bitmap blocks

(BMBs) for the tracking and managing utilization of blocks within that segment.Whenever a block becomes more full or less full, the bitmap is updated accordingly. This eliminates the need to specify the PCTUSED, FREELISTS, and FREELIST GROUPS parameters.

- **Automatic undo management (AUM)** This only requires that you specify a tablespace with adequate space for the undo (rollback) segment creation; you do not have to create and size rollback segments manually. You also do not have to tune rollback segment attributes to strike a balance between space consumption and performance via block contention. With AUM, Oracle creates, extends, and allocates undo segments within the space available in the undo tablespace. AUM eliminates the need for you to explicitly assign large rollback segments for batch transactions and for you to concern yourself with running out of space when different kinds of transactions occur concurrently. Oracle still uses rollback segments for storing undo information, but these segments are created and managed by Oracle.
- **Bitmap join index** For every value in a join column of a table, a bitmap join index stores the ROWIDs of corresponding rows in one or more join tables.
- **BLOB** Binary Large Objects is an Oracle datatype for storing large binary data up to 4G.
- **Block media recovery** Enables you to back up specific blocks in a datafile without taking the database offline. The default backup method is datafile media recovery. You can use the new BLOCKRECOVER statement to perform block media recovery, and you can restore and recover just those blocks that are corrupted.
- **Cache fusion block transfer** A direct cache-to-cache block transfer concept.
- **Change vector** A change vector tracks a specific change that is made to a single data segment block, the rollback segment block, and the transaction table of rollback segments. The change vector is the smallest unit of change that can be recorded. Changes are recorded in the redo log as redo entries, which are comprised of a set of change vectors.
- **Checkpoint** The highest system change number (SCN) at a given point in time when Oracle records the checkpoint. The checkpoint serves as an indicator that all datablocks below or at that SCN have been written out to disk. Frequent checkpointing reduces (improves) the instance recovery time, but adversely impacts performance.

- **CLOB** Character Large Objects is an Oracle datatype for storing large character data up to 4G.
- **Coalesce function** This function returns the first expression in the comma-separated list that is not a NULL.
- **Composite column** A set of columns that is treated as one group in generating group-based aggregate information.
- **Concatenated groupings** These enable you to specify combinations of groupings along a dimension of a cube, as opposed to a simple expression.
- **Configuration object** This represents a collection of site objects in a dataguard database solution.
- **Connection pooling** This enables you to use one physical connection to service multiple user sessions. This has a particular value in hosted web application servers, where many clients connect to the middle-tier web application server and this middle-tier application has a connection to the database server. Similar to the Oracle Shared Server, connection pooling eliminates the need for establishing one connection to the database server for every incoming user session.
- **Cost-based optimizer (CBO)** This generates alternative execution plans and determines the least cost alternative.
- **CREATE USER . . . TEMPORARY TABLESPACE** When you create users, you can specify a TEMPORARY TABLESPACE clause in the CREATE USER command to specify the tablespace to be used for sort operations. If you omit the TEMPORARY TABLESPACE clause, Oracle defaults to SYSTEM tablespace for sort operations. The use of the SYSTEM tablespace for sorts is not recommended.
- **Cross join** The cross product, which is also called a Cartesian product.
- **Cursor sharing** This enables you to share statements that are exactly the same. When parsing a statement, Oracle verifies if a totally identical statement exists in the shared SQL pool. If it does exist, Oracle will use (share) the statement in the shared pool. If the executing statement differs from the existing statement in the shared pool even in the smallest detail, Oracle will not share the statement.
- **Database Configuration Assistant (DBCA)** A graphical user interface (GUI) tool for creating a database.
- **Database Resource Manager** This gives the Oracle database server a greater degree of control over resource management than the operating

system (OS) would. Because the OS does not know about the architecture of the database server, it is inefficient in managing resources that pertain to the database.

- **Database resource object** This represents a primary or standby database instance in a dataguard solution; it is at the lowest level in the object hierarchy.
- **Datablock** Oracle manages its space within datafiles in units called datablocks; it is the finest level of granularity for space management. An Oracle datablock is the smallest unit for input/output (I/O) interactions with the operating system (OS). The DB_BLOCK_SIZE initialization parameter specifies the standard Oracle datablock size.
- **Data divergence** The primary database and the standby database are data divergent when they are not totally synchronized. When the standby database is unavailable or the connectivity to the standby database is unavailable, redo log transactions will be applied against the primary database, but they cannot be applied on the standby database; this results in data divergence. You also encounter data divergence between the primary and standby databases when you configure the log writer and/or the archiver for the asynchronous archival of the redo logs.
- **Datafile** Oracle uses operating system (OS) files called datafiles to store and manage all information related to the database.
- **Data Guard** This automates the tasks required to establish and manage a standby database solution. The tasks include setting up standby databases, managing standby databases, transferring the redo logs, and applying the logs to the standby database. Data Guard technology is a critical component of the Oracle database availability solution.
- **Data Guard Monitor** The component of the Data Guard Broker that is responsible for actually managing and monitoring the configuration.
- **Data loss** You encounter data loss when you failover from a primary database to a standby database that is in a data divergent state.
- **DBMS_FGA** The package that contains interfaces to specify auditing requirements.
- **DBMS_OBFUSCATION_TOOLKIT** A package that enables you to perform encryption and decryption on the server as opposed to the client machine.
- **DBMS_SESSION** An Oracle-supplied package that provides a number of interfaces that enable the application to set and manage global application context.

- **Dedicated server architecture** This requires a dedicated server process for each user connection.
- **DDL** The Data Definition Language is a subset of the SQL language set used to CREATE, ALTER, and DROP database objects.
- **Deep data protection** The Oracle9*i* approach to assuring security by establishing multiple layers of security tools. The approach ensures that security is not compromised even if one security tool is not effective in a given situation.
- **DEFAULT TEMPORARY TABLESPACE** Users for whom you did not specify a TEMPORARY TABLESPACE will default to the DEFAULT TEMPORARY TABLESPACE instead of cluttering up the SYSTEM tablespace.
- **Delayed Protection mode** You can specify a time lag from the point when you archive the redo log on the primary database, within which you cannot apply the redo logs on the standby database. This time lag can help by not propagating errors that may get fixed within the time lag specified.
- **Dirty buffer block** A block in the data cache in memory that contains changes that have not yet been written to disk.
- **DML** The Data Manipulation Language is a subset of the SQL language set used to query a database object, add data (INSERT INTO), UPDATE data, and DELETE data.
- **EXPLAIN_MVIEW** A procedure in the DBMS_MVIEW package that enables you to analyze why an existing or a potential materialized view is not fast refreshable.
- **Extent** A number of contiguous datablocks that can be allocated at a time. The extent is the next highest level of granularity after the datablock. Oracle requests a number of contiguous blocks from the operating system (OS), collectively called an *extent*. Oracle allocates one extent of additional space when the extents in a segment are full. Because space is allocated one extent at a time, there is a high probability that the extents will not be contiguous.
- **External procedures** These enable you to create C functions as Procedural Language/SQL (PL/SQL) bodies. In other words, it enables you to call C functions from PL/SQL. An external procedure is an external language procedure that is stored in a Dynamic Link Library (DLL) or in a libunit if you are using a Java class method.
- **External tables** These are read-only tables whose data resides in an external OS flat file, and whose definition is stored inside the database. You can query the data in an external table as if it were a regular database table.

- **Failover** A role transition that occurs to the standby database due to failure of the primary database.
- **Fast start checkpointing** Performs incremental checkpointing; it writes the oldest dirty blocks first to ensure that the more recent dirty blocks are associated with a higher SCN.
- **FAST_START_MTTR_TARGET** An initialization parameter used to specify the target mean time to recover for instance recovery. It takes a value between 0 and 3,600 seconds; when set to 0, Oracle9*i* will not use this parameter to manage instance recovery time.
- **Fine-grained access control** The concept of implementing a more granular level of access control beyond the standard password-based access control.
- **Fine-grained auditing (FGA)** The concept of auditing a query whenever the audit policy condition is satisfied.
- **FIPS** The Federal Information Processing Standard.
- **Flashback** Enables you to query the database as of a certain time or a specific system change number (SCN) in the past.
- **Forced failover** You use the forced failover transition option if the standby redo logs are not available.
- **GETKEY** A random number generator with a strong key; it is specified by the Federal Information Processing Standard (FIPS) 140. GETKEY is a part of the DBMS_OBFUSCATION_TOOLKIT package.
- **Global application context** This uses connection pooling and enables many connections to the middle tier to share and reuse application contexts.
- **Global Cache Service (GCS)** This service manages access to shared resources in the cluster; the most popular resource request by the instances is for datablocks. The GCS ensures that the different instances have appropriate access to the shared database buffer caches, even though you may have different versions of a datablock in existence.
- **Globalization support architecture** Oracle's globalization support architecture enables characters, numbers, money, time, calendar dates, and error messages to automatically adapt to the local native language and the locale. In previous releases, globalization support was called national language support (NLS).
- **Graceful failover** The failover operation is initiated when the primary database is not available or not accessible. You failover the primary

database to a standby database. This failover can be either a zero data loss or a minimal data loss failover, depending on the data availability mode the configuration was operating in prior to the failover. If the standby redo logs are available, then you must use the graceful failover option.

- **GROUPING SETs** These greatly enhance the GROUP BY clause; you can specify multiple groupings of data for aggregation, and just the groupings that you are interested in. Oracle does not have to aggregate based on every combination of the expressions in the CUBE or ROLLUP operation. Hence, GROUPING SETS are more efficient. Oracle applies the groupings specified in the GROUPING SETS and combines the result with an implied UNION ALL.
- **Guaranteed Protection mode** The most conservative of the data availability modes, it assures that the primary and standby databases are totally synchronized at all times. This is a zero divergence mode; you are assured that every transaction, up to the last transaction that has been committed on the primary database, has also been applied to the standby database.
- **Heterogeneous Service (HS) agents** These enable you to coordinate the different applications and separate components of applications that are running heterogeneous database systems in an enterprise business environment. For example, HS agents maintain transaction consistency and integrity across database applications.
- **Index monitoring** When you execute a Structured Query Language (SQL) statement, the cost-based optimizer steers the SQL statement execution away from nonselective indexes. Even though the index is not used, Oracle continues to maintain the indexes. These indexes constitute an overhead on memory, input/output (I/O), and central processing unit (CPU) resources because the index has to be updated for Data Manipulation Language (DML) operations. Index monitoring provides the capability to monitor index utilization. If it is determined that an index is not being used, then it can be dropped, thus eliminating unnecessary statement overhead. You can review the utilization information and drop indexes that are not being used in order to improve performance.
- **Instant Protection mode** Like the Guaranteed Protection mode, the Instant Protection mode assures you that database modifications made to the primary database, up to the last committed transaction, are also available on at least one standby database site by the log writer, even if the transactions have not yet been applied to the standby database. But, unlike the Guaranteed Protection mode, the Instant Protection mode enables

temporary data divergence. In a failover situation, the configuration retains full capability to synchronize the standby database.

- **INTERVAL DAY TO SECOND datatype** This datatype can store a time interval value in terms of days, hours, minutes, and seconds. You can specify the precision for the number of days in a range from 0 to 9, the default being 2.
- **INTERVAL YEAR TO MONTH datatype** This datatype can store a time interval value in terms of years and months. You can specify the precision for the number of years in a range from 0 to 9, the default being 2.
- **Label Security** Oracle Label Security is an optional add-on product that is part of Oracle9*i*'s advanced security architecture. Oracle Label Security enables you to specify labels based on the data in the row labels and associates the corresponding label security policy with a table or view.
- **List partitioning** This enables you to partition a table's data based on discrete column values; it gives you explicit control over how rows map to partitions. This differs from range partitioning where a range of values is associated with a partition, and from hash partitioning where you have no control over the row-to-partition mapping.
- **Log application service** This service applies the archived redo logs to the standby database; this action synchronizes the standby with the primary database in a dataguard solution.
- **LogMiner** An Oracle tool that reviews and analyzes the contents of both online and archived redo log files.
- **Log transport service** This service archives the redo logs from the primary database onto each standby database, performs error handling, takes care of input/output (I/O) contingencies, and automatically restarts the log transport process. It also automatically detects archive log gaps, goes about resolving them, and implements guaranteed zero data loss protection for data.
- **Materialized views (MV)** This is a replica of a master table at a master site or a master materialized view at a materialized view site at a specific point in time. Although the tables in a multimaster replication configuration are updated automatically on an ongoing basis to reflect the changes to the master, you need to refresh a materialized view periodically to reflect the changes to the master tables or master materialized views.
- **MERGE** The MERGE statement enables you to retrieve rows from a source table and either update existing rows or insert new rows into a destination table.

- **Minimal I/O Recovery** A tool for recovering rapidly from an outage by optimizing the speed with which it can apply redo logs. More specifically, minimal I/O recovery minimizes the number of redo entries that must be read and applied.
- **MV_CAPABILITIES_TABLE** After EXPLAIN_MVIEW completes the analysis, it posts the results in MV_CAPABILITIES_TABLE.
- **NATURAL JOIN** The NATURAL JOIN matches rows that have equal values in all columns that have the same name. Oracle assumes that the matching columns with the same name also have the same datatype. If they have different datatypes, you will encounter an error. Depending on the datatypes of the different columns, you could get the ORA-01722: invalid number error.
- **NULLIF function** This returns a NULL if the two expressions are equal; otherwise, Oracle will return the first expression.
- **Online index rebuilding** The capability to rebuild the index while the users continue to have access to the data in the tables. In the past, the entire table had to be locked when performing such actions.
- **Online redo logs** The files where Oracle records the changes to the database as they are made. In the event of a failure, Oracle will read these redo logs to recover the database. The redo logs also track the rollback segments in the database.
- **Oracle Application Server (OAS)** Middleware software that services database requests.
- **Oracle Enterprise Login Assistant (ELA)** A tool that enables Oracle to authenticate a user for enterprise-wide application logins.
- **Oracle-managed files (OMFs)** Oracle automatically creates and manages operating system (OS) files; the database administrator (DBA) managed these files manually in previous versions. The DBA does not have to specify filenames while creating database, tablespace, and redo log groups, and they do not have to delete files that are not needed anymore, such as datafiles corresponding to dropped tablespaces. With Oracle9*i*, the DBA configures the database in terms of database objects like tablespaces without having to be concerned about operating system (OS) filenames. Oracle creates the data files, redo log files, and control files automatically using standard file system interfaces.
- **OS authentication** This enables you to authenticate an Oracle user based on their operating system (OS) login.

- **OSDBA** Operating system (OS) authentication for database administrators involves putting the OS login name in a special OSDBA group. Then you get the SYSDBA privileges.
- **OSOPER** Operating system (OS) authentication for database operators involves putting the OS login name in a special OSOPER group. Then you get the SYSOPER privileges.
- **Outer joins** These enable you to retrieve rows that satisfy the join condition as well as rows in a table where no rows from the other table satisfy the join condition. Even when the American National Standards Institute (ANSI) and International Organization for Standardization (ISO) standards for outer joins did not exist, many past versions of Oracle enabled you to specify the outer join with the (+) qualifier. You could only specify one (+) qualifier to give you a left or a right outer join. In Oracle9*i*, you can use the SQL:99 specification for the outer join, where you can explicitly use the keywords OUTER JOIN instead of the not-so-readable (+) qualifier.
- **Partitioned fine-grained access control** You can associate multiple security policies into a security policy group, which you can associate with an application context (also called an driving application context). When accessing a table or view, Oracle refers to the driving application context to identify the associated security policy group and enforces all the policies in the associated security policy group to implement partitioned fine-grained access control.
- **Pending area** A staging area where you can specify your resource solutions and validate them before you submit them to be implemented. You must create a pending area before you can either create a new plan or update an existing plan; otherwise, it will result in a "pending area not active" error.
- **PGA_AGGREGATE_TARGET** A new instance-level parameter that specifies the total memory in KB, MB, or GB for the program global area (PGA) of all sessions combined. The default value for this parameter is 0; this 0 value specifies that automatic work area management be disabled. Setting this parameter to a nonzero value enables automatic work area management; the range of possible values is 10 MB to 4 TB.
- **Policy Manager** A GUI tool used to create and manage security policies; it is part of the Oracle Enterprise Manager (OEM).
- **Predicate of a query** The condition or criteria in the where clause of Structured Query Language (SQL) statement.

- **Program global area (PGA)** The part of the organized memory that contains the data and control-related information for a process on the server. Oracle creates a PGA when you start a process on the server. PGA memory is organized into two parts: tunable memory for SQL areas and nontunable memory for everything else. Oracle9*i*'s automatic work management only tunes the tunable part of PGA memory.
- **Rapid Protection mode** This mode improves the performance of the primary database as compared to the instant mode; the log writer sends modifications on the primary database to the standby database site as soon as it gets a chance. Data divergence is enabled here.
- **Real application clusters (RACs)** The RAC configuration is a set of interconnected clusters of nodes with the database residing on a set of shared disks. A node is one instance that runs on a set of processors, shared memory, and shared disks. A cluster is a set of loosely coupled nodes.
- **Recovery Manager (RMAN)** A client-side application or utility that enables you to perform backup and recovery operations.
- **Recovery window policy** You can use the CONFIGURE command to specify a recovery window policy that establishes the number of days the backups are to be retained.
- **Redo entries** Also known as redo records, they document changes made to the database as a set of change vectors.
- **Redundancy policy** You can use the CONFIGURE command to specify a redundancy policy that establishes the number of backup files and control files you want to retain.
- **Replicated database** Built upon distributed database technology, it synchronizes objects and data across databases.
- **Replication group** A collection of related replication objects. A replication object can only belong to one replication group.
- **Replication object** A replicated object is a database object that you have configured to be replicated.
- **Resource consumer groups** A resource plan can have many resource consumer groups, each of which represents a group of sessions that has a common set of resource requirements.
- **Resource plan** This is associated with resource plan directives, each of which specifies which resources are allocated to a resource consumer group.

- **Resource plan directives** These directives associate a resource consumer group with a resource plan, and specify the resources that must be allocated to the group.
- **Resumable space allocation** This suspends a large operation in the event of a space allocation failure so you can take corrective action; execution resumes automatically once the action is corrected.
- **Role management service (RMS)** This enables you to change the database role from primary to standby, and from standby to primary in a dataguard database solution.
- **Role transition** The change of roles between primary and standby databases. The role management service (RMS) enables you to change the role of a database from primary to standby or from standby to primary.
- **Scalar subquery** A query that only selects one column or expression and returns just one row. If the scalar subquery does not select any rows, Oracle will use a NULL value for the output of the scalar subquery. The scalar subquery enables you to treat the output of a subquery as a column or expression within a SELECT statement.
- **Schema** An Oracle structure that serves as a collection or grouping of database objects such as tables, views, and stored procedures.
- **Searched CASE statement** The searched CASE expression is very similar to the format for the simple CASE expression. There is one difference: you compare the CASE expression to the comparison_expression in the WHEN clause to determine your course of action. In the searched CASE expression, you do not specify a CASE expression, and you specify any condition or predicate instead of a comparison_expression after the WHEN keyword.
- **Secure application context** This enables an application to tailor access control based on using the attributes of the user's session. This results in a virtual private database (VPD) that is customized to the specific security needs of the application.
- **Secure application role** Oracle9*i* takes the concept of the application context one step further; it provides a means of associating the application context with the security role to give you the secure application role.
- **Security policy** The ability to define an access restriction and associate it with a database object. When that object is accessed, the associated security policy is enforced.

- **Security policy group** Oracle gives you the ability to combine a number of security policies into a security policy group, which you can associate with an application context (also called the driving application context).
- **Segment** A set or collection of extents. Oracle uses data segments, index segments, rollback segments, and temporary segments to manage information. The segment is the next highest level of granularity after the extent.
- **Server Manager utility** This is deprecated in Oracle9*i*. You can use SQL*Plus to issue STARTUP and SHUTDOWN commands, and to perform most Server Manager line-mode scripts.
- **Server parameter file (SPFILE)** A binary file that serves as a storage facility for initialization parameters.
- **Shared Server architecture** This Oracle architecture enables you to share one server process with multiple user sessions. An idle server process from a server process pool services a user session from a user request queue.
- **Simple CASE statement** The simple CASE expression is very similar to the DECODE statement that uses value and substitution expression pairs. The simple CASE expression enables you to specify a number of WHEN . . . THEN . . . pairs. For each WHEN clause, Oracle will perform that use_expression if the CASE expression is equal to that comparison_expression. You can also specify an ELSE clause, which is a catchall clause. If none of the WHEN . . . conditions are met, the CASE expression performs the default_use_expression specified in the ELSE clause; Oracle will give you a NULL value if you did not specify an ELSE clause.
- **Single sign-on (SSO)** This enables you to sign on only once into the Oracle application server and to access a number of different Web-based applications. This eliminates the need to have a password for every single application.
- **Site object** This represents a collection of database resource objects that are resident on a single host system in a dataguard database solution.
- **SPACE_USAGE procedure** Part of the DBMS_SPACE package, it enables you to obtain information about the free blocks in automatically space-managed segments.
- **SQL** Stands for Structured Query Language. It is the American National Standards Institute (ANSI) standard language of choice to interact with relational databases and object-relational databases. Standards bodies such

as ANSI and the International Organization for Standardization (ISO) enhance the SQL language on a regular basis.

- **SQL99** The most recent official release of the SQL language, it was officially adopted in July 1999. SQL:99 represents both the International Organization for Standardization/Interexchange Carrier (ISO/IEC) 9075-1:1999 and American National Standards Institute (ANSI) x3.135-1999 standards.
- **Switchover** A planned role transition.
- **SYSDBA** A privilege that enables a user to perform database administration. The SYSDBA privilege is a superset of the SYSOPER privilege. Besides all the SYSOPER privileges, SYSDBA enables you to use CREATE DATABASE and to connect as user SYS.
- **SYS_DEFAULT policy group** The default group whose policies are always enforced whenever Oracle enforces the policies in the associated security policy group of the driving application context.
- **SYSOPER** A privilege that enables a user to perform operational tasks such as startup/shutdown, CREATE SPFILE, ALTER DATABASE (open/mount/backup), ARCHIVELOG, and RECOVERY. It also includes the RESTRICTED SESSION privilege.
- **Tablespace** An Oracle structure that serves as a grouping for other logical structures and objects.
- **TIMESTAMP Datatype** This is very much like the DATE datatype; it can store both the date and time values. Unlike the DATE datatype, you can specify the precision of the fractional seconds value in the TIMESTAMP datatype.
- **TIMESTAMP WITH LOCAL TIME ZONE Datatype** This is a variant of the TIMESTAMP datatype. Much like the TIMESTAMP WITH TIME ZONE datatype, the TIMESTAMP WITH LOCAL TIME ZONE includes time zone information. Unlike the TIMESTAMP WITH TIME ZONE datatype, the TIMESTAMP WITH LOCAL TIME ZONE does not store the time zone displacement in additional bytes of storage. Instead, it stores the time values normalized in terms of the database's time zone.
- **TIMESTAMP WITH TIME ZONE Datatype** This datatype adds a slight twist to the TIMESTAMP datatype. In addition to the date and time, you can store the time zone displacement (or offset), which requires additional bytes of storage. The time zone displacement is the difference in hours and minutes between the local time and the Universal Time (Coordinated) (UTC), which formerly was the Greenwich Meridian Time (GMT).

- **Trial recovery** This enables the database administrator (DBA) to anticipate problems before performing the recovery. You can mark the datablocks that cannot be recovered as corrupted, and you can perform trial recovery to determine if additional problems exist.
- **UNDO_POOL parameter** This specifies the maximum size (in KB) of the undo space that the group can use, which in turn sets a limit on the amount of undo entries corresponding to the consumer group. The default for the UNDO_POOL parameter is UNLIMITED.
- **UNDO_RETENTION initialization parameter** This specifies how long (in seconds) undo data must be retained in the undo tablespace before it is overwritten. This parameter enables you to minimize the chance that long-running queries encounter the "snapshot too old" error.
- **Unicode** Unicode is a 2-byte or 16-bit encoded character set that can take on one of 65,536 values and can represent most of the language characters of the world. Alternatively, the American Standard Code for Information Interchange (ASCII) set is an 1-byte or 8-bit encoded character set that can take on one of 256 values (0 to 255); each value represents an English character or a special character such as the TAB key or CTRL character.
- **Virtual private database (VPD)** This enables a number of clients to access data stored on a common, shared hosted database server, while limiting each client to their own data.
- **WHERE clause** The clause in the Structured Query Language (SQL) statement where you specify the criteria or condition.
- **Workspace** A virtual database facility that enables you to maintain multiple versions of one row of data and enables each workspace context to reference a different version of this row as compared to another workspace context. In other words, the workspace context enables you to work with one version of the database in one workspace context, and with another version of the database in another workspace context, without compromising transactional integrity across the database.
- **Workspace Manager** This provides you with a virtual workspace where the domain of data is constant, even though other user changes may be changing the data in this domain. The Workspace Manager also enables you to return to this domain of data at a future point in time.
- **Zero data divergence** This implies that the primary and secondary databases must be synchronized at all times. In other words, you cannot commit a transaction on the primary database until you are sure that it has also been applied on at least one standby database. Zero data divergence

also implies that if you are unable to apply transactions to the standby database, you must cease making changes to the primary database.

- **Zero data loss** This implies that all transactions on the primary database must also be available on at least one standby database, even if it has not been applied to the standby database yet.

Index

A

B

C

D

E

J–K

L

M

N

O

P

Q

R

S

T

U

V

W

Z

INTERNATIONAL CONTACT INFORMATION

AUSTRALIA
McGraw-Hill Book Company Australia Pty. Ltd.
TEL +61-2-9417-9899
FAX +61-2-9417-5687
http://www.mcgraw-hill.com.au
books-it_sydney@mcgraw-hill.com

CANADA
McGraw-Hill Ryerson Ltd.
TEL +905-430-5000
FAX +905-430-5020
http://www.mcgrawhill.ca

GREECE, MIDDLE EAST, NORTHERN AFRICA
McGraw-Hill Hellas
TEL +30-1-656-0990-3-4
FAX +30-1-654-5525

MEXICO (Also serving Latin America)
McGraw-Hill Interamericana Editores S.A. de C.V.
TEL +525-117-1583
FAX +525-117-1589
http://www.mcgraw-hill.com.mx
fernando_castellanos@mcgraw-hill.com

SINGAPORE (Serving Asia)
McGraw-Hill Book Company
TEL +65-863-1580
FAX +65-862-3354
http://www.mcgraw-hill.com.sg
mghasia@mcgraw-hill.com

SOUTH AFRICA
McGraw-Hill South Africa
TEL +27-11-622-7512
FAX +27-11-622-9045
robyn_swanepoel@mcgraw-hill.com

UNITED KINGDOM & EUROPE (Excluding Southern Europe)
McGraw-Hill Education Europe
TEL +44-1-628-502500
FAX +44-1-628-770224
http://www.mcgraw-hill.co.uk
computing_neurope@mcgraw-hill.com

ALL OTHER INQUIRIES Contact:
Osborne/McGraw-Hill
TEL +1-510-549-6600
FAX +1-510-883-7600
http://www.osborne.com
omg_international@mcgraw-hill.com

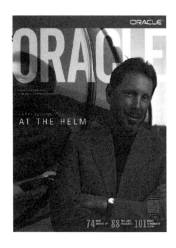

FREE SUBSCRIPTION

○ Yes, please send me a FREE subscription to *Oracle Magazine* ○ NO

To receive a free subscription to *Oracle Magazine*, you must fill out the entire card, sign it, and date it (incomplete cards cannot be processed or acknowledged). You can also fax your application to +1.847.647.9735.

Or subscribe at our Web site at www.oracle.com/oraclemagazine/

○ From time to time, Oracle Publishing allows our partners exclusive access to our e-mail addresses for special promotions and announcements. To be included in this program, please check this box.

○ Oracle Publishing allows sharing of our mailing list with selected third parties. If you prefer your mailing address not to be included in this program, please check here. If at any time you would like to be removed from this mailing list, please contact Customer Service at +1.847.647.9630 or send an e-mail to oracle@halldata.com.

signature (required) date

X

name title

company e-mail address

street/p.o. box

city/state/zip or postal code telephone

country fax

YOU MUST ANSWER ALL NINE QUESTIONS BELOW

① WHAT IS THE PRIMARY BUSINESS ACTIVITY OF YOUR FIRM AT THIS LOCATION? (check one only)

- □ 01 Application Service Provider
- □ 02 Communications
- □ 03 Consulting, Training
- □ 04 Data Processing
- □ 05 Education
- □ 06 Engineering
- □ 07 Financial Services
- □ 08 Government (federal, local, state, other)
- □ 09 Government (military)
- □ 10 Health Care
- □ 11 Manufacturing (aerospace, defense)
- □ 12 Manufacturing (computer hardware)
- □ 13 Manufacturing (noncomputer)
- □ 14 Research & Development
- □ 15 Retailing, Wholesaling, Distribution
- □ 16 Software Development
- □ 17 Systems Integration, VAR, VAD, OEM
- □ 18 Transportation
- □ 19 Utilities (electric, gas, sanitation)
- □ 98 Other Business and Services

② WHICH OF THE FOLLOWING BEST DESCRIBES YOUR PRIMARY JOB FUNCTION? (check one only)

Corporate Management/Staff

- □ 01 Executive Management (President, Chair, CEO, CFO, Owner, Partner, Principal)
- □ 02 Finance/Administrative Management (VP/Director/ Manager/Controller, Purchasing, Administration)
- □ 03 Sales/Marketing Management (VP/Director/Manager)
- □ 04 Computer Systems/Operations Management (CIO/VP/Director/ Manager MIS, Operations)

IS/IT Staff

- □ 05 Systems Development/ Programming Management
- □ 06 Systems Development/ Programming Staff
- □ 07 Consulting
- □ 08 DBA/Systems Administrator
- □ 09 Education/Training
- □ 10 Technical Support Director/Manager
- □ 11 Other Technical Management/Staff
- □ 98 Other

③ WHAT IS YOUR CURRENT PRIMARY OPERATING PLATFORM? (select all that apply)

- □ 01 Digital Equipment UNIX
- □ 02 Digital Equipment VAX VMS
- □ 03 HP UNIX
- □ 04 IBM AIX
- □ 05 IBM UNIX
- □ 06 Java
- □ 07 Linux
- □ 08 Macintosh
- □ 09 MS-DOS
- □ 10 MVS
- □ 11 NetWare
- □ 12 Network Computing
- □ 13 OpenVMS
- □ 14 SCO UNIX
- □ 15 Sequent DYNIX/ptx
- □ 16 Sun Solaris/SunOS
- □ 17 SVR4
- □ 18 UnixWare
- □ 19 Windows
- □ 20 Windows NT
- □ 21 Other UNIX
- □ 98 Other
- 99 □ None of the above

④ DO YOU EVALUATE, SPECIFY, RECOMMEND, OR AUTHORIZE THE PURCHASE OF ANY OF THE FOLLOWING? (check all that apply)

- □ 01 Hardware
- □ 02 Software
- □ 03 Application Development Tools
- □ 04 Database Products
- □ 05 Internet or Intranet Products
- 99 □ None of the above

⑤ IN YOUR JOB, DO YOU USE OR PLAN TO PURCHASE ANY OF THE FOLLOWING PRODUCTS? (check all that apply)

Software

- □ 01 Business Graphics
- □ 02 CAD/CAE/CAM
- □ 03 CASE
- □ 04 Communications
- □ 05 Database Management
- □ 06 File Management
- □ 07 Finance
- □ 08 Java
- □ 09 Materials Resource Planning
- □ 10 Multimedia Authoring
- □ 11 Networking
- □ 12 Office Automation
- □ 13 Order Entry/Inventory Control
- □ 14 Programming
- □ 15 Project Management
- □ 16 Scientific and Engineering
- □ 17 Spreadsheets
- □ 18 Systems Management
- □ 19 Workflow

Hardware

- □ 20 Macintosh
- □ 21 Mainframe
- □ 22 Massively Parallel Processing
- □ 23 Minicomputer
- □ 24 PC
- □ 25 Network Computer
- □ 26 Symmetric Multiprocessing
- □ 27 Workstation

Peripherals

- □ 28 Bridges/Routers/Hubs/Gateways
- □ 29 CD-ROM Drives
- □ 30 Disk Drives/Subsystems
- □ 31 Modems
- □ 32 Tape Drives/Subsystems
- □ 33 Video Boards/Multimedia

Services

- □ 34 Application Service Provider
- □ 35 Consulting
- □ 36 Education/Training
- □ 37 Maintenance
- □ 38 Online Database Services
- □ 39 Support
- □ 40 Technology-Based Training
- □ 98 Other
- 99 □ None of the above

⑥ WHAT ORACLE PRODUCTS ARE IN USE AT YOUR SITE? (check all that apply)

Software

- □ 01 Oracle9i
- □ 02 Oracle9i Lite
- □ 03 Oracle8
- □ 04 Oracle8i
- □ 05 Oracle8i Lite
- □ 06 Oracle7
- □ 07 Oracle9i Application Server
- □ 08 Oracle9i Application Server Wireless
- □ 09 Oracle Data Mart Suites
- □ 10 Oracle Internet Commerce Server
- □ 11 Oracle interMedia
- □ 12 Oracle Lite
- □ 13 Oracle Payment Server
- □ 14 Oracle Video Server
- □ 15 Oracle Rdb

Tools

- □ 16 Oracle Darwin
- □ 17 Oracle Designer
- □ 18 Oracle Developer
- □ 19 Oracle Discoverer
- □ 20 Oracle Express
- □ 21 Oracle JDeveloper
- □ 22 Oracle Reports
- □ 23 Oracle Portal
- □ 24 Oracle Warehouse Builder
- □ 25 Oracle Workflow

Oracle E-Business Suite

- □ 26 Oracle Advanced Planning/Scheduling
- □ 27 Oracle Business Intelligence
- □ 28 Oracle E-Commerce
- □ 29 Oracle Exchange
- □ 30 Oracle Financials
- □ 31 Oracle Human Resources
- □ 32 Oracle Interaction Center
- □ 33 Oracle Internet Procurement
- □ 34 Oracle Manufacturing
- □ 35 Oracle Marketing
- □ 36 Oracle Order Management
- □ 37 Oracle Professional Services Automation
- □ 38 Oracle Projects
- □ 39 Oracle Sales
- □ 40 Oracle Service
- □ 41 Oracle Small Business Suite
- □ 42 Oracle Supply Chain Management
- □ 43 Oracle Travel Management
- □ 44 Oracle Treasury

Oracle Services

- □ 45 Oracle.com Online Services
- □ 46 Oracle Consulting
- □ 47 Oracle Education
- □ 48 Oracle Support
- □ 98 ther
- 99 □ None of the above

⑦ WHAT OTHER DATABASE PRODUCTS ARE IN USE AT YOUR SITE? (check all that apply)

- □ 01 Access
- □ 02 Baan
- □ 03 dbase
- □ 04 Gupta
- □ 05 BM DB2
- □ 06 Informix
- □ 07 Ingres
- □ 08 Microsoft Access
- □ 09 Microsoft SQL Server
- □ 10 PeopleSoft
- □ 11 Progress
- □ 12 SAP
- □ 13 Sybase
- □ 14 VSAM
- □ 98 Other
- 99 □ None of the above

⑧ DURING THE NEXT 12 MONTHS, HOW MUCH DO YOU ANTICIPATE YOUR ORGANIZATION WILL SPEND ON COMPUTER HARDWARE, SOFTWARE, PERIPHERALS, AND SERVICES FOR YOUR LOCATION? (check only one)

- □ 01 Less than $10,000
- □ 02 $10,000 to $49,999
- □ 03 $50,000 to $99,999
- □ 04 $100,000 to $499,999
- □ 05 $500,000 to $999,999
- □ 06 $1,000,000 and over

⑨ WHAT IS YOUR COMPANY'S YEARLY SALES REVENUE? (please choose one)

- □ 01 $500, 000, 000 and above
- □ 02 $100, 000, 000 to $500, 000, 000
- □ 03 $50, 000, 000 to $100, 000, 000
- □ 04 $5, 000, 000 to $50, 000, 000
- □ 05 $1, 000, 000 to $5, 000, 000

123101

About the BeachFrontQuizzer™ CD-ROM

BeachFrontQuizzer provides interactive certification exams to help you prepare for certification. With the enclosed CD, you can test your knowledge of the topics covered in this book with more than 175 multiple choice questions.

Installation

To install BeachFrontQuizzer:

1. **Insert the CD-ROM in your CD-ROM drive.**
2. **Follow the Setup steps in the displayed Installation Wizard. (When the Setup is finished, you may immediately begin using BeachFrontQuizzer.)**
3. **To begin using BeachFrontQuizzer, enter the 12-digit license key number of the exam you want to take:**

   OCP Oracle 9*i* Database: New Features for Administrators
   Exam Guide   242985728690

Study Sessions

BeachFrontQuizzer tests your knowledge as you learn about new subjects through interactive quiz sessions. Study Session Questions are selected from a single database for each session, dependent on the subcategory selected and the number of times each question has been previously answered correctly. In this way, questions you have answered correctly are not repeated until you have answered all the new questions. Questions that you have missed previously will reappear in later sessions and keep coming back to haunt you until you get the question correct. In addition, you can track your progress by displaying the number of questions you have answered with the Historical Analysis option. You can reset the progress tracking by clicking on the Clear History button. Each time a question is presented the answers are randomized so you will memorize a pattern or letter that goes with the question. You will start to memorize the correct answer that goes with the question concept.

Practice Exams

For advanced users, BeachFrontQuizzer also provides Simulated and Adaptive certification exams. Questions are chosen at random from the database. The Simulated Exam presents a specific number of questions directly related to the real exam. After you finish the exam, BeachFrontQuizzer displays your score and the passing score required for the test. You may display the exam results of this specific exam from this menu. You may review each question and display the correct answer.

NOTE
For further details of the feature functionality of this BeachFrontQuizzer software, consult the online instructions by choosing Contents from the BeachFrontQuizzer Help menu.

Technical Support

If you experience technical difficulties, please call (888) 992-3131. Outside the United States call (281) 992-3131. Or, you may e-mail **bfquiz@swbell.net**.

LICENSE AGREEMENT

THIS PRODUCT (THE "PRODUCT") CONTAINS PROPRIETARY SOFTWARE, DATA AND INFORMATION (INCLUDING DOCUMENTATION) OWNED BY THE McGRAW-HILL COMPANIES, INC. ("McGRAW-HILL") AND ITS LICENSORS. YOUR RIGHT TO USE THE PRODUCT IS GOVERNED BY THE TERMS AND CONDITIONS OF THIS AGREEMENT.

LICENSE: Throughout this License Agreement, "you" shall mean either the individual or the entity whose agent opens this package. You are granted a non-exclusive and non-transferable license to use the Product subject to the following terms:

(i) If you have licensed a single user version of the Product, the Product may only be used on a single computer (i.e., a single CPU). If you licensed and paid the fee applicable to a local area network or wide area network version of the Product, you are subject to the terms of the following subparagraph (ii).

(ii) If you have licensed a local area network version, you may use the Product on unlimited workstations located in one single building selected by you that is served by such local area network. If you have licensed a wide area network version, you may use the Product on unlimited workstations located in multiple buildings on the same site selected by you that is served by such wide area network; provided, however, that any building will not be considered located in the same site if it is more than five (5) miles away from any building included in such site. In addition, you may only use a local area or wide area network version of the Product on one single server. If you wish to use the Product on more than one server, you must obtain written authorization from McGraw-Hill and pay additional fees.

(iii) You may make one copy of the Product for back-up purposes only and you must maintain an accurate record as to the location of the back-up at all times.

COPYRIGHT; RESTRICTIONS ON USE AND TRANSFER: All rights (including copyright) in and to the Product are owned by McGraw-Hill and its licensors. You are the owner of the enclosed disc on which the Product is recorded. You may not use, copy, decompile, disassemble, reverse engineer, modify, reproduce, create derivative works, transmit, distribute, sublicense, store in a database or retrieval system of any kind, rent or transfer the Product, or any portion thereof, in any form or by any means (including electronically or otherwise) except as expressly provided for in this License Agreement. You must reproduce the copyright notices, trademark notices, legends and logos of McGraw-Hill and its licensors that appear on the Product on the back-up copy of the Product which you are permitted to make hereunder. All rights in the Product not expressly granted herein are reserved by McGraw-Hill and its licensors.

TERM: This License Agreement is effective until terminated. It will terminate if you fail to comply with any term or condition of this License Agreement. Upon termination, you are obligated to return to McGraw-Hill the Product together with all copies thereof and to purge all copies of the Product included in any and all servers and computer facilities.

DISCLAIMER OF WARRANTY: THE PRODUCT AND THE BACK-UP COPY ARE LICENSED "AS IS." McGRAW-HILL, ITS LICENSORS AND THE AUTHORS MAKE NO WARRANTIES, EXPRESS OR IMPLIED, AS TO THE RESULTS TO BE OBTAINED BY ANY PERSON OR ENTITY FROM USE OF THE PRODUCT, ANY INFORMATION OR DATA INCLUDED THEREIN AND/OR ANY TECHNICAL SUPPORT SERVICES PROVIDED HEREUNDER, IF ANY ("TECHNICAL SUPPORT SERVICES"). McGRAW-HILL, ITS LICENSORS AND THE AUTHORS MAKE NO EXPRESS OR IMPLIED WARRANTIES OF MERCHANTABILITY OR FITNESS FOR A PARTICULAR PURPOSE OR USE WITH RESPECT TO THE PRODUCT. McGRAW-HILL, ITS LICENSORS, AND THE AUTHORS MAKE NO GUARANTEE THAT YOU WILL PASS ANY CERTIFICATION EXAM WHATSOEVER BY USING THIS PRODUCT. NEITHER McGRAW-HILL, ANY OF ITS LICENSORS NOR THE AUTHORS WARRANT THAT THE FUNCTIONS CONTAINED IN THE PRODUCT WILL MEET YOUR REQUIREMENTS OR THAT THE OPERATION OF THE PRODUCT WILL BE UNINTERRUPTED OR ERROR FREE. YOU ASSUME THE ENTIRE RISK WITH RESPECT TO THE QUALITY AND PERFORMANCE OF THE PRODUCT.

LIMITED WARRANTY FOR DISC: To the original licensee only, McGraw-Hill warrants that the enclosed disc on which the Product is recorded is free from defects in materials and workmanship under normal use and service for a period of ninety (90) days from the date of purchase. In the event of a defect in the disc covered by the foregoing warranty, McGraw-Hill will replace the disc.

LIMITATION OF LIABILITY: NEITHER McGRAW-HILL, ITS LICENSORS NOR THE AUTHORS SHALL BE LIABLE FOR ANY INDIRECT, SPECIAL OR CONSEQUENTIAL DAMAGES, SUCH AS BUT NOT LIMITED TO, LOSS OF ANTICIPATED PROFITS OR BENEFITS, RESULTING FROM THE USE OR INABILITY TO USE THE PRODUCT EVEN IF ANY OF THEM HAS BEEN ADVISED OF THE POSSIBILITY OF SUCH DAMAGES. THIS LIMITATION OF LIABILITY SHALL APPLY TO ANY CLAIM OR CAUSE WHATSOEVER WHETHER SUCH CLAIM OR CAUSE ARISES IN CONTRACT, TORT, OR OTHERWISE. Some states do not allow the exclusion or limitation of indirect, special or consequential damages, so the above limitation may not apply to you.

U.S. GOVERNMENT RESTRICTED RIGHTS: Any software included in the Product is provided with restricted rights subject to subparagraphs (c), (1) and (2) of the Commercial Computer Software-Restricted Rights clause at 48 C.F.R. 52.227-19. The terms of this Agreement applicable to the use of the data in the Product are those under which the data are generally made available to the general public by McGraw-Hill. Except as provided herein, no reproduction, use, or disclosure rights are granted with respect to the data included in the Product and no right to modify or create derivative works from any such data is hereby granted.

GENERAL: This License Agreement constitutes the entire agreement between the parties relating to the Product. The terms of any Purchase Order shall have no effect on the terms of this License Agreement. Failure of McGraw-Hill to insist at any time on strict compliance with this License Agreement shall not constitute a waiver of any rights under this License Agreement. This License Agreement shall be construed and governed in accordance with the laws of the State of New York. If any provision of this License Agreement is held to be contrary to law, that provision will be enforced to the maximum extent permissible and the remaining provisions will remain in full force and effect.